THE HEROIC LEGEND OF
ARSLAN

STORY BY
YOSHIKI TANAKA

MANGA BY
HIROMU ARAKAWA

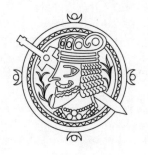

15

The Heroic Legend of
ARSLAN

Table of Contents

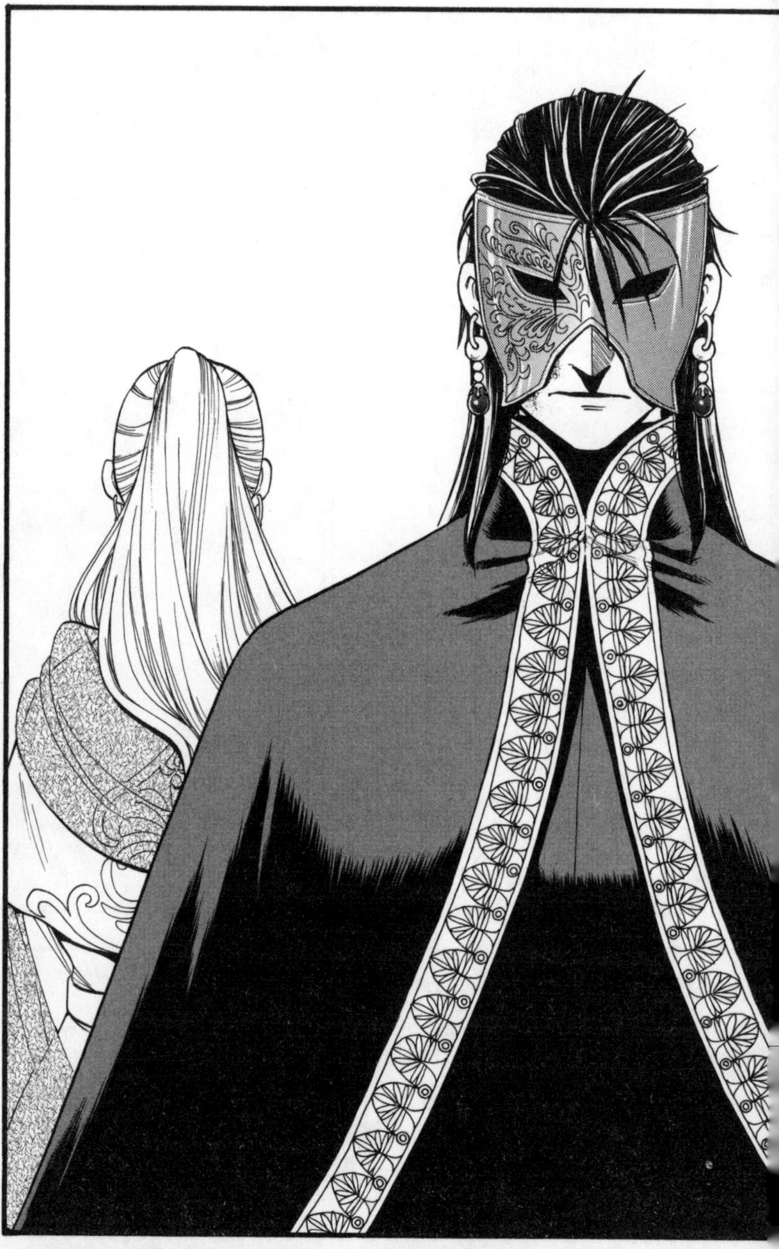

Chapter 89: The Pathos of Reminiscence

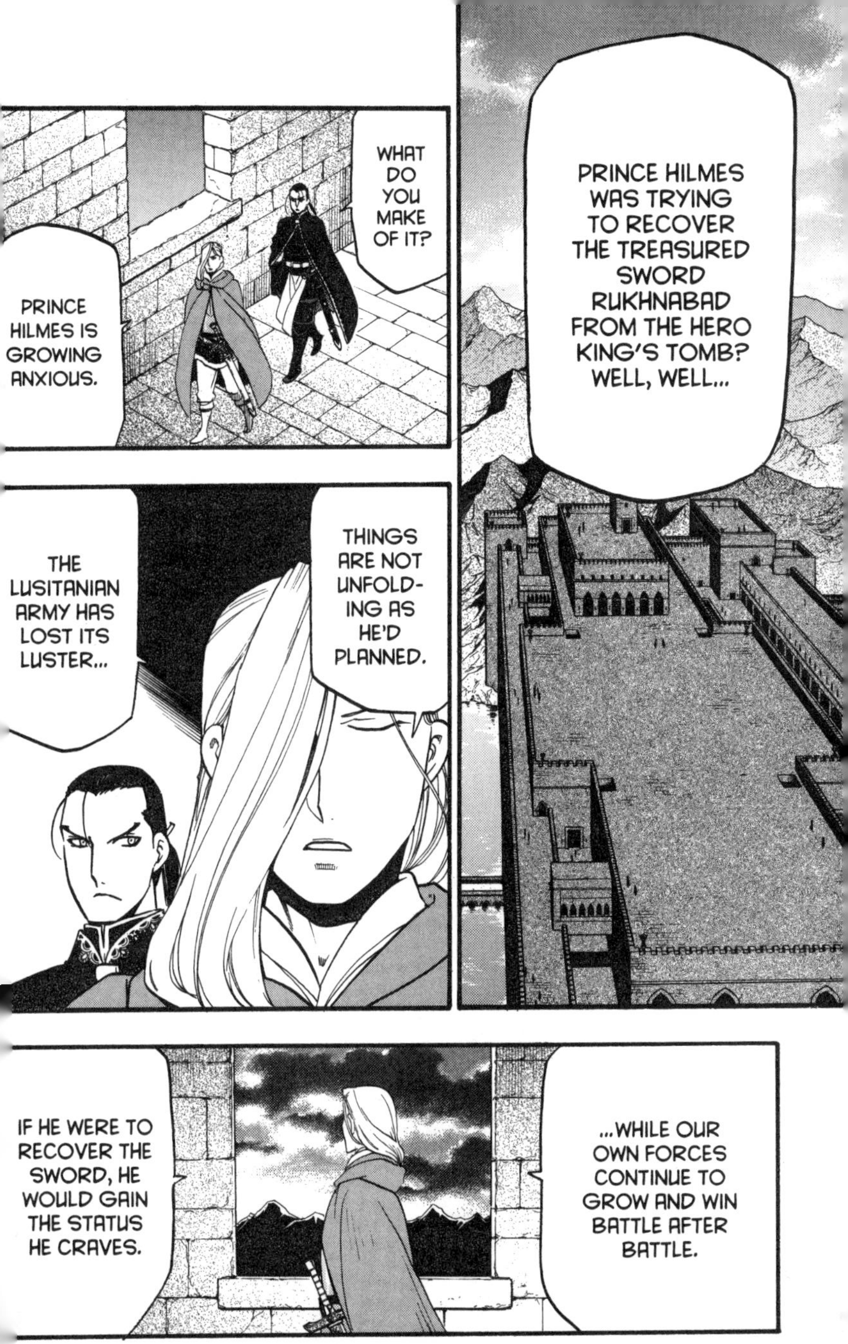
PRINCE HILMES WAS TRYING TO RECOVER THE TREASURED SWORD RUKHNABAD FROM THE HERO KING'S TOMB? WELL, WELL...
WHAT DO YOU MAKE OF IT?
PRINCE HILMES IS GROWING ANXIOUS.
THINGS ARE NOT UNFOLDING AS HE'D PLANNED.
THE LUSITANIAN ARMY HAS LOST ITS LUSTER...
...WHILE OUR OWN FORCES CONTINUE TO GROW AND WIN BATTLE AFTER BATTLE.
IF HE WERE TO RECOVER THE SWORD, HE WOULD GAIN THE STATUS HE CRAVES.

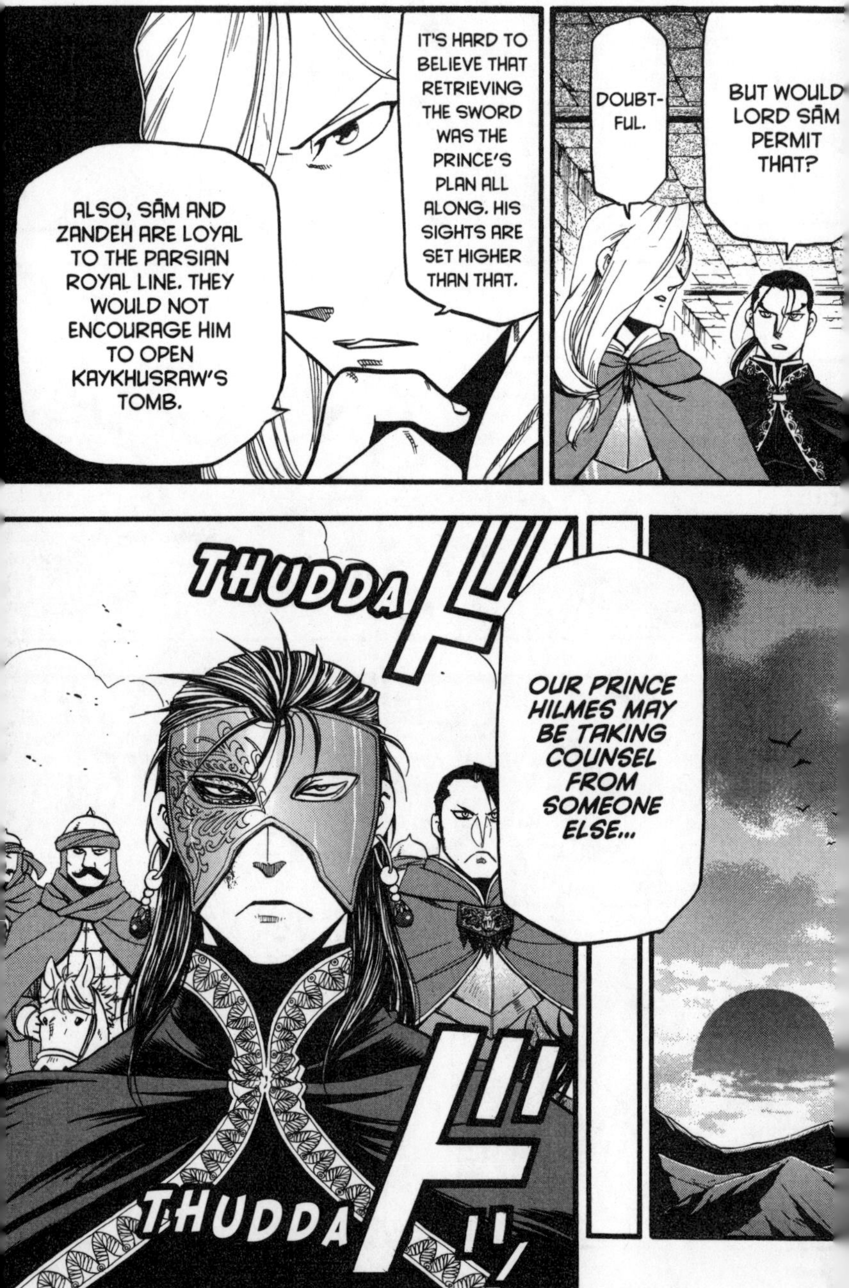
BUT WOULD LORD SĀM PERMIT THAT?
DOUBT-FUL.
IT'S HARD TO BELIEVE THAT RETRIEVING THE SWORD WAS THE PRINCE'S PLAN ALL ALONG. HIS SIGHTS ARE SET HIGHER THAN THAT.
ALSO, SĀM AND ZANDEH ARE LOYAL TO THE PARSIAN ROYAL LINE. THEY WOULD NOT ENCOURAGE HIM TO OPEN KAYKHUSRAW'S TOMB.
OUR PRINCE HILMES MAY BE TAKING COUNSEL FROM SOMEONE ELSE...
THUDDA
THUDDA

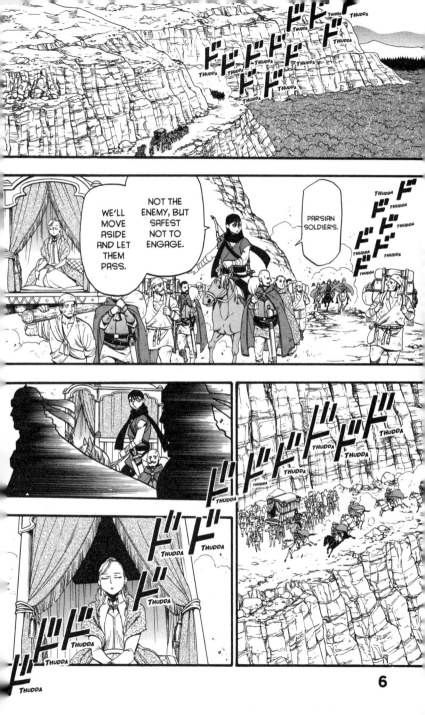

WE'LL MOVE ASIDE AND LET THEM PASS.

NOT THE ENEMY, BUT SAFEST NOT TO ENGAGE.

PARSIAN SOLDIERS.

ド ド ド ド ド
THUDDA THUDDA THUDDA THUDDA
ド ド
THUDDA THUDDA

THUDDA ド THUDDA
ド ド THUDDA
THUDDA ド
ド ド
THUDDA

ド ド ド ド
THUDDA ド ド THUDDA
ド ド THUDDA
THUDDA

ド ド
THUDDA THUDDA
ド
THUDDA

ド ド
THUDDA

ド
THUDDA

6

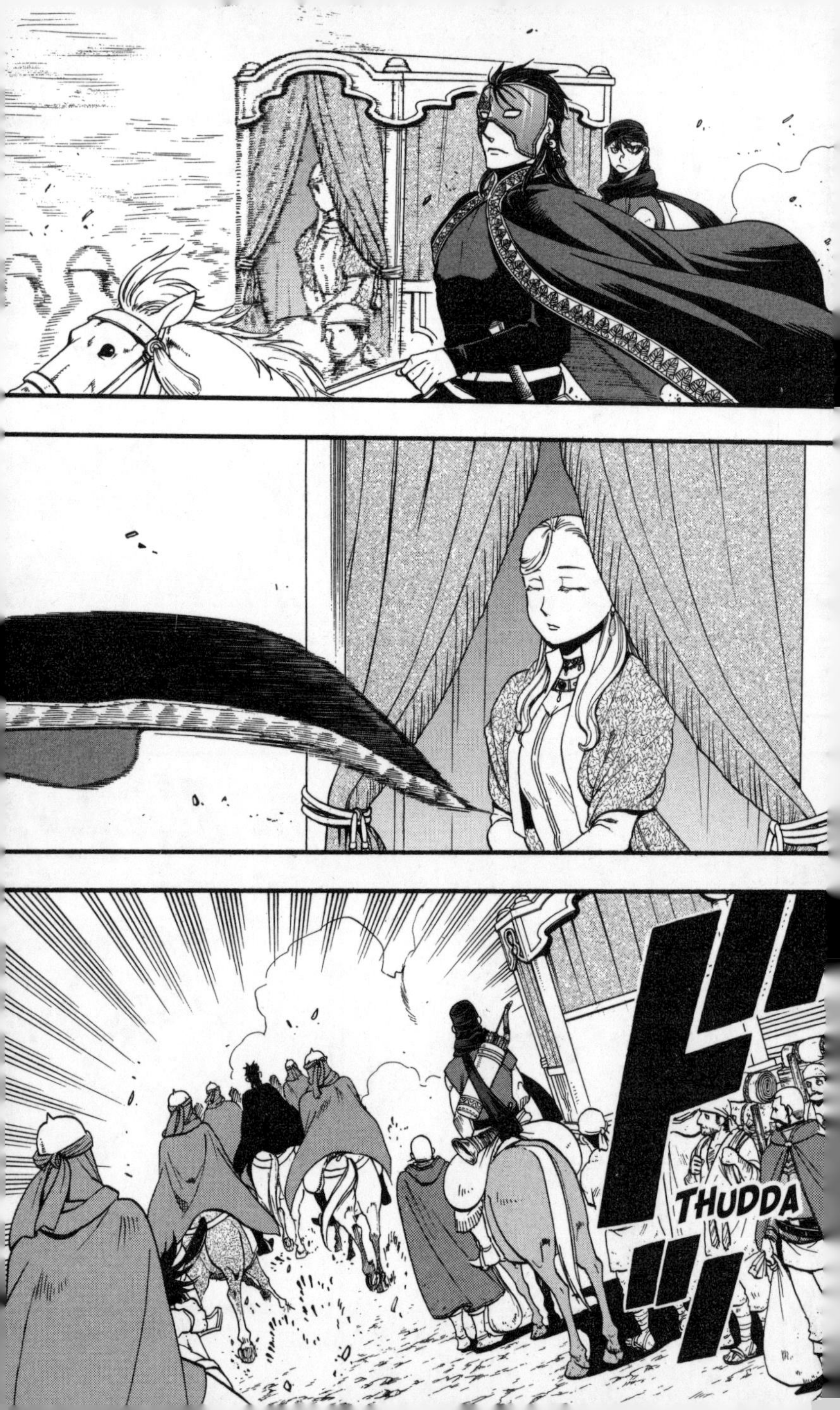
THUDDA

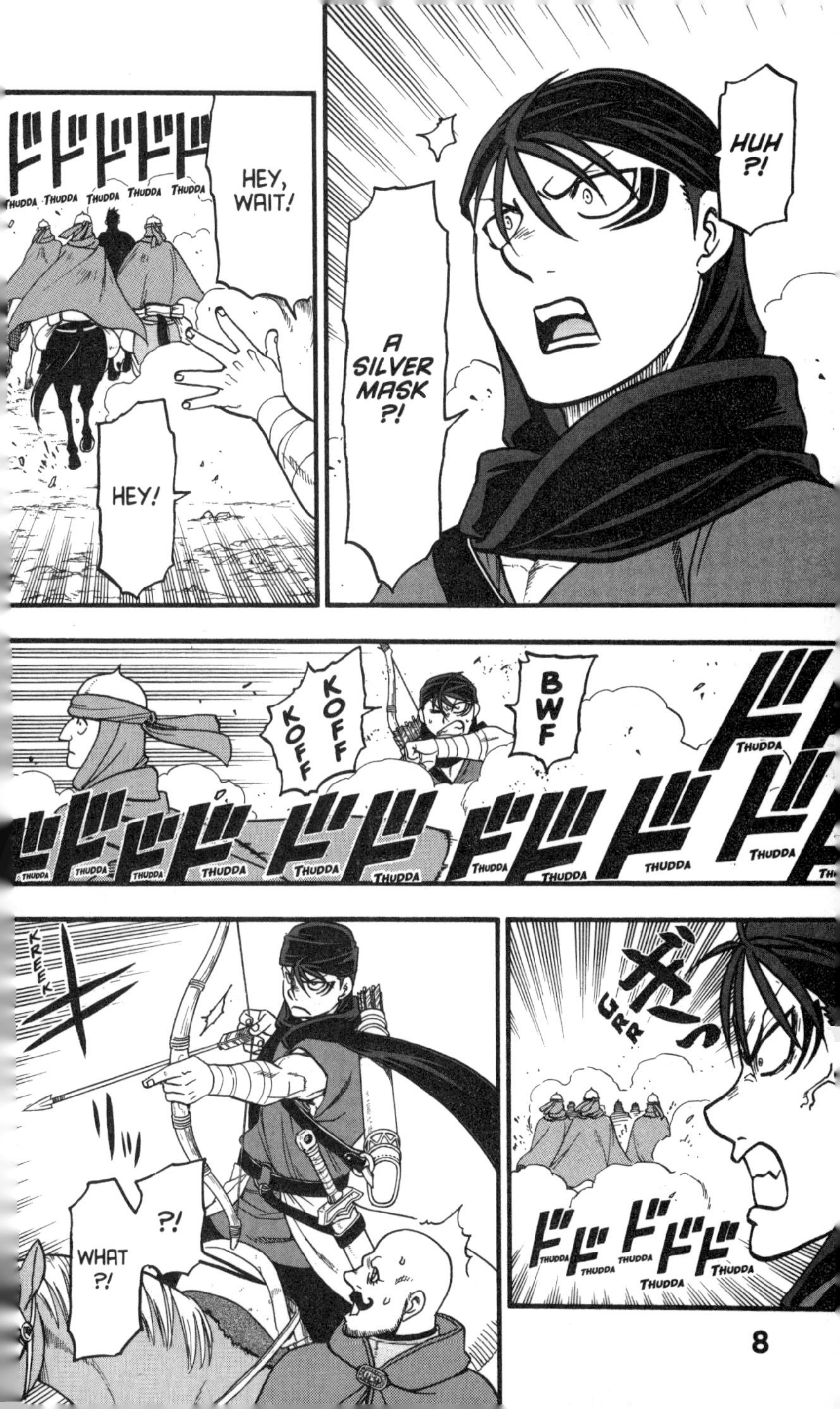
HUH ?!
A SILVER MASK ?!
ドドドドド
THUDDA THUDDA THUDDA THUDDA THUDDA
HEY, WAIT!
HEY!
ドドドドドドドドドドドド
THUDDA THUDDA THUDDA THUDDA THUDDA THUDDA THUDDA THUDDA THUDDA THUDDA THUDDA THUDDA
BWF
KOFF KOFF
GRR
ドドドドド
THUDDA THUDDA THUDDA THUDDA THUDDA
KREEK
?!
WHAT ?!

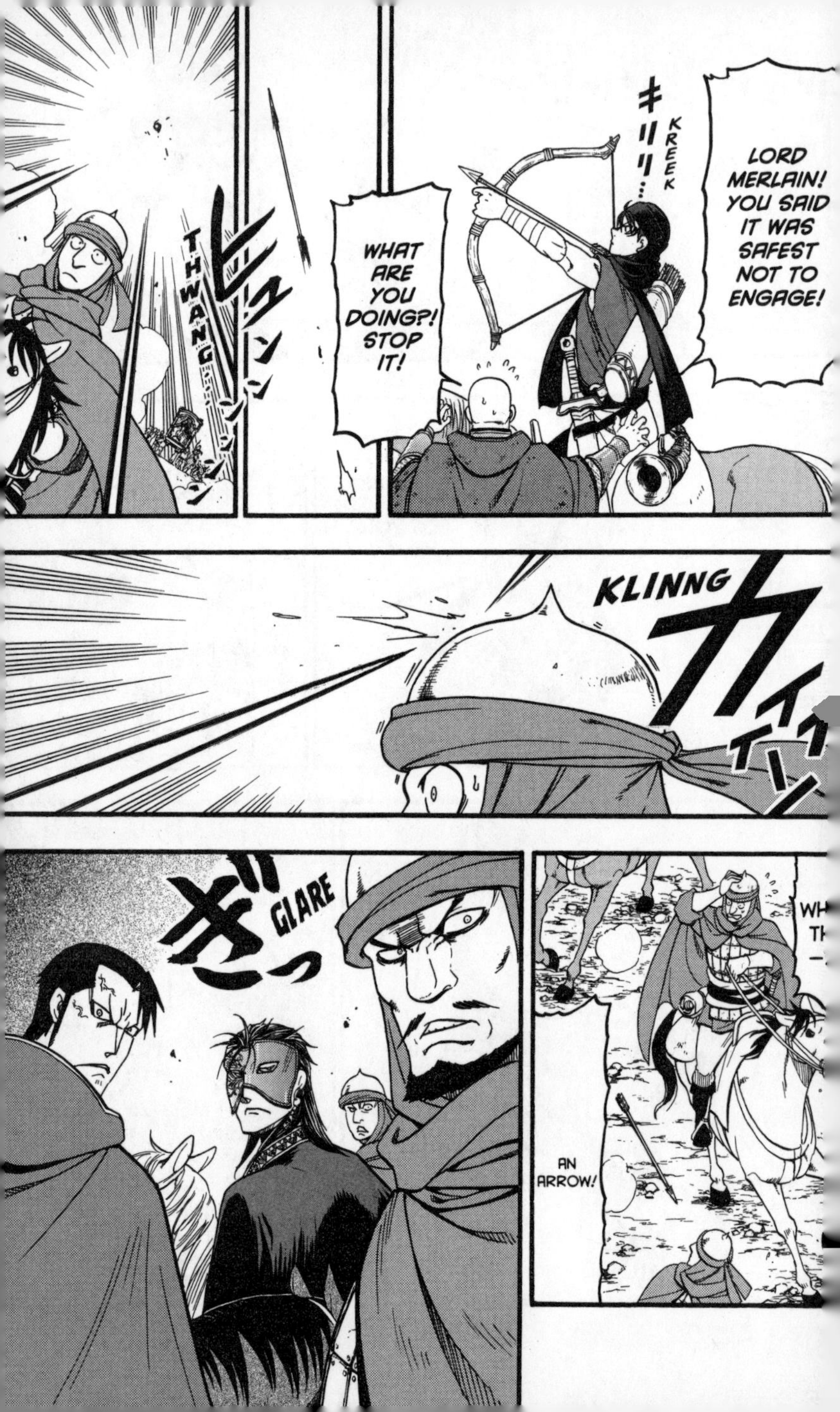
LORD MERLAIN! YOU SAID IT WAS SAFEST NOT TO ENGAGE!
キリリ…
KREEK
WHAT ARE YOU DOING?! STOP IT!
THWANG
KLINNG
AN ARROW!
GLARE

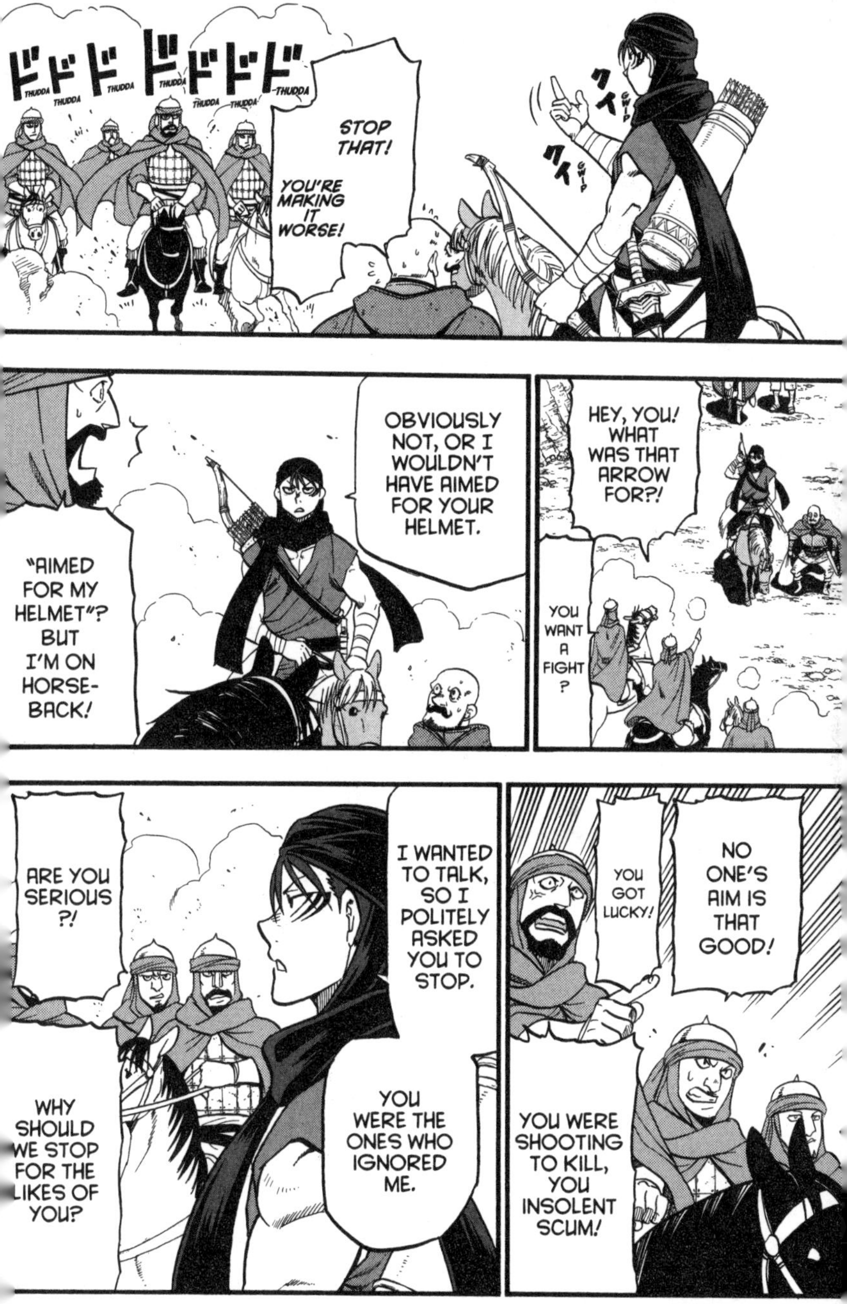
クイ
GWIP
クイ
GWIP
STOP THAT!
YOU'RE MAKING IT WORSE!
ドドドドドドド
THUDDA THUDDA THUDDA THUDDA THUDDA THUDDA THUDDA
HEY, YOU! WHAT WAS THAT ARROW FOR?!
YOU WANT A FIGHT?
OBVIOUSLY NOT, OR I WOULDN'T HAVE AIMED FOR YOUR HELMET.
"AIMED FOR MY HELMET"? BUT I'M ON HORSE-BACK!
NO ONE'S AIM IS THAT GOOD!
YOU GOT LUCKY!
YOU WERE SHOOTING TO KILL, YOU INSOLENT SCUM!
I WANTED TO TALK, SO I POLITELY ASKED YOU TO STOP.
ARE YOU SERIOUS?!
YOU WERE THE ONES WHO IGNORED ME.
WHY SHOULD WE STOP FOR THE LIKES OF YOU?

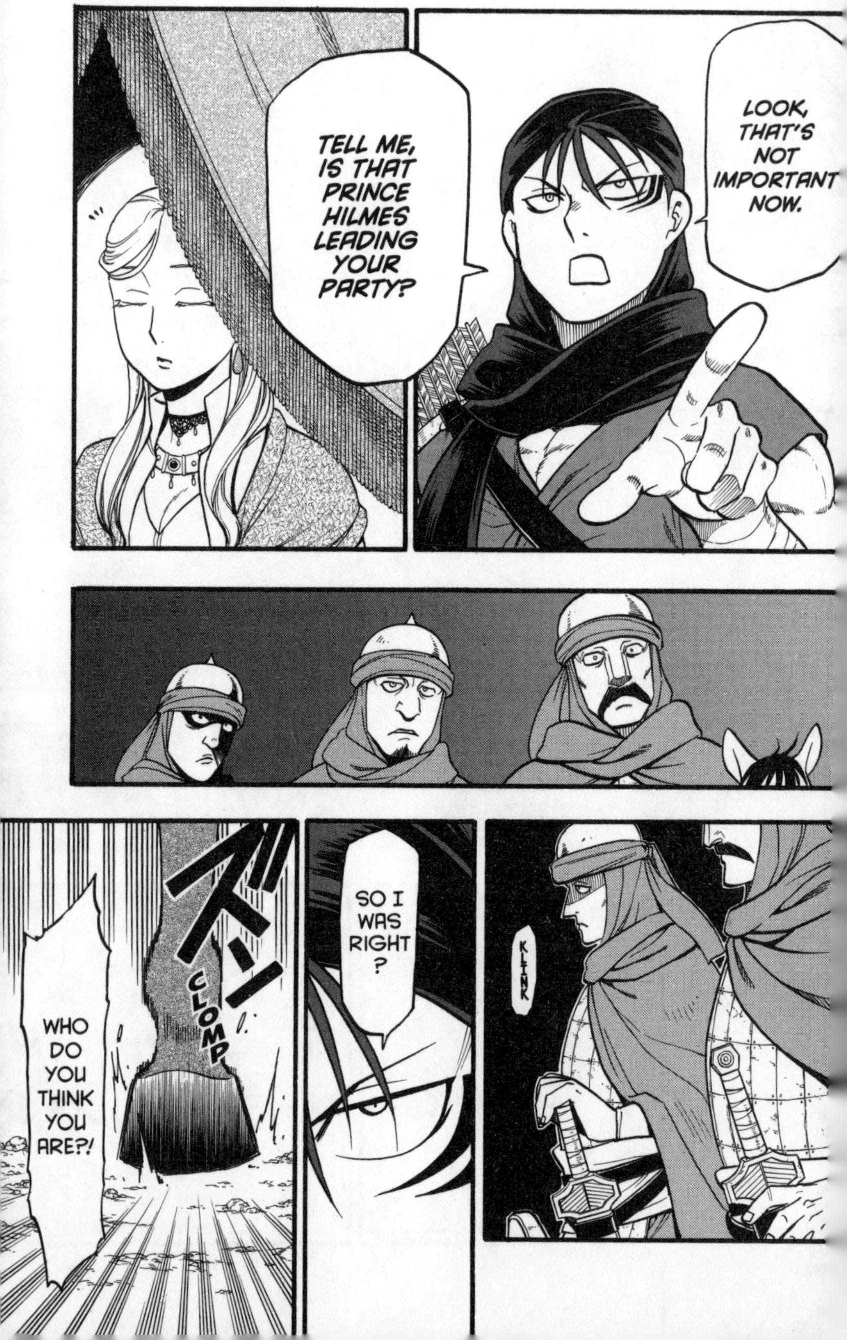
LOOK, THAT'S NOT IMPORTANT NOW.
TELL ME, IS THAT PRINCE HILMES LEADING YOUR PARTY?
KLINK
SO I WAS RIGHT?
CLOMP
WHO DO YOU THINK YOU ARE?!

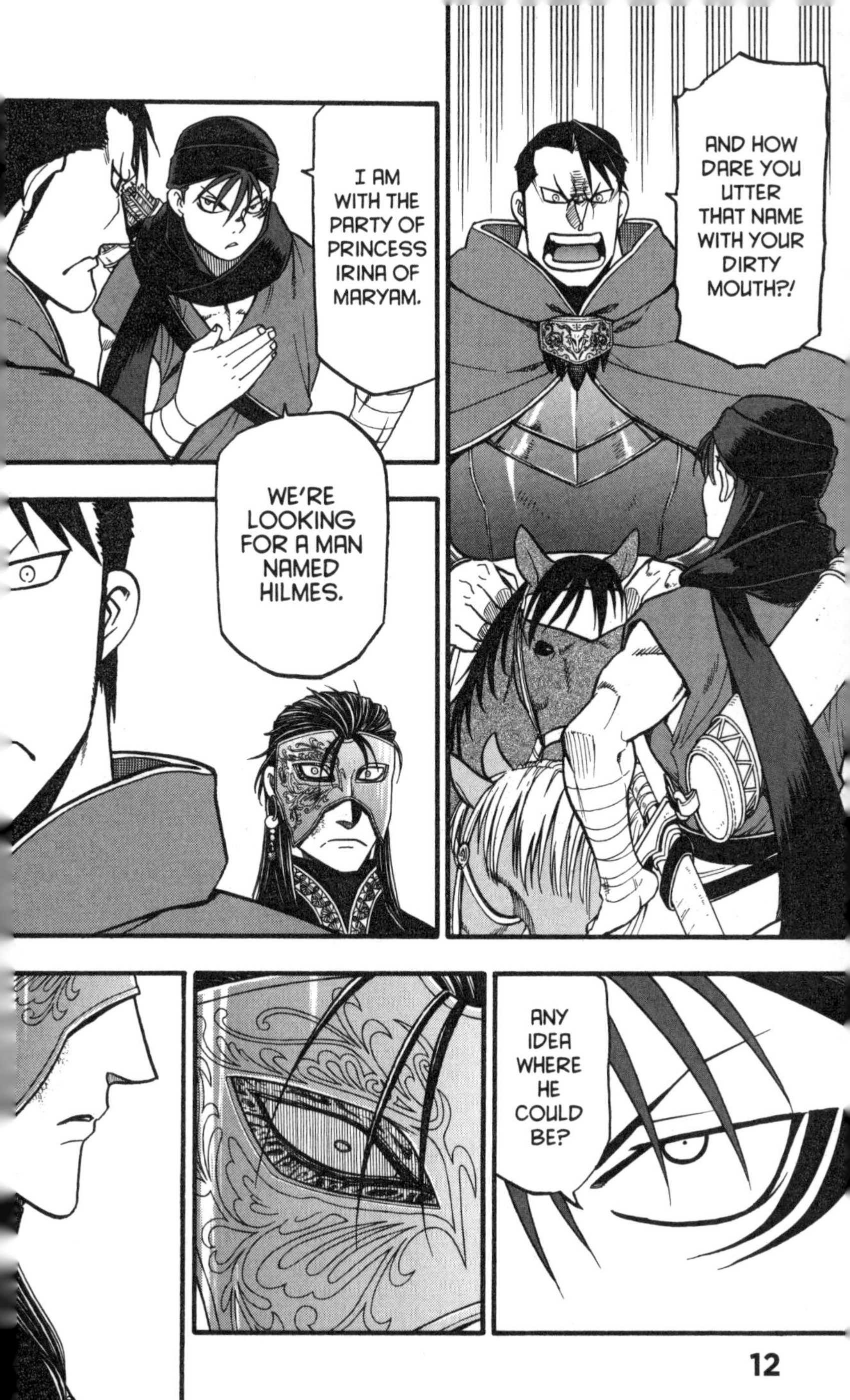
AND HOW DARE YOU UTTER THAT NAME WITH YOUR DIRTY MOUTH?!
I AM WITH THE PARTY OF PRINCESS IRINA OF MARYAM.
WE'RE LOOKING FOR A MAN NAMED HILMES.
ANY IDEA WHERE HE COULD BE?

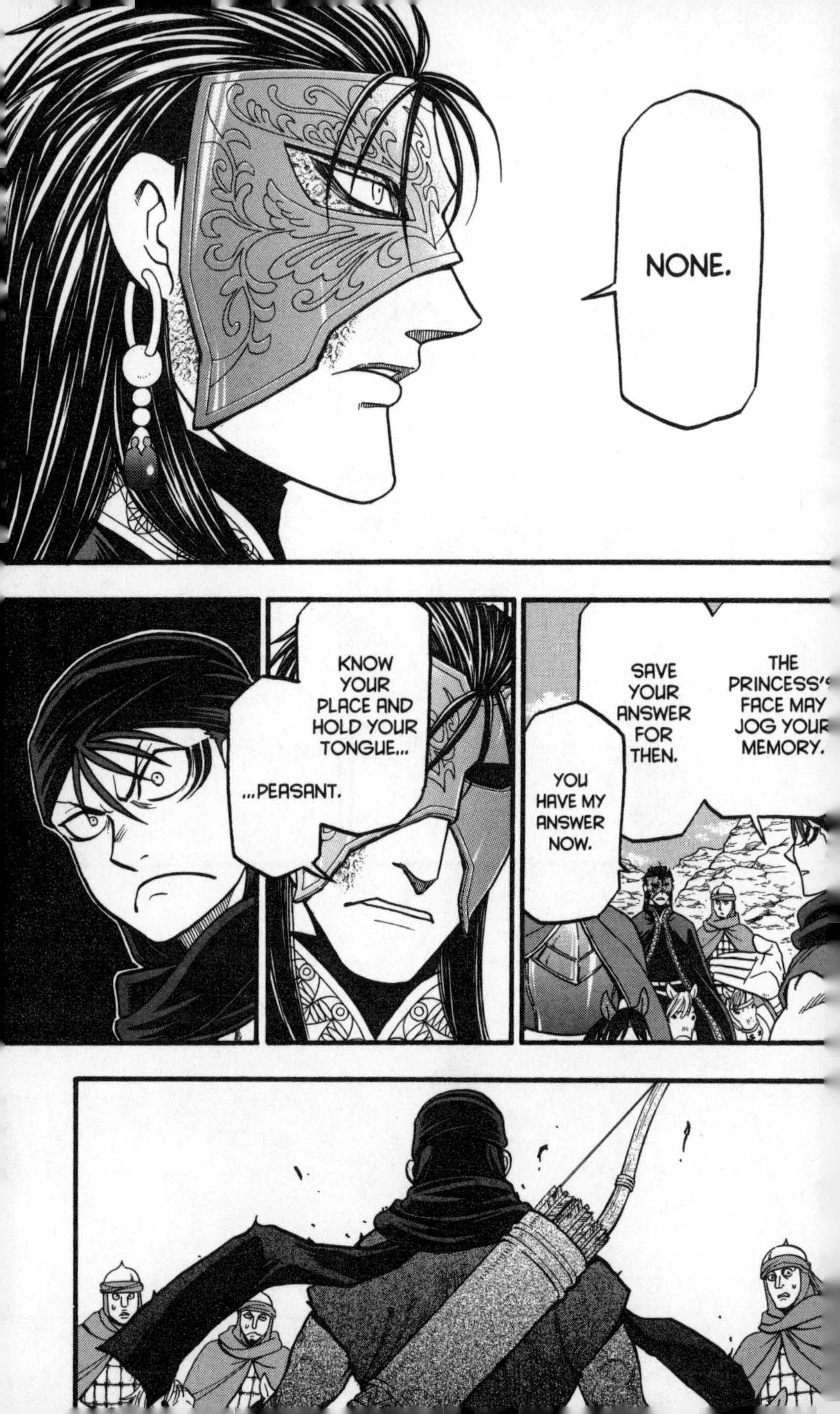
NONE.
THE PRINCESS'S FACE MAY JOG YOUR MEMORY.
SAVE YOUR ANSWER FOR THEN.
YOU HAVE MY ANSWER NOW.
KNOW YOUR PLACE AND HOLD YOUR TONGUE...
...PEASANT.

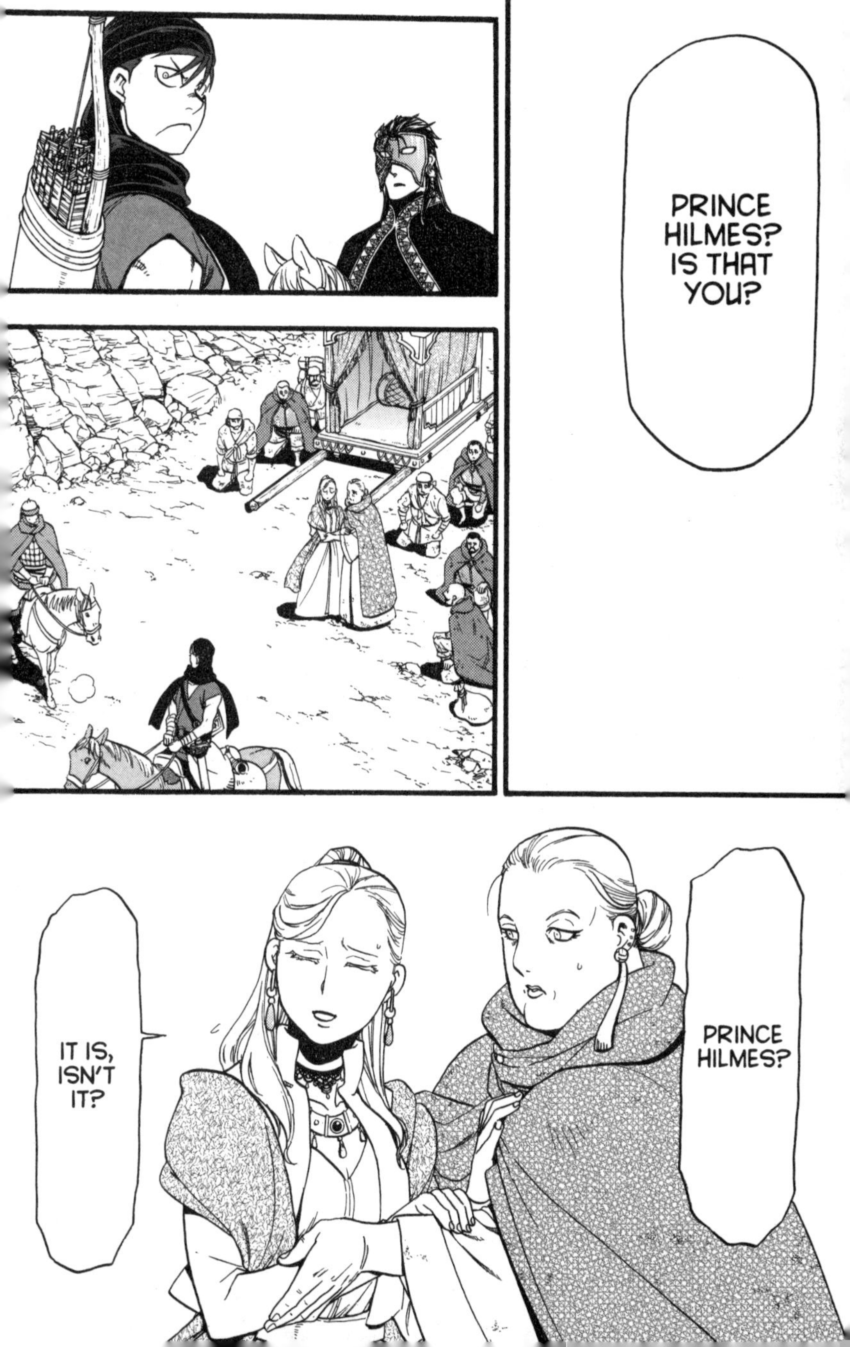
PRINCE HILMES? IS THAT YOU?
PRINCE HILMES?
IT IS, ISN'T IT?

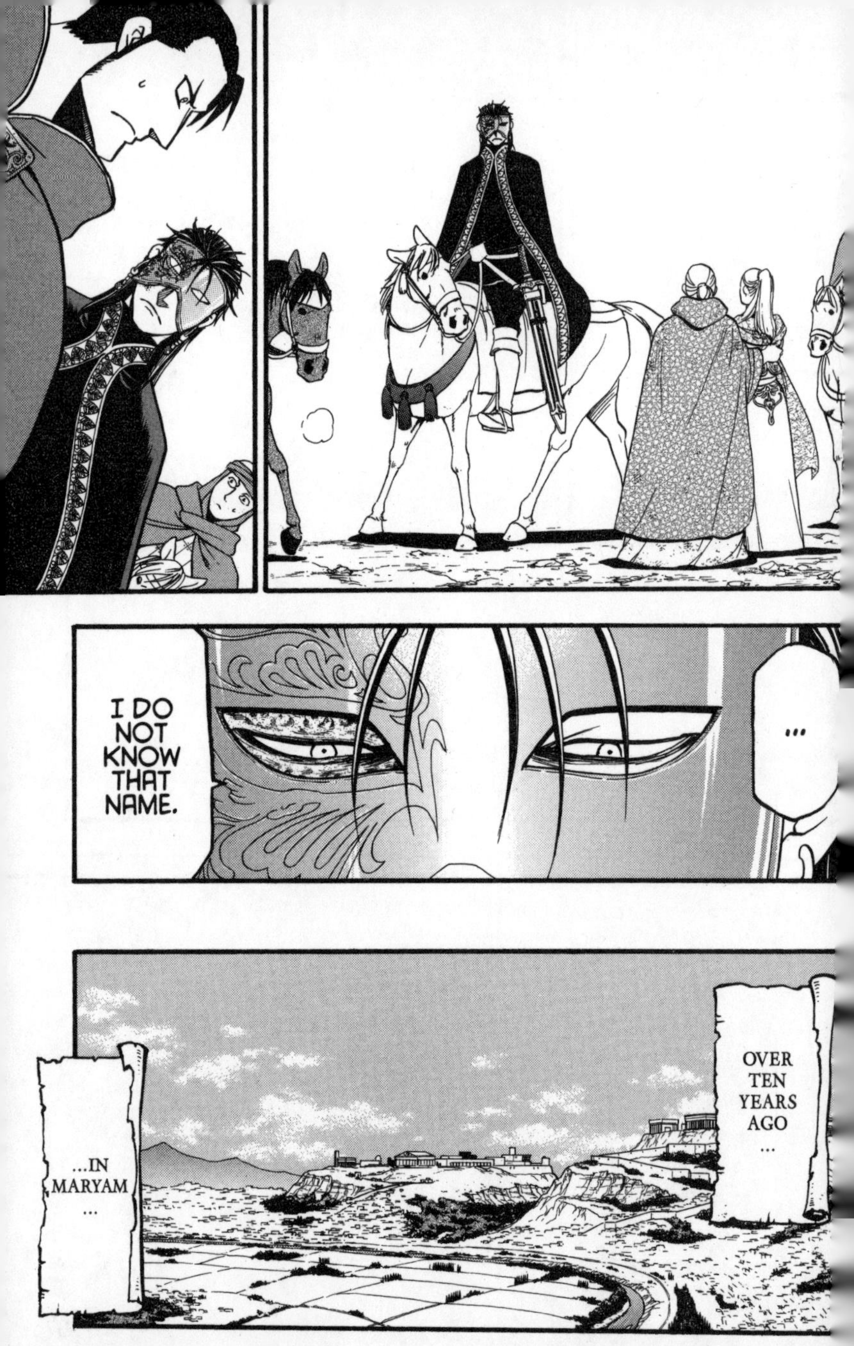
...
I DO NOT KNOW THAT NAME.
OVER TEN YEARS AGO ...
...IN MARYAM ...

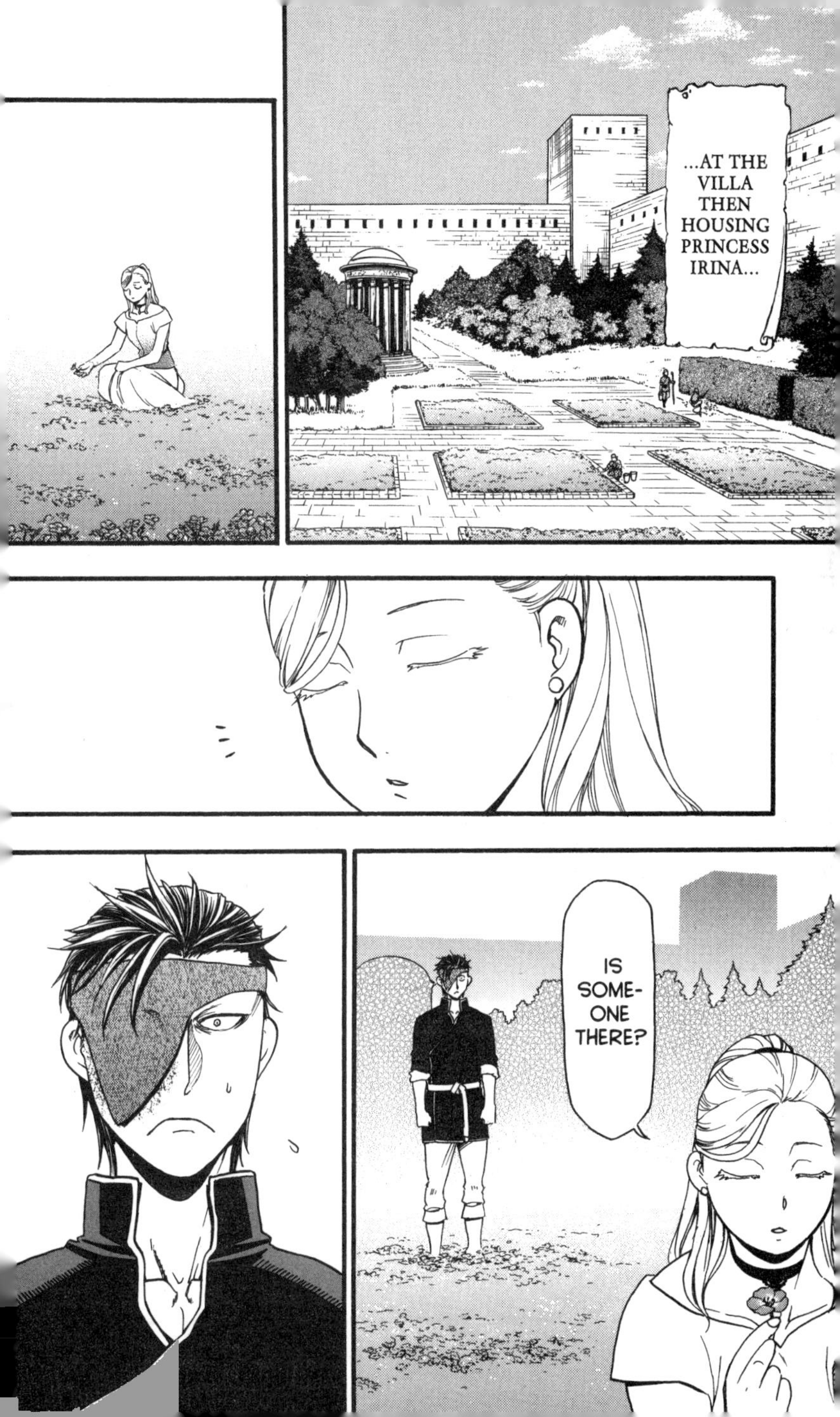
...AT THE VILLA THEN HOUSING PRINCESS IRINA...
IS SOME-ONE THERE?

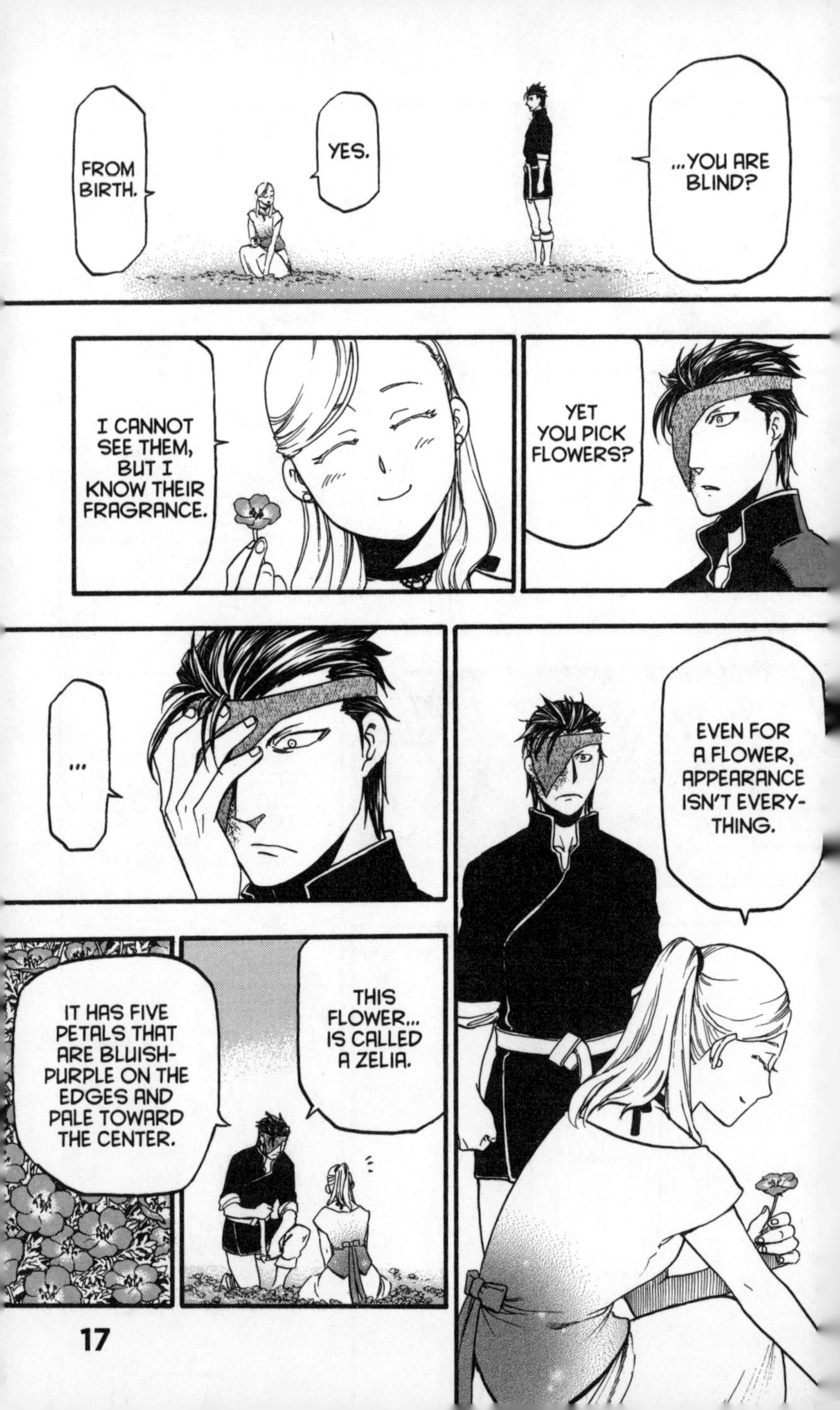
...YOU ARE BLIND?
YES.
FROM BIRTH.
YET YOU PICK FLOWERS?
I CANNOT SEE THEM, BUT I KNOW THEIR FRAGRANCE.
EVEN FOR A FLOWER, APPEARANCE ISN'T EVERYTHING.
...
THIS FLOWER... IS CALLED A ZELIA.
IT HAS FIVE PETALS THAT ARE BLUISH-PURPLE ON THE EDGES AND PALE TOWARD THE CENTER.

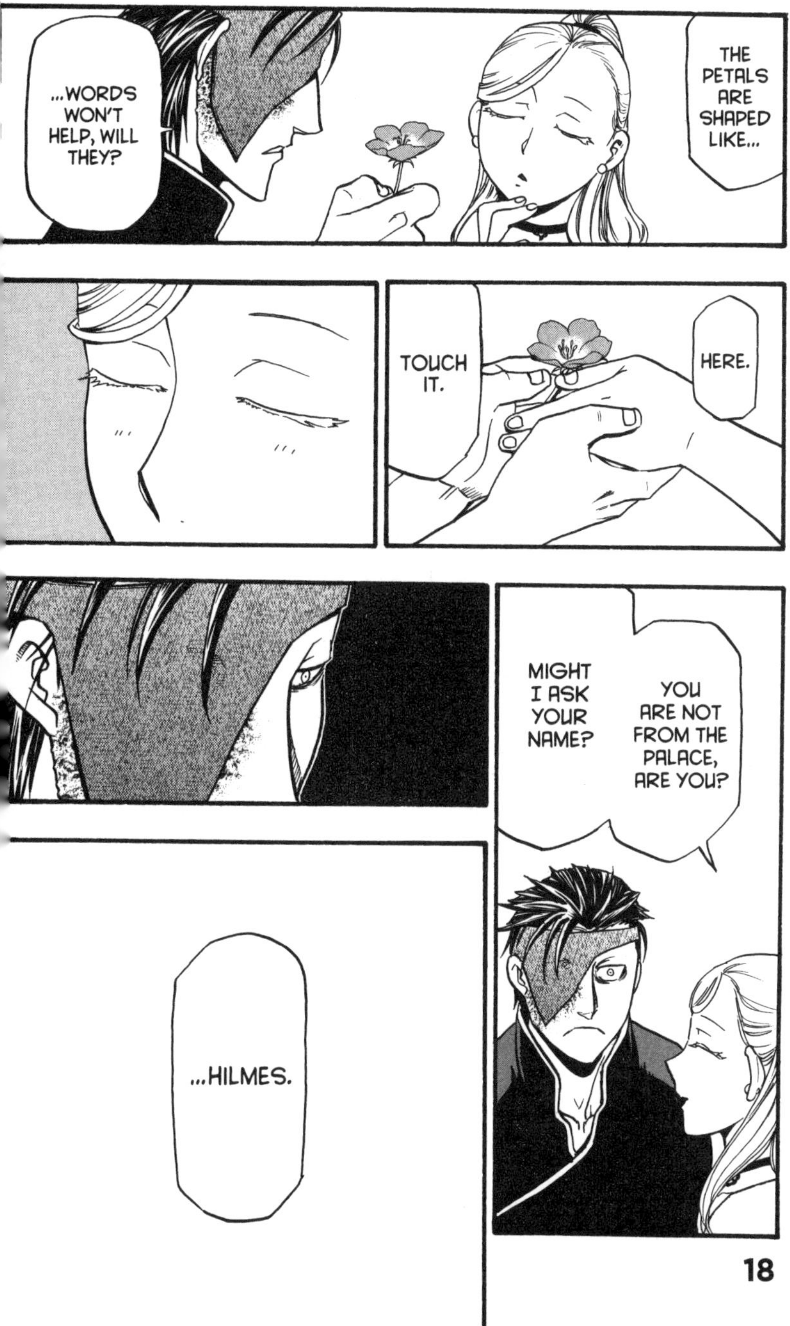
THE PETALS ARE SHAPED LIKE...
...WORDS WON'T HELP, WILL THEY?
HERE.
TOUCH IT.
YOU ARE NOT FROM THE PALACE, ARE YOU?
MIGHT I ASK YOUR NAME?
...HILMES.

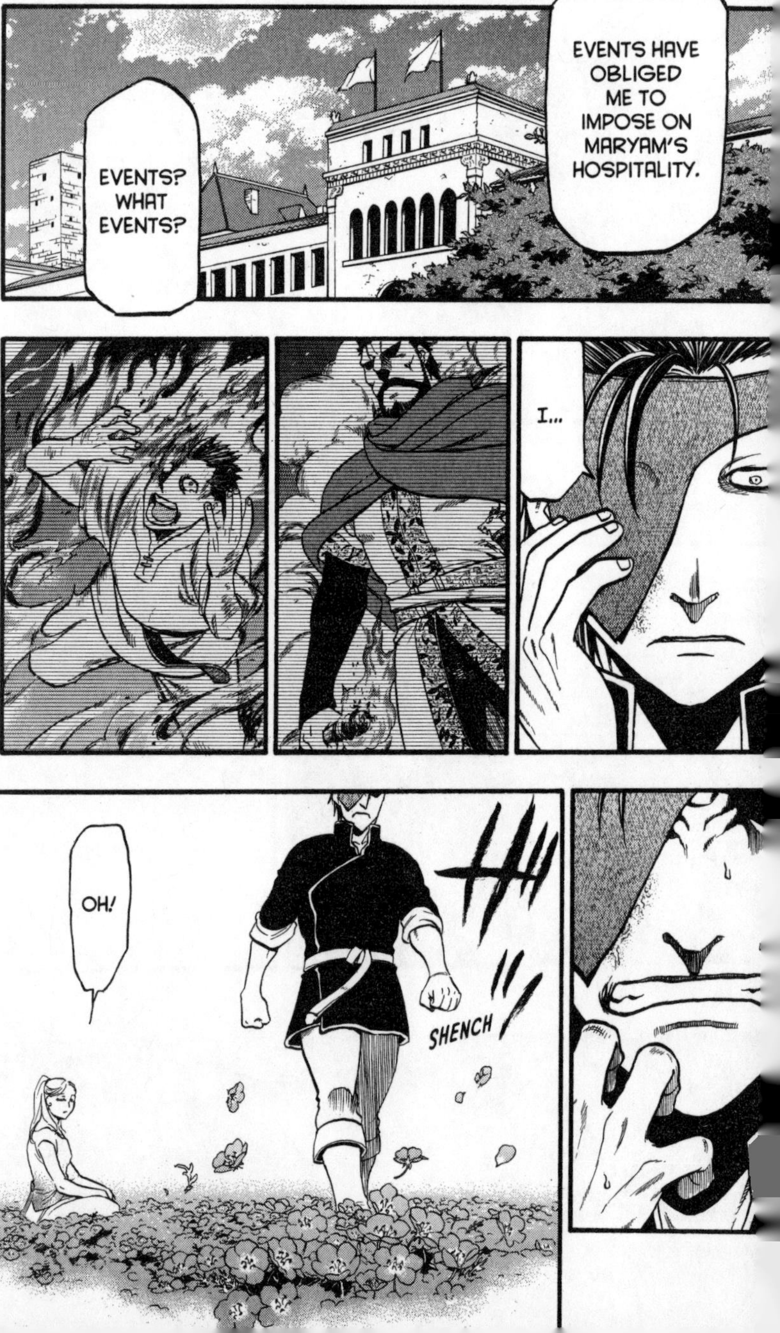
EVENTS HAVE OBLIGED ME TO IMPOSE ON MARYAM'S HOSPITALITY.
EVENTS? WHAT EVENTS?
I...
SHENCH
OH!

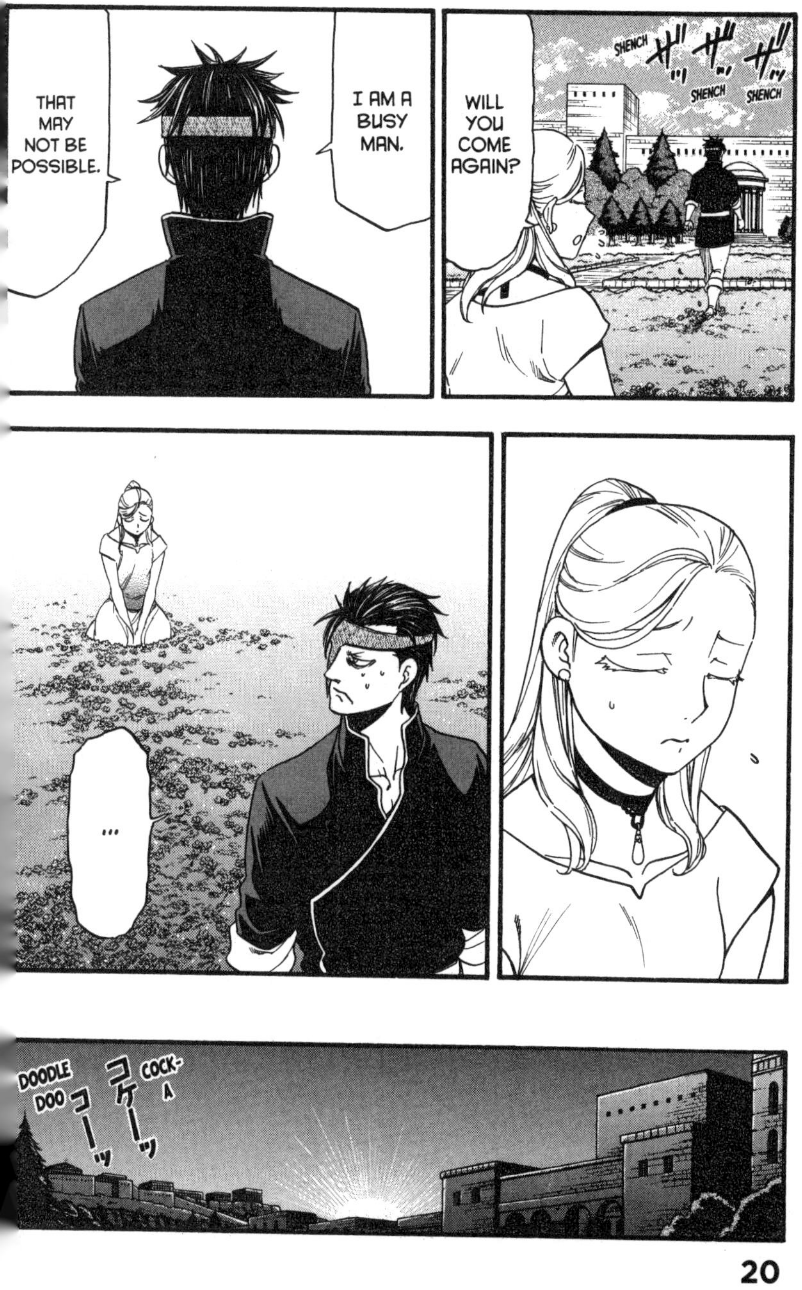
WILL YOU COME AGAIN?
ザッ
SHENCH
ザッ
SHENCH
ザッ
SHENCH
I AM A BUSY MAN.
THAT MAY NOT BE POSSIBLE.
...
COCK-A
コケーッ
DOODLE DOO
コーッ

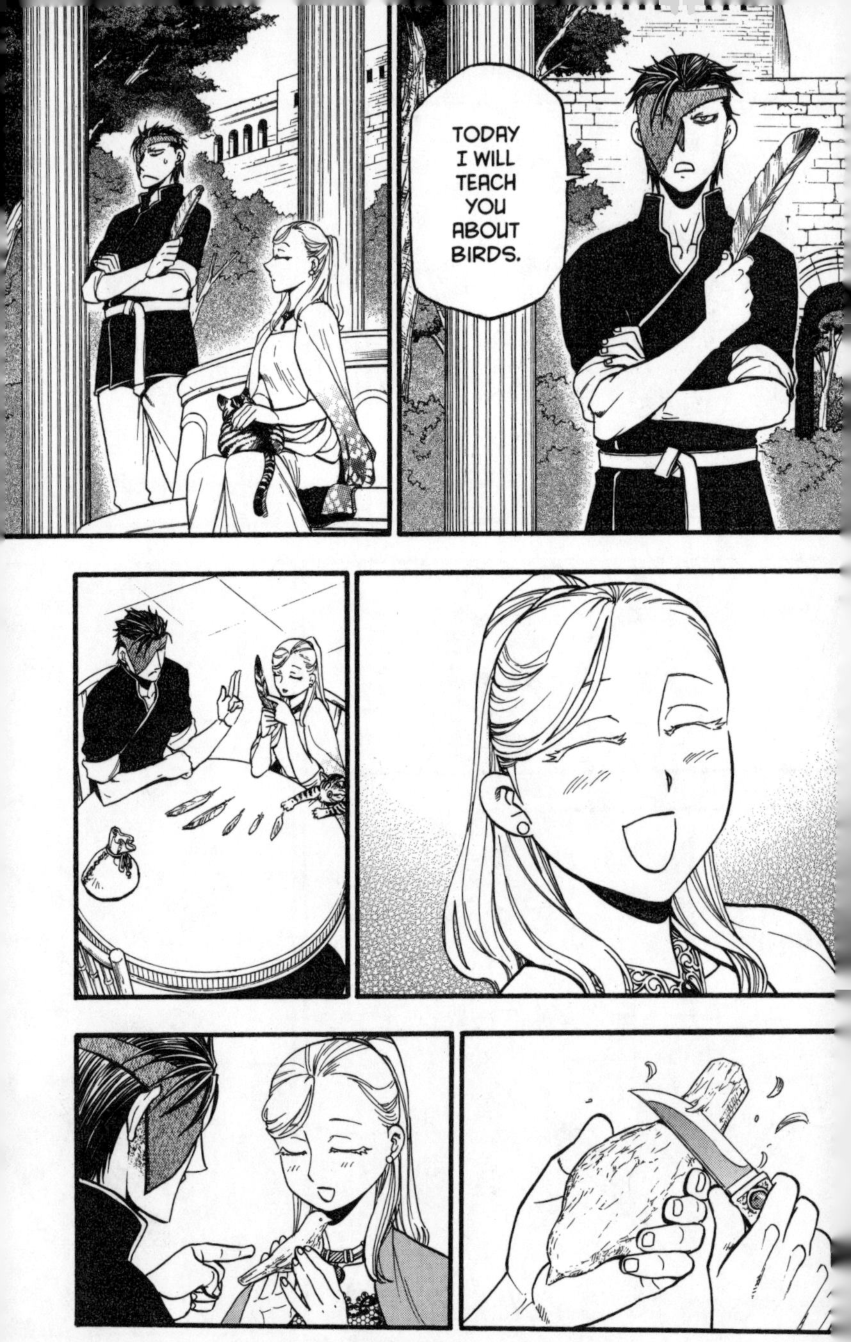
TODAY I WILL TEACH YOU ABOUT BIRDS.

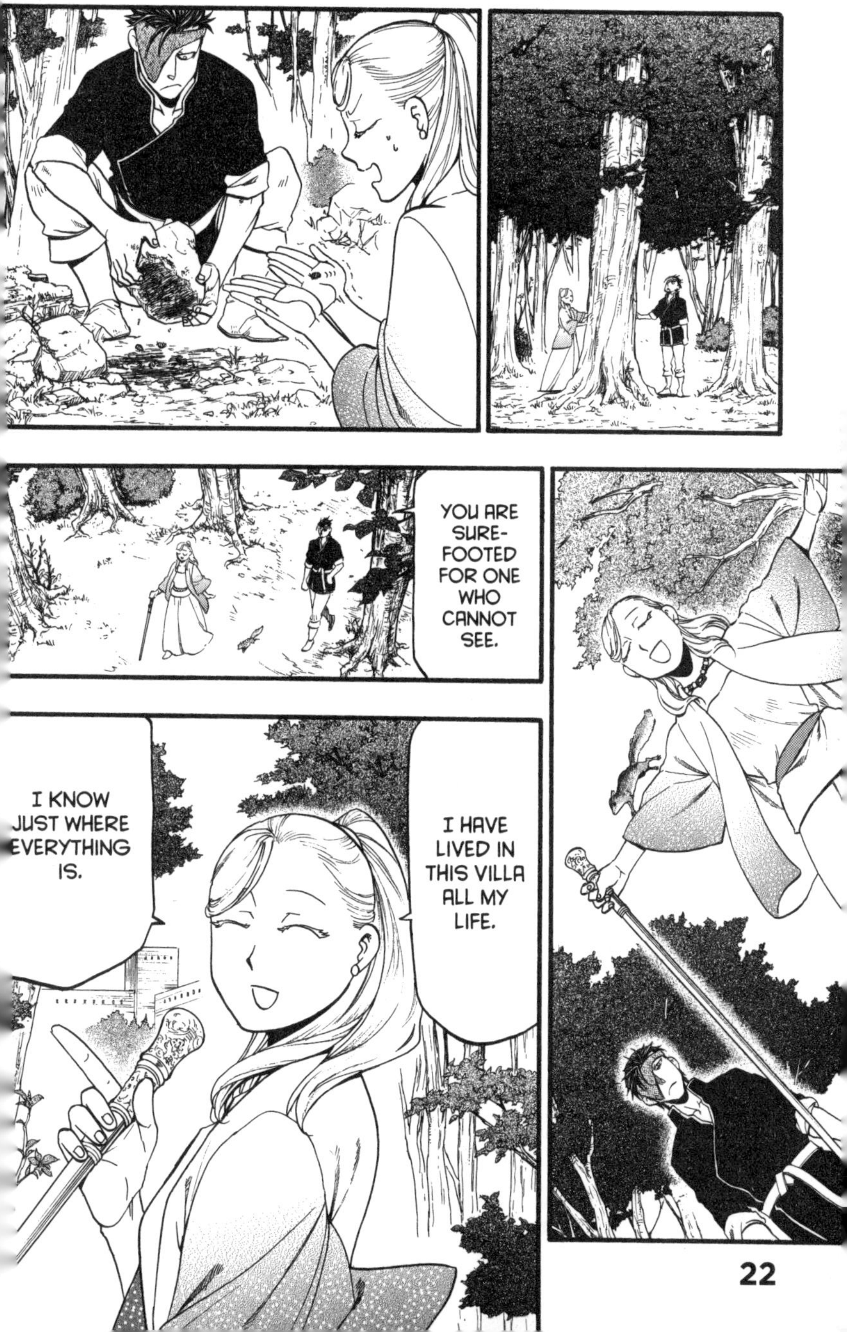
YOU ARE SURE-FOOTED FOR ONE WHO CANNOT SEE.
I HAVE LIVED IN THIS VILLA ALL MY LIFE.
I KNOW JUST WHERE EVERYTHING IS.

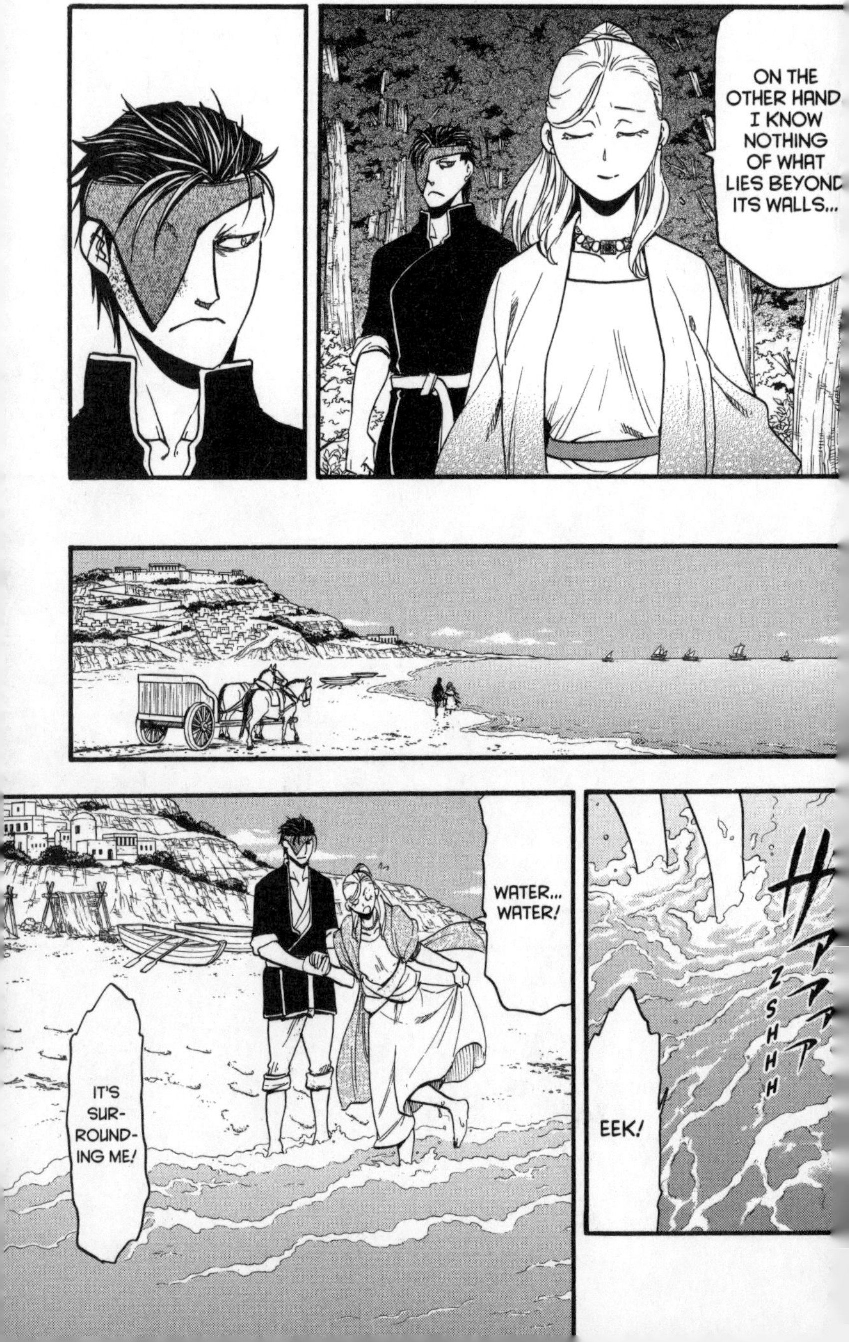
ON THE OTHER HAND I KNOW NOTHING OF WHAT LIES BEYOND ITS WALLS...
ZSHHH
EEK!
WATER... WATER!
IT'S SUR-ROUND-ING ME!

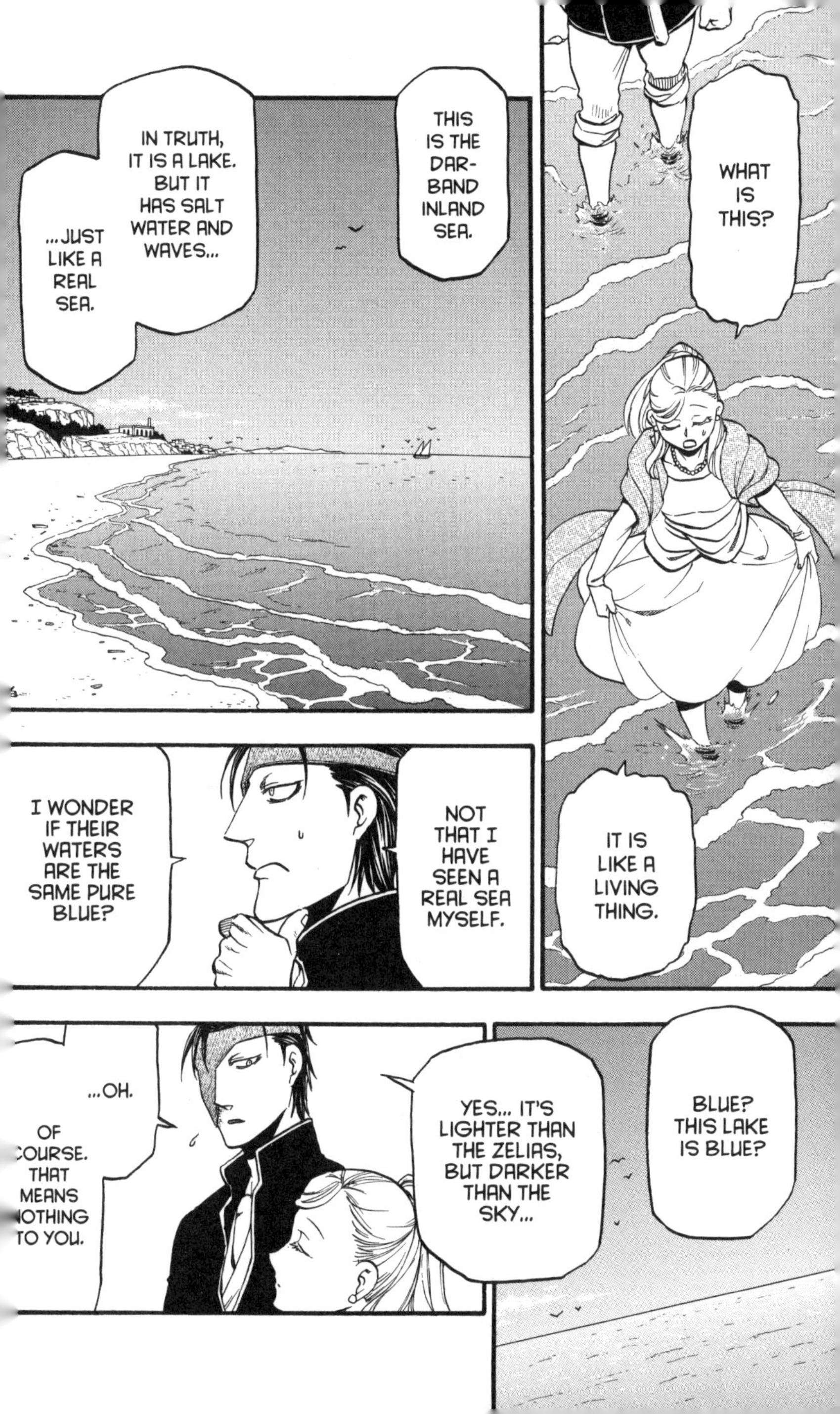
WHAT IS THIS?
IT IS LIKE A LIVING THING.
THIS IS THE DAR-BAND INLAND SEA.
IN TRUTH, IT IS A LAKE. BUT IT HAS SALT WATER AND WAVES...
...JUST LIKE A REAL SEA.
NOT THAT I HAVE SEEN A REAL SEA MYSELF.
I WONDER IF THEIR WATERS ARE THE SAME PURE BLUE?
BLUE? THIS LAKE IS BLUE?
YES... IT'S LIGHTER THAN THE ZELIAS, BUT DARKER THAN THE SKY...
...OH.
OF COURSE. THAT MEANS NOTHING TO YOU.

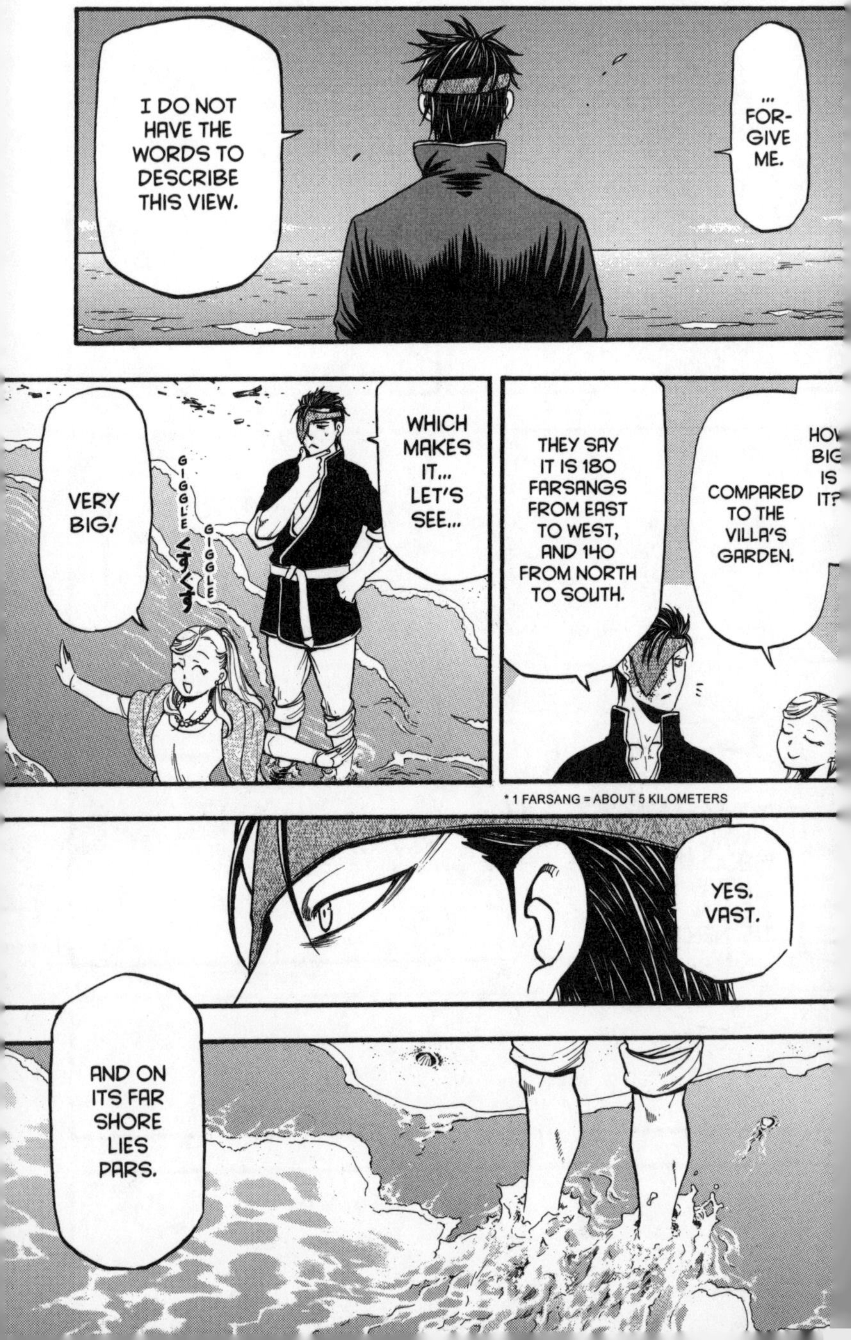

... FOR-GIVE ME.
I DO NOT HAVE THE WORDS TO DESCRIBE THIS VIEW.
HOW BIG IS IT?
COMPARED TO THE VILLA'S GARDEN.
THEY SAY IT IS 180 FARSANGS FROM EAST TO WEST, AND 140 FROM NORTH TO SOUTH.
WHICH MAKES IT... LET'S SEE...
GIGGLE GIGGLE くすくす
VERY BIG!
* 1 FARSANG = ABOUT 5 KILOMETERS
YES. VAST.
AND ON ITS FAR SHORE LIES PARS.

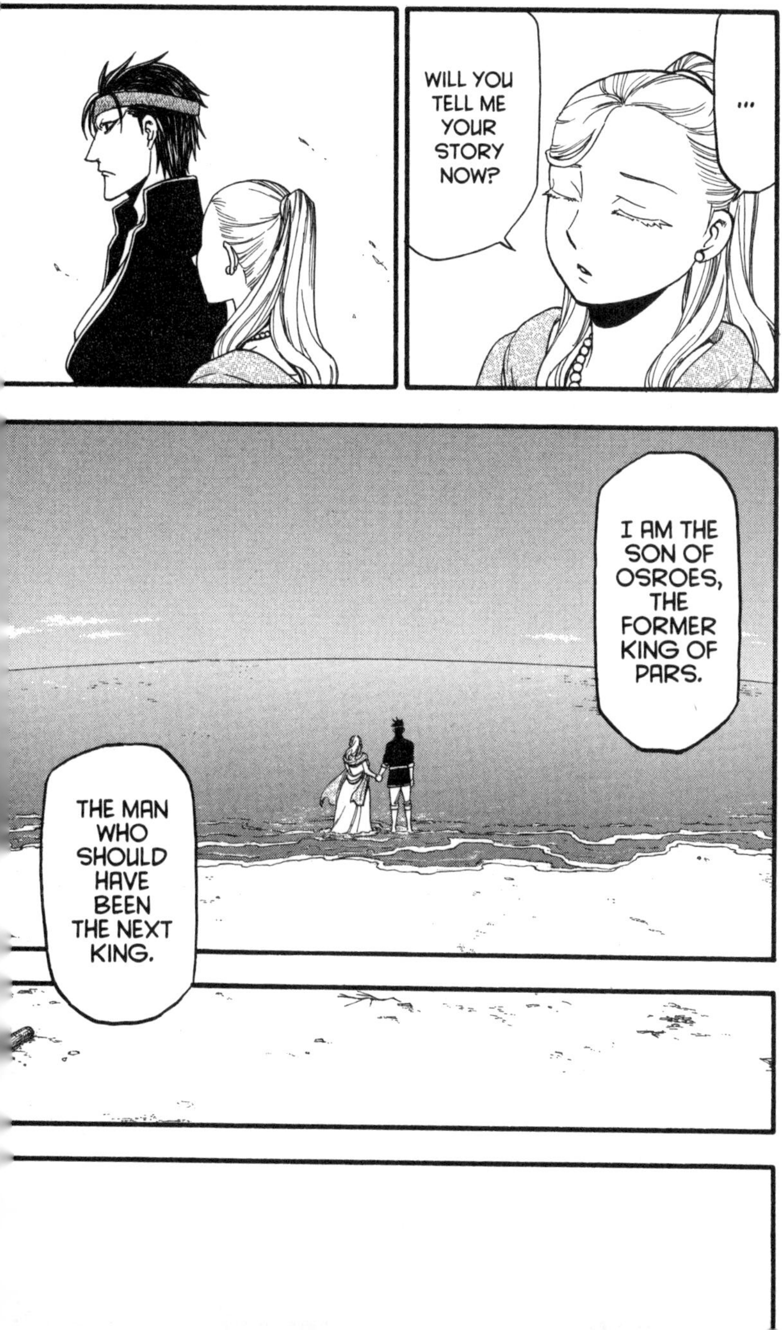
...
WILL YOU TELL ME YOUR STORY NOW?
I AM THE SON OF OSROES, THE FORMER KING OF PARS.
THE MAN WHO SHOULD HAVE BEEN THE NEXT KING.

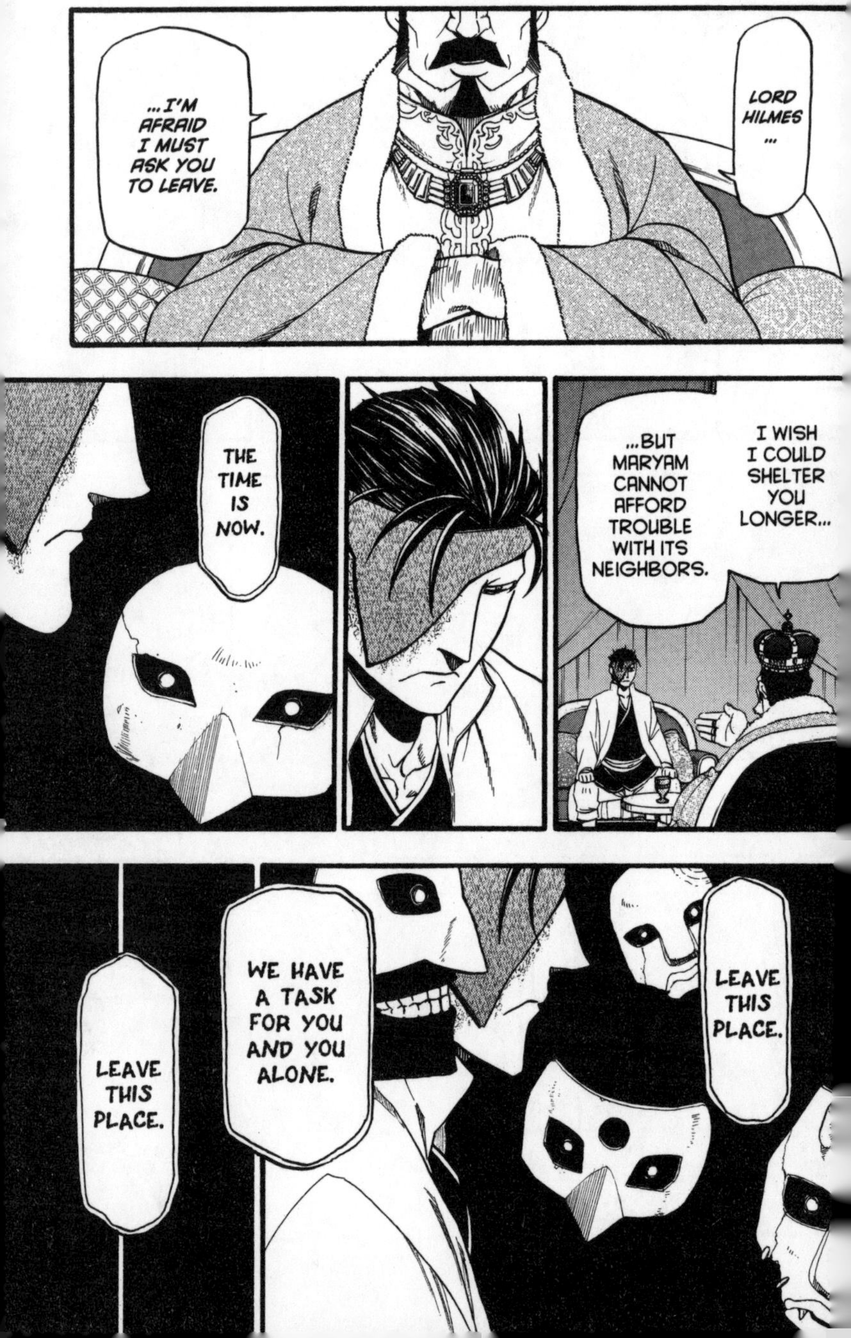
LORD HILMES ...
...I'M AFRAID I MUST ASK YOU TO LEAVE.
I WISH I COULD SHELTER YOU LONGER...
...BUT MARYAM CANNOT AFFORD TROUBLE WITH ITS NEIGHBORS.
THE TIME IS NOW.
LEAVE THIS PLACE.
WE HAVE A TASK FOR YOU AND YOU ALONE.
LEAVE THIS PLACE.

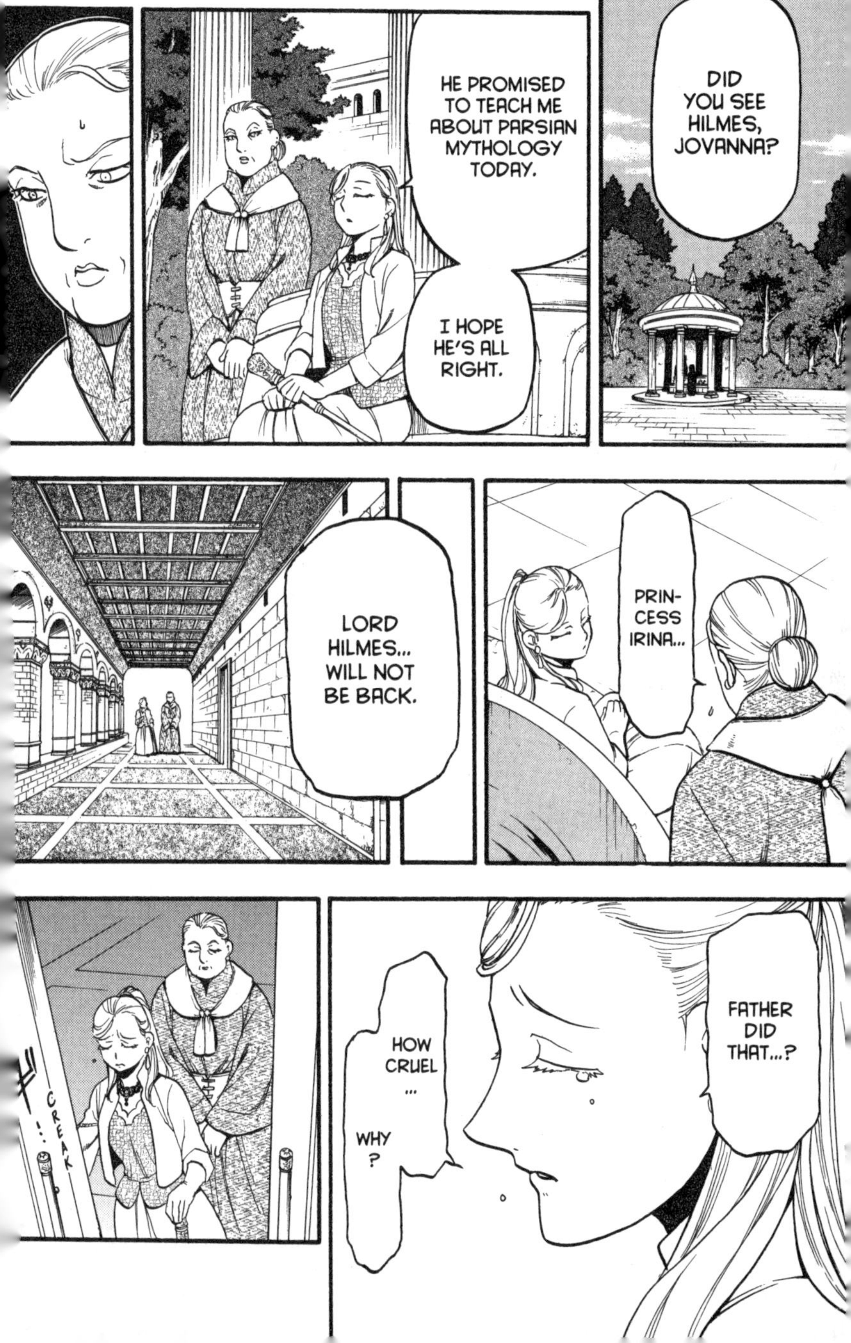
DID YOU SEE HILMES, JOVANNA?
HE PROMISED TO TEACH ME ABOUT PARSIAN MYTHOLOGY TODAY.
I HOPE HE'S ALL RIGHT.
PRIN-CESS IRINA...
LORD HILMES... WILL NOT BE BACK.
FATHER DID THAT...?
HOW CRUEL...
WHY?
CREAK

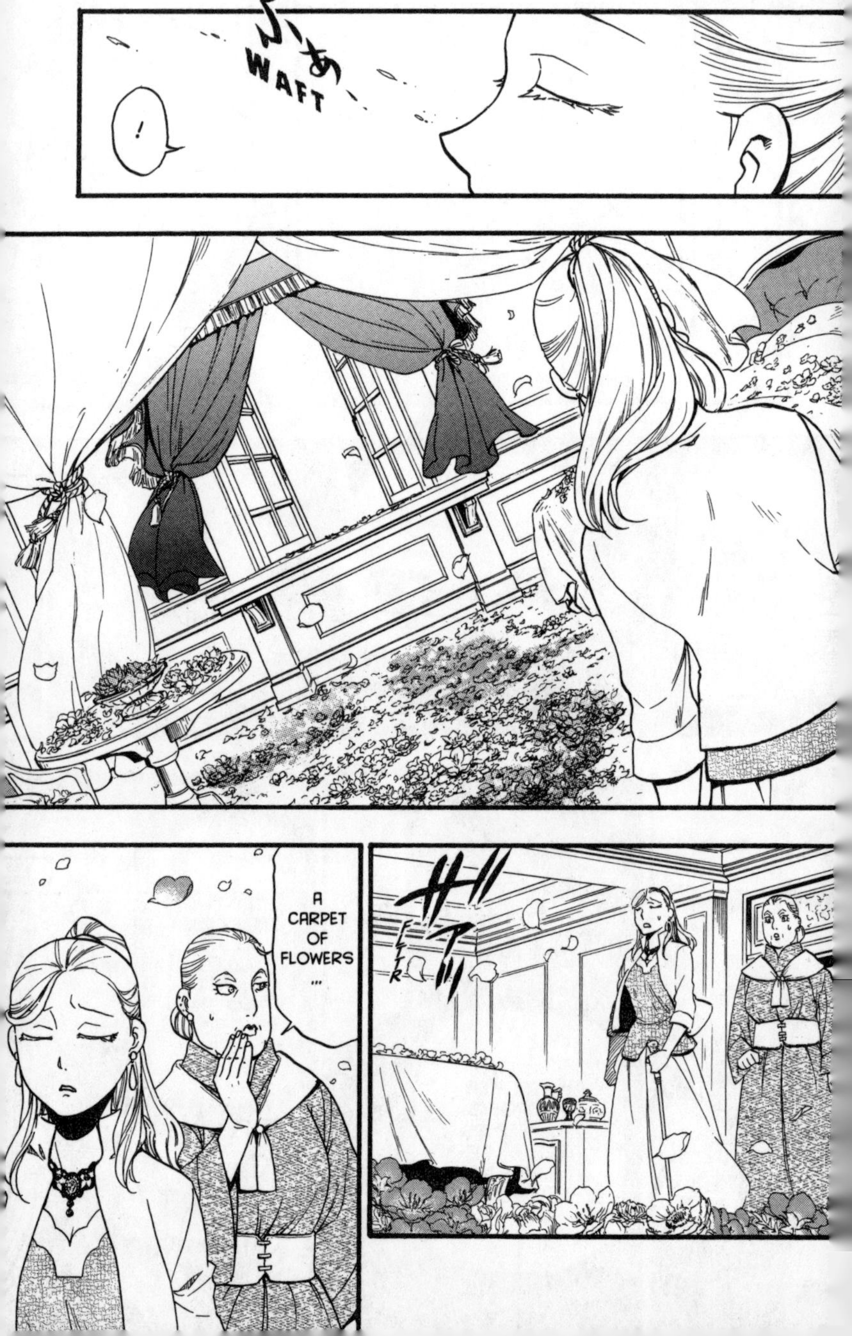
ふあ
WAFT
!
ザァ
FLTTR
A CARPET OF FLOWERS ...

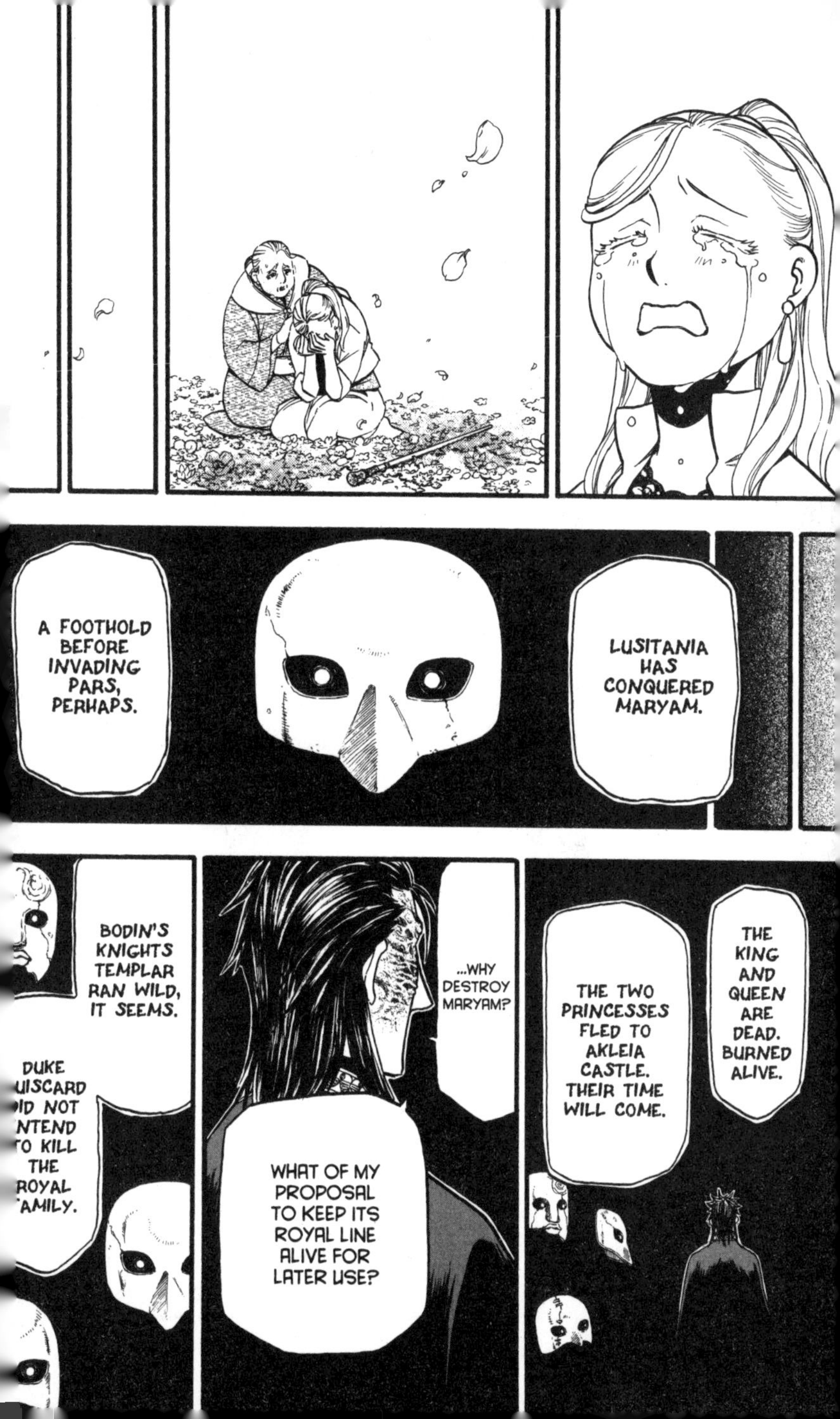
LUSITANIA HAS CONQUERED MARYAM.
A FOOTHOLD BEFORE INVADING PARS, PERHAPS.
THE KING AND QUEEN ARE DEAD. BURNED ALIVE.
THE TWO PRINCESSES FLED TO AKLEIA CASTLE. THEIR TIME WILL COME.
...WHY DESTROY MARYAM?
WHAT OF MY PROPOSAL TO KEEP ITS ROYAL LINE ALIVE FOR LATER USE?
BODIN'S KNIGHTS TEMPLAR RAN WILD, IT SEEMS.
DUKE UISCARD ID NOT NTEND O KILL THE ROYAL AMILY.

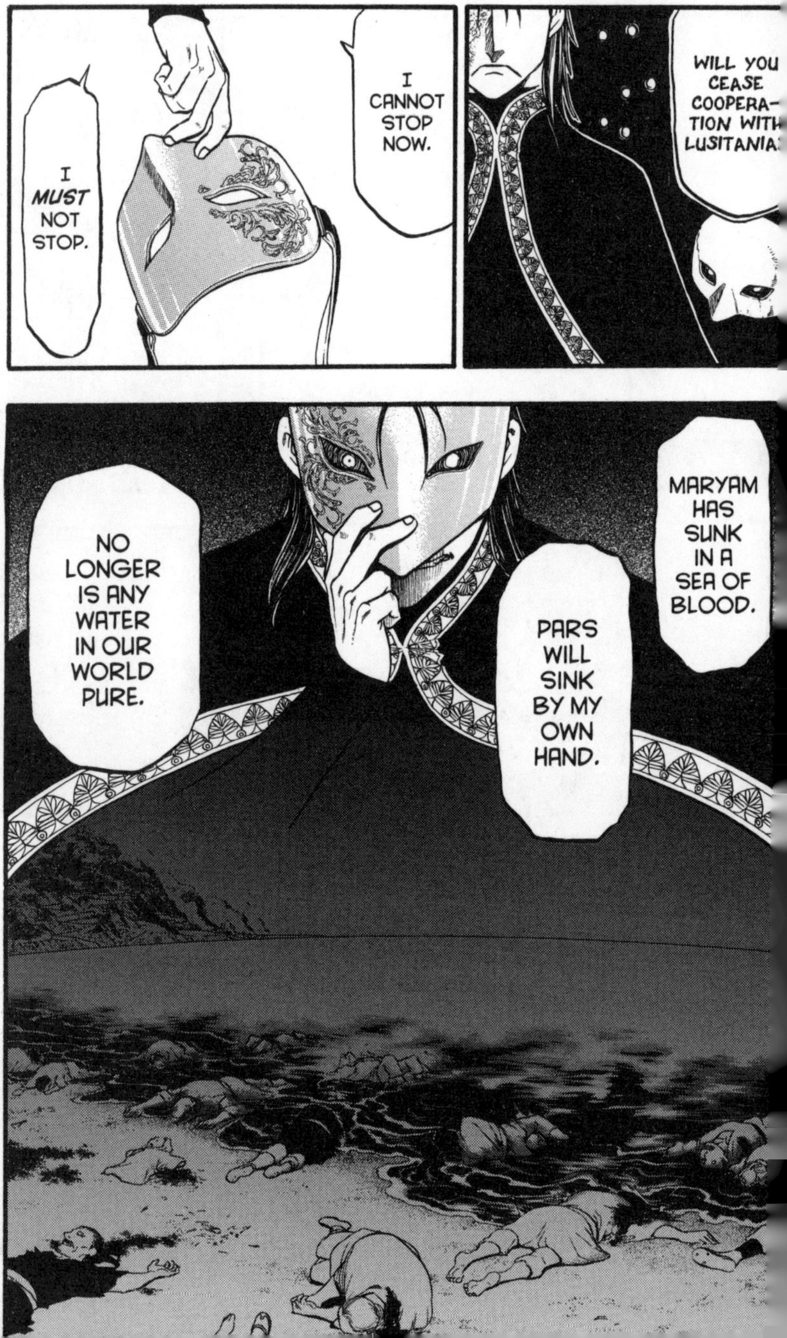
WILL YOU CEASE COOPERATION WITH LUSITANIA
I CANNOT STOP NOW.
I *MUST* NOT STOP.
MARYAM HAS SUNK IN A SEA OF BLOOD.
PARS WILL SINK BY MY OWN HAND.
NO LONGER IS ANY WATER IN OUR WORLD PURE.

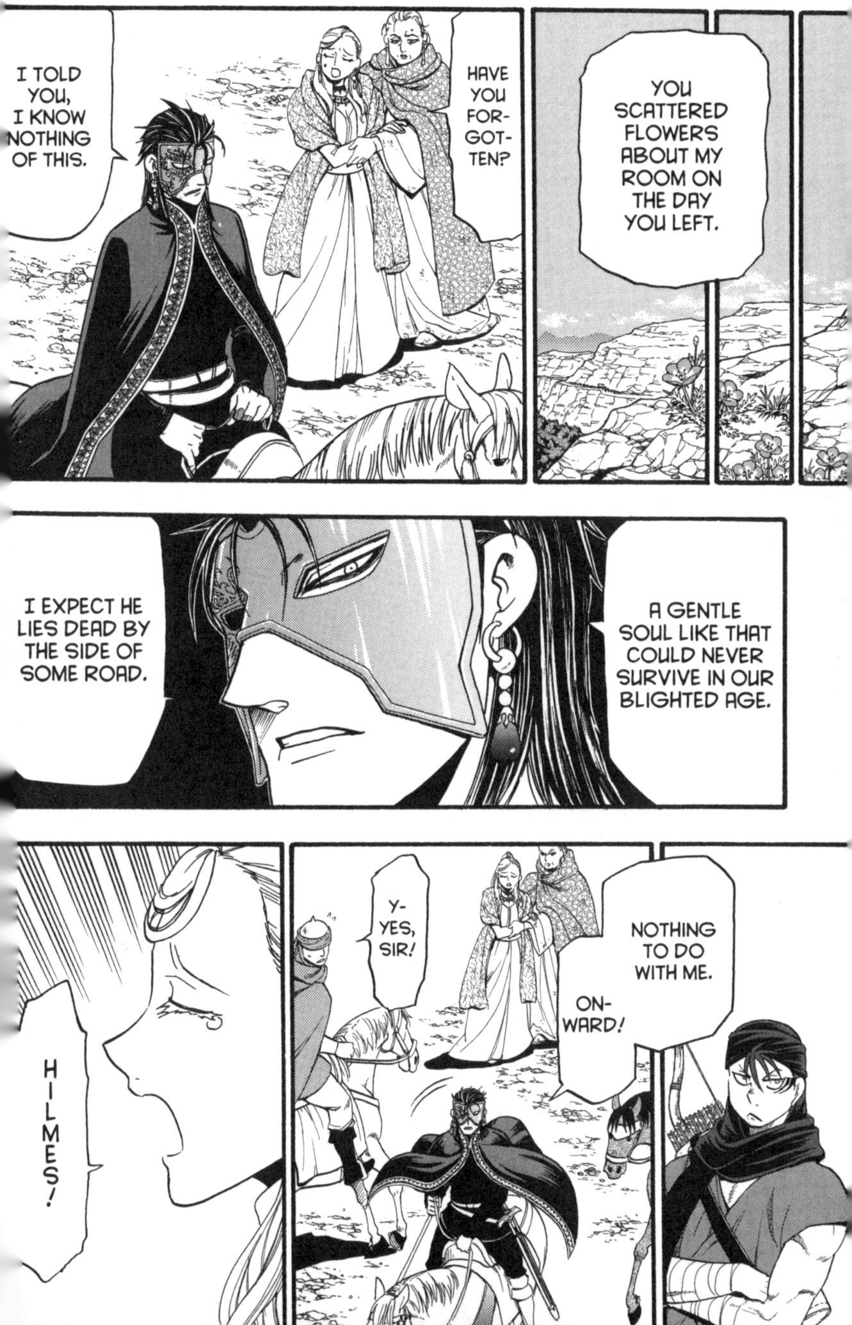
YOU SCATTERED FLOWERS ABOUT MY ROOM ON THE DAY YOU LEFT.
HAVE YOU FOR-GOT-TEN?
I TOLD YOU, I KNOW NOTHING OF THIS.
A GENTLE SOUL LIKE THAT COULD NEVER SURVIVE IN OUR BLIGHTED AGE.
I EXPECT HE LIES DEAD BY THE SIDE OF SOME ROAD.
NOTHING TO DO WITH ME.
ON-WARD!
Y-YES, SIR!
HILMES!

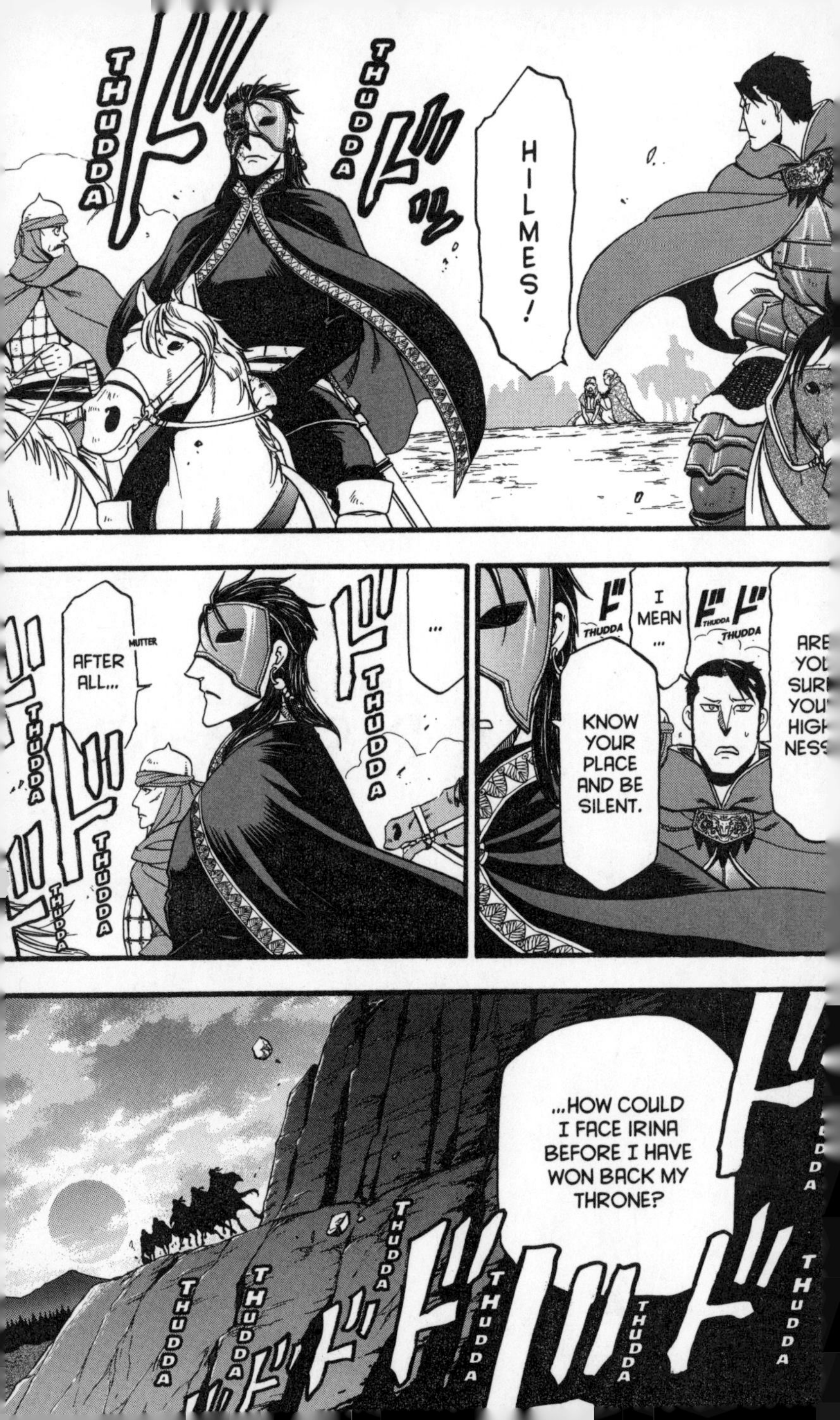
HILMES!
THUDDA
THUDDA
ARE YOU SURE YOUR HIGHNESS
THUDDA
THUDDA
I MEAN ...
THUDDA
KNOW YOUR PLACE AND BE SILENT.
...
THUDDA
MUTTER
AFTER ALL...
THUDDA
THUDDA
THUDDA
THUDDA
THUDDA
THUDDA
...HOW COULD I FACE IRINA BEFORE I HAVE WON BACK MY THRONE?
THUDDA
THUDDA
THUDDA
THUDDA

THE HEROIC LEGEND OF
ARSLAN

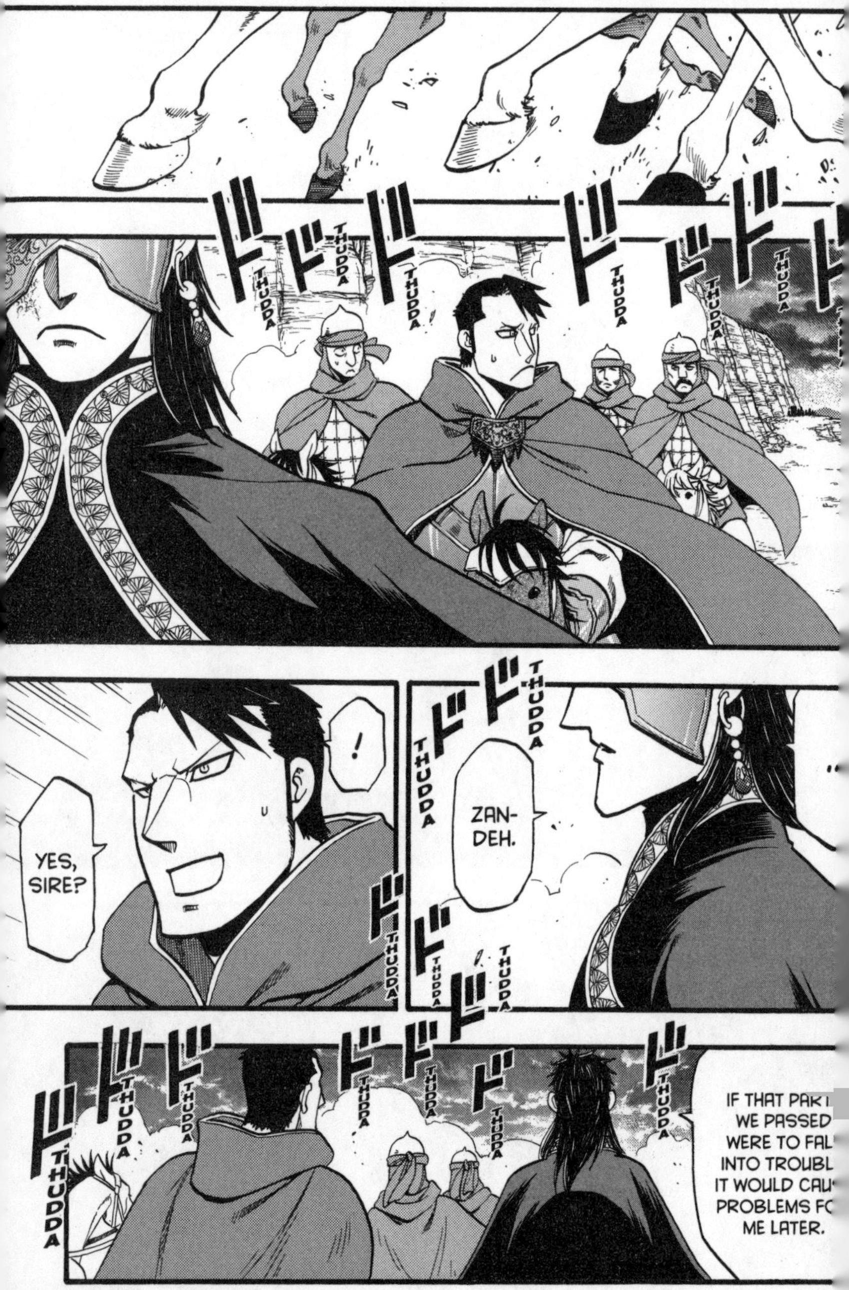

ドドドド
THUDDA
THUDDA
THUDDA
THUDDA
THUDDA
THUDDA
ドド
THUDDA
THUDDA
ZAN-DEH.
ドド
THUDDA
THUDDA
!
YES, SIRE?
ド
THUDDA
IF THAT PAR
WE PASSED
WERE TO FAL
INTO TROUBL
IT WOULD CAU
PROBLEMS FO
ME LATER.
ドドドドドドドド
THUDDA
THUDDA
THUDDA
THUDDA
THUDDA
THUDDA
THUDDA

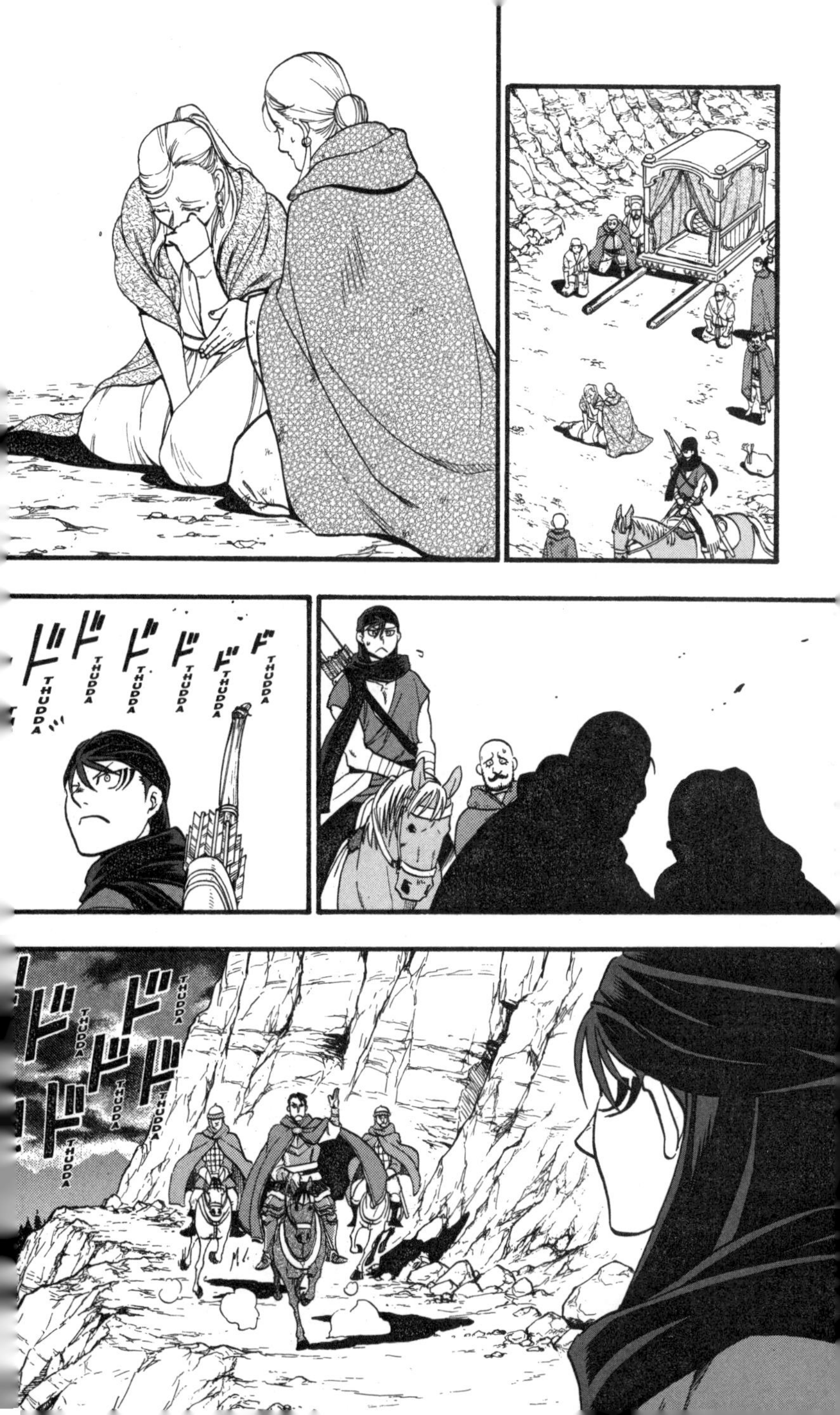
ド THUDDA
ド THUDDA
ド THUDDA
ド THUDDA
ド THUDDA
ド THUDDA
ド THUDDA
ド THUDDA
ド THUDDA
ド THUDDA
ド THUDDA

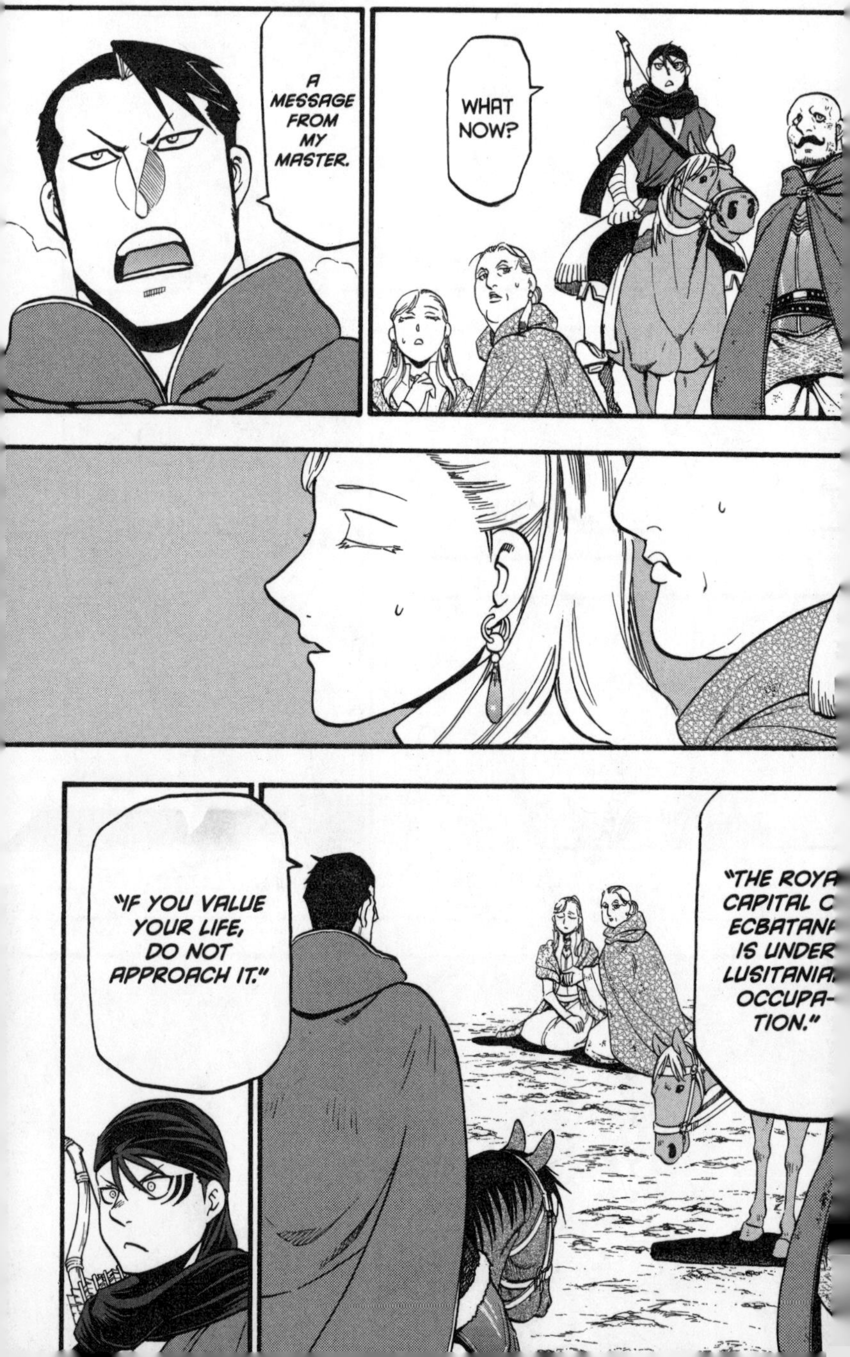
WHAT NOW?
A MESSAGE FROM MY MASTER.
"THE ROYA CAPITAL ECBATAN IS UNDER LUSITANIA OCCUPA-TION."
"IF YOU VALUE YOUR LIFE, DO NOT APPROACH IT."

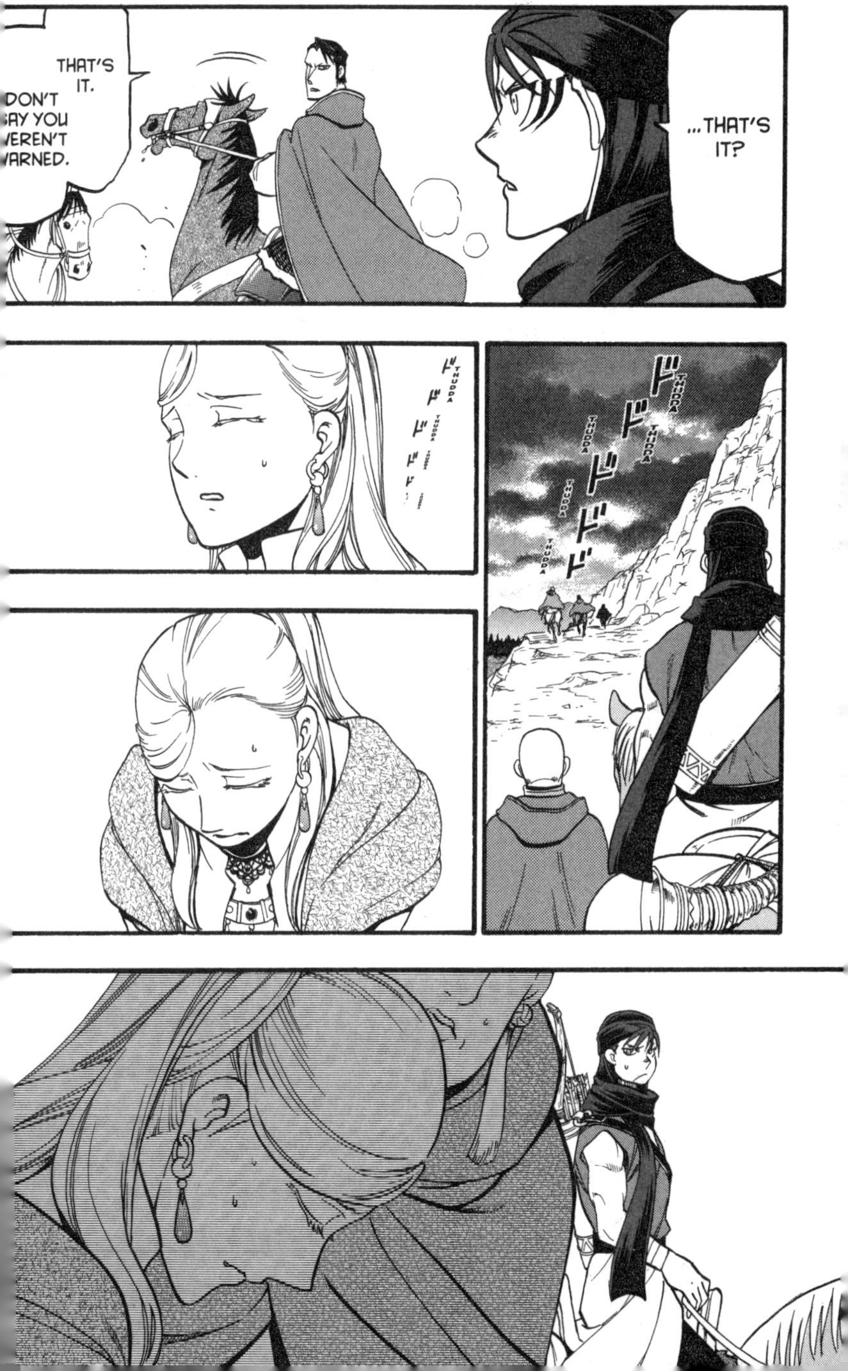
...THAT'S IT?
THAT'S IT. DON'T SAY YOU WEREN'T WARNED.
ドドドドド
THUDDA THUDDA THUDDA THUDDA
ドドドドド
THUDDA THUDDA THUDDA

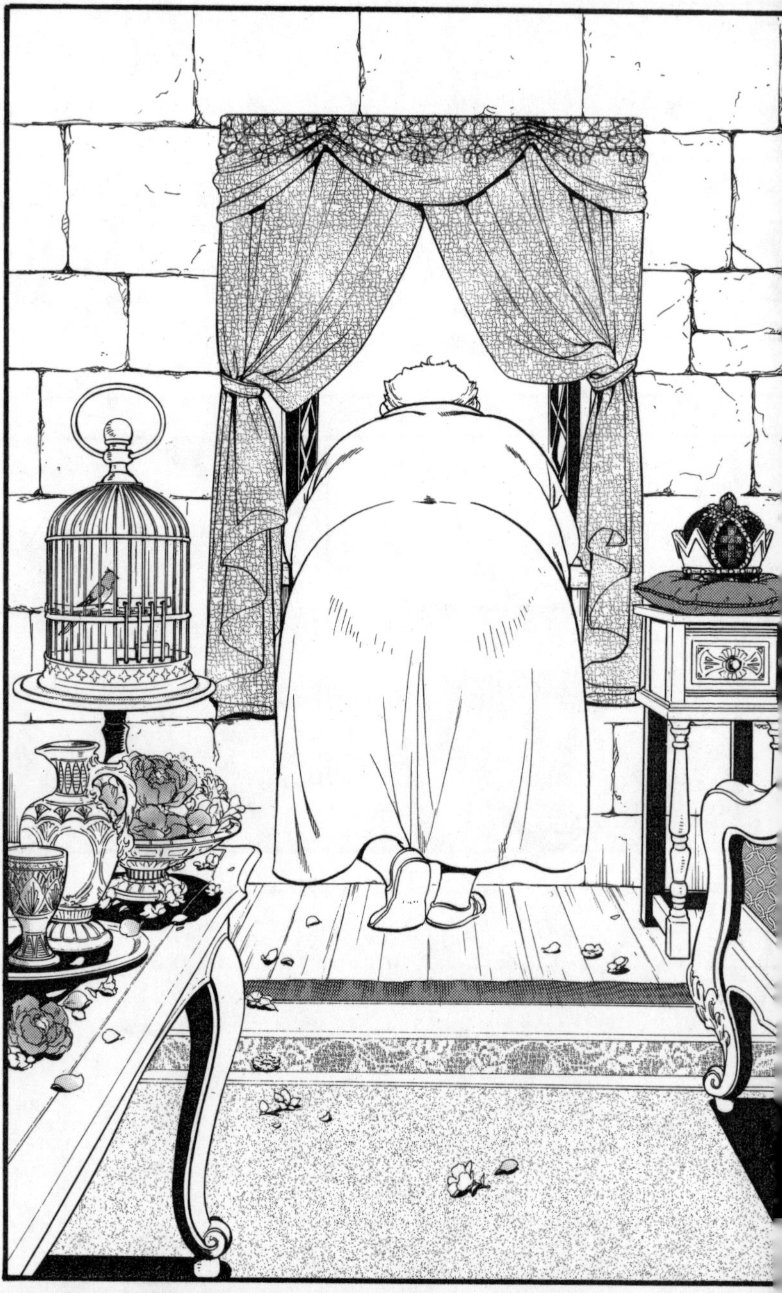

Chapter 90: At Journey's End

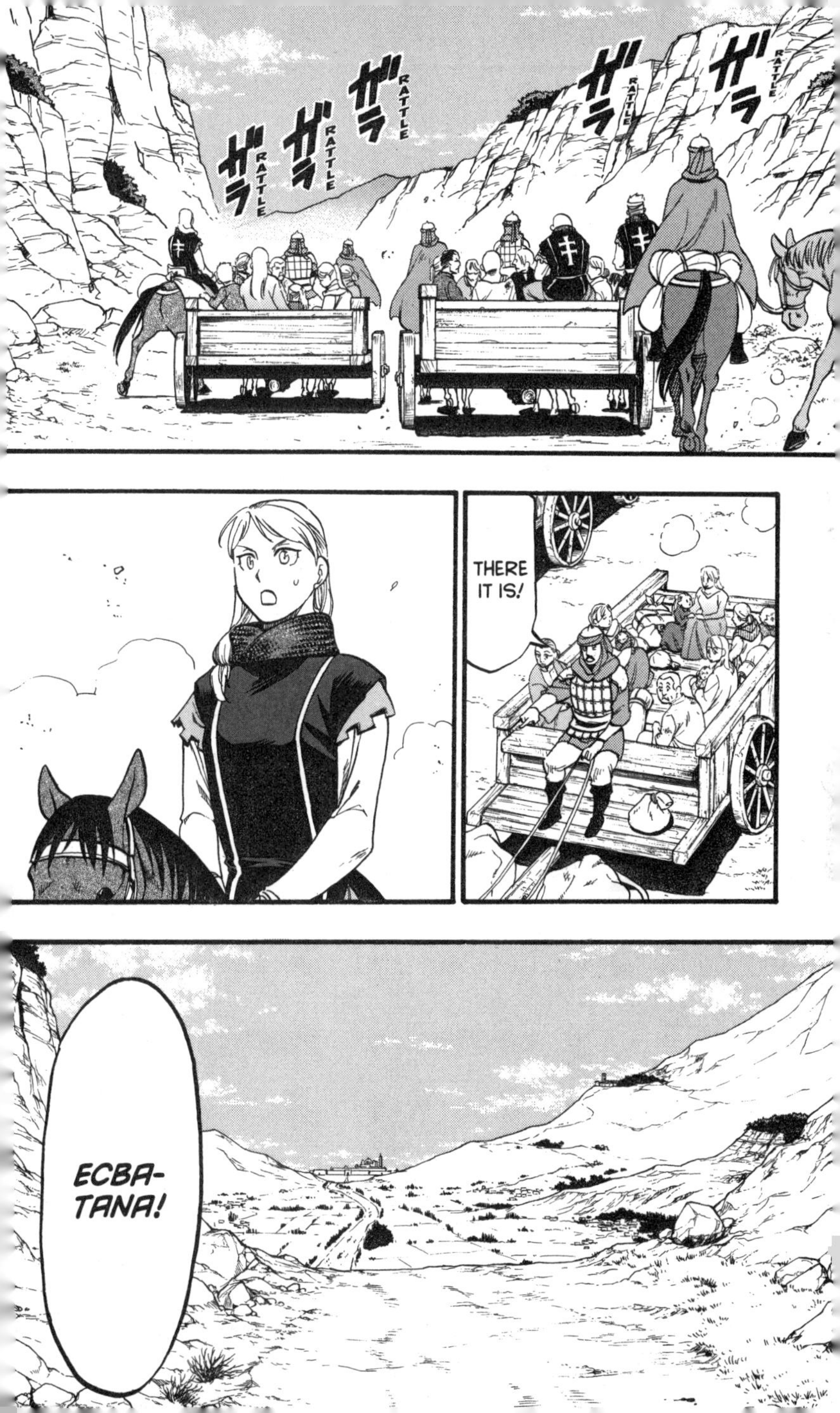
ガラ RATTLE
ガラ RATTLE
ガラ RATTLE
ガラ RATTLE
ガラ RATTLE
THERE IT IS!
ECBA-TANA!

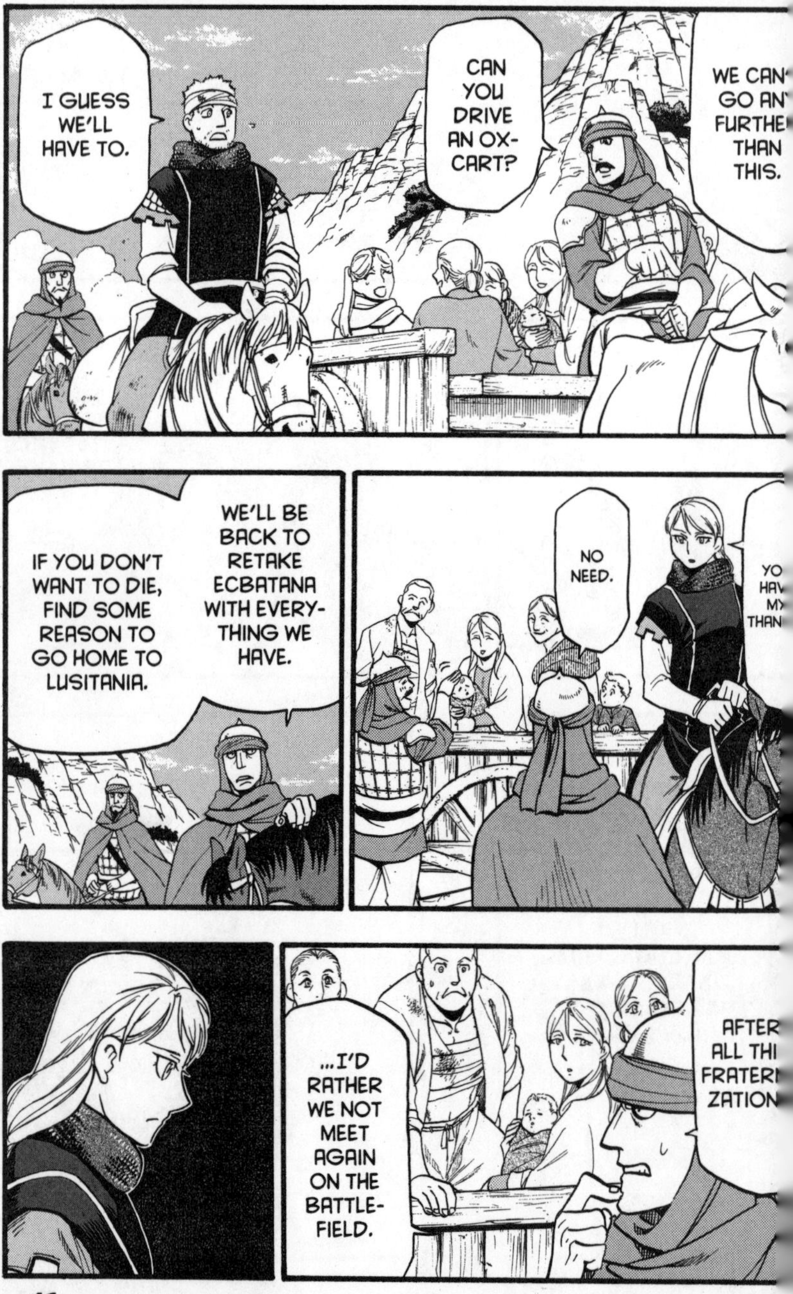

WE CAN GO AN FURTHE THAN THIS.
CAN YOU DRIVE AN OX-CART?
I GUESS WE'LL HAVE TO.
YO HAV MY THAN
NO NEED.
WE'LL BE BACK TO RETAKE ECBATANA WITH EVERY-THING WE HAVE.
IF YOU DON'T WANT TO DIE, FIND SOME REASON TO GO HOME TO LUSITANIA.
AFTER ALL THI FRATERN ZATION
...I'D RATHER WE NOT MEET AGAIN ON THE BATTLE-FIELD.

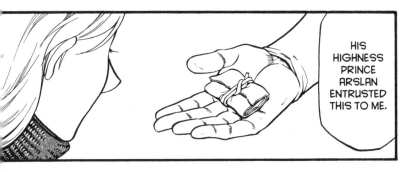

HIS HIGHNESS PRINCE ARSLAN ENTRUSTED THIS TO ME.

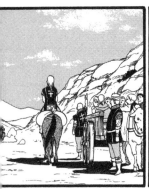

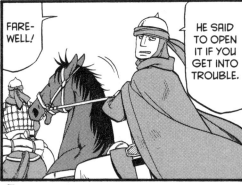

FARE-WELL!

HE SAID TO OPEN IT IF YOU GET INTO TROUBLE.

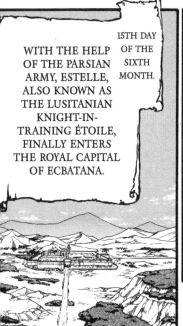

15TH DAY OF THE SIXTH MONTH.

WITH THE HELP OF THE PARSIAN ARMY, ESTELLE, ALSO KNOWN AS THE LUSITANIAN KNIGHT-IN-TRAINING ÉTOILE, FINALLY ENTERS THE ROYAL CAPITAL OF ECBATANA.

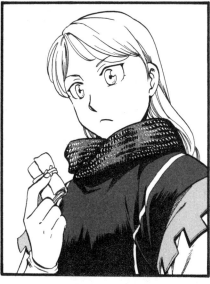

42

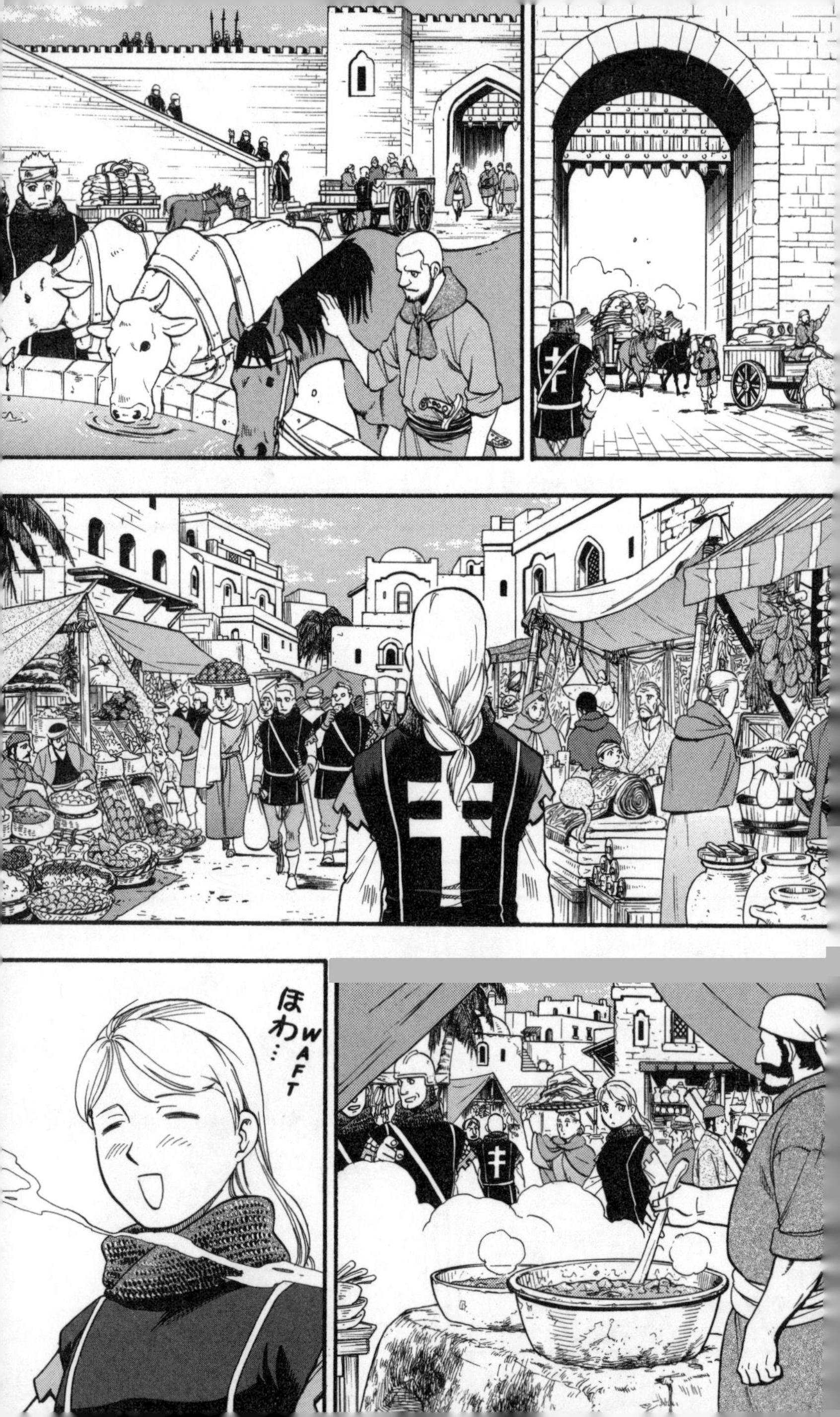
ほわ…
WAFT

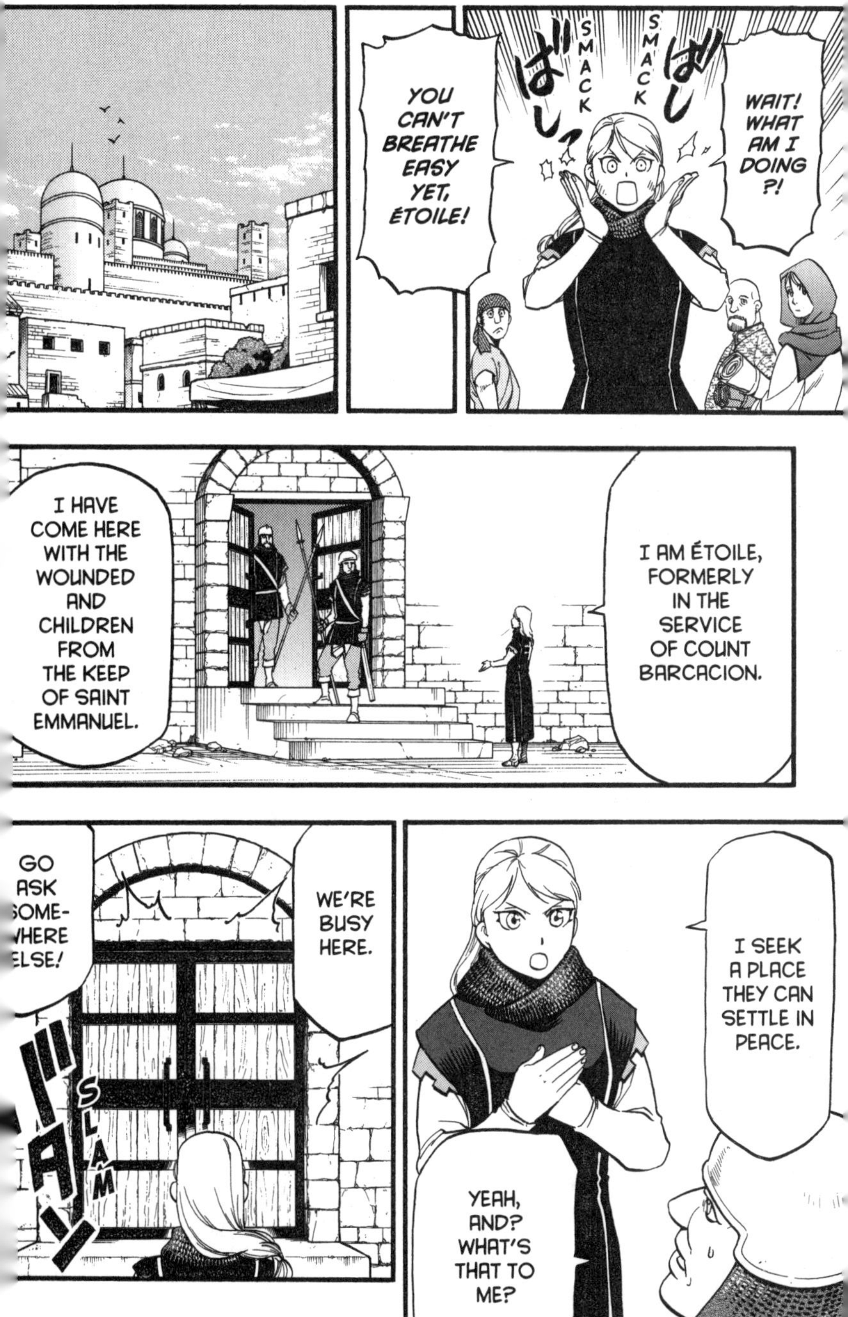
WAIT! WHAT AM I DOING?!
ぱし
SMACK
ぱしっ
SMACK
YOU CAN'T BREATHE EASY YET, ÉTOILE!
I AM ÉTOILE, FORMERLY IN THE SERVICE OF COUNT BARCACION.
I HAVE COME HERE WITH THE WOUNDED AND CHILDREN FROM THE KEEP OF SAINT EMMANUEL.
I SEEK A PLACE THEY CAN SETTLE IN PEACE.
YEAH, AND? WHAT'S THAT TO ME?
WE'RE BUSY HERE.
GO ASK SOME-WHERE ELSE!
SLAM

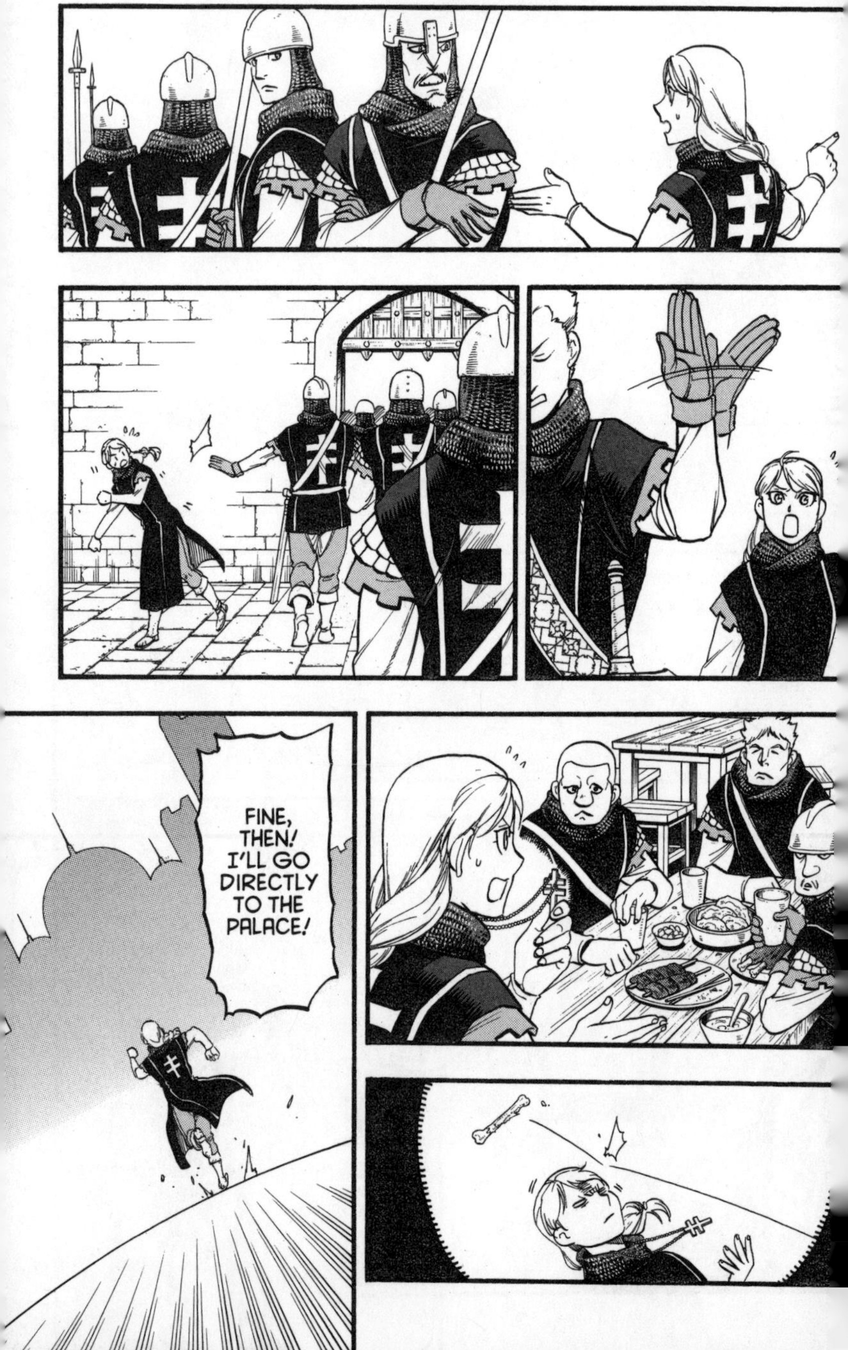
FINE, THEN! I'LL GO DIRECTLY TO THE PALACE!

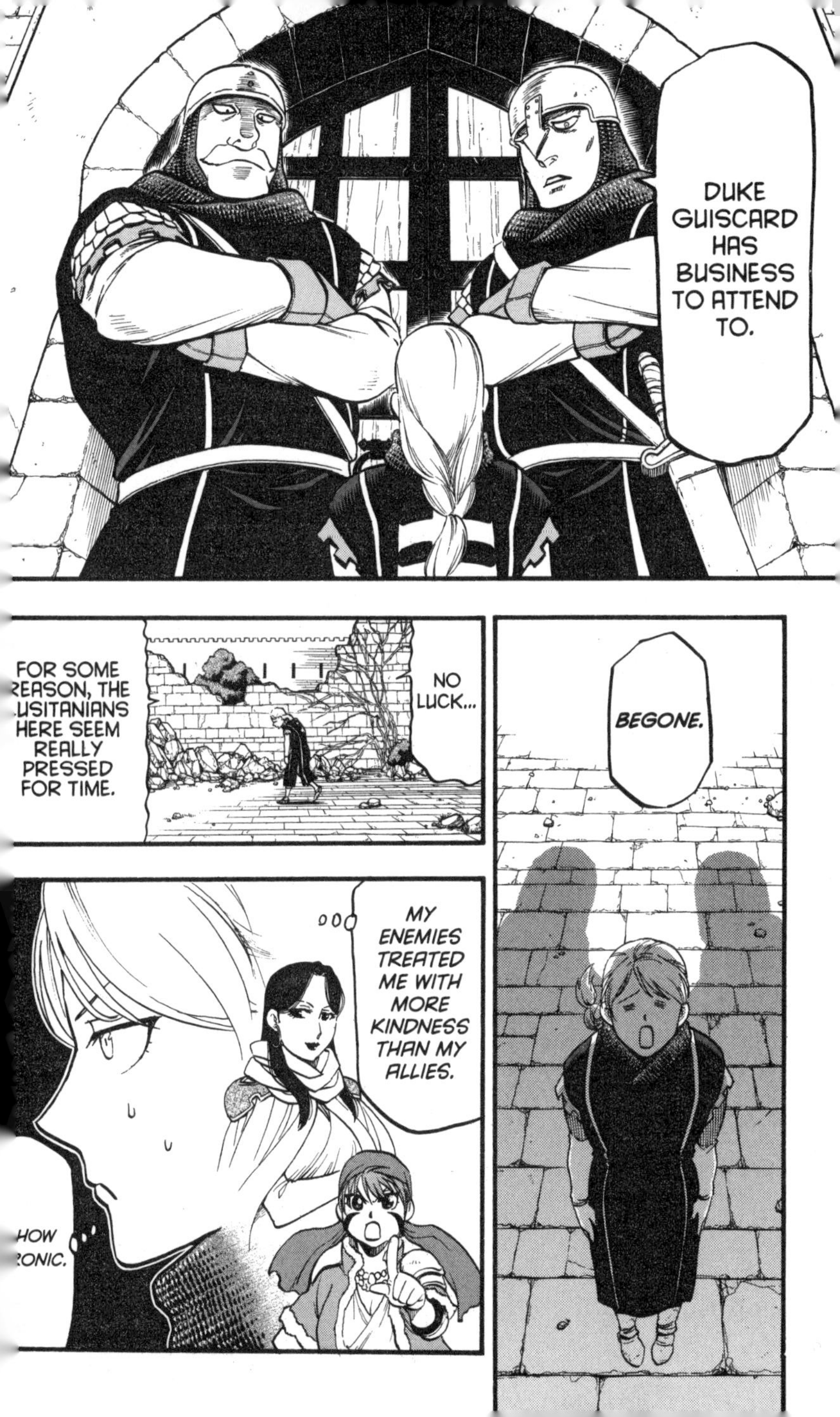
DUKE GUISCARD HAS BUSINESS TO ATTEND TO.
BEGONE.
NO LUCK...
FOR SOME REASON, THE LUSITANIANS HERE SEEM REALLY PRESSED FOR TIME.
MY ENEMIES TREATED ME WITH MORE KINDNESS THAN MY ALLIES.
HOW IRONIC.

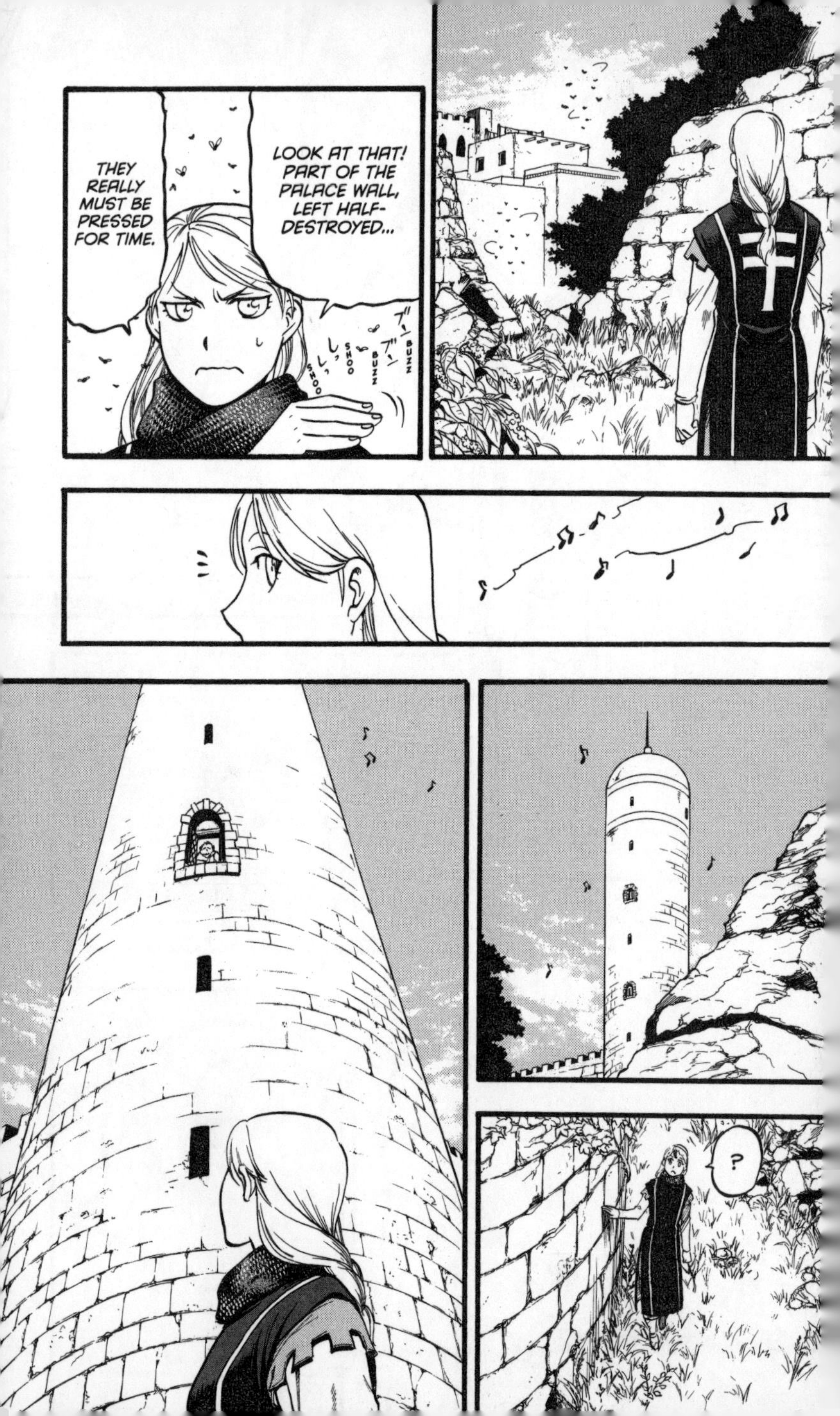
LOOK AT THAT! PART OF THE PALACE WALL, LEFT HALF-DESTROYED...
THEY REALLY MUST BE PRESSED FOR TIME.
BUZZ
BUZZ
SHOO
SHOO
?

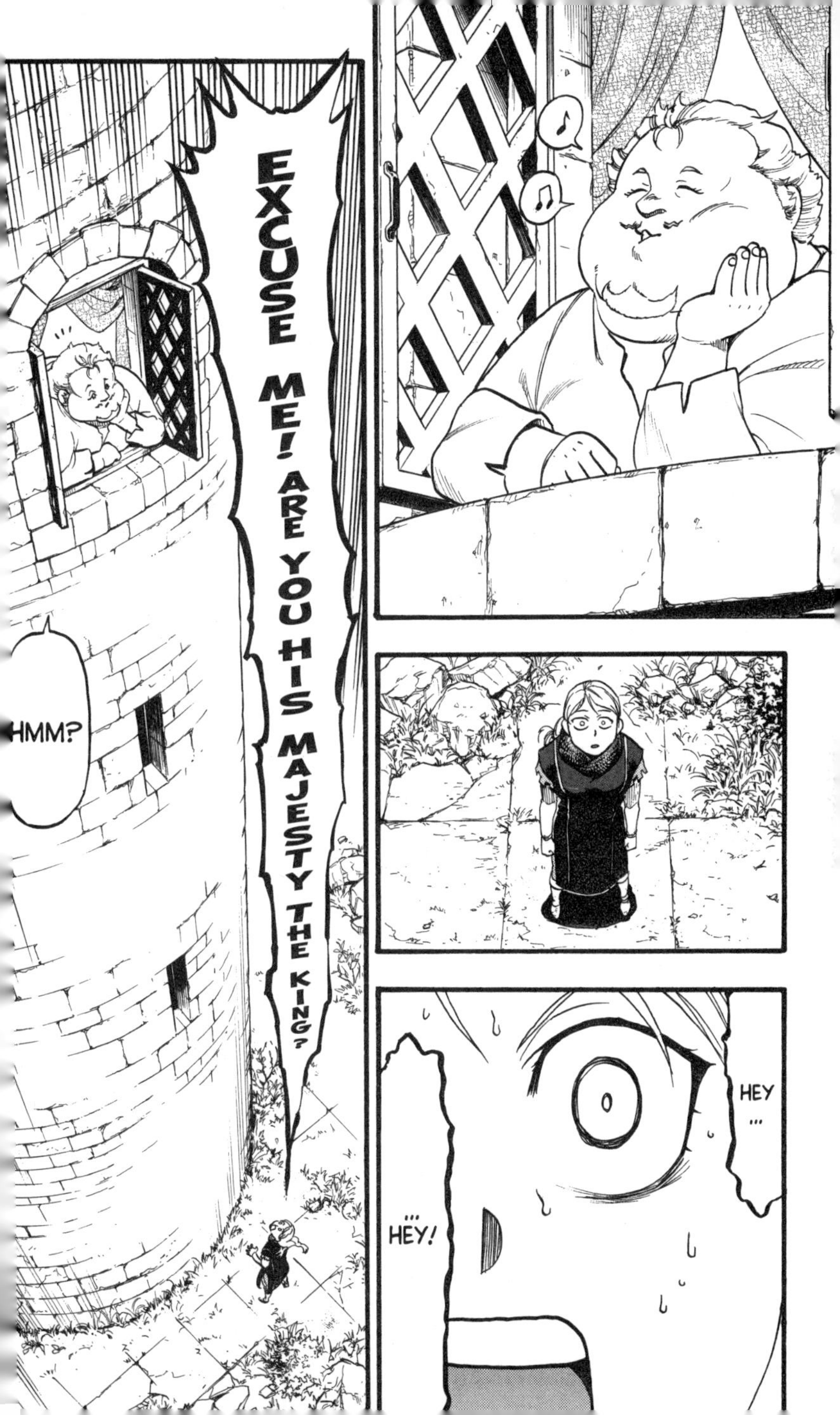
HEY ...
... HEY!
EXCUSE ME! ARE YOU HIS MAJESTY THE KING?
HMM?

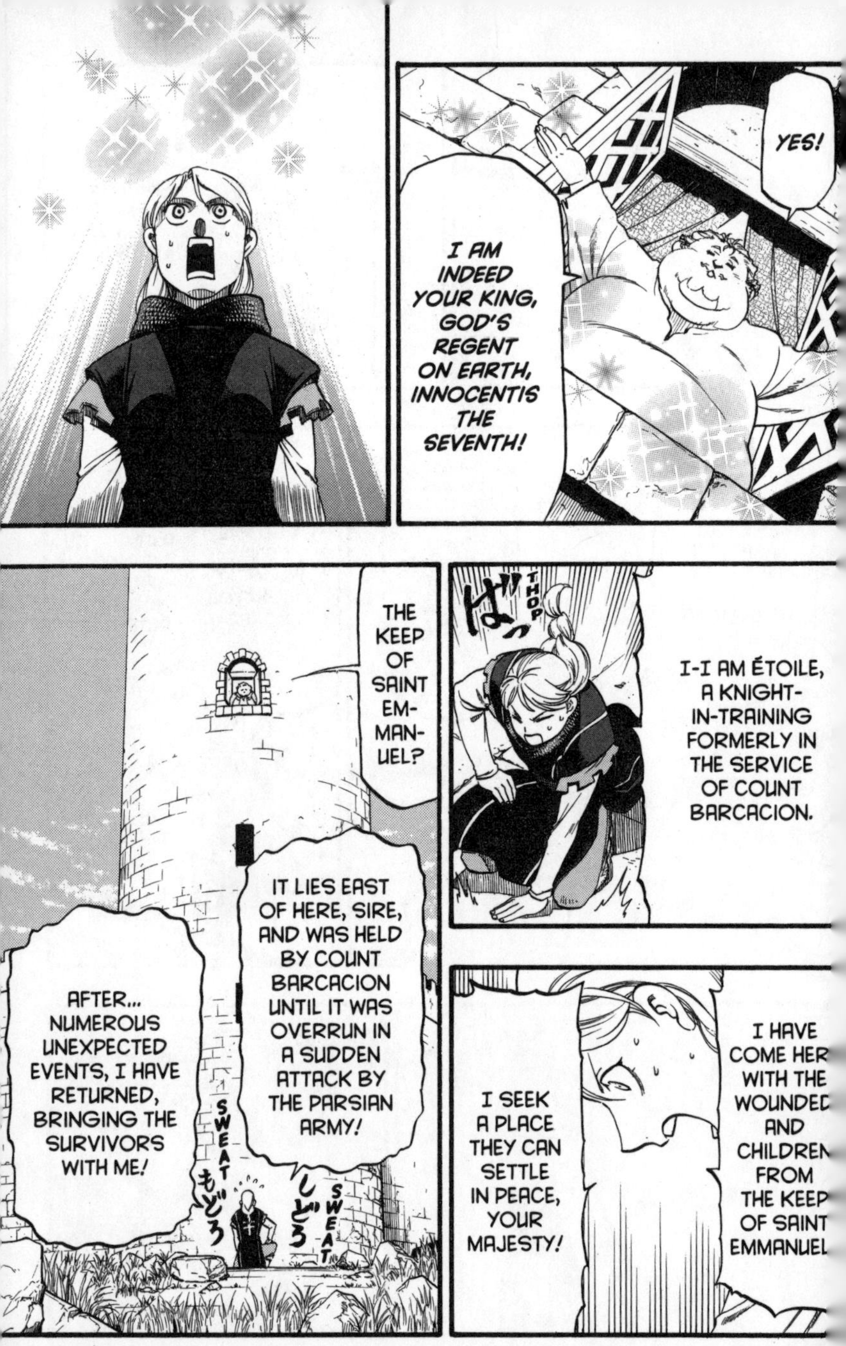
YES!
I AM INDEED YOUR KING, GOD'S REGENT ON EARTH, INNOCENTIS THE SEVENTH!
ぱっ THOP
I-I AM ÉTOILE, A KNIGHT-IN-TRAINING FORMERLY IN THE SERVICE OF COUNT BARCACION.
I HAVE COME HER WITH THE WOUNDED AND CHILDREN FROM THE KEEP OF SAINT EMMANUEL
I SEEK A PLACE THEY CAN SETTLE IN PEACE, YOUR MAJESTY!
THE KEEP OF SAINT EM-MAN-UEL?
IT LIES EAST OF HERE, SIRE, AND WAS HELD BY COUNT BARCACION UNTIL IT WAS OVERRUN IN A SUDDEN ATTACK BY THE PARSIAN ARMY!
AFTER... NUMEROUS UNEXPECTED EVENTS, I HAVE RETURNED, BRINGING THE SURVIVORS WITH ME!
しどろ SWEAT
もどろ SWEAT

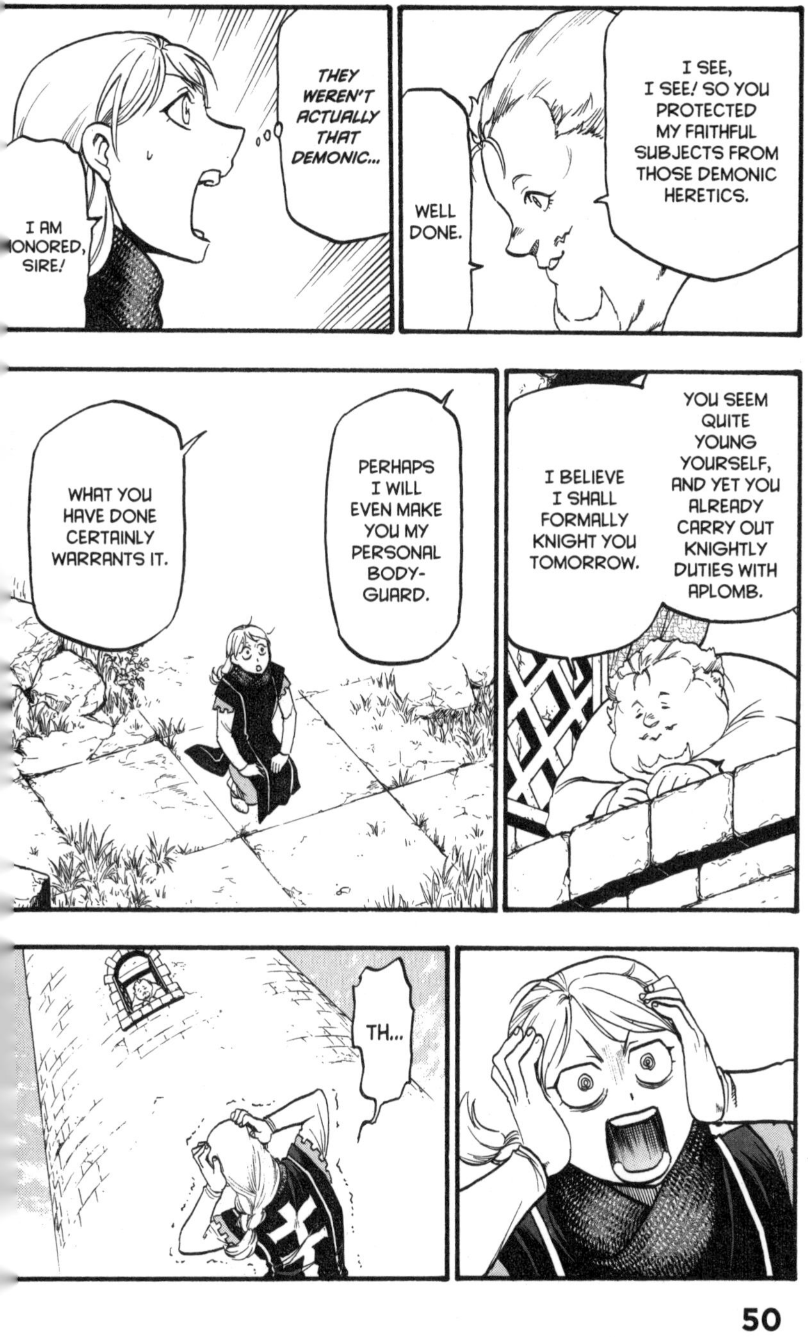
I SEE, I SEE! SO YOU PROTECTED MY FAITHFUL SUBJECTS FROM THOSE DEMONIC HERETICS.
WELL DONE.
THEY WEREN'T ACTUALLY THAT DEMONIC...
I AM HONORED, SIRE!
YOU SEEM QUITE YOUNG YOURSELF, AND YET YOU ALREADY CARRY OUT KNIGHTLY DUTIES WITH APLOMB.
I BELIEVE I SHALL FORMALLY KNIGHT YOU TOMORROW.
PERHAPS I WILL EVEN MAKE YOU MY PERSONAL BODY-GUARD.
WHAT YOU HAVE DONE CERTAINLY WARRANTS IT.
TH...

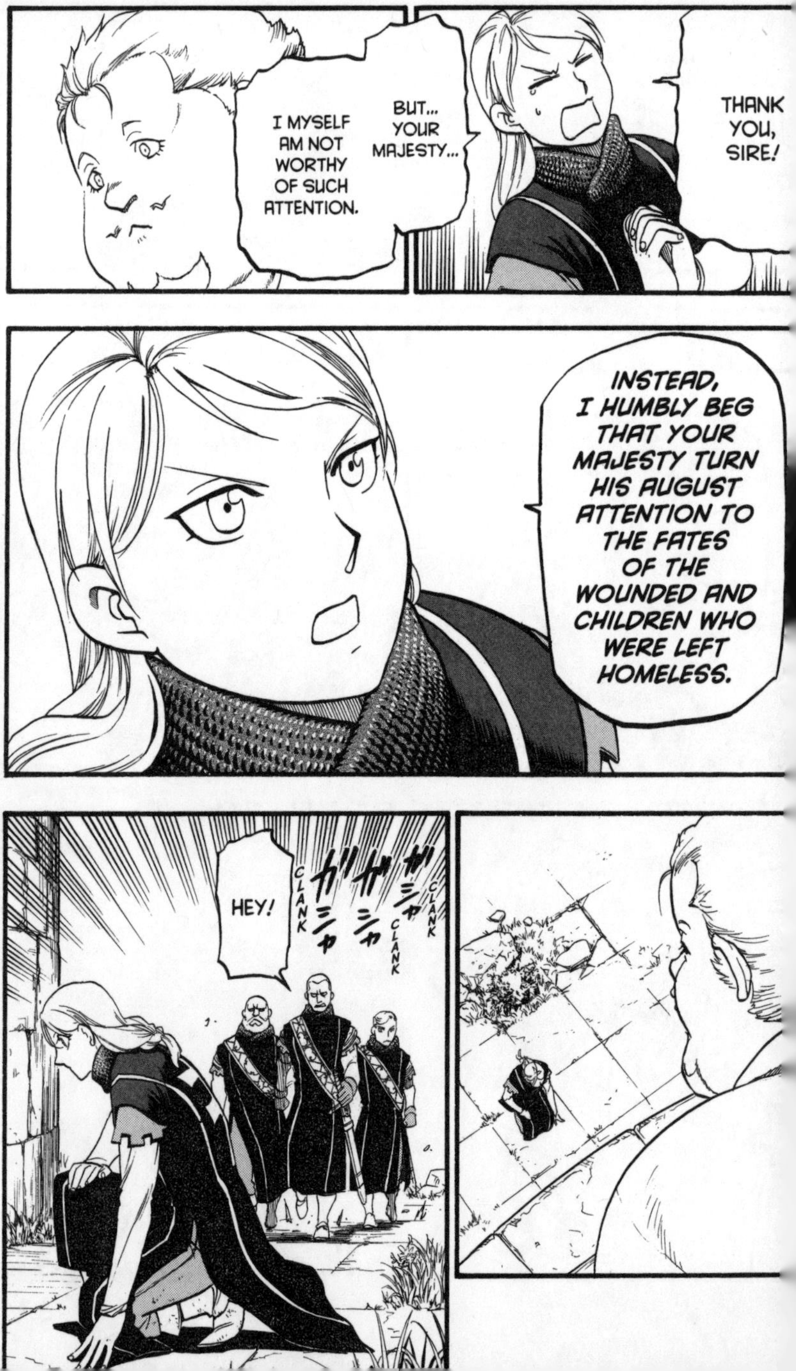
THANK YOU, SIRE!
BUT... YOUR MAJESTY...
I MYSELF AM NOT WORTHY OF SUCH ATTENTION.
INSTEAD, I HUMBLY BEG THAT YOUR MAJESTY TURN HIS AUGUST ATTENTION TO THE FATES OF THE WOUNDED AND CHILDREN WHO WERE LEFT HOMELESS.
ガシャ
CLANK
ガシャ
CLANK
ガシャ
CLANK
HEY!

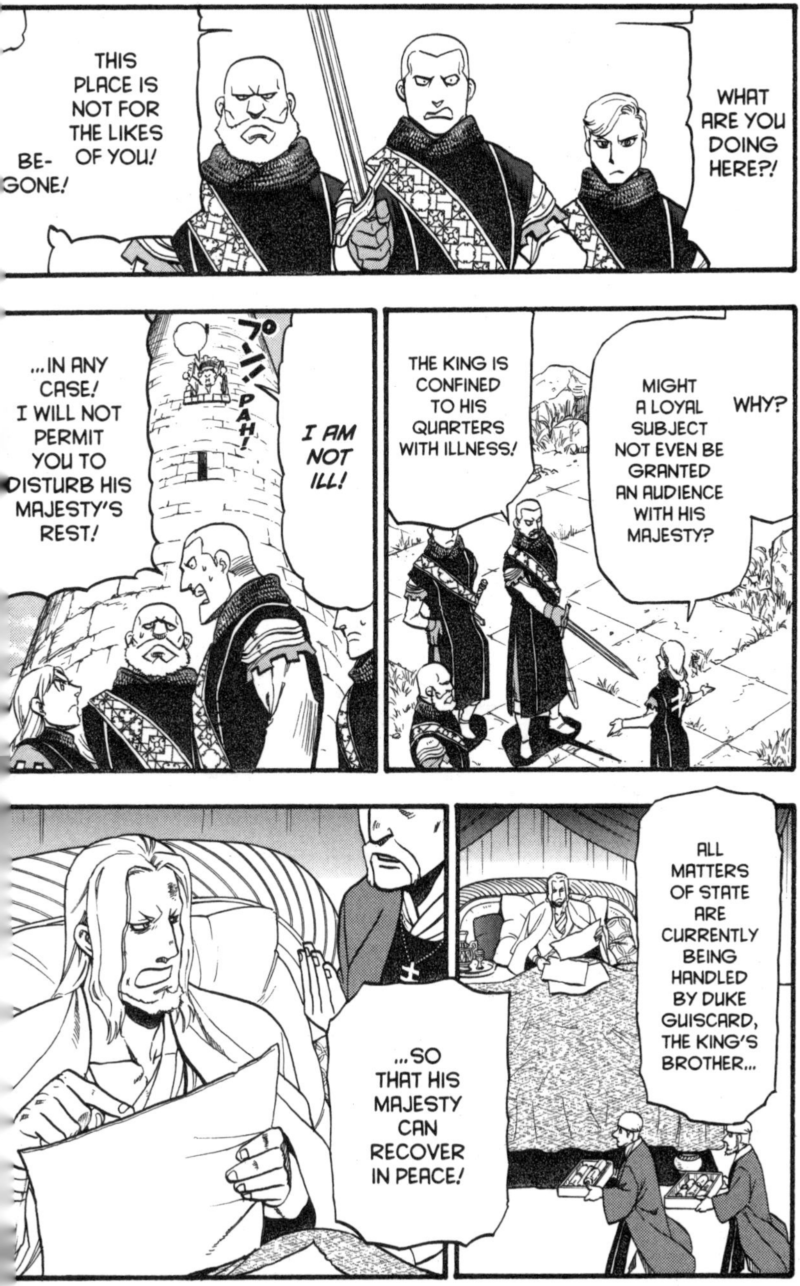
WHAT ARE YOU DOING HERE?!
THIS PLACE IS NOT FOR THE LIKES OF YOU!
BE-GONE!
WHY?
MIGHT A LOYAL SUBJECT NOT EVEN BE GRANTED AN AUDIENCE WITH HIS MAJESTY?
THE KING IS CONFINED TO HIS QUARTERS WITH ILLNESS!
I AM NOT ILL!
PAH!
...IN ANY CASE! I WILL NOT PERMIT YOU TO DISTURB HIS MAJESTY'S REST!
ALL MATTERS OF STATE ARE CURRENTLY BEING HANDLED BY DUKE GUISCARD, THE KING'S BROTHER...
...SO THAT HIS MAJESTY CAN RECOVER IN PEACE!

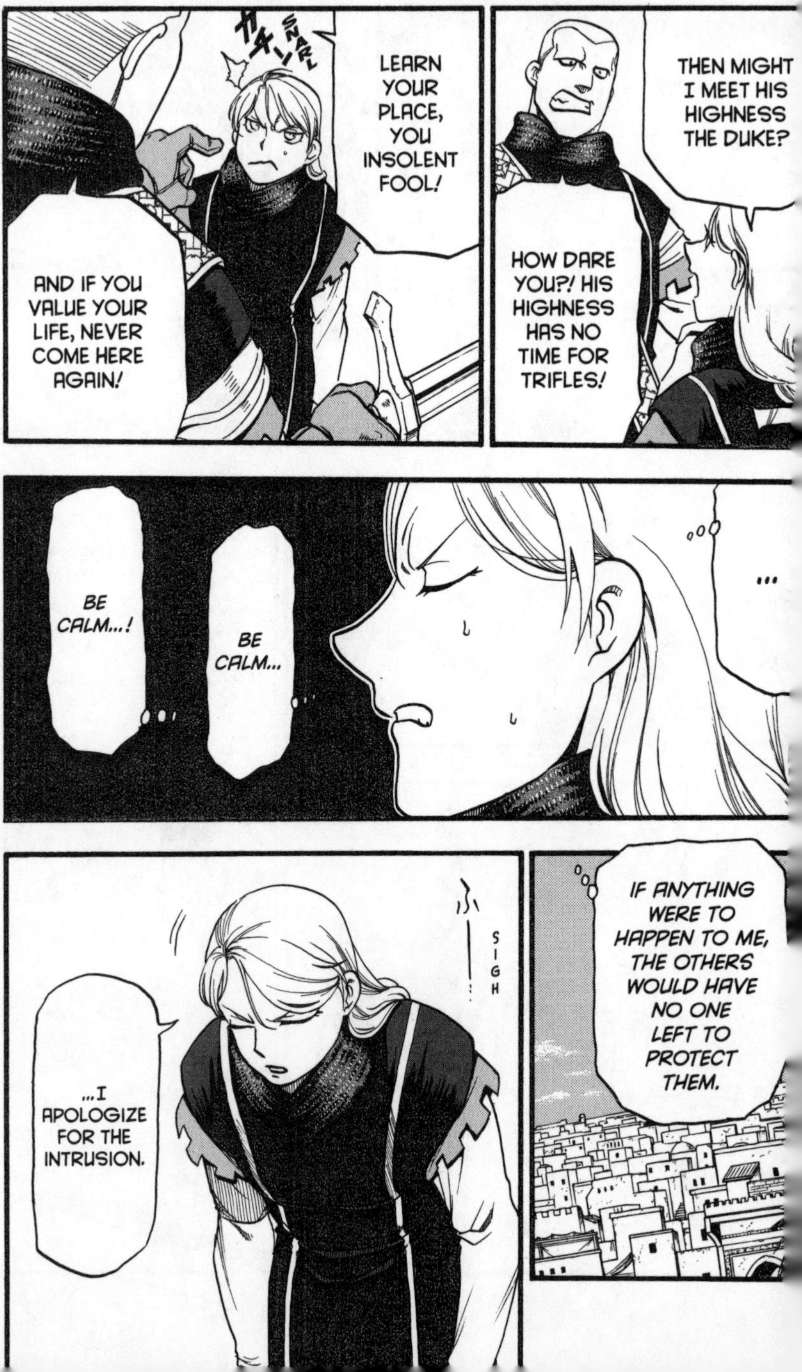
THEN MIGHT I MEET HIS HIGHNESS THE DUKE?
HOW DARE YOU?! HIS HIGHNESS HAS NO TIME FOR TRIFLES!
SNARL
LEARN YOUR PLACE, YOU INSOLENT FOOL!
AND IF YOU VALUE YOUR LIFE, NEVER COME HERE AGAIN!
...
BE CALM...
BE CALM...!
IF ANYTHING WERE TO HAPPEN TO ME, THE OTHERS WOULD HAVE NO ONE LEFT TO PROTECT THEM.
SIGH
...I APOLOGIZE FOR THE INTRUSION.

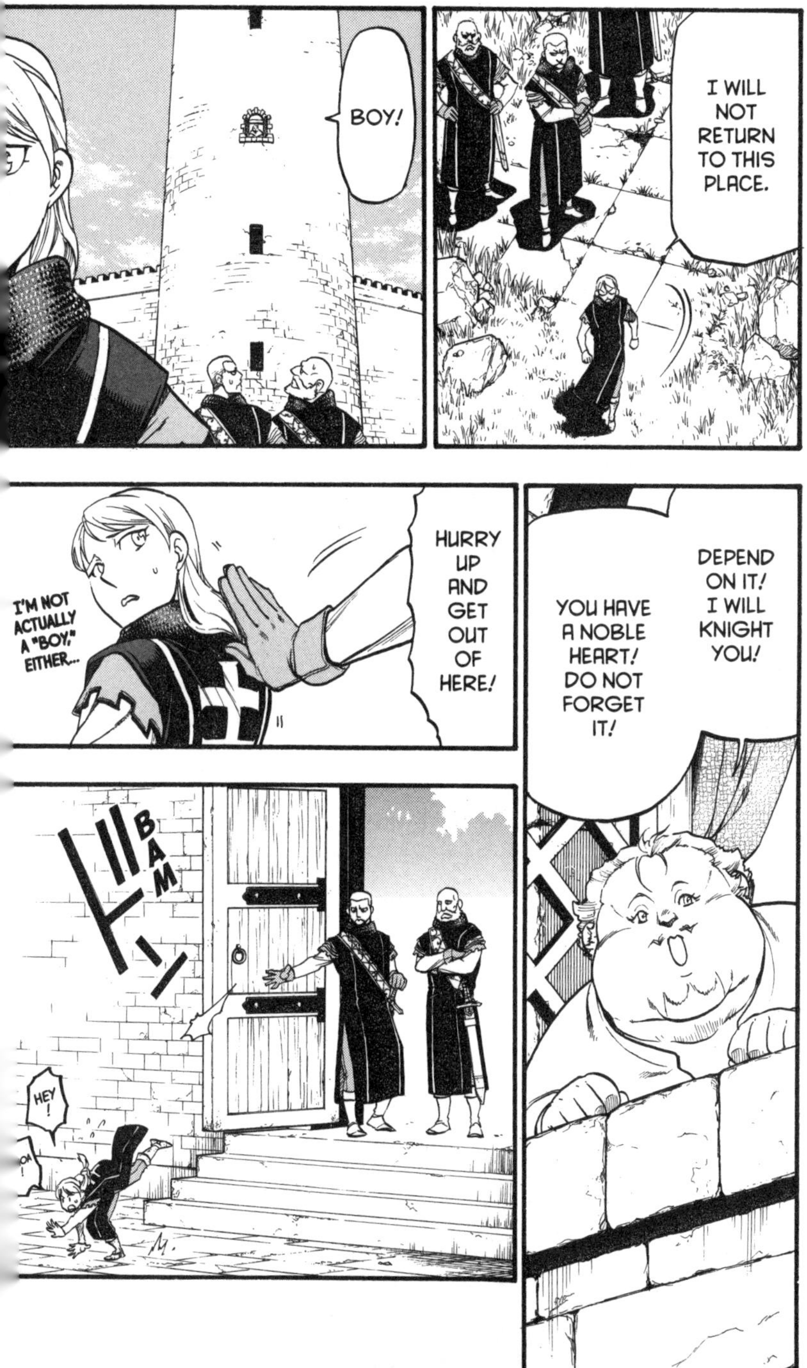
I WILL NOT RETURN TO THIS PLACE.
BOY!
DEPEND ON IT! I WILL KNIGHT YOU!
YOU HAVE A NOBLE HEART! DO NOT FORGET IT!
HURRY UP AND GET OUT OF HERE!
I'M NOT ACTUALLY A "BOY," EITHER...
BAM
HEY!

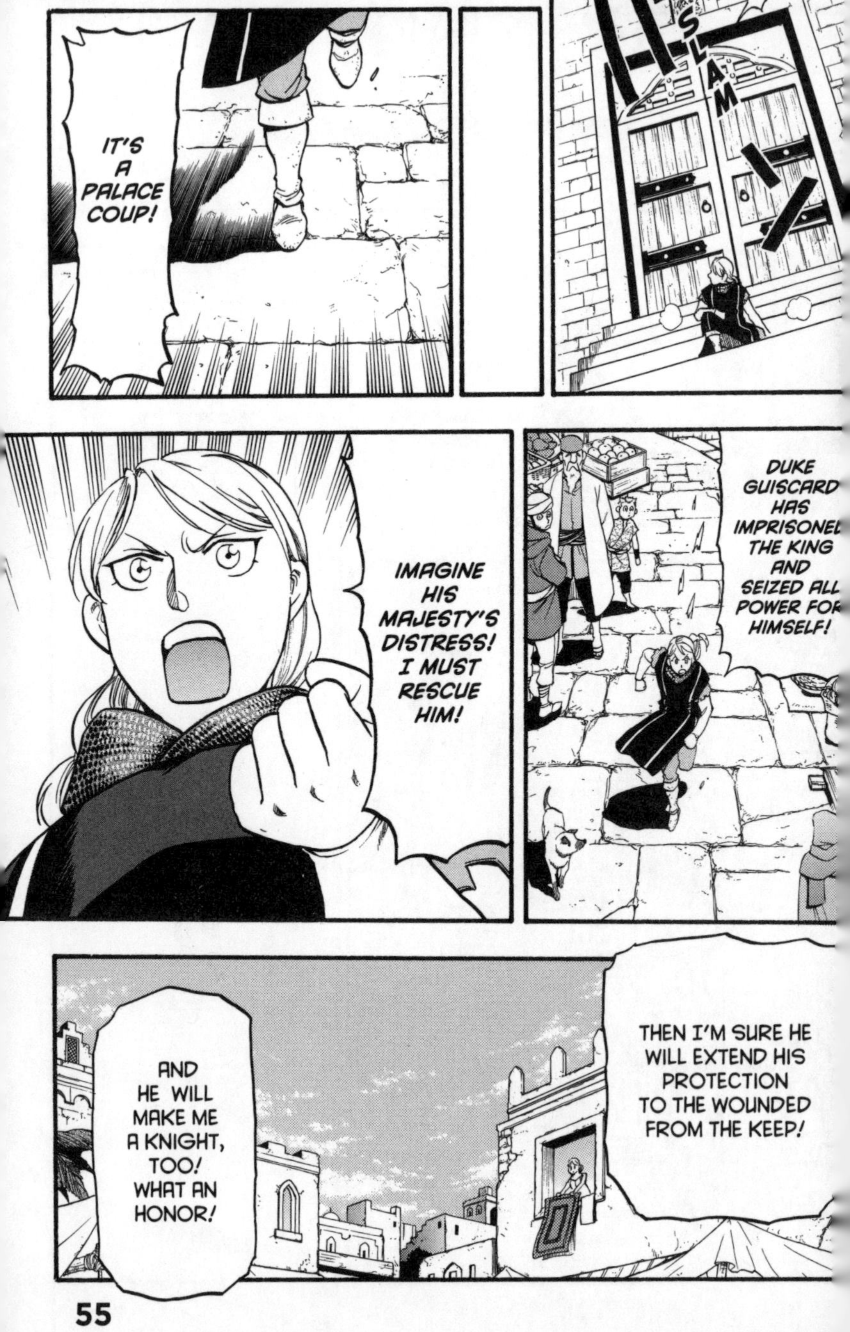
SLAM
IT'S A PALACE COUP!
DUKE GUISCARD HAS IMPRISONED THE KING AND SEIZED ALL POWER FOR HIMSELF!
IMAGINE HIS MAJESTY'S DISTRESS! I MUST RESCUE HIM!
THEN I'M SURE HE WILL EXTEND HIS PROTECTION TO THE WOUNDED FROM THE KEEP!
AND HE WILL MAKE ME A KNIGHT, TOO! WHAT AN HONOR!

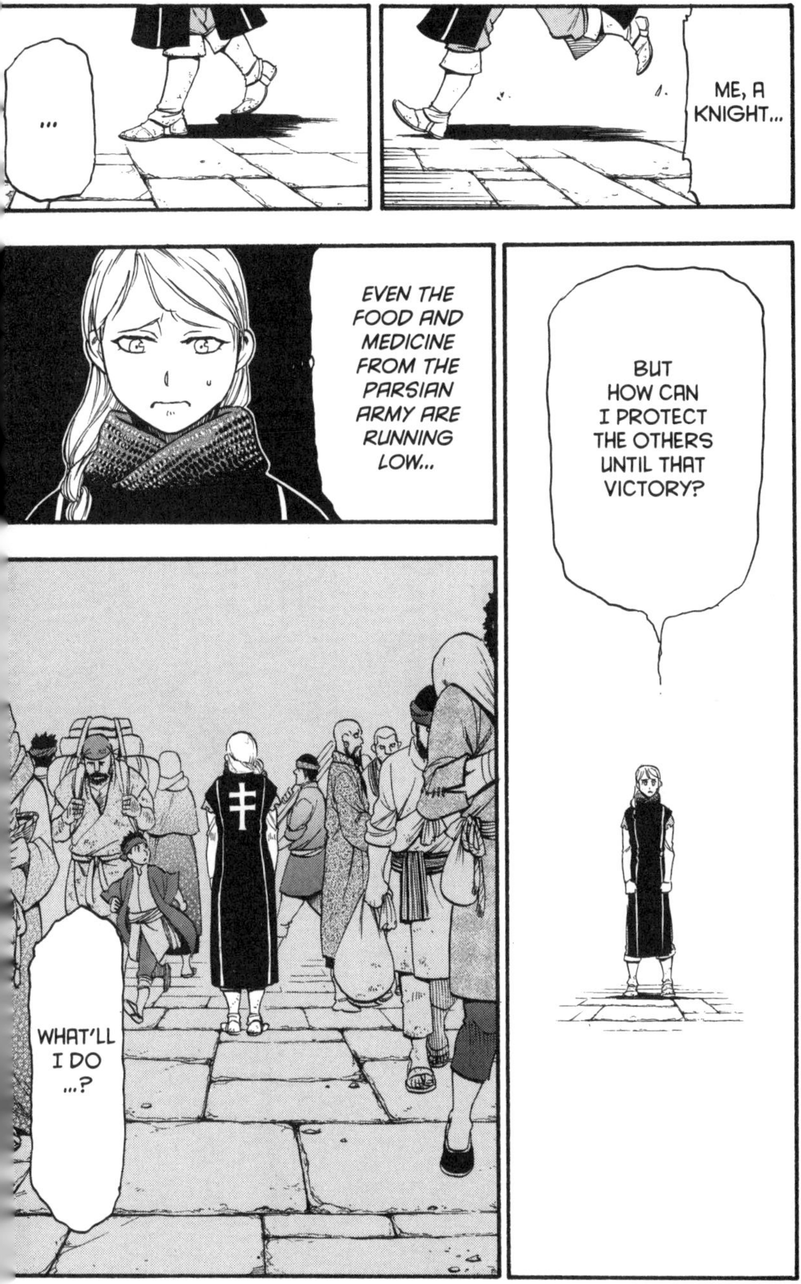
ME, A KNIGHT...
...
BUT HOW CAN I PROTECT THE OTHERS UNTIL THAT VICTORY?
EVEN THE FOOD AND MEDICINE FROM THE PARSIAN ARMY ARE RUNNING LOW...
WHAT'LL I DO ...?

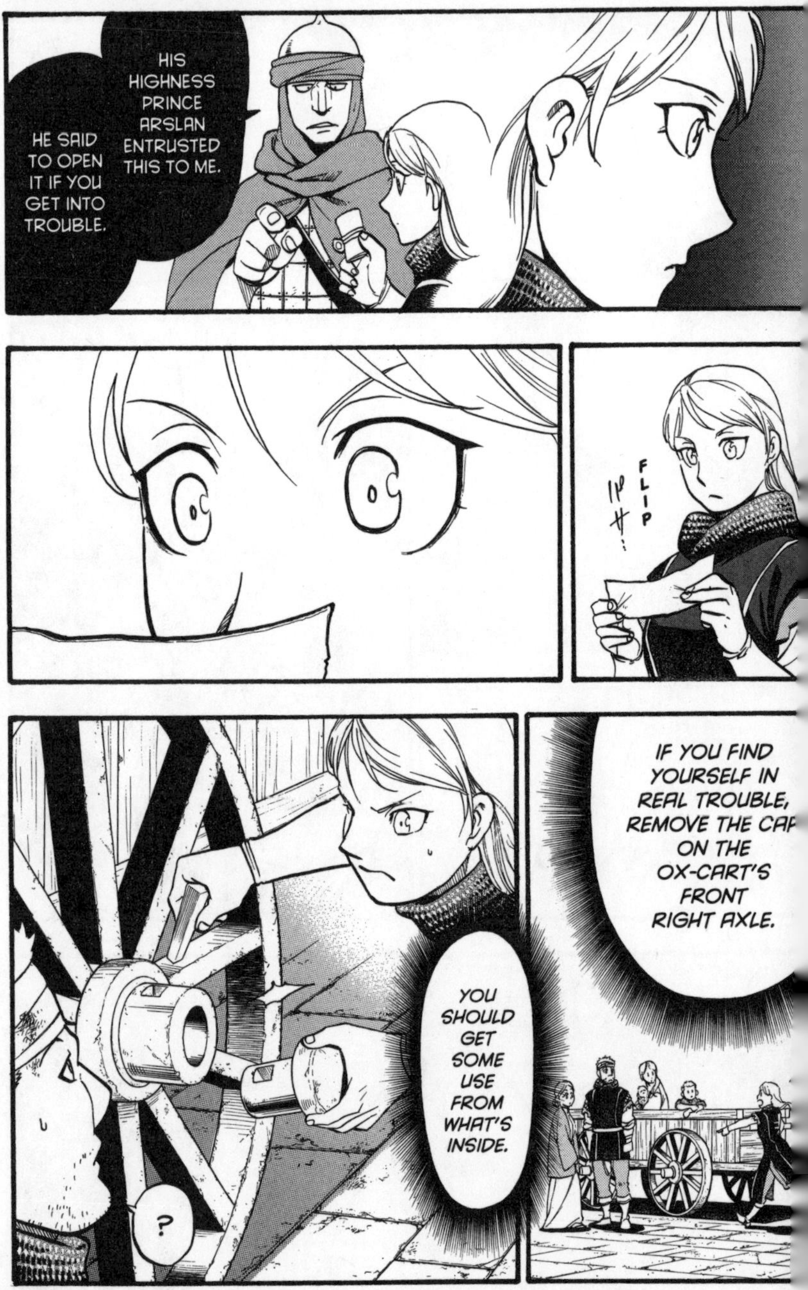
HIS HIGHNESS PRINCE ARSLAN ENTRUSTED THIS TO ME.
HE SAID TO OPEN IT IF YOU GET INTO TROUBLE.
FLIP
IF YOU FIND YOURSELF IN REAL TROUBLE, REMOVE THE CAP ON THE OX-CART'S FRONT RIGHT AXLE.
YOU SHOULD GET SOME USE FROM WHAT'S INSIDE.
?

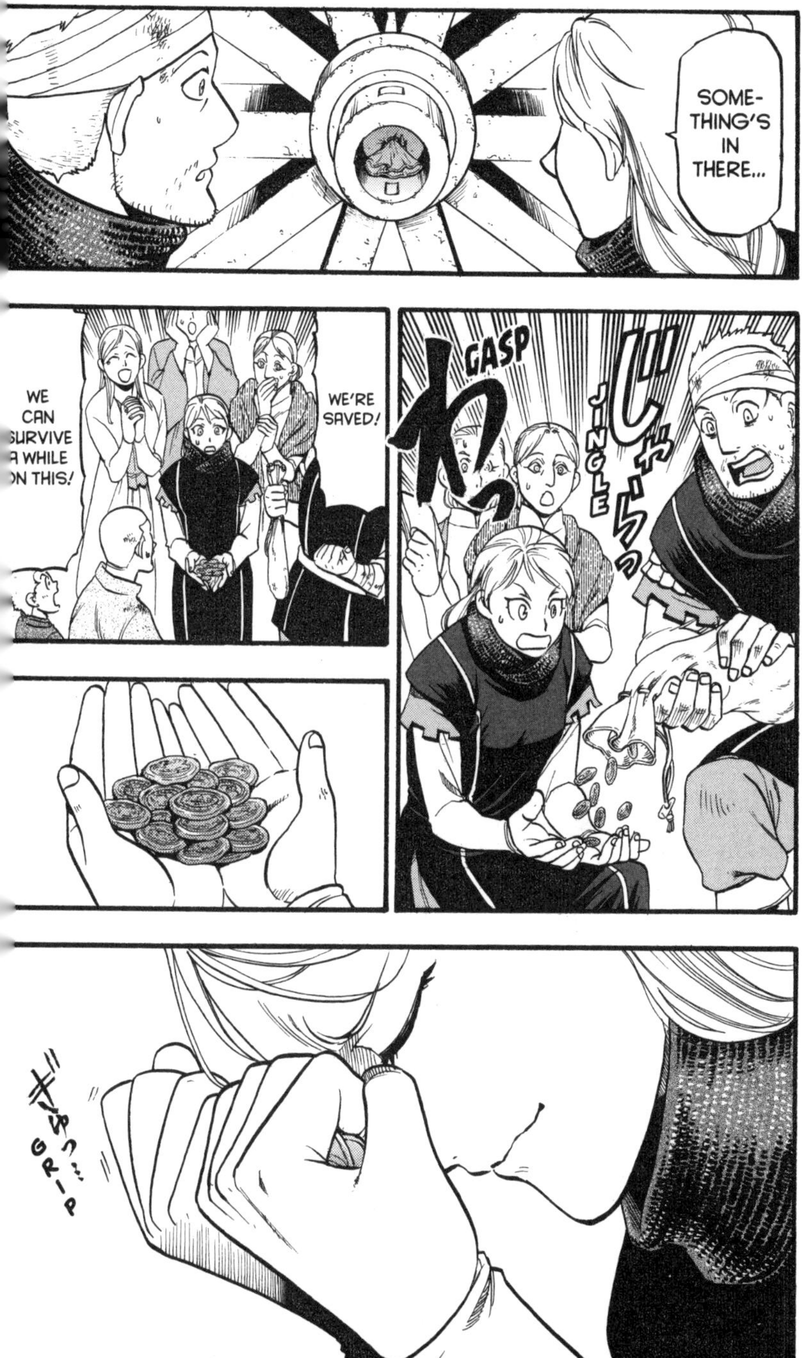
SOME-THING'S IN THERE...
GASP
JINGLE
WE'RE SAVED!
WE CAN SURVIVE A WHILE ON THIS!
GRIP

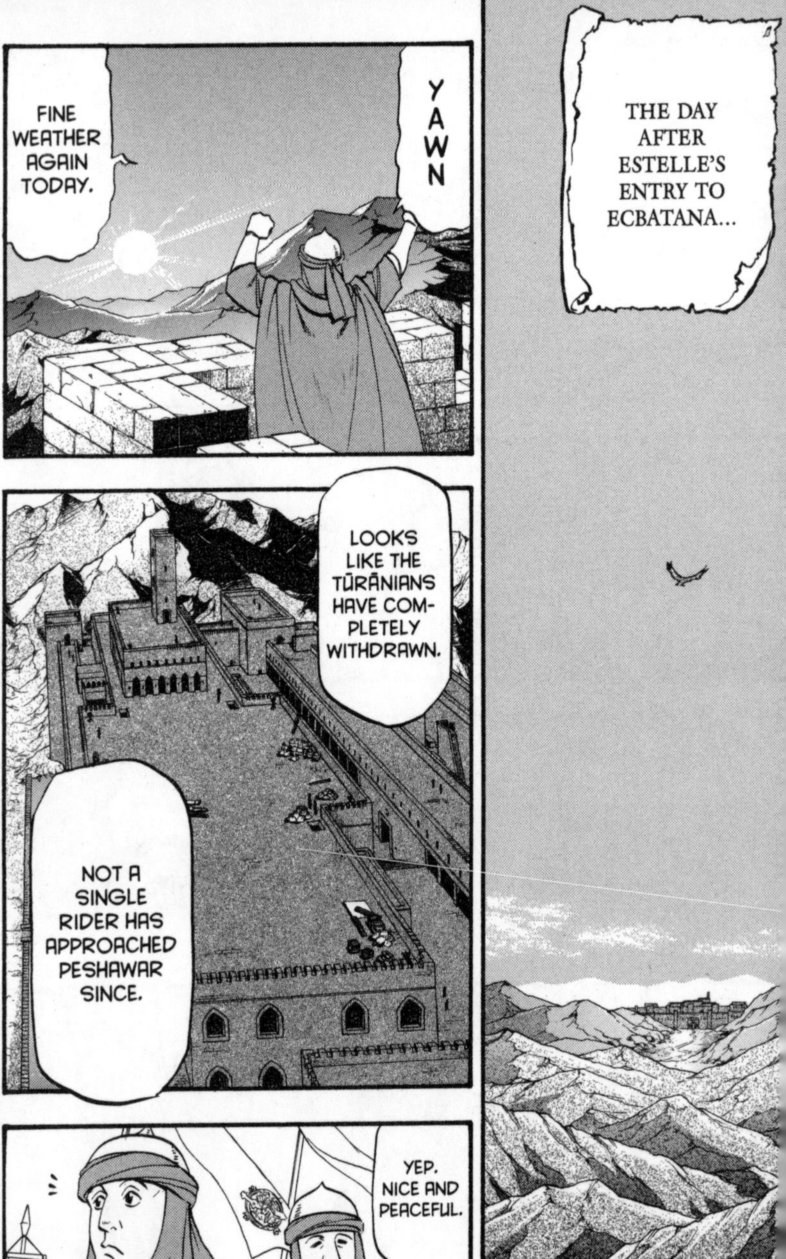
THE DAY AFTER ESTELLE'S ENTRY TO ECBATANA...
YAWN
FINE WEATHER AGAIN TODAY.
LOOKS LIKE THE TŪRĀNIANS HAVE COM-PLETELY WITHDRAWN.
NOT A SINGLE RIDER HAS APPROACHED PESHAWAR SINCE.
YEP. NICE AND PEACEFUL.

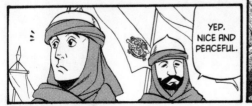

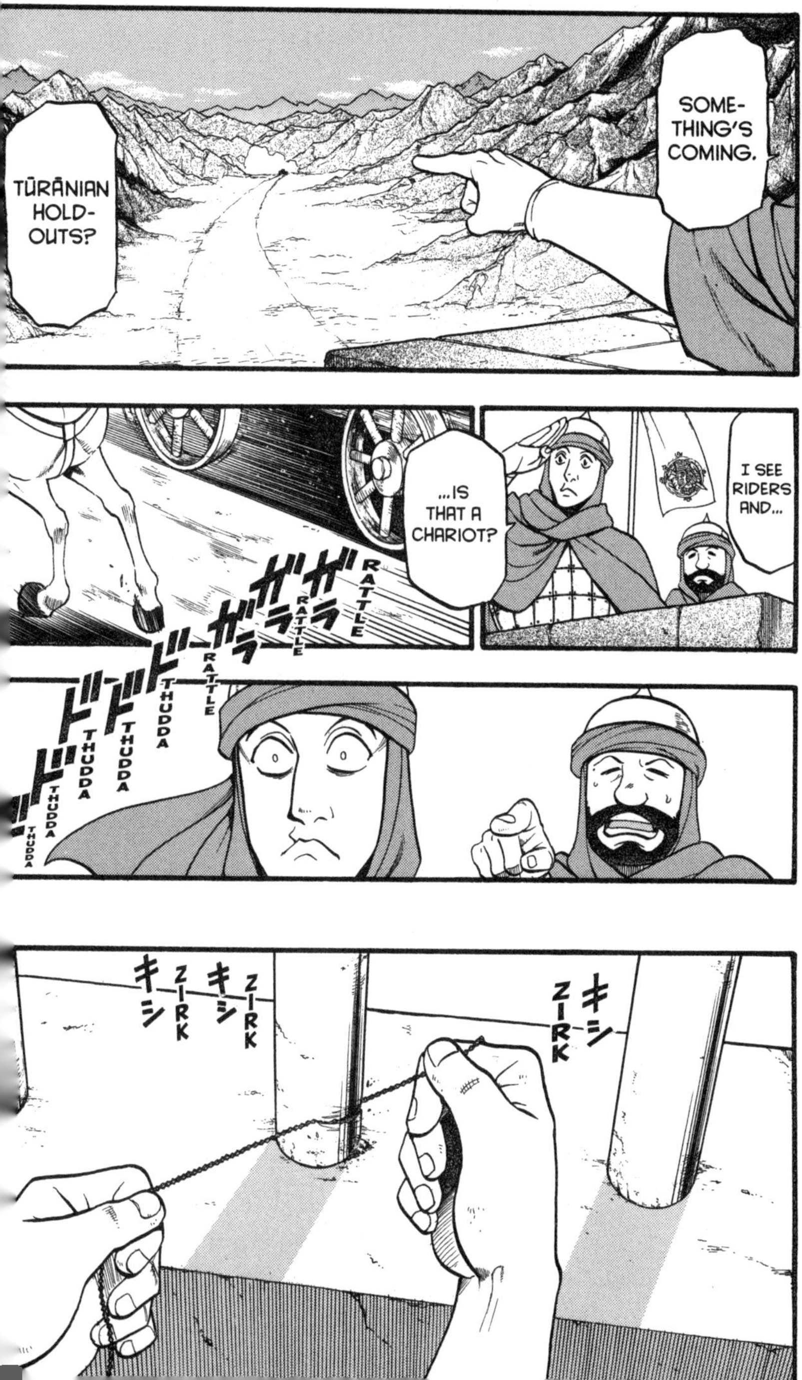
SOME-THING'S COMING.
TŪRĀNIAN HOLD-OUTS?
I SEE RIDERS AND...
...IS THAT A CHARIOT?
ガラガラ
RATTLE RATTLE RATTLE
ドドド
THUDDA THUDDA THUDDA THUDDA THUDDA
キシ ZIRK
キシ ZIRK
キシ ZIRK

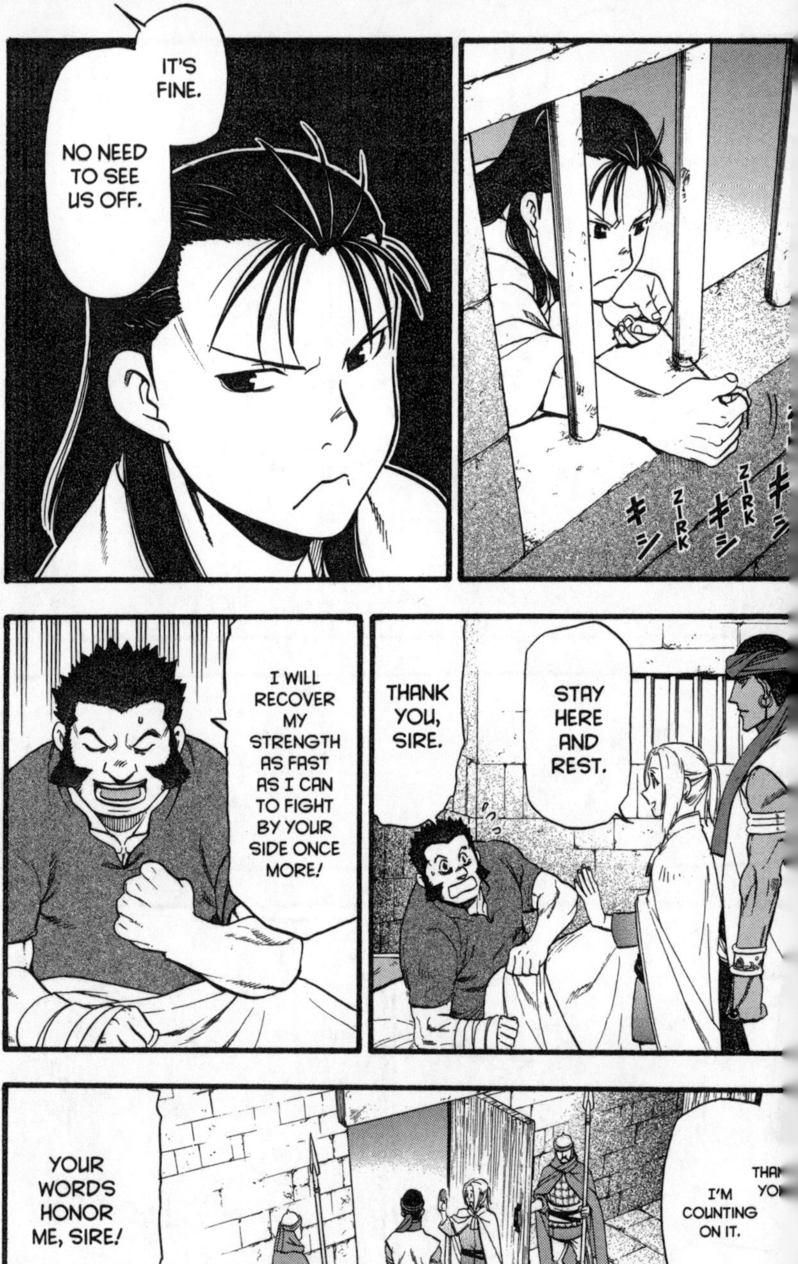
ZIRK
ZIRK
IT'S FINE.
NO NEED TO SEE US OFF.
STAY HERE AND REST.
THANK YOU, SIRE.
I WILL RECOVER MY STRENGTH AS FAST AS I CAN TO FIGHT BY YOUR SIDE ONCE MORE!
I'M COUNTING ON IT.
YOUR WORDS HONOR ME, SIRE!

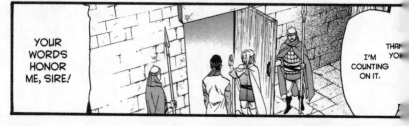

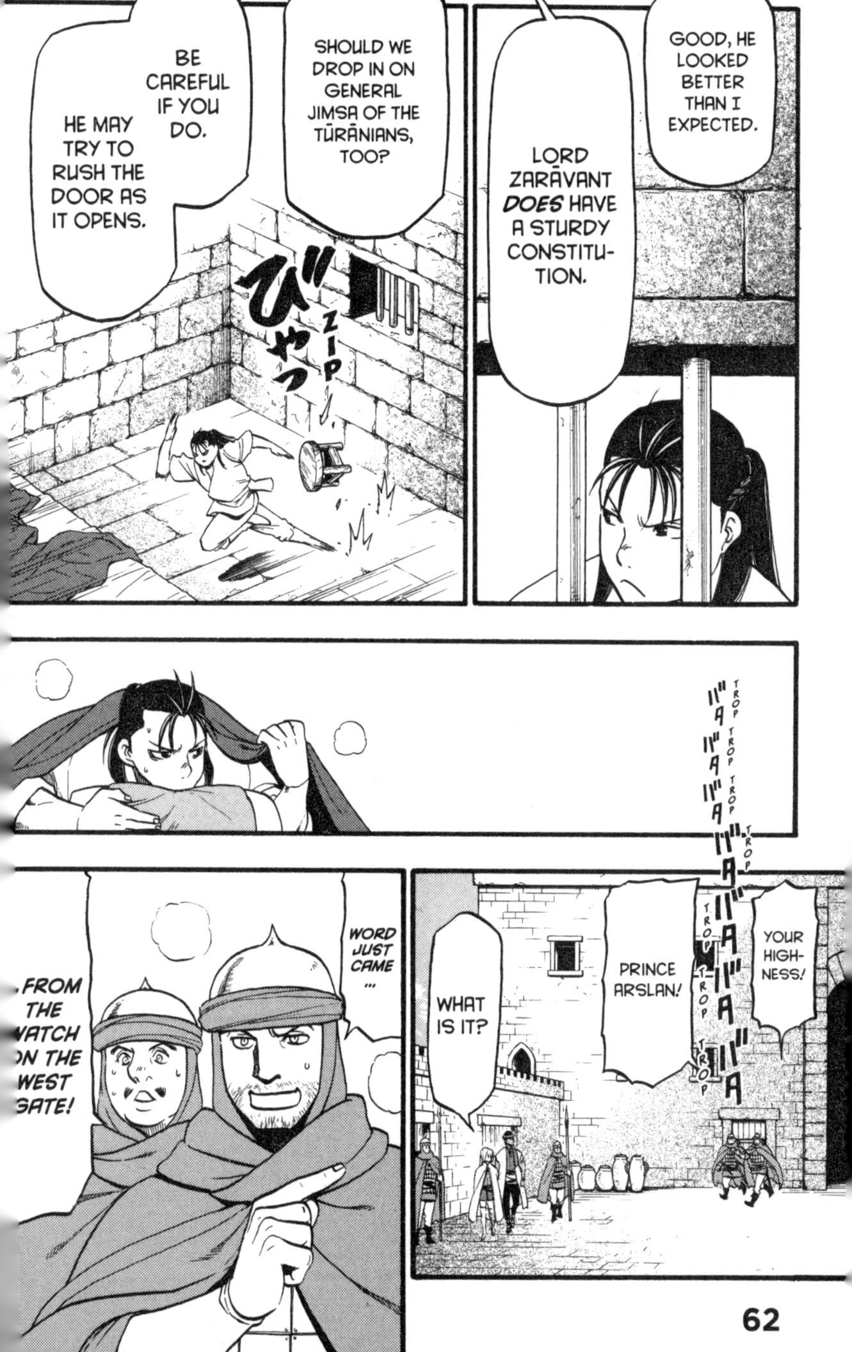
GOOD, HE LOOKED BETTER THAN I EXPECTED.
LORD ZARĀVANT *DOES* HAVE A STURDY CONSTITUTION.
SHOULD WE DROP IN ON GENERAL JIMSA OF THE TŪRĀNIANS, TOO?
BE CAREFUL IF YOU DO.
HE MAY TRY TO RUSH THE DOOR AS IT OPENS.
びゅっ
ZIP
バババババババババ
TROP TROP TROP TROP TROP TROP
YOUR HIGHNESS!
PRINCE ARSLAN!
WHAT IS IT?
WORD JUST CAME ...
...FROM THE WATCH ON THE WEST GATE!

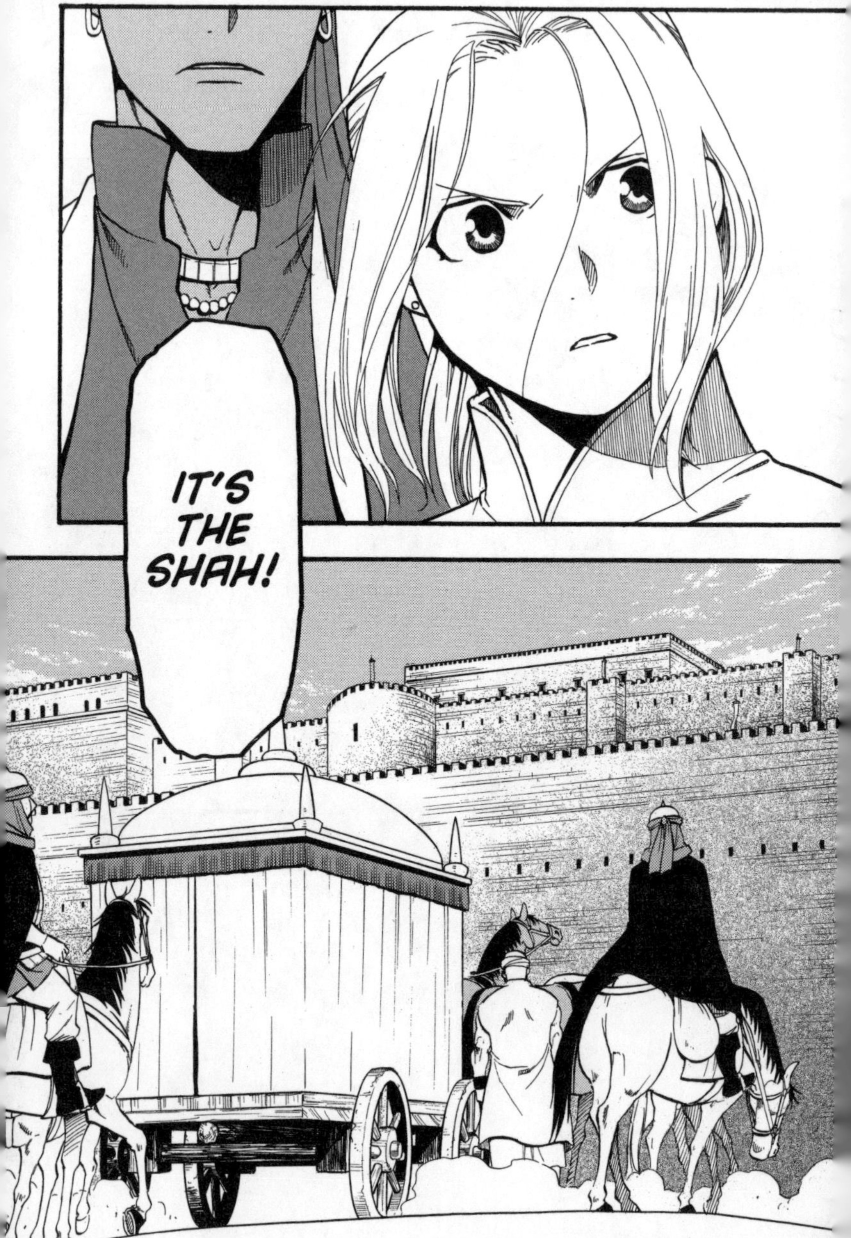
IT'S THE SHAH!

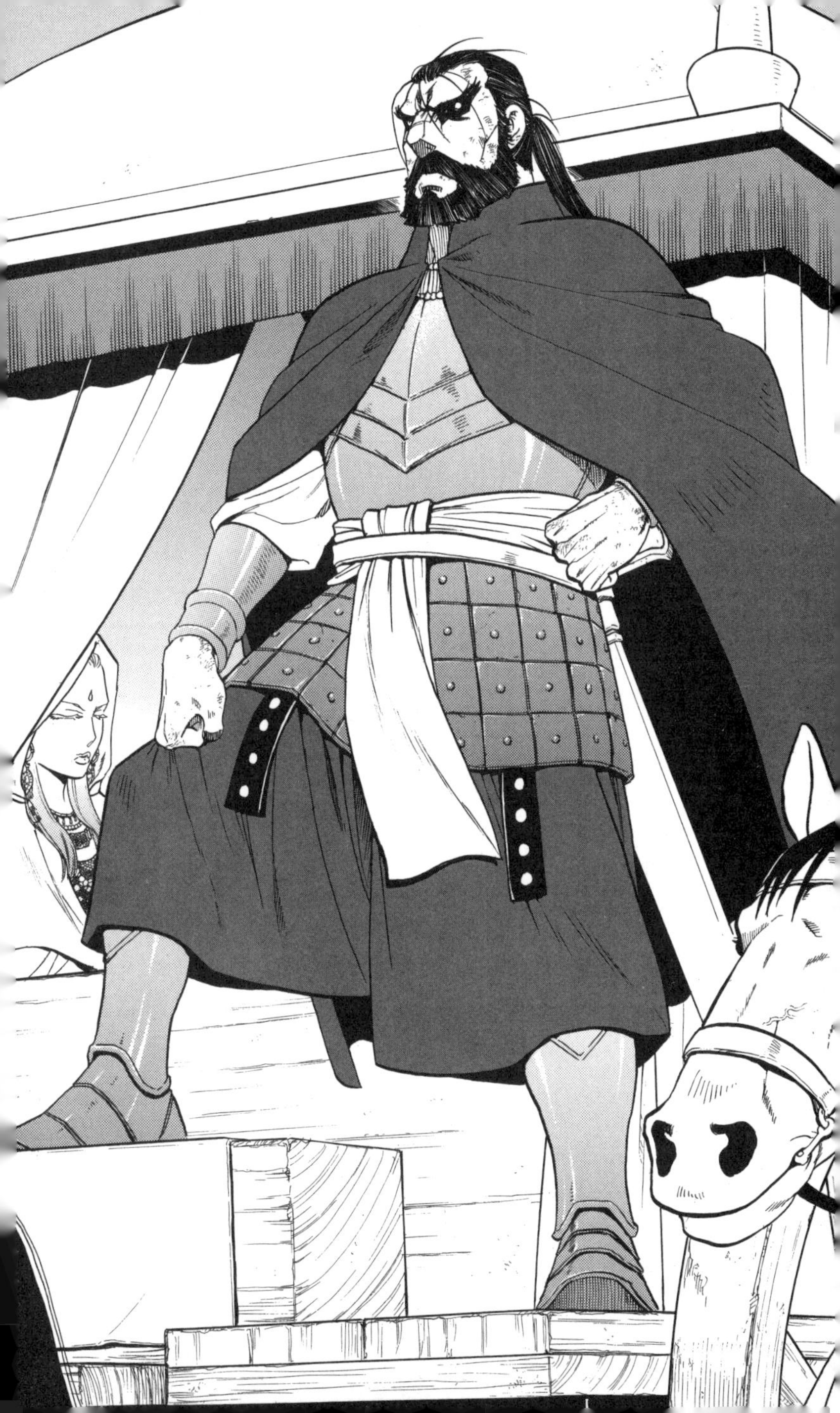

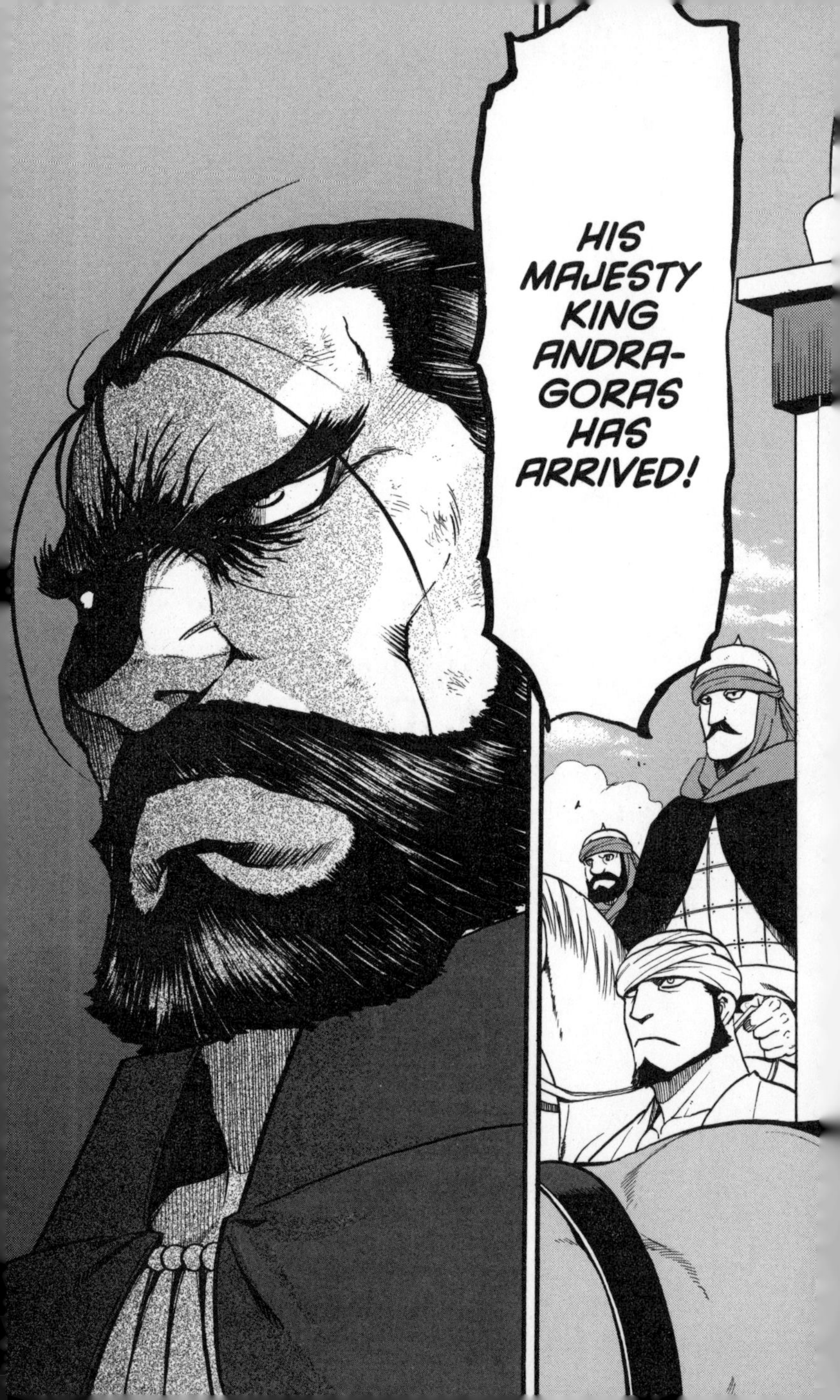
HIS MAJESTY KING ANDRA-GORAS HAS ARRIVED!

THE HEROIC LEGEND OF
ARSLAN

Chapter 91: Only One Shah

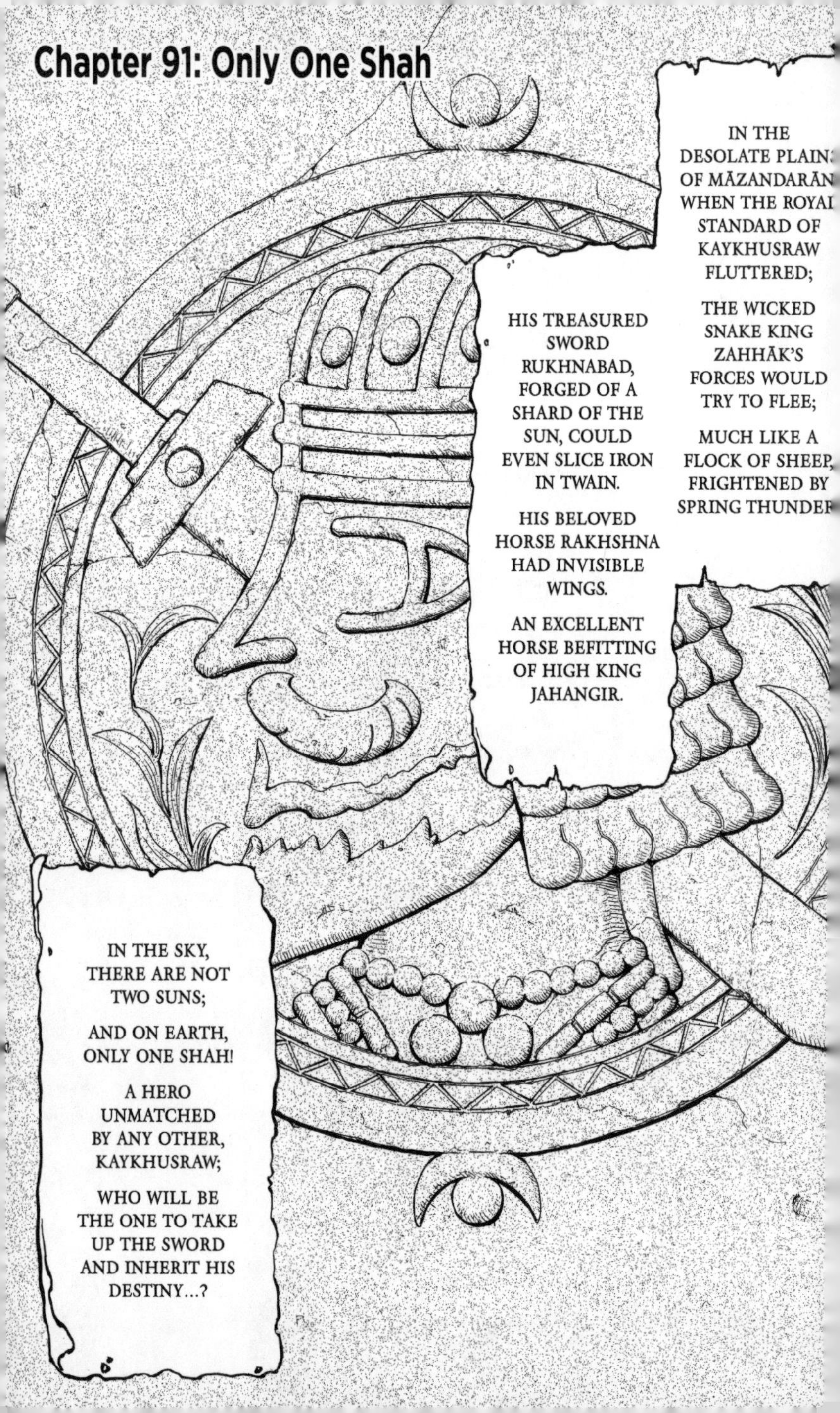
IN THE DESOLATE PLAINS OF MĀZANDARĀN WHEN THE ROYAL STANDARD OF KAYKHUSRAW FLUTTERED;
THE WICKED SNAKE KING ZAHHĀK'S FORCES WOULD TRY TO FLEE;
MUCH LIKE A FLOCK OF SHEEP, FRIGHTENED BY SPRING THUNDER
HIS TREASURED SWORD RUKHNABAD, FORGED OF A SHARD OF THE SUN, COULD EVEN SLICE IRON IN TWAIN.
HIS BELOVED HORSE RAKHSHNA HAD INVISIBLE WINGS.
AN EXCELLENT HORSE BEFITTING OF HIGH KING JAHANGIR.
IN THE SKY, THERE ARE NOT TWO SUNS;
AND ON EARTH, ONLY ONE SHAH!
A HERO UNMATCHED BY ANY OTHER, KAYKHUSRAW;
WHO WILL BE THE ONE TO TAKE UP THE SWORD AND INHERIT HIS DESTINY...?

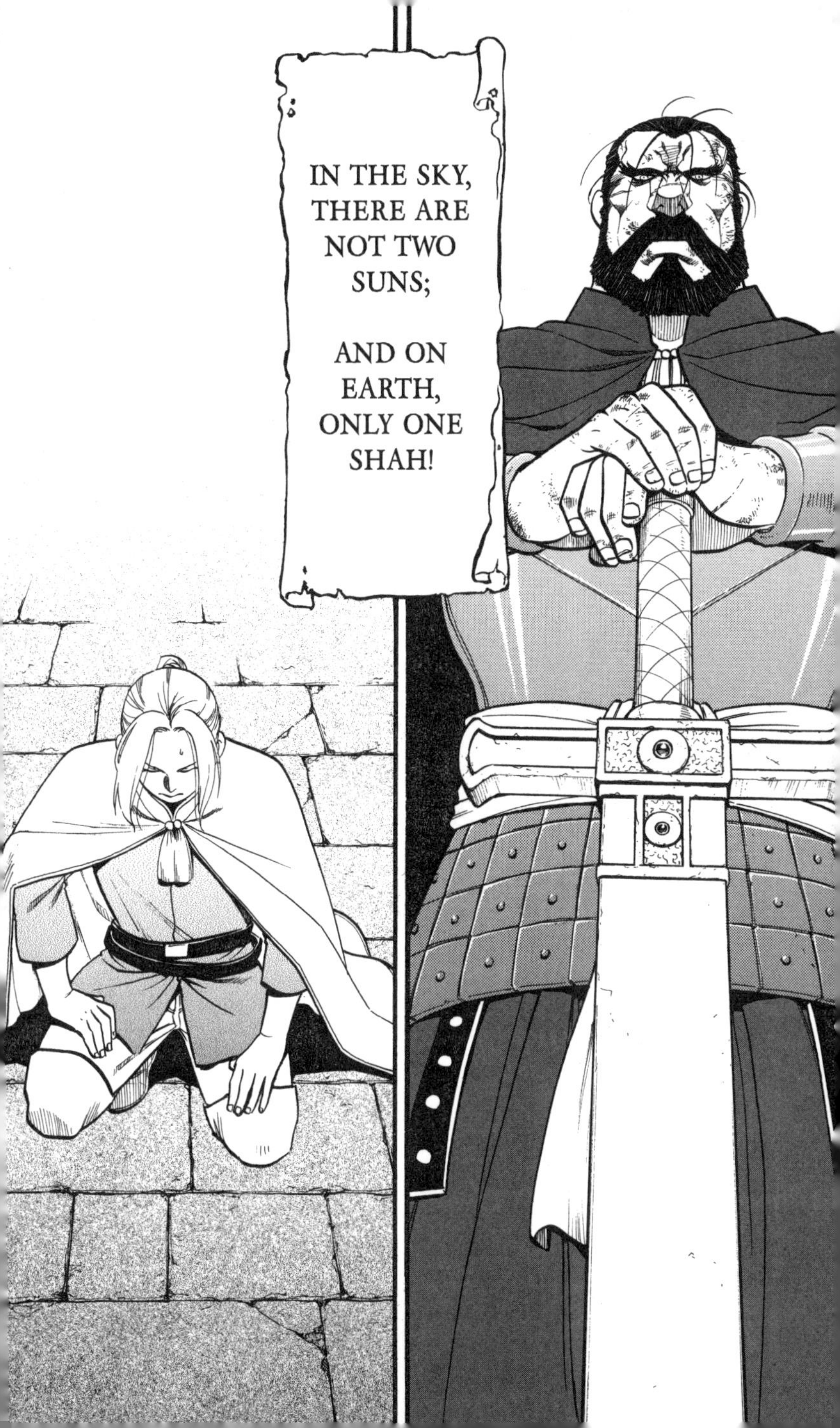
IN THE SKY, THERE ARE NOT TWO SUNS;
AND ON EARTH, ONLY ONE SHAH!

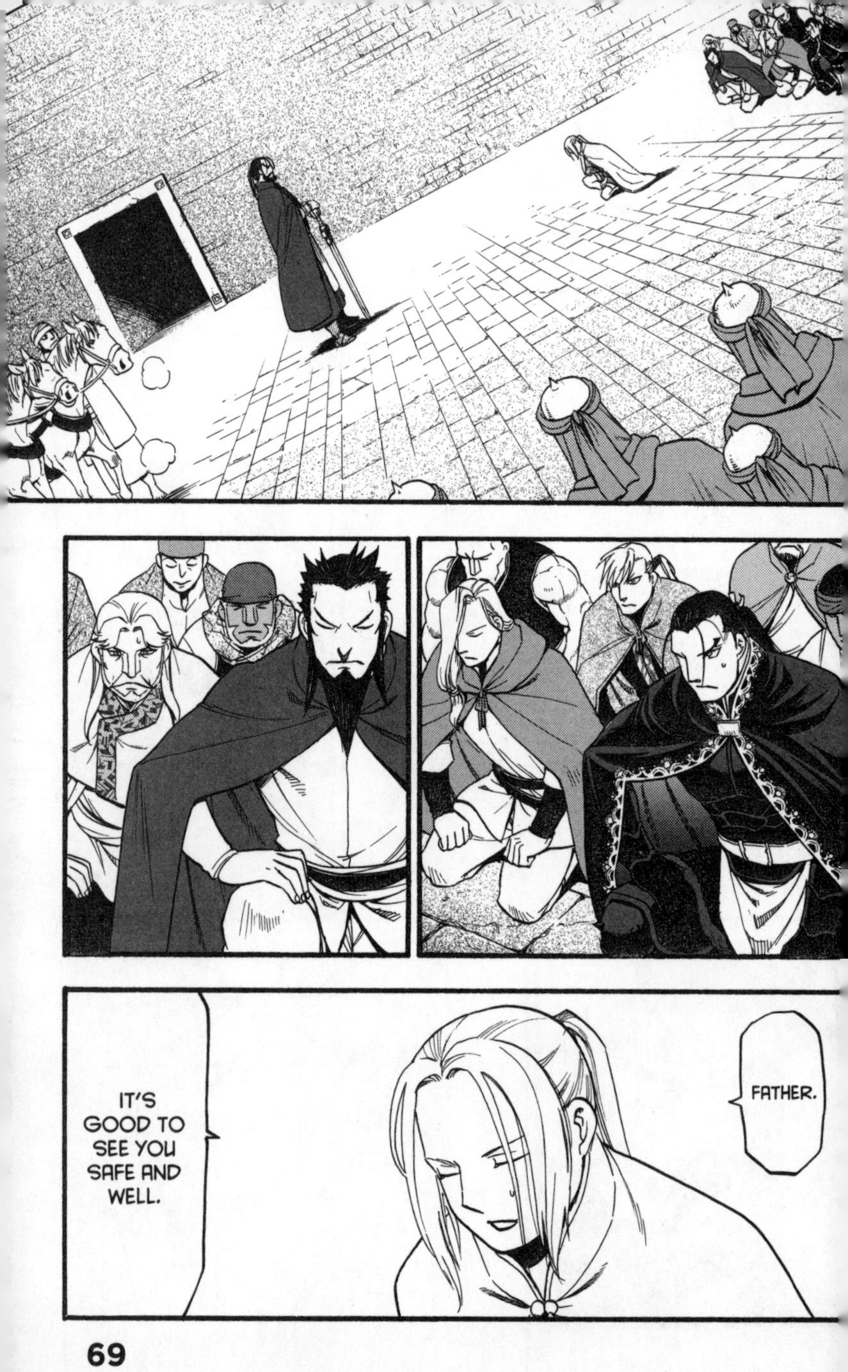
FATHER.
IT'S GOOD TO SEE YOU SAFE AND WELL.

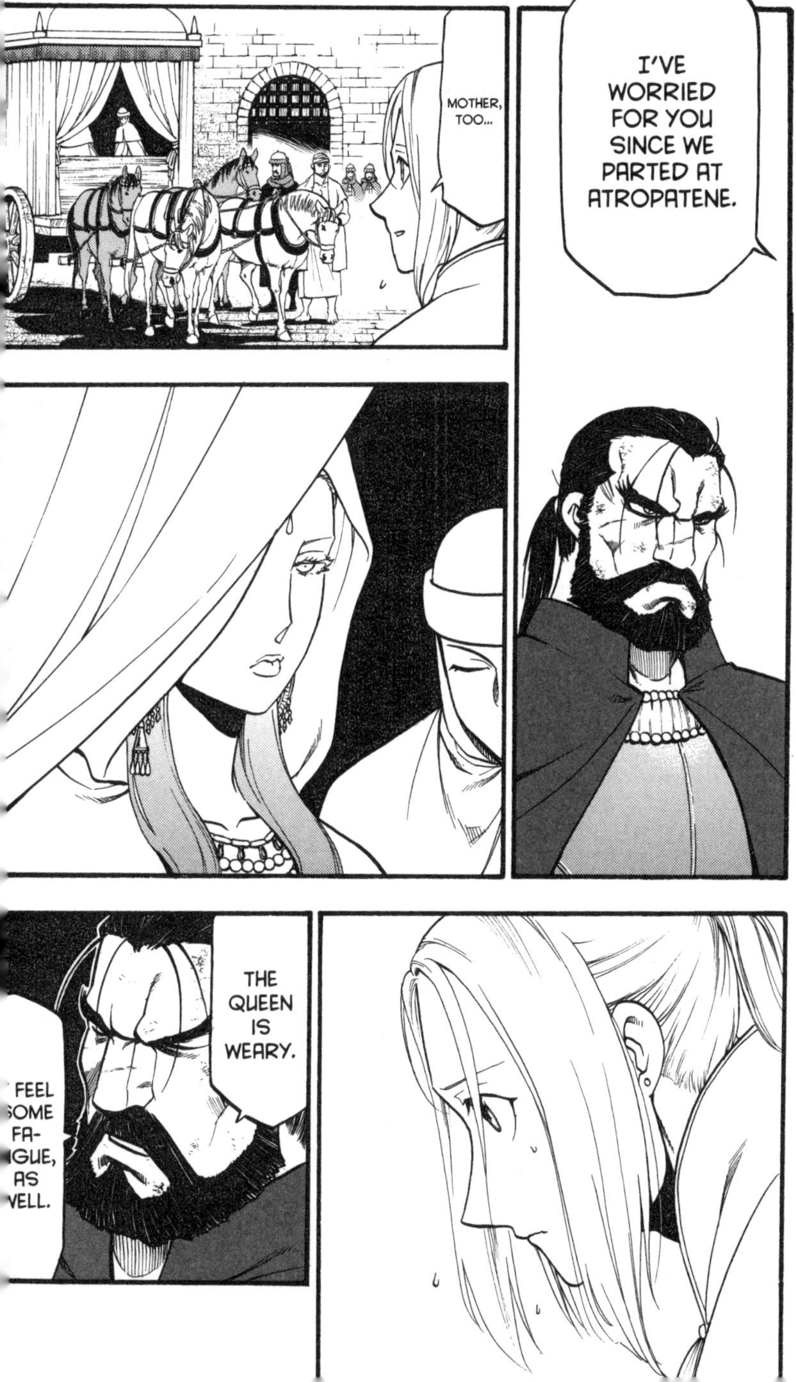
I'VE WORRIED FOR YOU SINCE WE PARTED AT ATROPATENE.
MOTHER, TOO...
THE QUEEN IS WEARY.
FEEL SOME FA- IGUE, AS VELL.

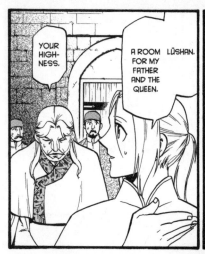

PREPAR A BED CHAMBE
TALK CAN WAIT UNTIL THE AFTER-NOON.
OF COURSE.
LŪSHAN.
A ROOM FOR MY FATHER AND THE QUEEN.
YOUR HIGH-NESS.
...
ざわ MURMUR
ざわ MURMUR
ざわ MURMUR
ざわ MURMUR
ざわ MURMUR

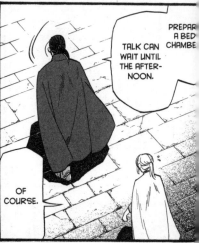

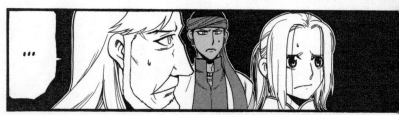

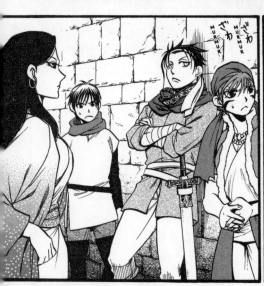

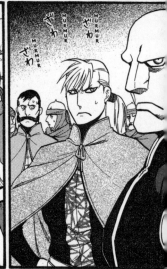

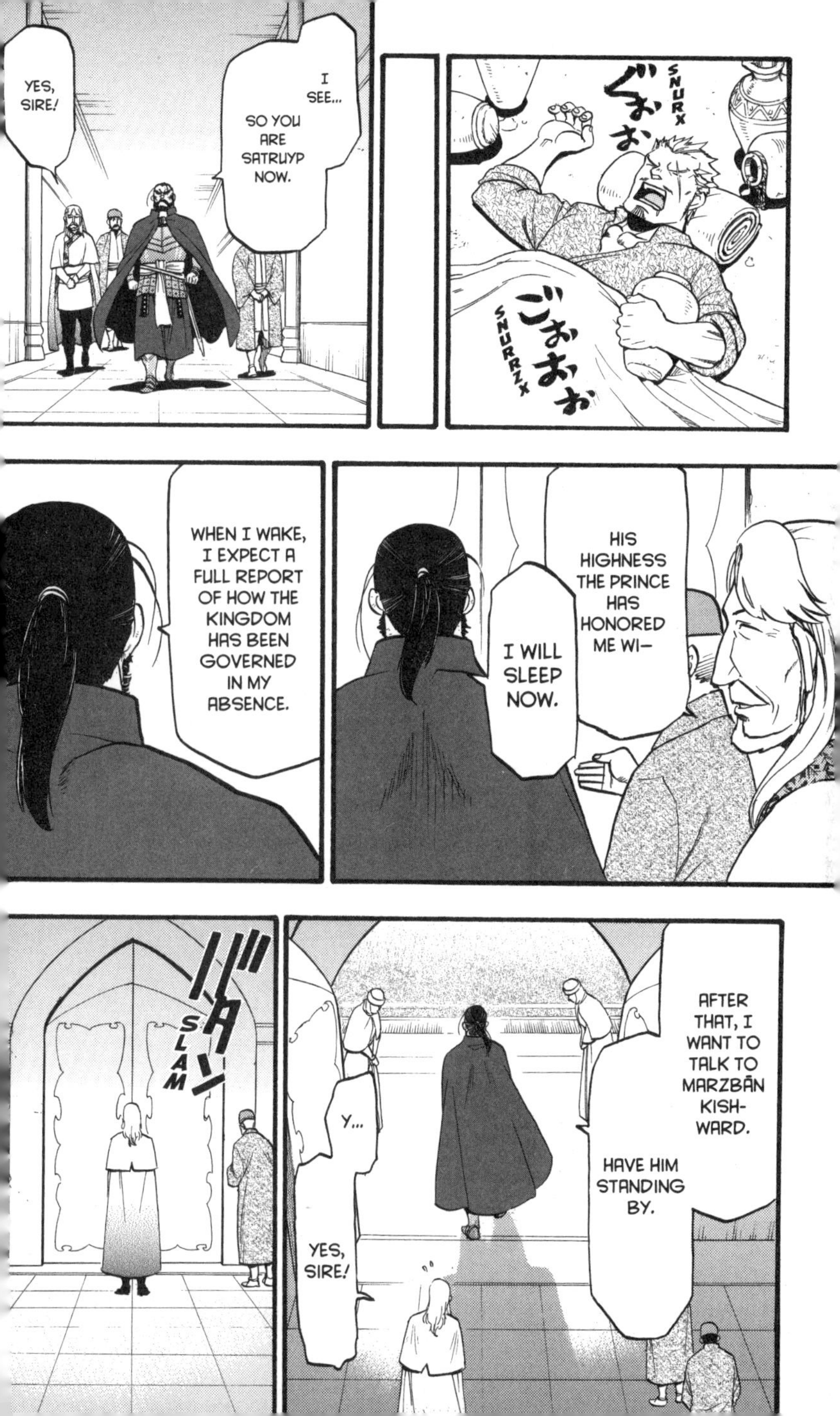
ぐおお
SNURX
ごおおお
SNURZX
I SEE...
SO YOU ARE SATRUYP NOW.
YES, SIRE!
HIS HIGHNESS THE PRINCE HAS HONORED ME WI—
I WILL SLEEP NOW.
WHEN I WAKE, I EXPECT A FULL REPORT OF HOW THE KINGDOM HAS BEEN GOVERNED IN MY ABSENCE.
AFTER THAT, I WANT TO TALK TO MARZBĀN KISH-WARD.
HAVE HIM STANDING BY.
Y...
YES, SIRE!
バタン
SLAM

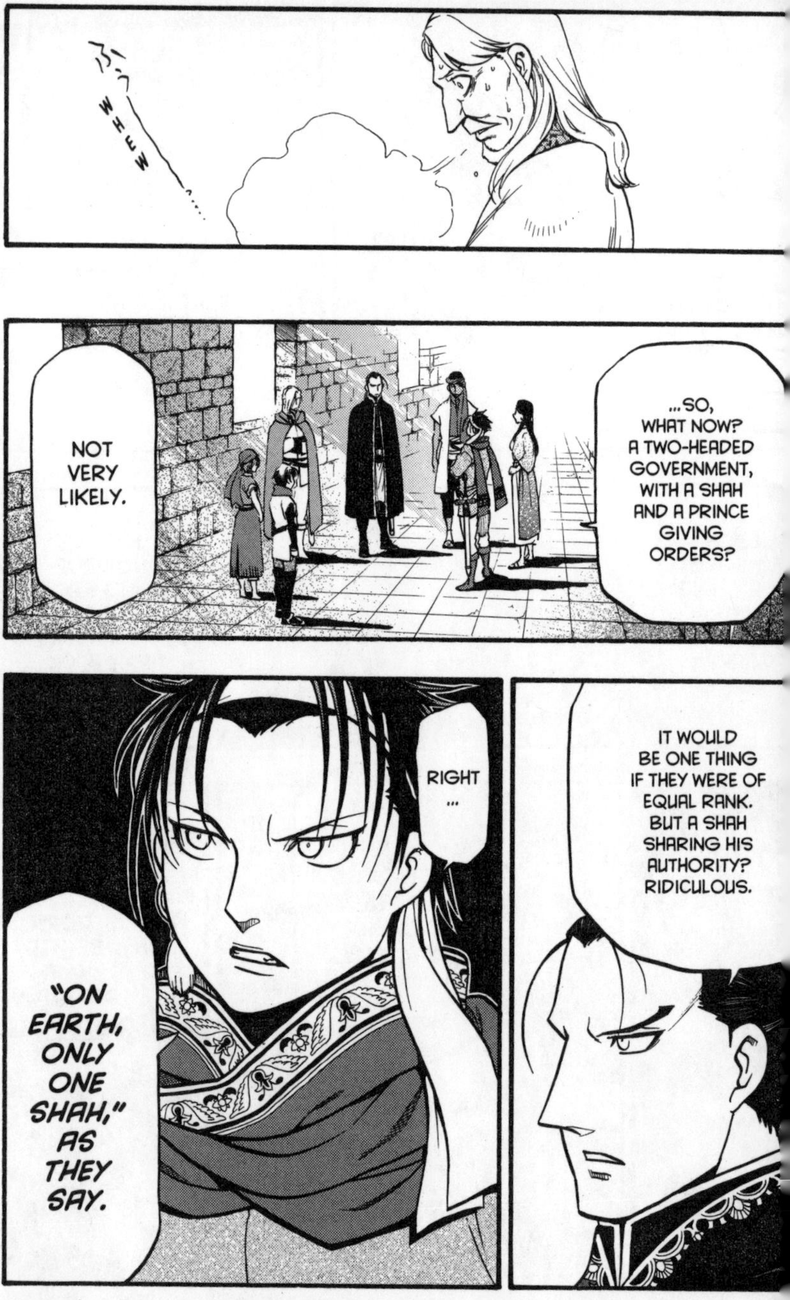
ふう
WHEW...
...SO, WHAT NOW? A TWO-HEADED GOVERNMENT, WITH A SHAH AND A PRINCE GIVING ORDERS?
NOT VERY LIKELY.
IT WOULD BE ONE THING IF THEY WERE OF EQUAL RANK. BUT A SHAH SHARING HIS AUTHORITY? RIDICULOUS.
RIGHT ...
"ON EARTH, ONLY ONE SHAH," AS THEY SAY.

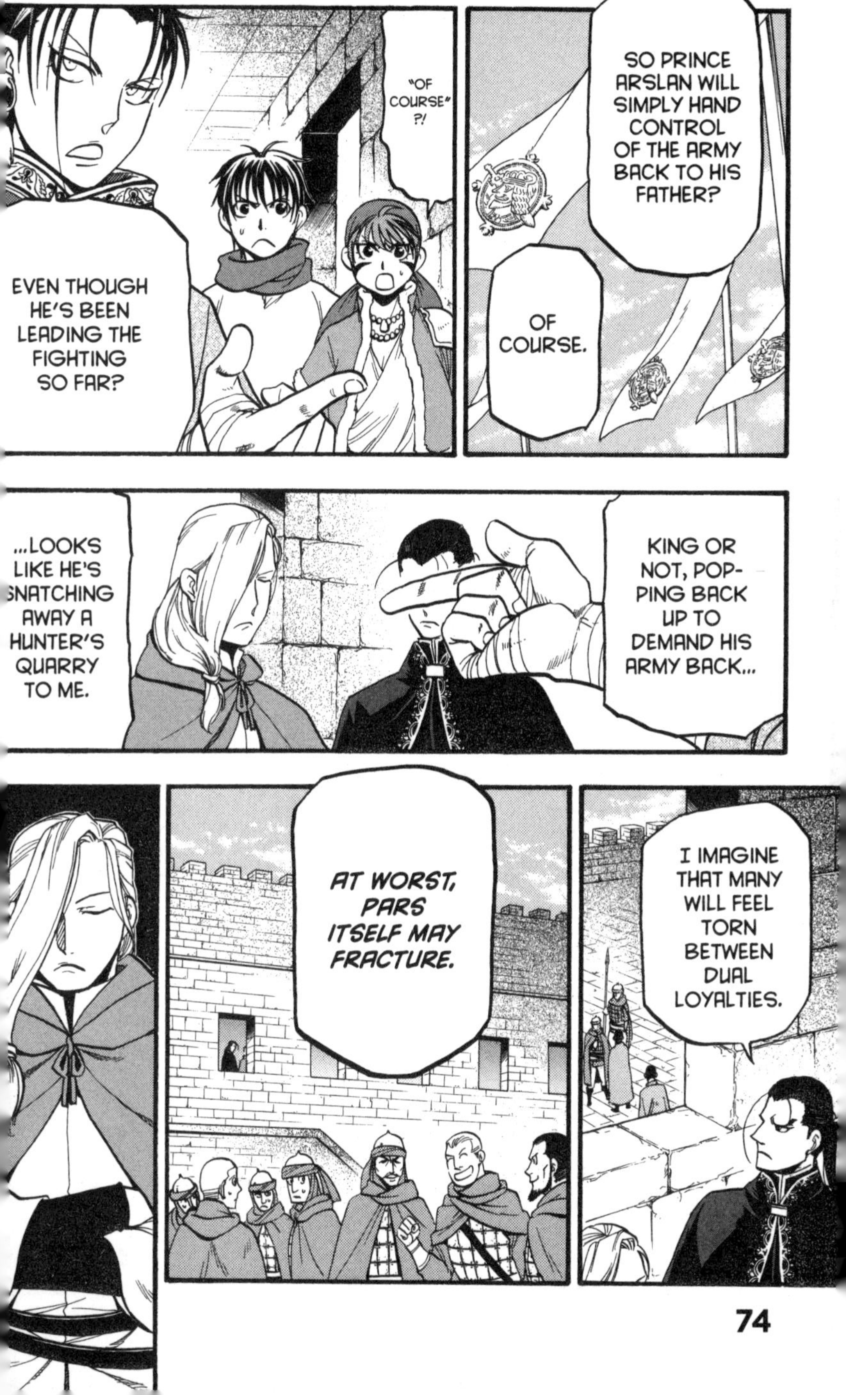
SO PRINCE ARSLAN WILL SIMPLY HAND CONTROL OF THE ARMY BACK TO HIS FATHER?
OF COURSE.
"OF COURSE"?!
EVEN THOUGH HE'S BEEN LEADING THE FIGHTING SO FAR?
KING OR NOT, POP-PING BACK UP TO DEMAND HIS ARMY BACK...
...LOOKS LIKE HE'S SNATCHING AWAY A HUNTER'S QUARRY TO ME.
I IMAGINE THAT MANY WILL FEEL TORN BETWEEN DUAL LOYALTIES.
AT WORST, PARS ITSELF MAY FRACTURE.

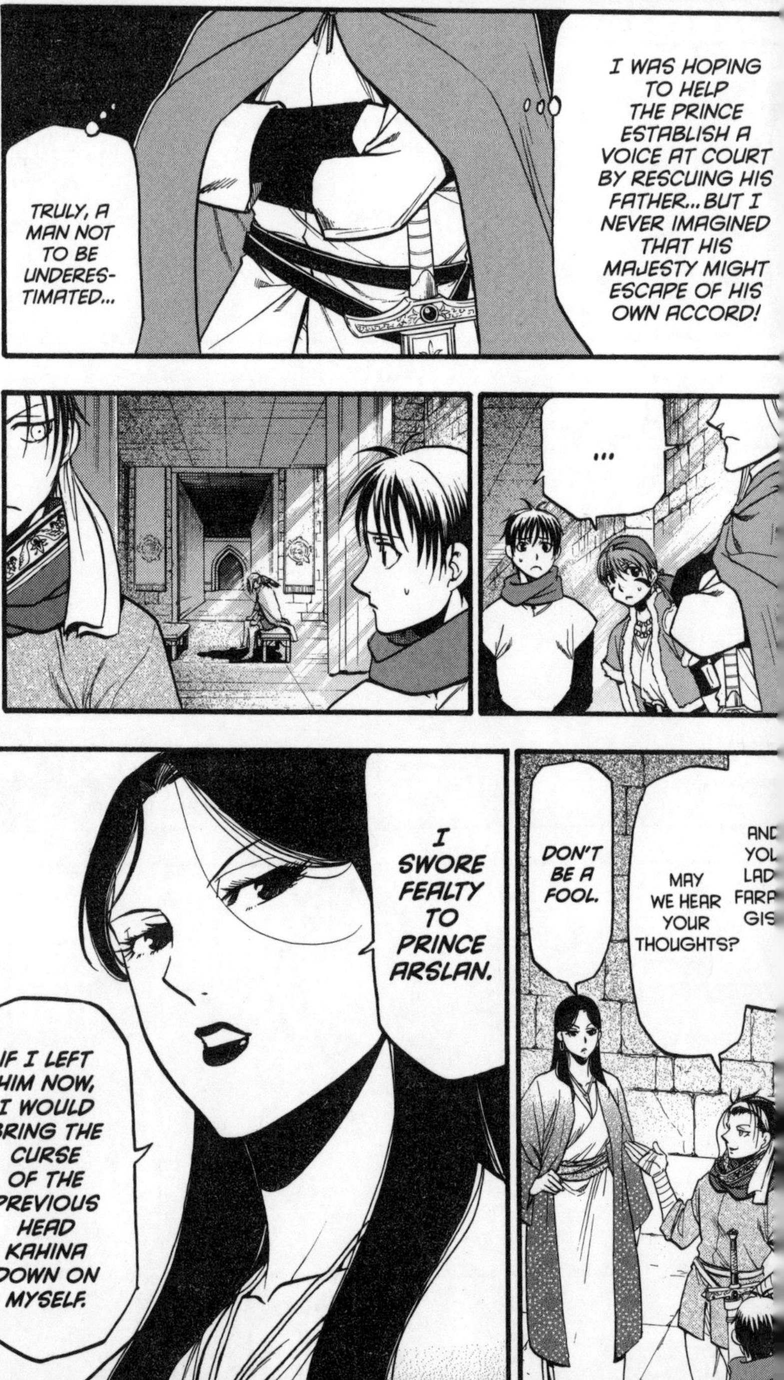
I WAS HOPING TO HELP THE PRINCE ESTABLISH A VOICE AT COURT BY RESCUING HIS FATHER... BUT I NEVER IMAGINED THAT HIS MAJESTY MIGHT ESCAPE OF HIS OWN ACCORD!
TRULY, A MAN NOT TO BE UNDERES-TIMATED...
...
MAY WE HEAR YOUR THOUGHTS?
DON'T BE A FOOL.
I SWORE FEALTY TO PRINCE ARSLAN.
IF I LEFT HIM NOW, I WOULD BRING THE CURSE OF THE PREVIOUS HEAD KAHINA DOWN ON MYSELF.

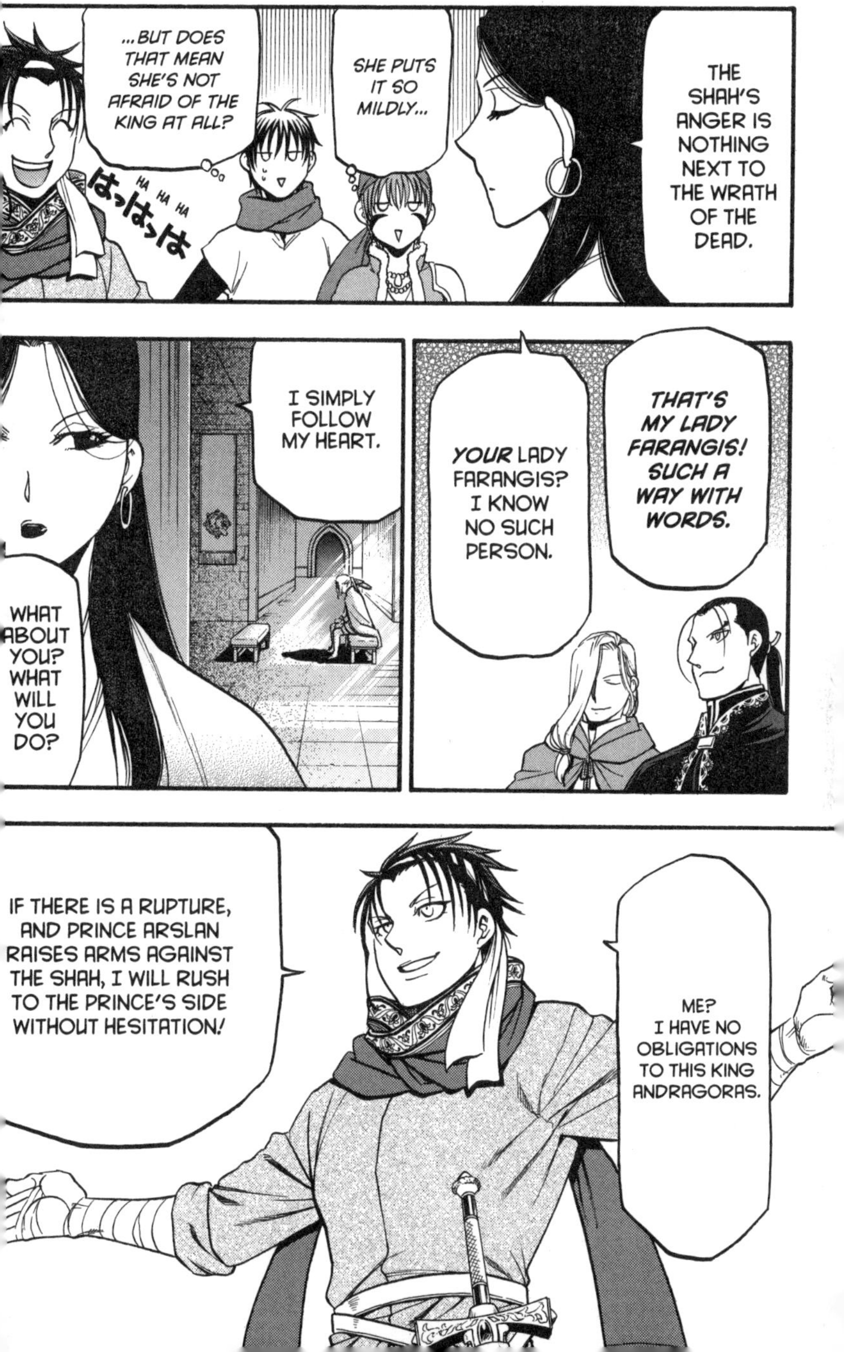
THE SHAH'S ANGER IS NOTHING NEXT TO THE WRATH OF THE DEAD.
SHE PUTS IT SO MILDLY...
...BUT DOES THAT MEAN SHE'S NOT AFRAID OF THE KING AT ALL?
はっはっは HA HA HA
THAT'S MY LADY FARANGIS! SUCH A WAY WITH WORDS.
YOUR LADY FARANGIS? I KNOW NO SUCH PERSON.
I SIMPLY FOLLOW MY HEART.
WHAT ABOUT YOU? WHAT WILL YOU DO?
ME? I HAVE NO OBLIGATIONS TO THIS KING ANDRAGORAS.
IF THERE IS A RUPTURE, AND PRINCE ARSLAN RAISES ARMS AGAINST THE SHAH, I WILL RUSH TO THE PRINCE'S SIDE WITHOUT HESITATION!

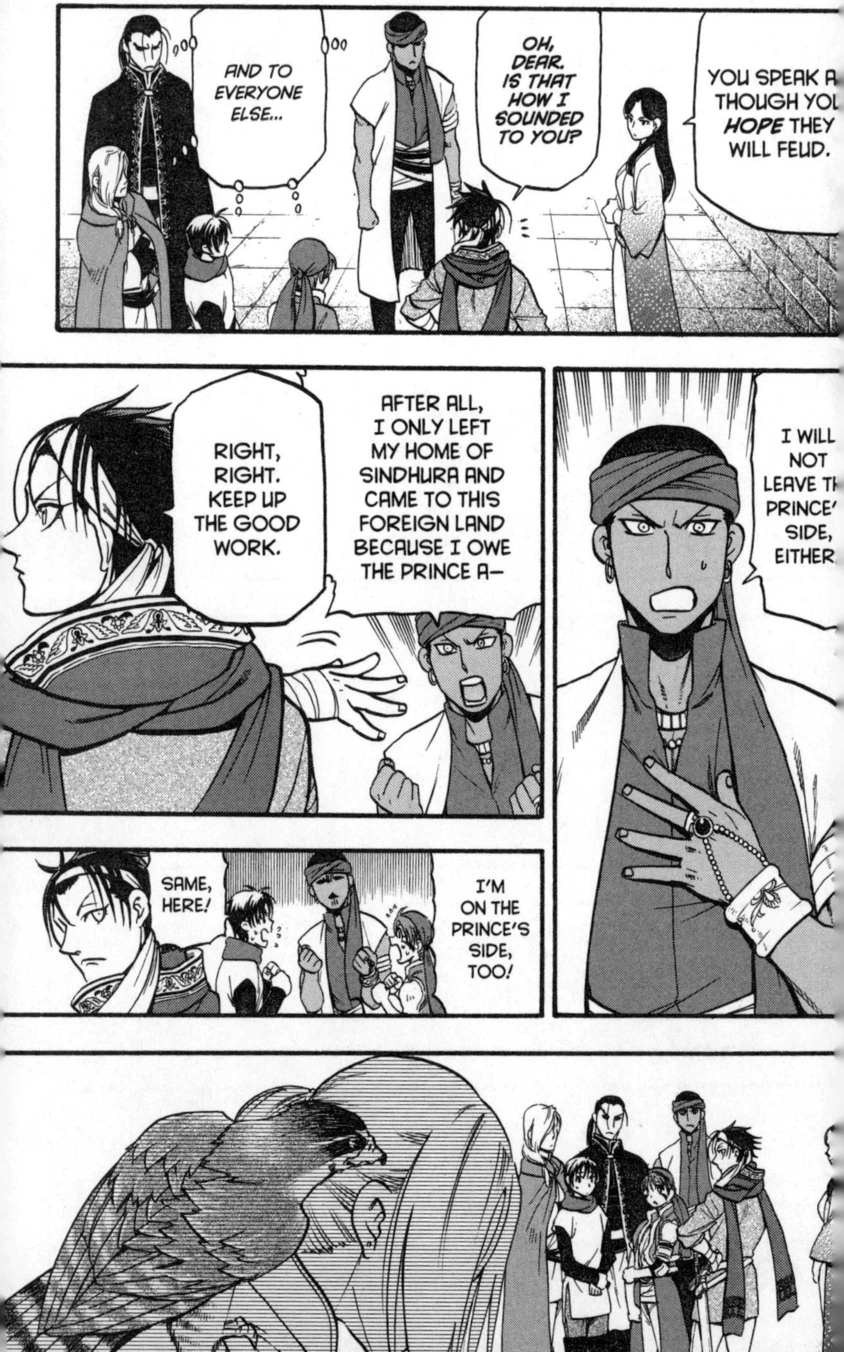
YOU SPEAK A THOUGH YO HOPE THEY WILL FEUD.
OH, DEAR. IS THAT HOW I SOUNDED TO YOU?
AND TO EVERYONE ELSE...
I WILL NOT LEAVE T PRINCE SIDE, EITHER
AFTER ALL, I ONLY LEFT MY HOME OF SINDHURA AND CAME TO THIS FOREIGN LAND BECAUSE I OWE THE PRINCE A—
RIGHT, RIGHT. KEEP UP THE GOOD WORK.
I'M ON THE PRINCE'S SIDE, TOO!
SAME, HERE!

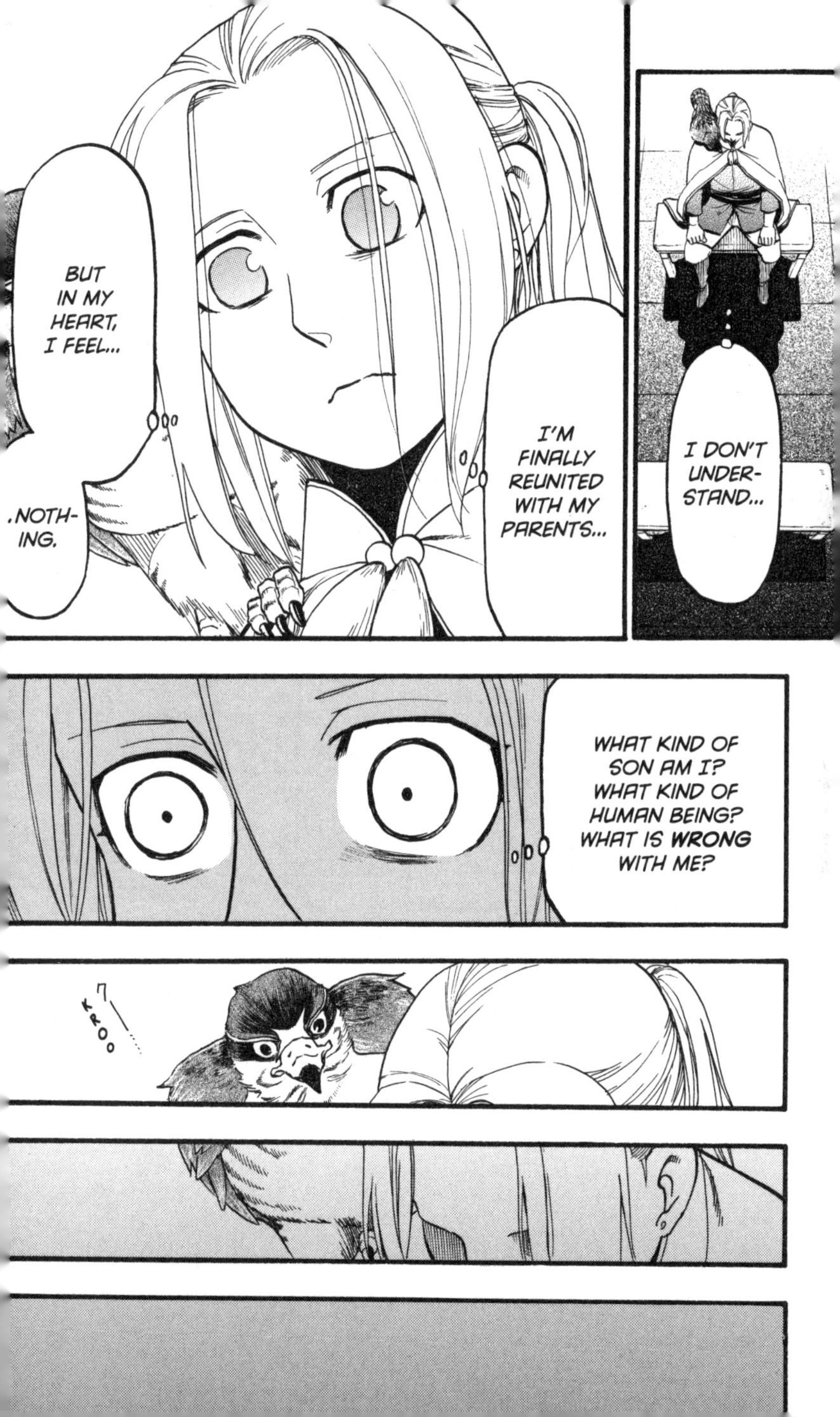
I DON'T UNDERSTAND...
I'M FINALLY REUNITED WITH MY PARENTS...
BUT IN MY HEART, I FEEL...
...NOTHING.
WHAT KIND OF SON AM I? WHAT KIND OF HUMAN BEING? WHAT IS **WRONG** WITH ME?
KROO...

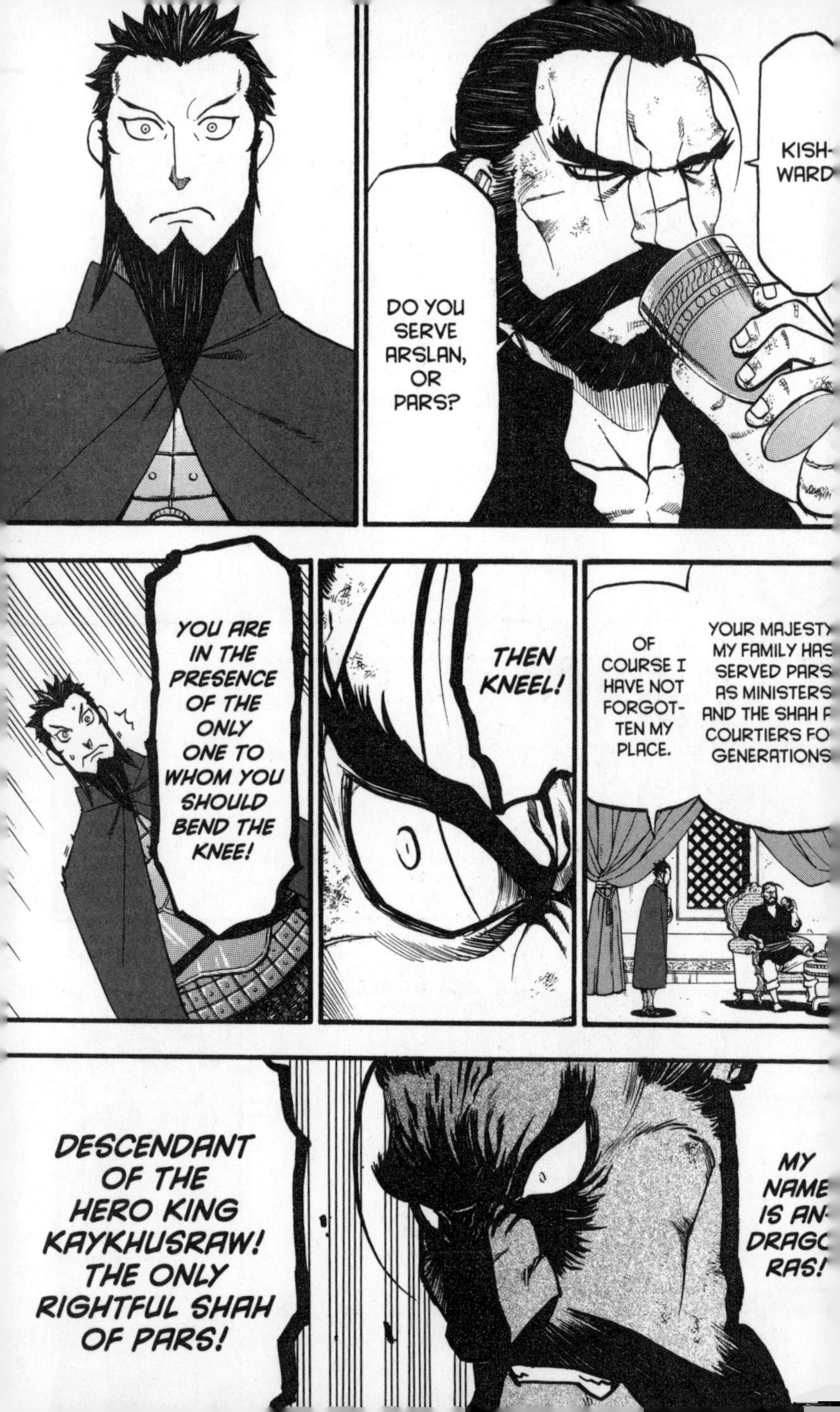
KISH-WARD
DO YOU SERVE ARSLAN, OR PARS?
YOUR MAJESTY MY FAMILY HAS SERVED PARS AS MINISTERS AND THE SHAH A COURTIERS FO GENERATIONS
OF COURSE I HAVE NOT FORGOT-TEN MY PLACE.
THEN KNEEL!
YOU ARE IN THE PRESENCE OF THE ONLY ONE TO WHOM YOU SHOULD BEND THE KNEE!
MY NAME IS AN-DRAGO RAS!
DESCENDANT OF THE HERO KING KAYKHUSRAW! THE ONLY RIGHTFUL SHAH OF PARS!

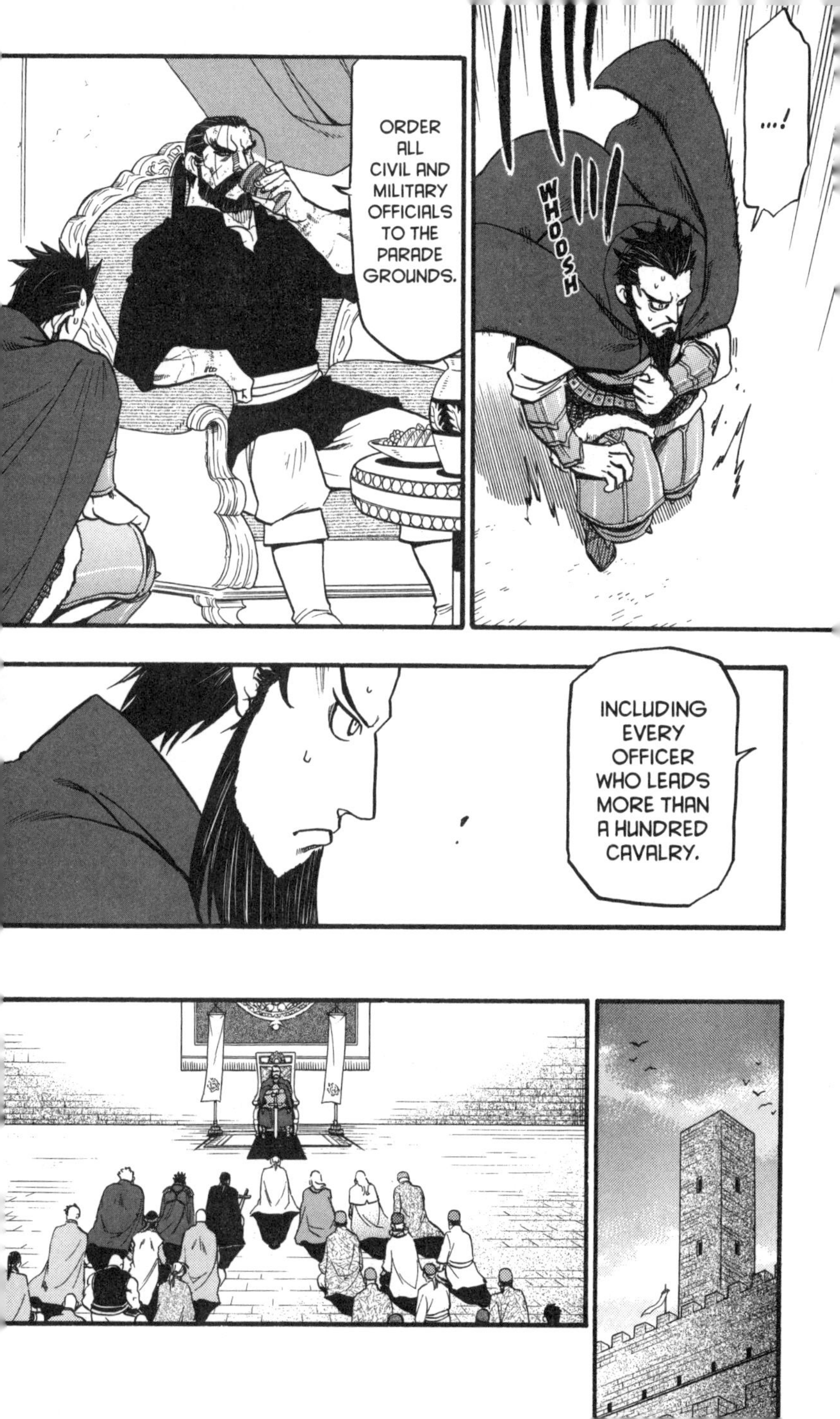
...!
WHOOSH
ORDER ALL CIVIL AND MILITARY OFFICIALS TO THE PARADE GROUNDS.
INCLUDING EVERY OFFICER WHO LEADS MORE THAN A HUNDRED CAVALRY.

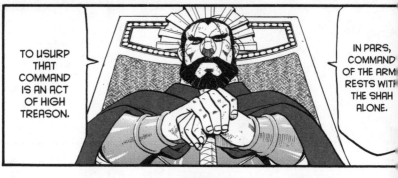

IN PARS, COMMAND OF THE ARM RESTS WITH THE SHAH ALONE.
TO USURP THAT COMMAND IS AN ACT OF HIGH TREASON.
YOU KNOW THIS, ARSLAN
YES...
...SIRE.
YOUR MAJESTY, IF I MAY!
IT WAS YOUR MAJESTY HIMSELF WHO MADE HIS HIGHNESS A CROWN PRINCE.
FOR A CROWN PRINCE TO ACT AS REGENT WHEN NECESSARY IS PERFECTLY PROPER!

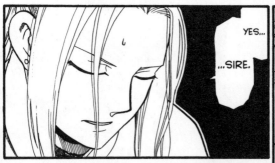

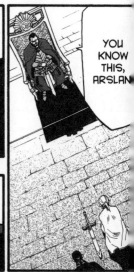

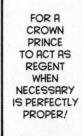

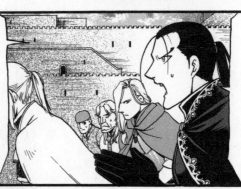

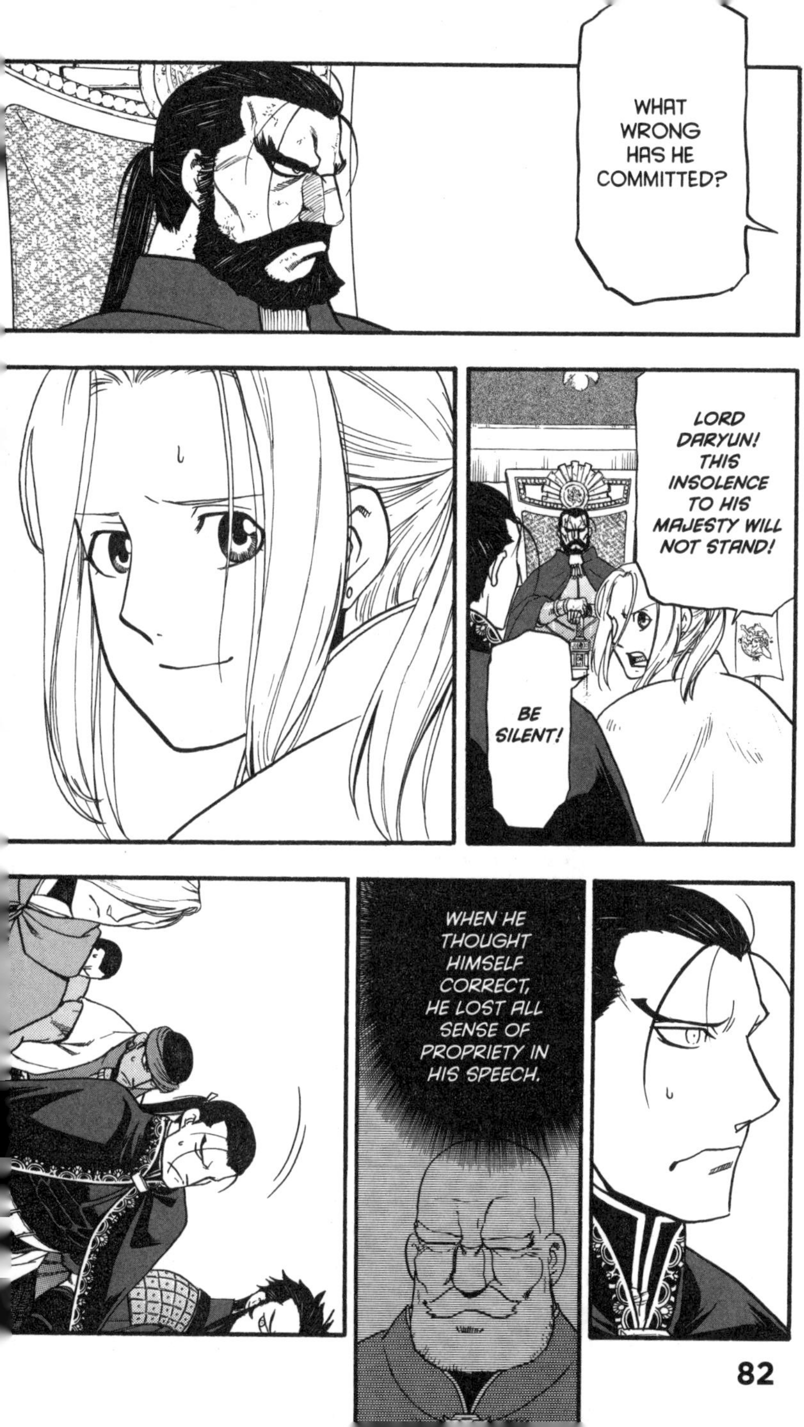
WHAT WRONG HAS HE COMMITTED?
LORD DARYUN! THIS INSOLENCE TO HIS MAJESTY WILL NOT STAND!
BE SILENT!
WHEN HE THOUGHT HIMSELF CORRECT, HE LOST ALL SENSE OF PROPRIETY IN HIS SPEECH.

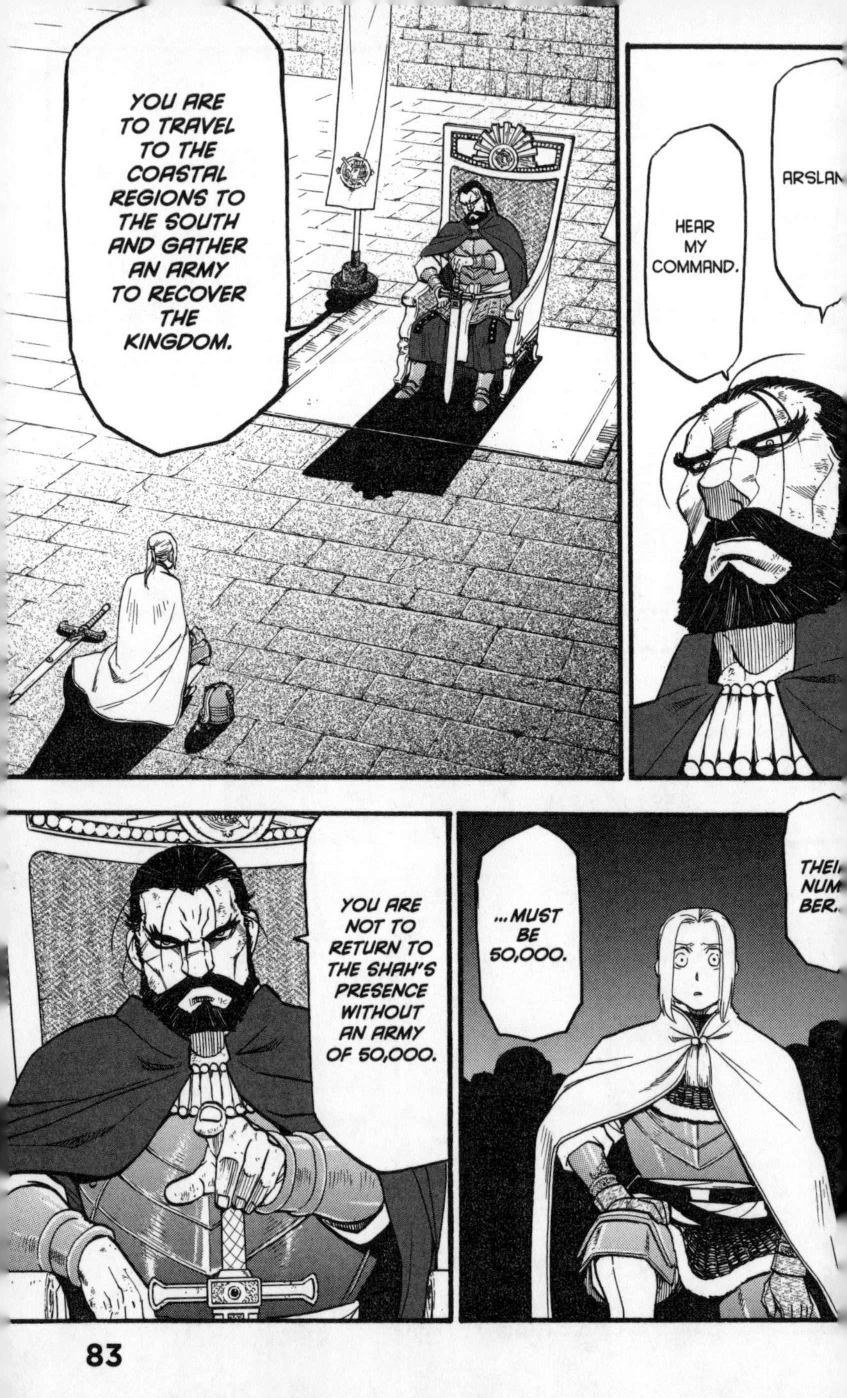
ARSLAN
HEAR MY COMMAND.
YOU ARE TO TRAVEL TO THE COASTAL REGIONS TO THE SOUTH AND GATHER AN ARMY TO RECOVER THE KINGDOM.
THEIR NUMBER...
...MUST BE 50,000.
YOU ARE NOT TO RETURN TO THE SHAH'S PRESENCE WITHOUT AN ARMY OF 50,000.

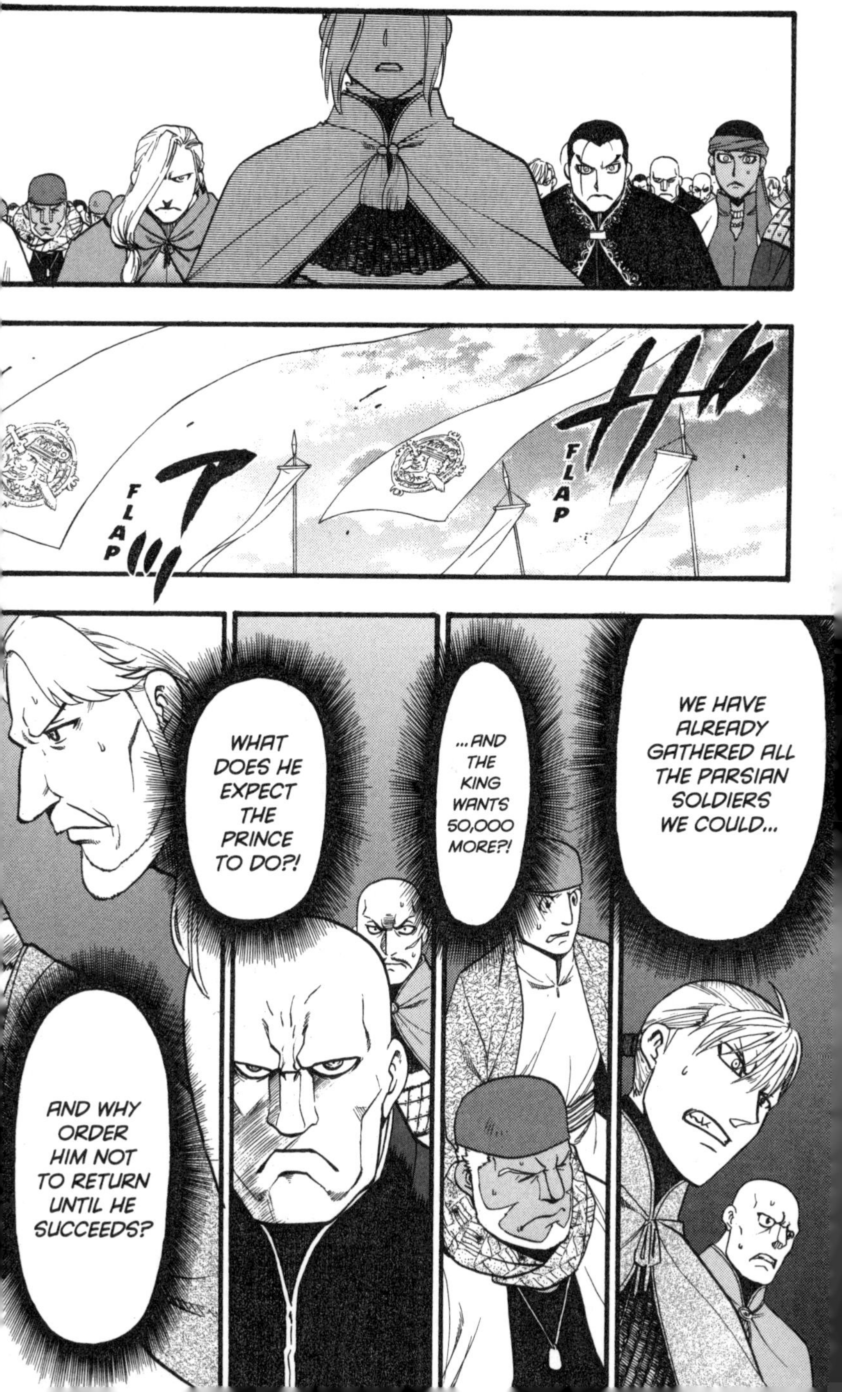
FLAP
FLAP
WE HAVE ALREADY GATHERED ALL THE PARSIAN SOLDIERS WE COULD...
...AND THE KING WANTS 50,000 MORE?!
WHAT DOES HE EXPECT THE PRINCE TO DO?!
AND WHY ORDER HIM NOT TO RETURN UNTIL HE SUCCEEDS?

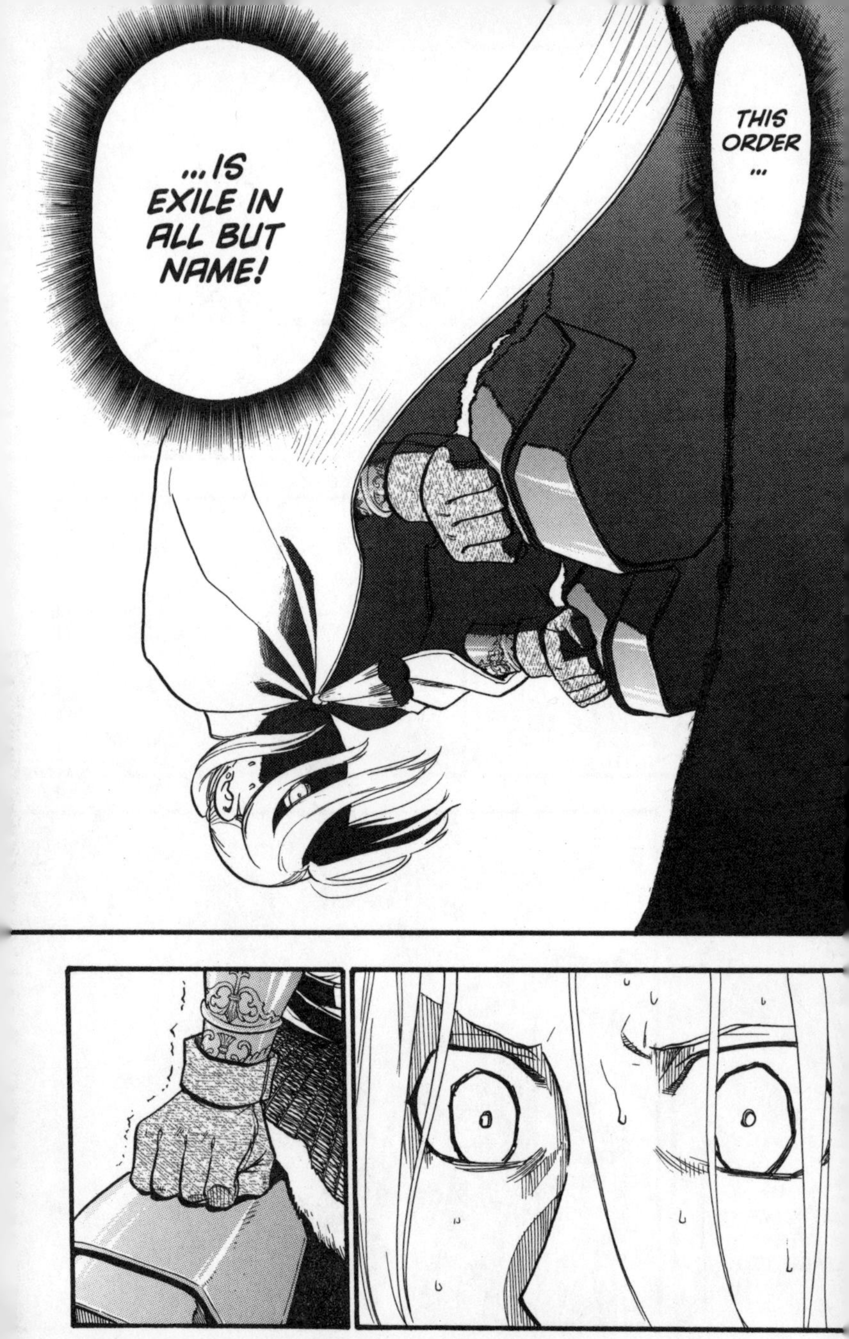
THIS ORDER ...
...IS EXILE IN ALL BUT NAME!

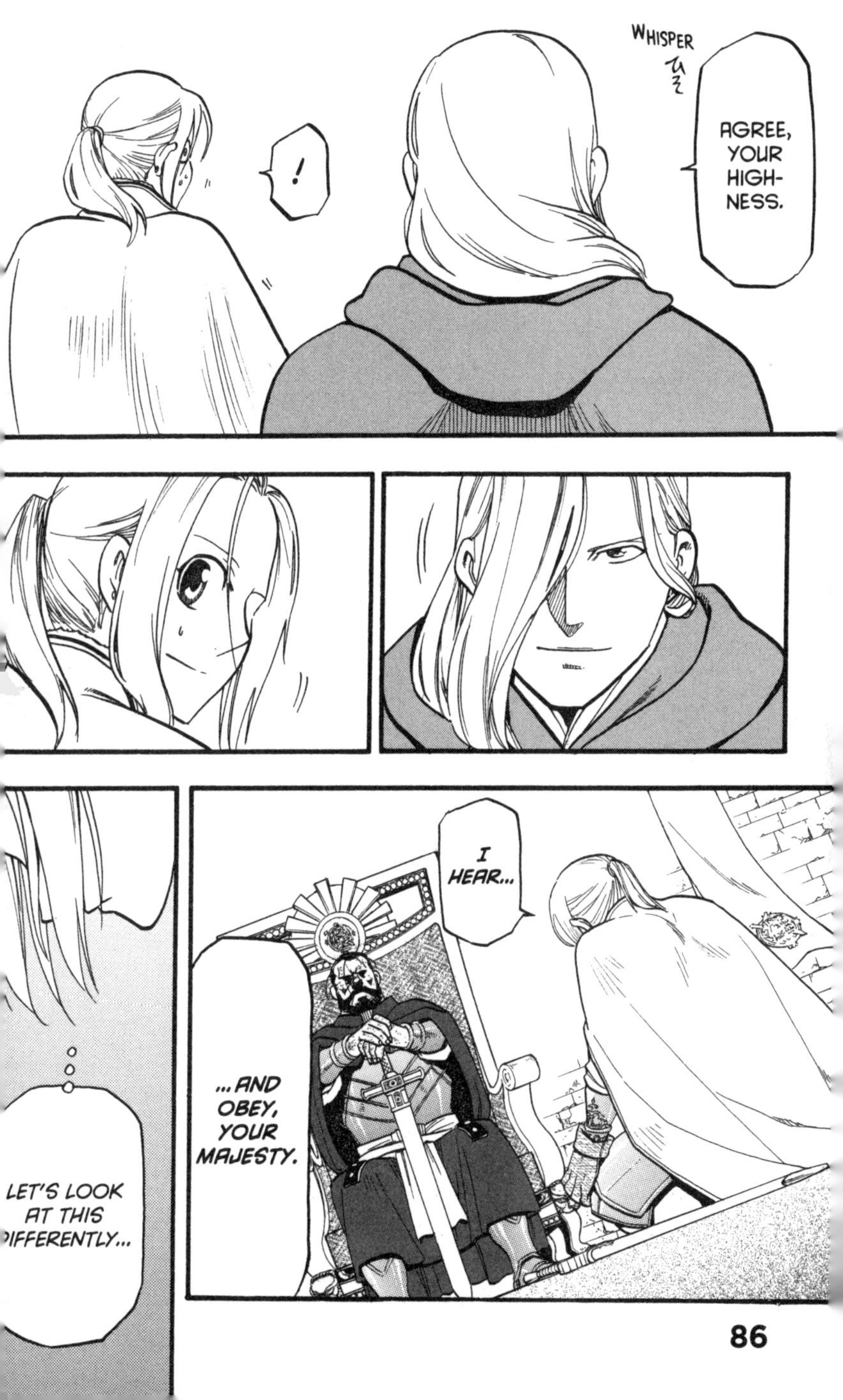
WHISPER
AGREE, YOUR HIGH-NESS.
!
I HEAR...
...AND OBEY, YOUR MAJESTY.
LET'S LOOK AT THIS IFFERENTLY...

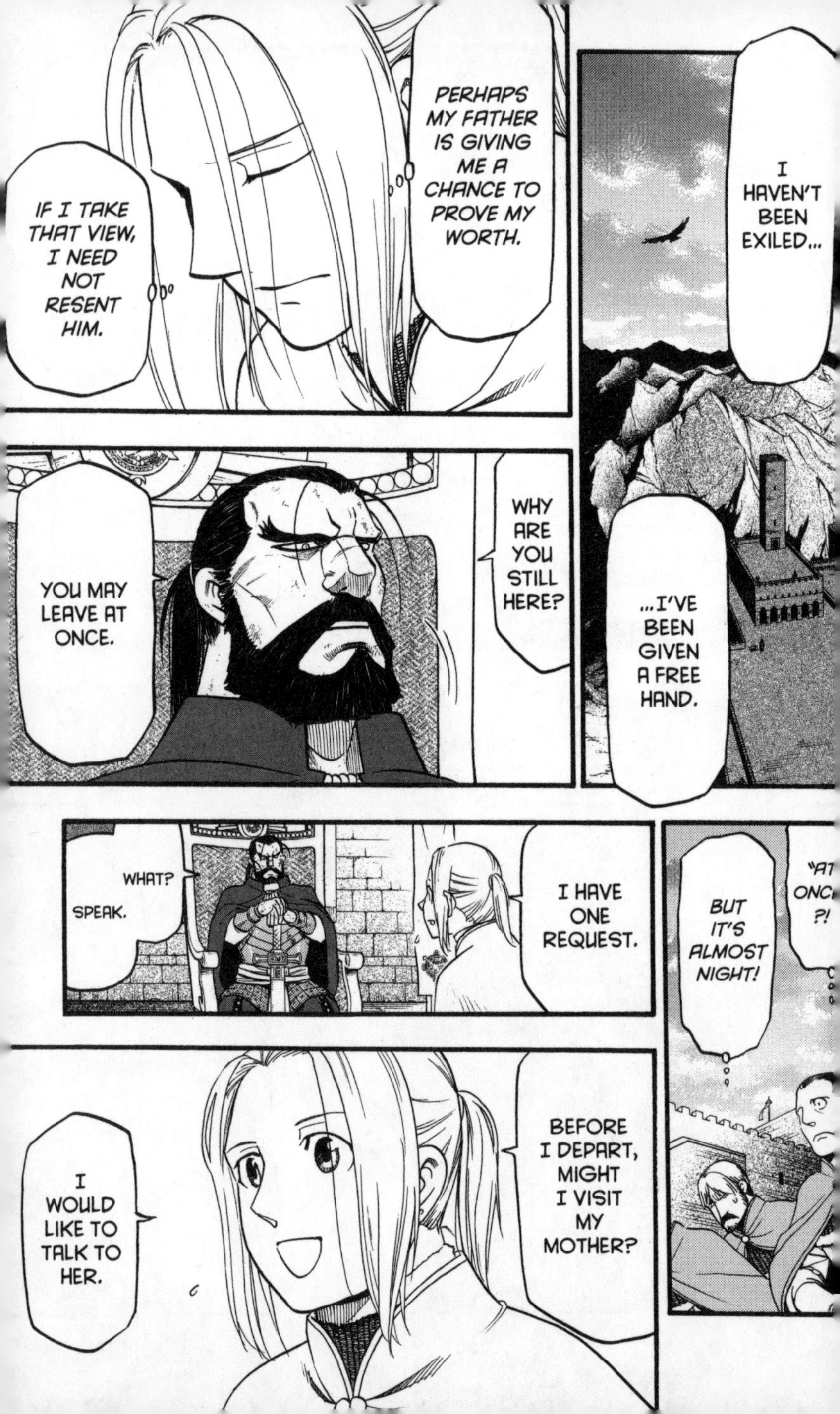
I HAVEN'T BEEN EXILED...
...I'VE BEEN GIVEN A FREE HAND.
PERHAPS MY FATHER IS GIVING ME A CHANCE TO PROVE MY WORTH.
IF I TAKE THAT VIEW, I NEED NOT RESENT HIM.
WHY ARE YOU STILL HERE?
YOU MAY LEAVE AT ONCE.
“AT ONC ?!
BUT IT'S ALMOST NIGHT!
I HAVE ONE REQUEST.
WHAT?
SPEAK.
BEFORE I DEPART, MIGHT I VISIT MY MOTHER?
I WOULD LIKE TO TALK TO HER.

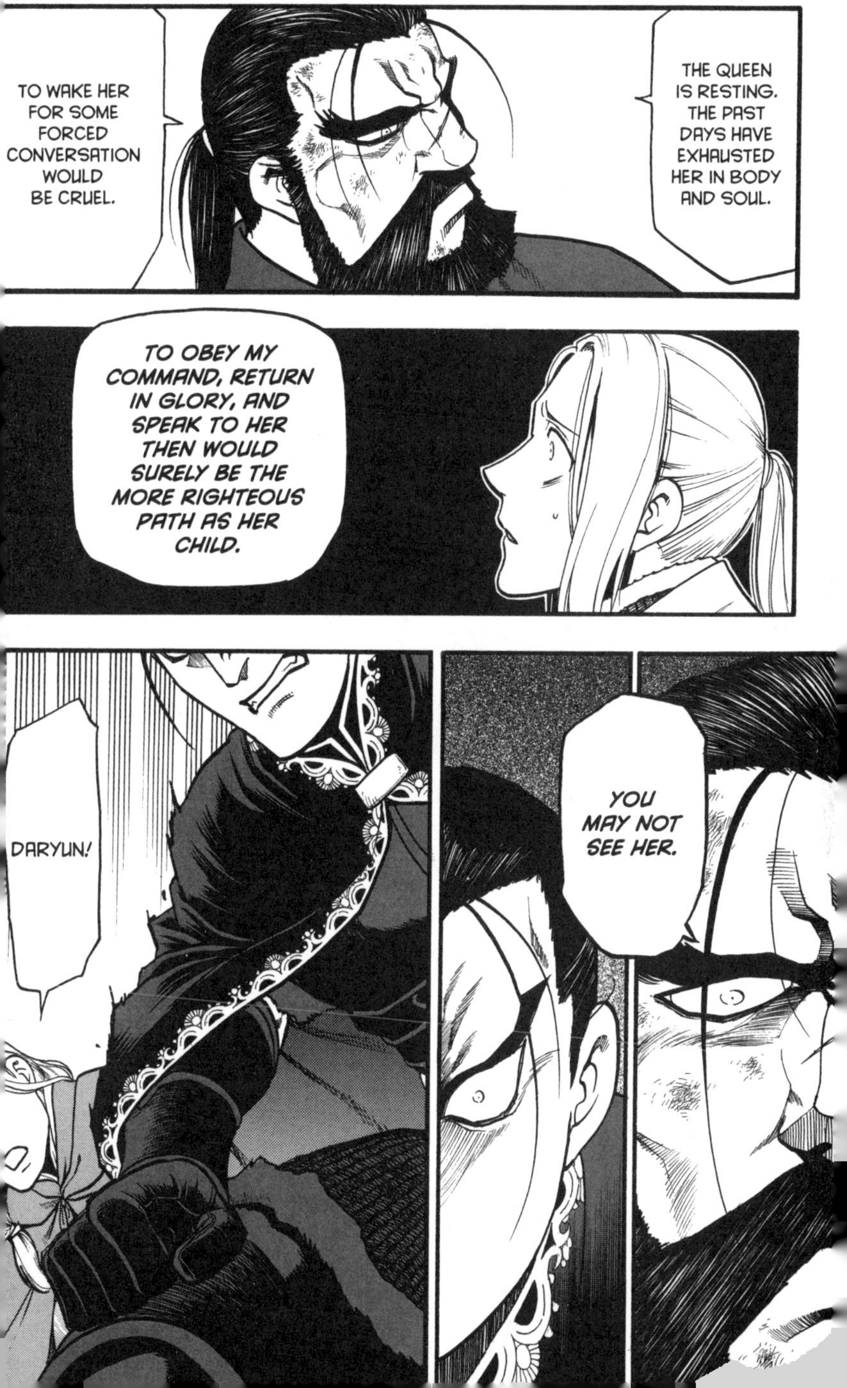
THE QUEEN IS RESTING. THE PAST DAYS HAVE EXHAUSTED HER IN BODY AND SOUL.
TO WAKE HER FOR SOME FORCED CONVERSATION WOULD BE CRUEL.
TO OBEY MY COMMAND, RETURN IN GLORY, AND SPEAK TO HER THEN WOULD SURELY BE THE MORE RIGHTEOUS PATH AS HER CHILD.
YOU MAY NOT SEE HER.
DARYUN!

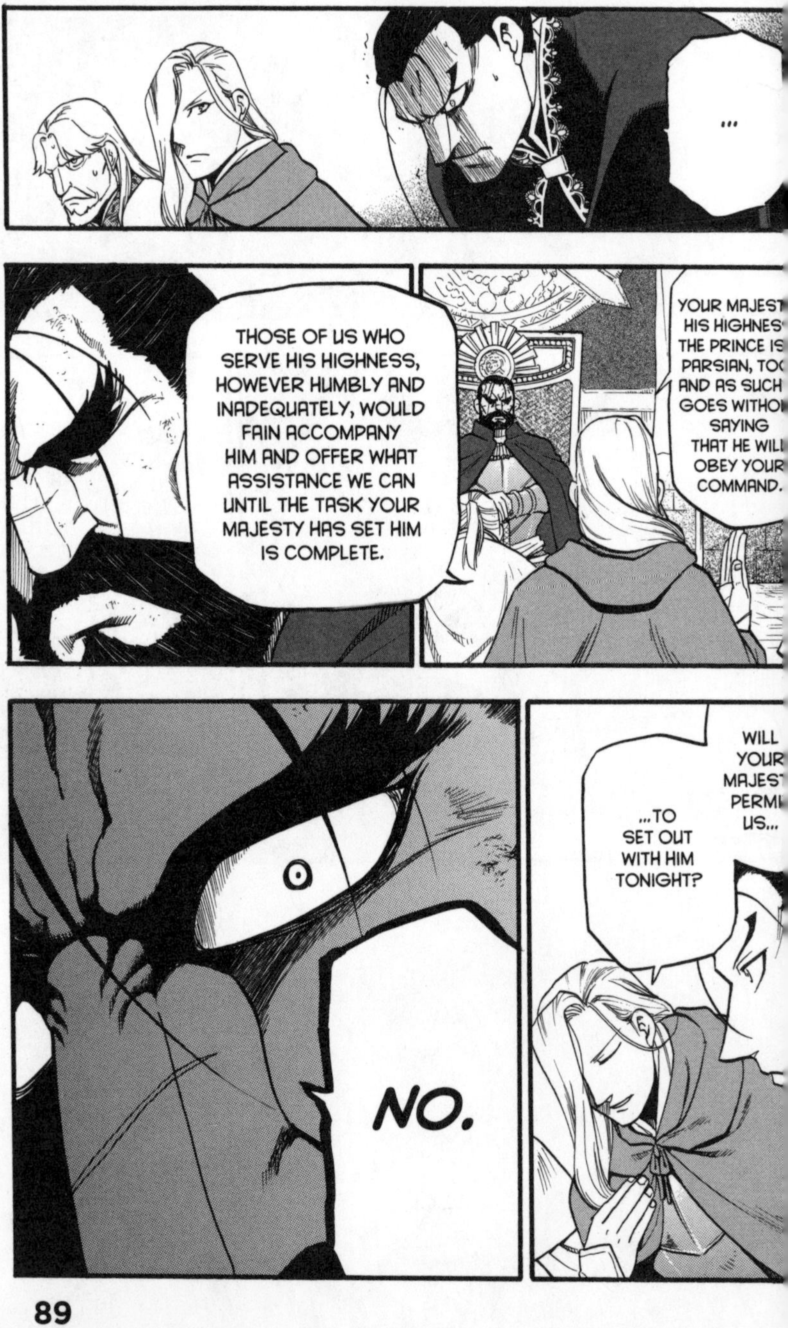
...
YOUR MAJEST HIS HIGHNES THE PRINCE IS PARSIAN, TO AND AS SUCH GOES WITHO SAYING THAT HE WILL OBEY YOUR COMMAND.
THOSE OF US WHO SERVE HIS HIGHNESS, HOWEVER HUMBLY AND INADEQUATELY, WOULD FAIN ACCOMPANY HIM AND OFFER WHAT ASSISTANCE WE CAN UNTIL THE TASK YOUR MAJESTY HAS SET HIM IS COMPLETE.
WILL YOUR MAJEST PERMI US...
...TO SET OUT WITH HIM TONIGHT?
NO.

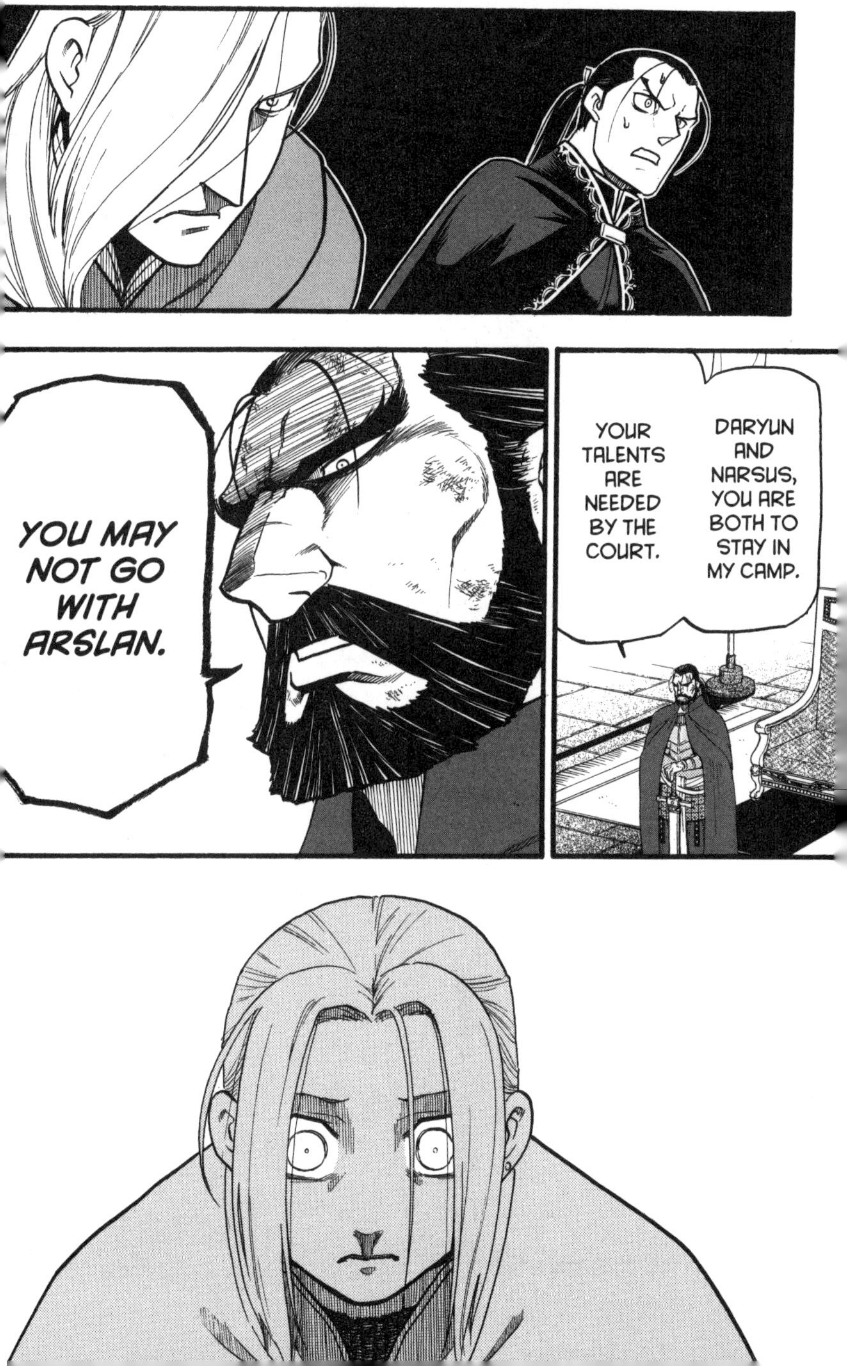
DARYUN AND NARSUS, YOU ARE BOTH TO STAY IN MY CAMP. YOUR TALENTS ARE NEEDED BY THE COURT.
YOU MAY NOT GO WITH ARSLAN.

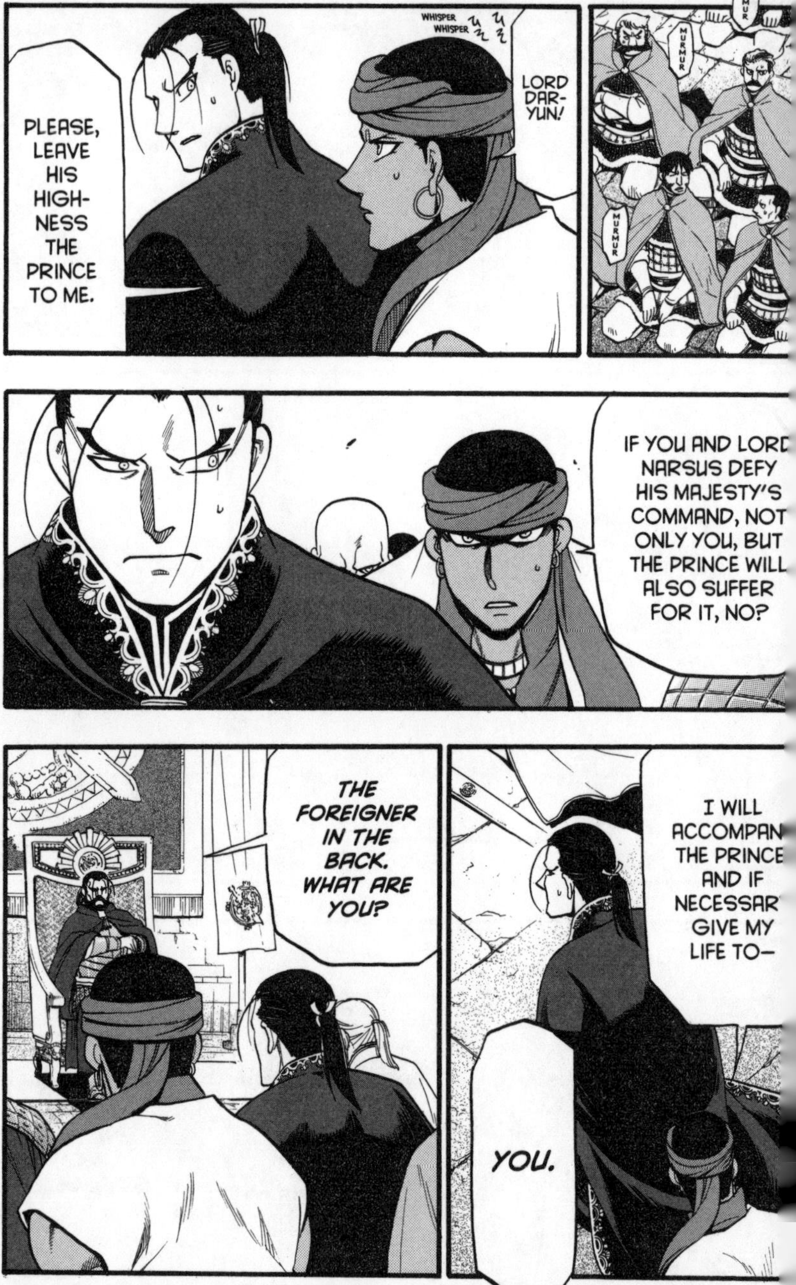
MURMUR
MURMUR
MURMUR
WHISPER WHISPER
LORD DARYUN!
PLEASE, LEAVE HIS HIGHNESS THE PRINCE TO ME.
IF YOU AND LORD NARSUS DEFY HIS MAJESTY'S COMMAND, NOT ONLY YOU, BUT THE PRINCE WILL ALSO SUFFER FOR IT, NO?
I WILL ACCOMPAN THE PRINCE AND IF NECESSAR GIVE MY LIFE TO—
YOU.
THE FOREIGNER IN THE BACK. WHAT ARE YOU?

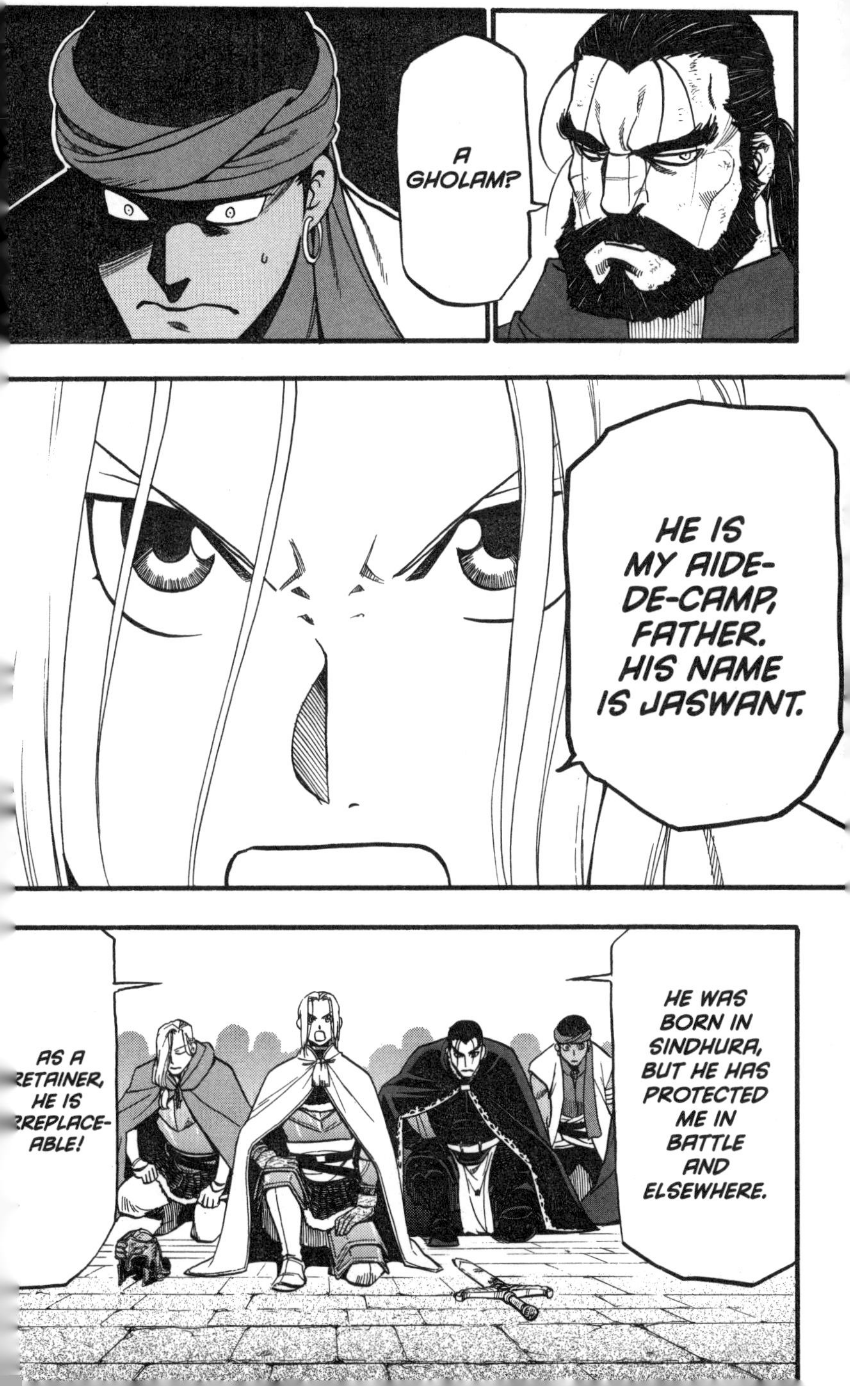
A GHOLAM?
HE IS MY AIDE-DE-CAMP, FATHER. HIS NAME IS JASWANT.
HE WAS BORN IN SINDHURA, BUT HE HAS PROTECTED ME IN BATTLE AND ELSEWHERE.
AS A RETAINER, HE IS RREPLACE-ABLE!

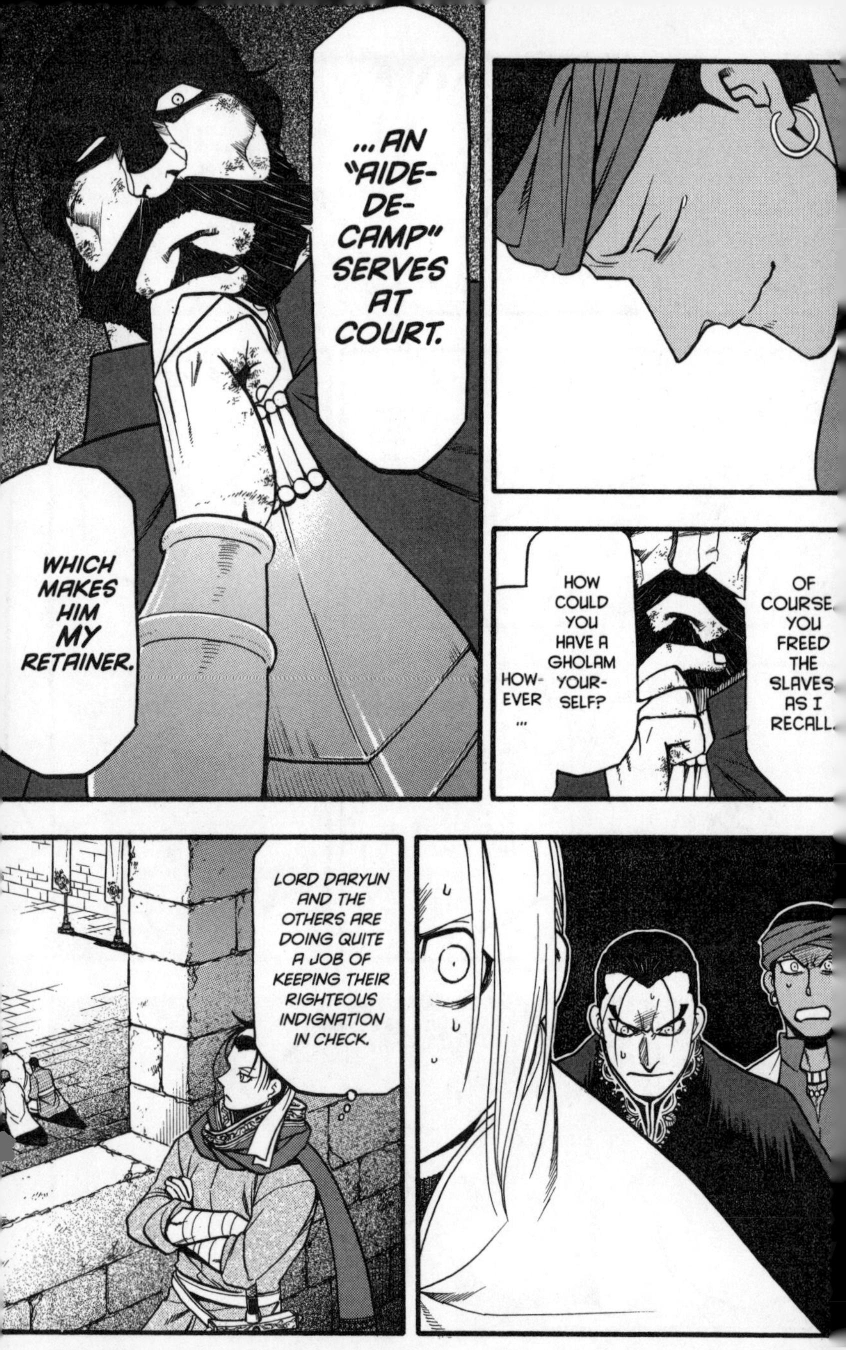
OF COURSE, YOU FREED THE SLAVES, AS I RECALL.
HOW COULD YOU HAVE A GHOLAM YOURSELF?
HOW-EVER ...
...AN "AIDE-DE-CAMP" SERVES AT COURT.
WHICH MAKES HIM MY RETAINER.
LORD DARYUN AND THE OTHERS ARE DOING QUITE A JOB OF KEEPING THEIR RIGHTEOUS INDIGNATION IN CHECK.

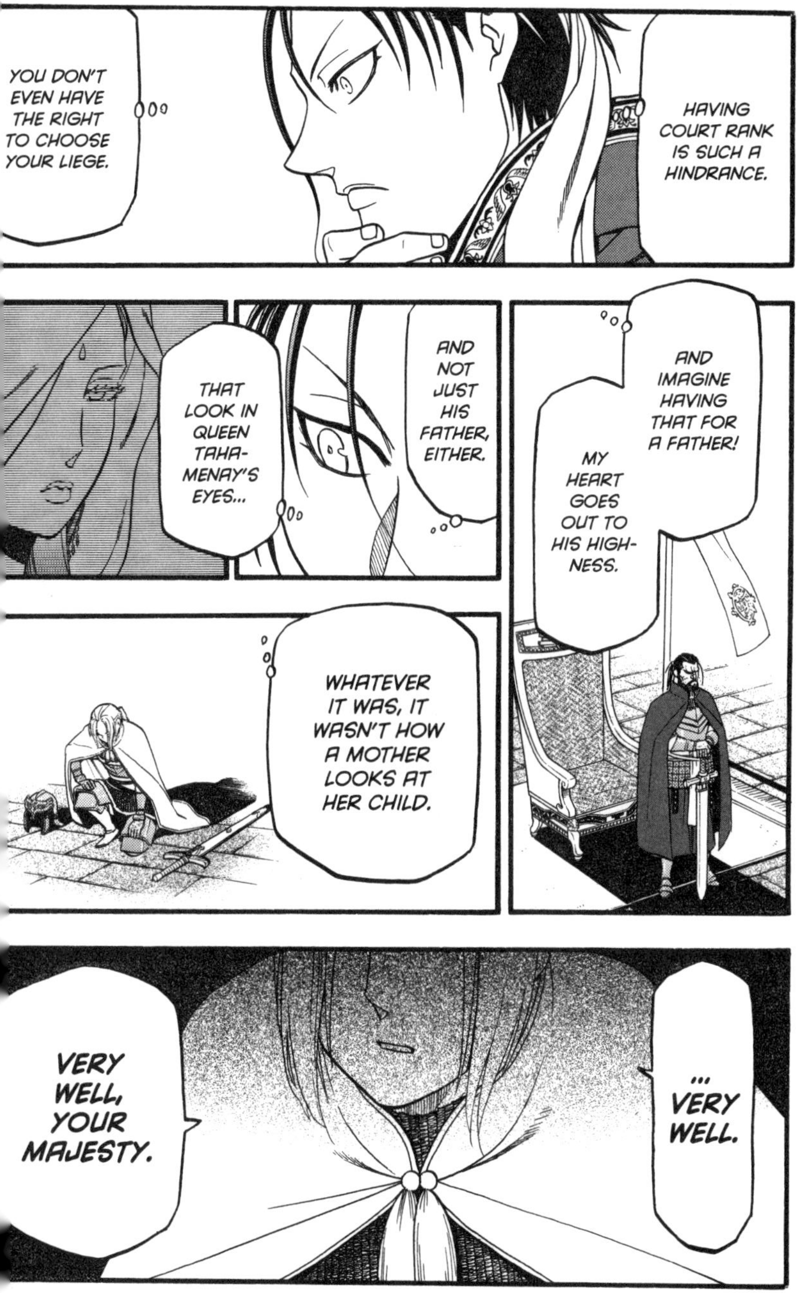
HAVING COURT RANK IS SUCH A HINDRANCE.
YOU DON'T EVEN HAVE THE RIGHT TO CHOOSE YOUR LIEGE.
AND IMAGINE HAVING THAT FOR A FATHER!
MY HEART GOES OUT TO HIS HIGH-NESS.
AND NOT JUST HIS FATHER, EITHER.
THAT LOOK IN QUEEN TAHA-MENAY'S EYES...
WHATEVER IT WAS, IT WASN'T HOW A MOTHER LOOKS AT HER CHILD.
...VERY WELL.
VERY WELL, YOUR MAJESTY.

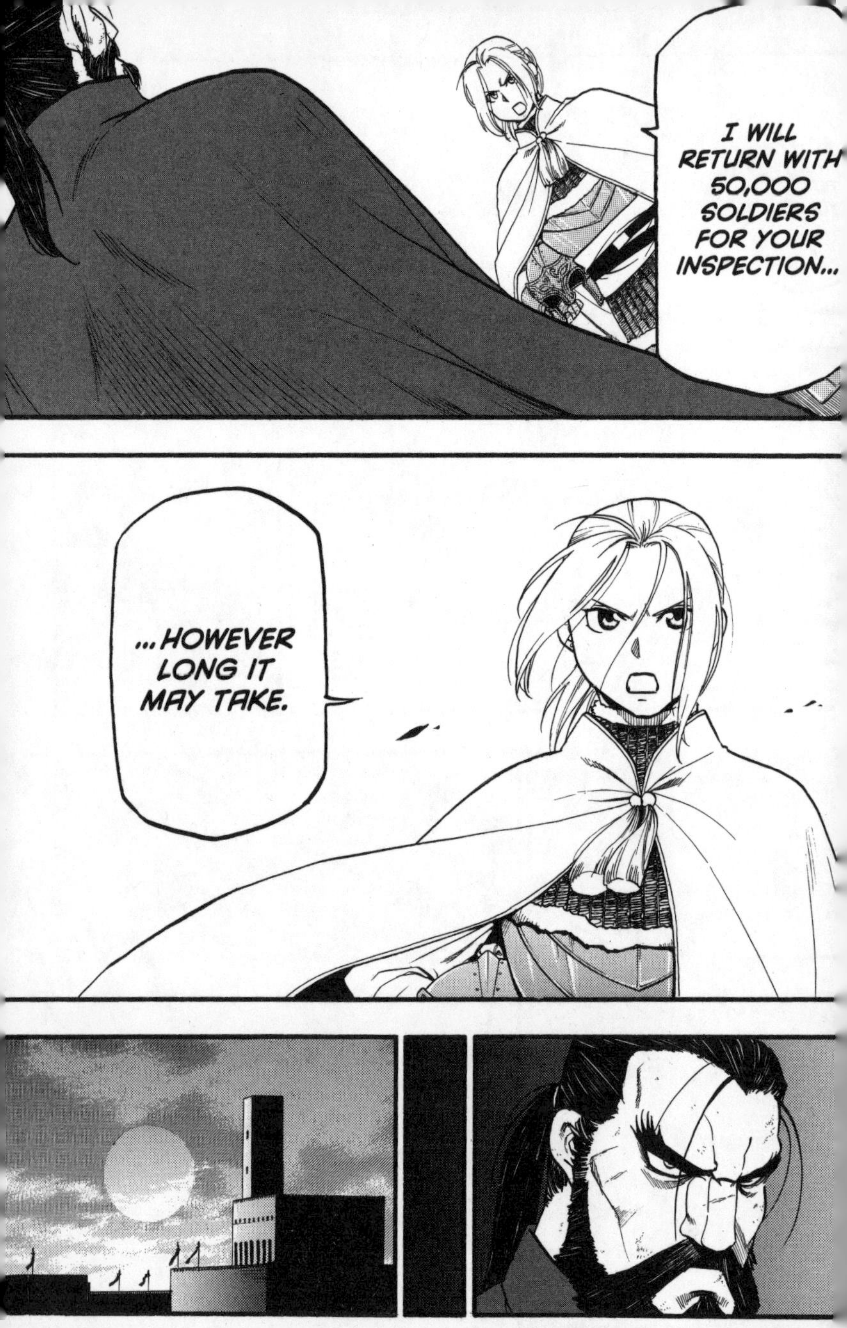
I WILL RETURN WITH 50,000 SOLDIERS FOR YOUR INSPECTION...
...HOWEVER LONG IT MAY TAKE.

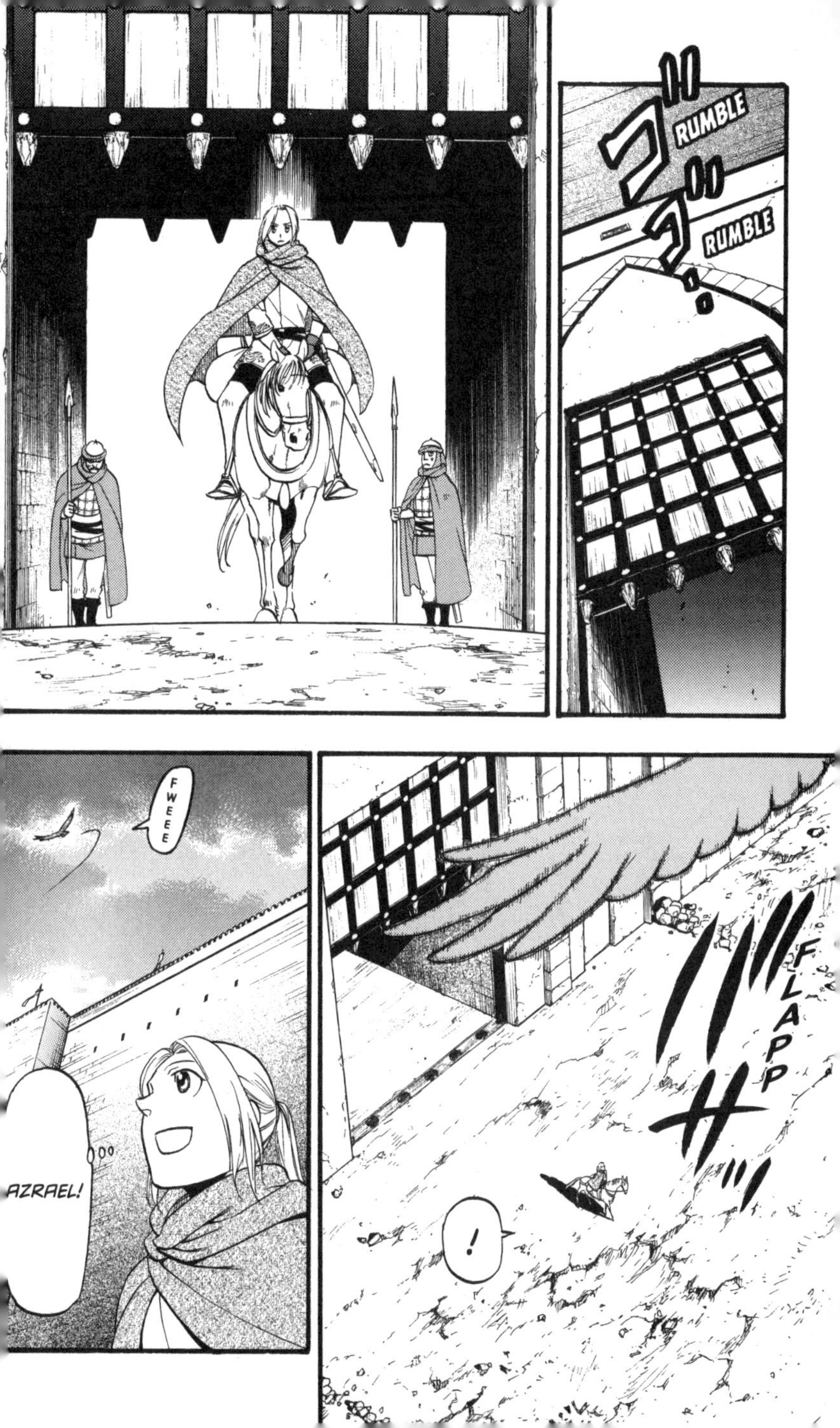
RUMBLE
RUMBLE
FLAPP
!
FWEEE
AZRAEL!

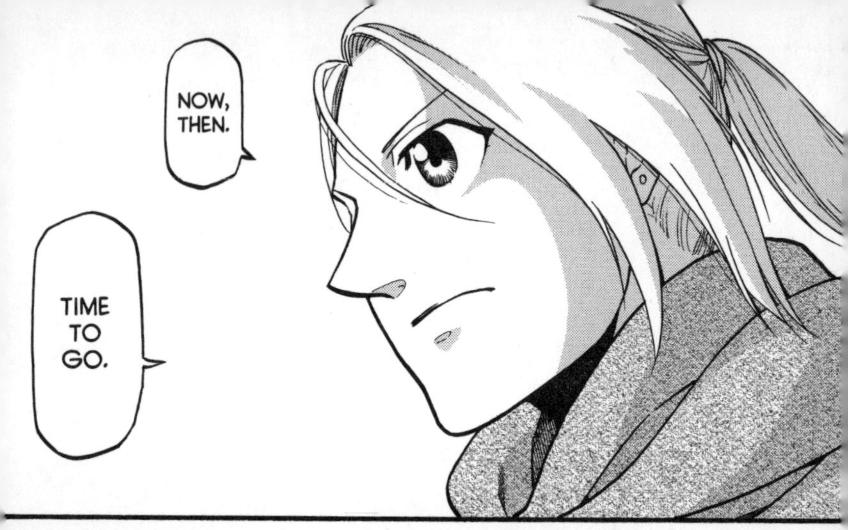
NOW, THEN.
TIME TO GO.
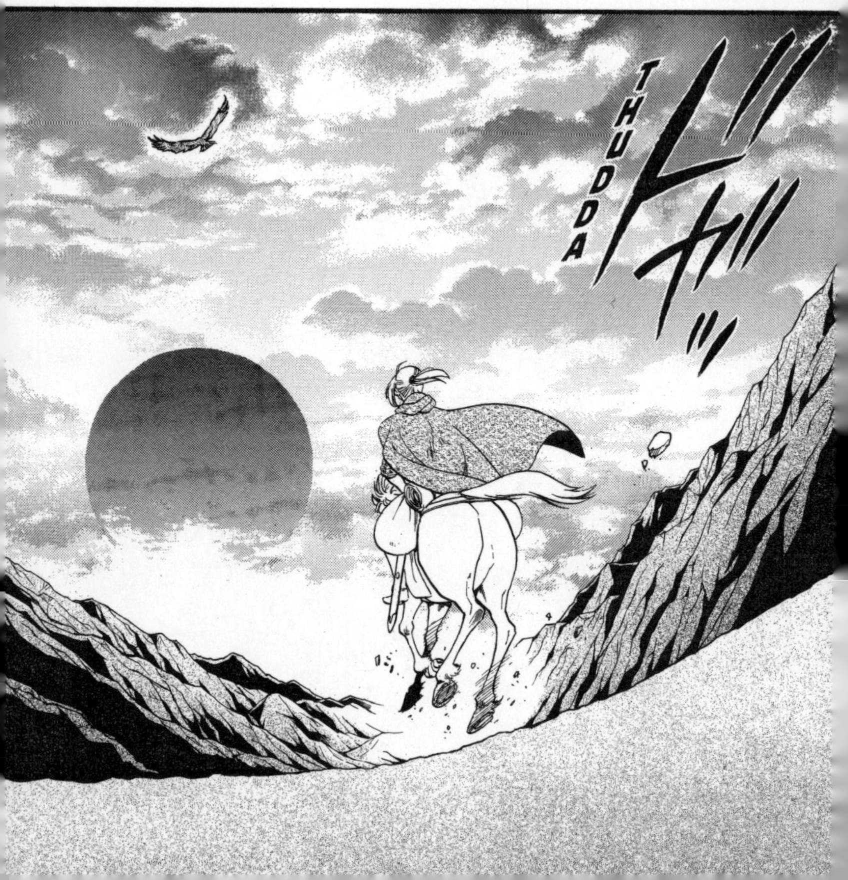
THUDDA

THE HEROIC LEGEND OF
ARSLAN

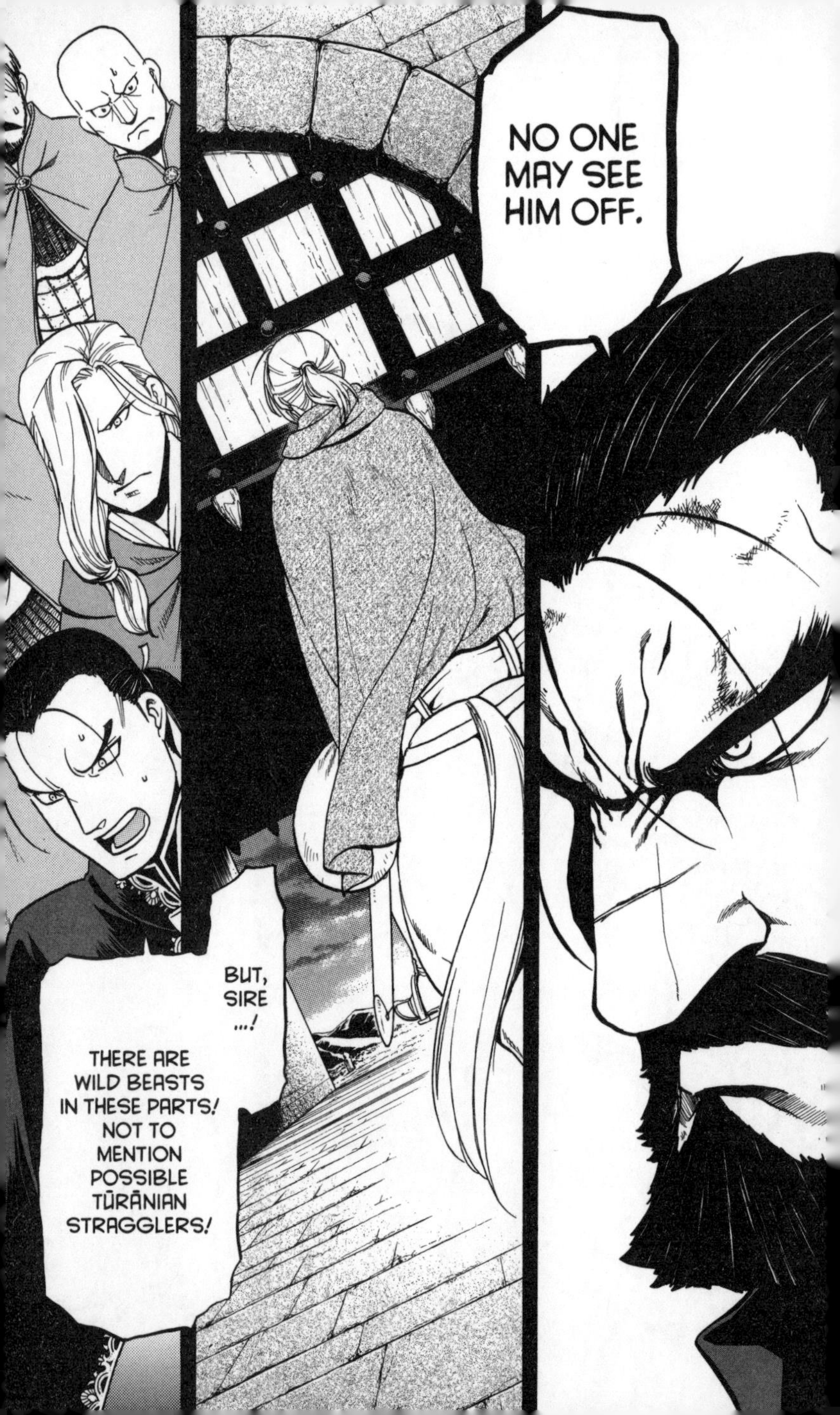
NO ONE MAY SEE HIM OFF.
BUT, SIRE ...!
THERE ARE WILD BEASTS IN THESE PARTS! NOT TO MENTION POSSIBLE TŪRĀNIAN STRAGGLERS!

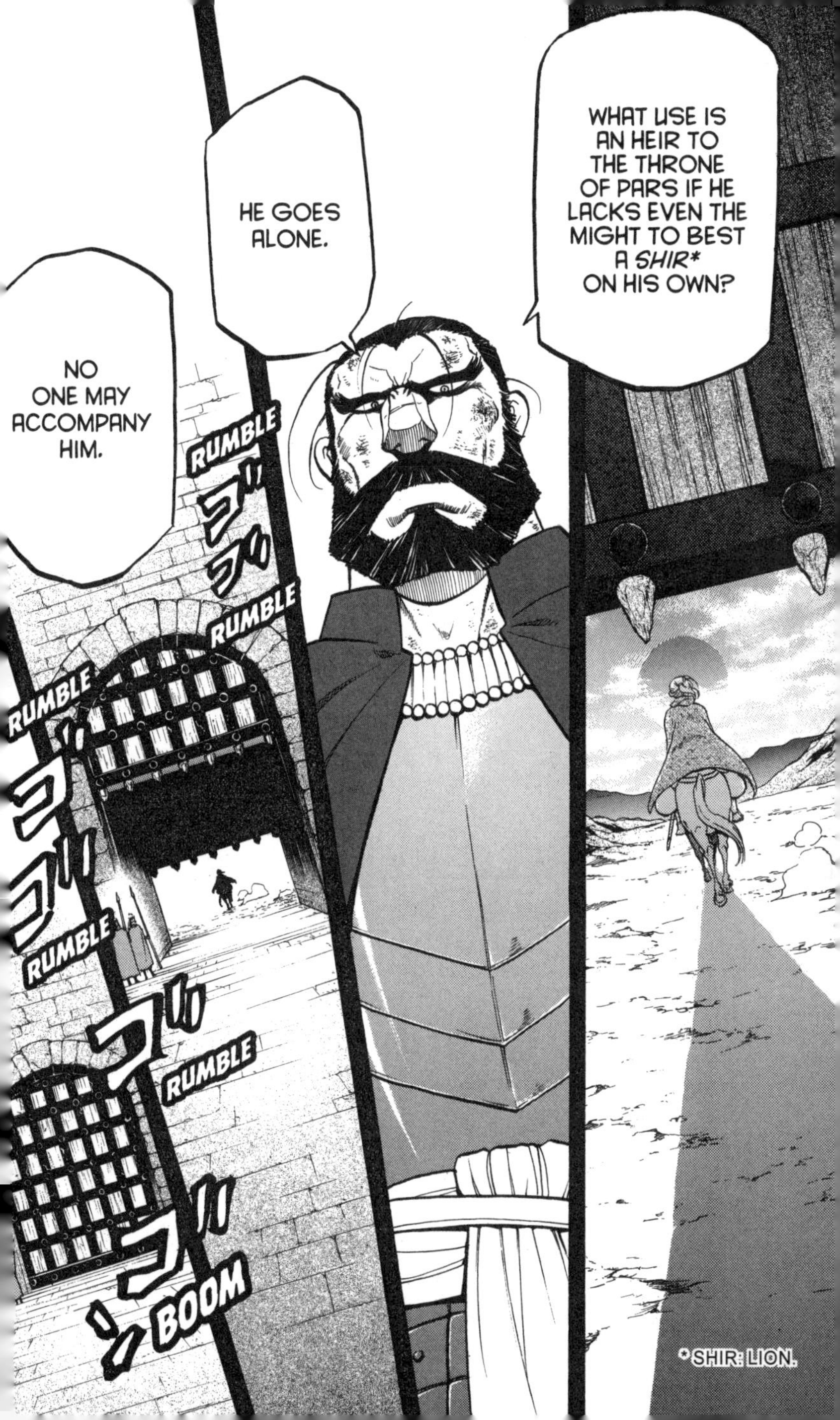
WHAT USE IS AN HEIR TO THE THRONE OF PARS IF HE LACKS EVEN THE MIGHT TO BEST A *SHIR** ON HIS OWN?
*SHIR: LION.
HE GOES ALONE.
NO ONE MAY ACCOMPANY HIM.
RUMBLE
RUMBLE
RUMBLE
RUMBLE
RUMBLE
BOOM

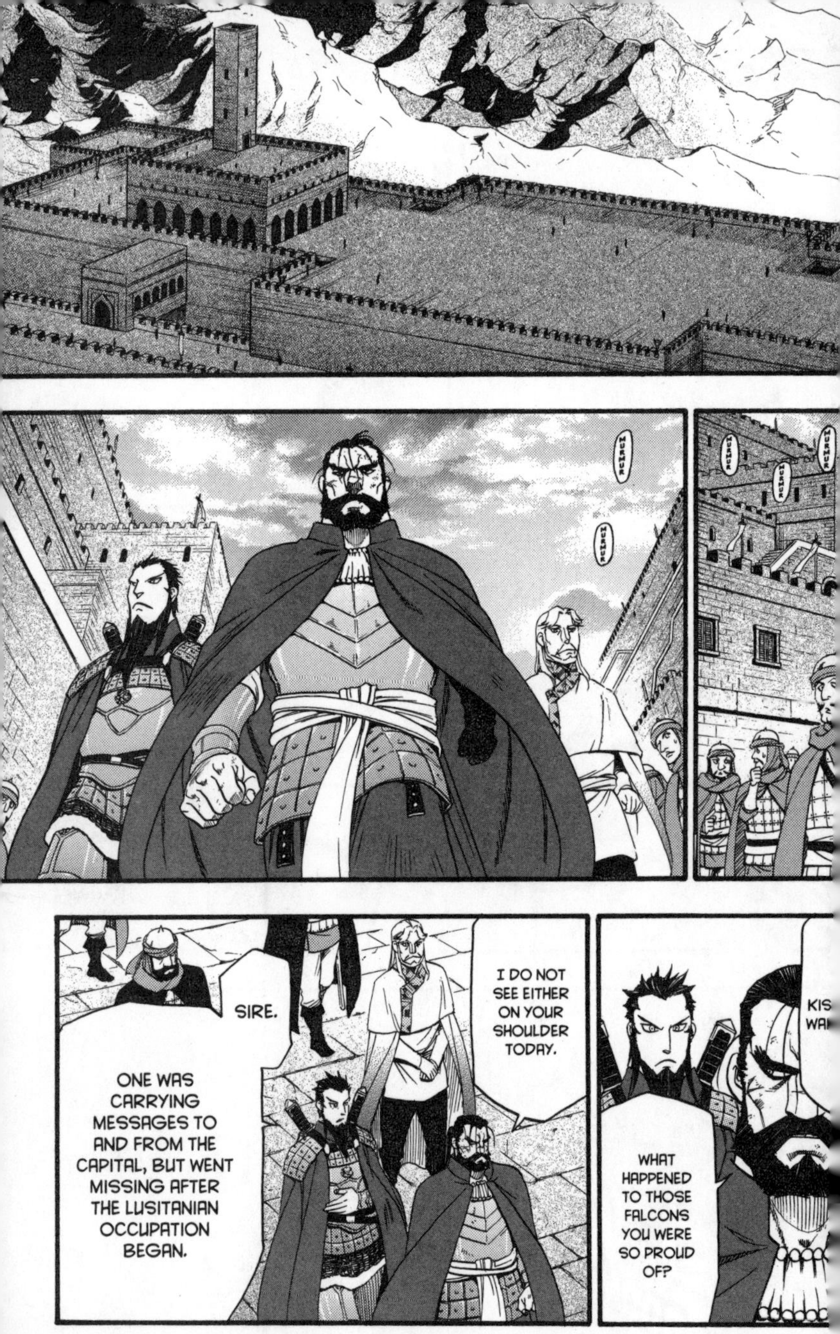
MURMUR
MURMUR
MURMUR
MURMUR
MURMUR
WHAT HAPPENED TO THOSE FALCONS YOU WERE SO PROUD OF?
I DO NOT SEE EITHER ON YOUR SHOULDER TODAY.
SIRE.
ONE WAS CARRYING MESSAGES TO AND FROM THE CAPITAL, BUT WENT MISSING AFTER THE LUSITANIAN OCCUPATION BEGAN.

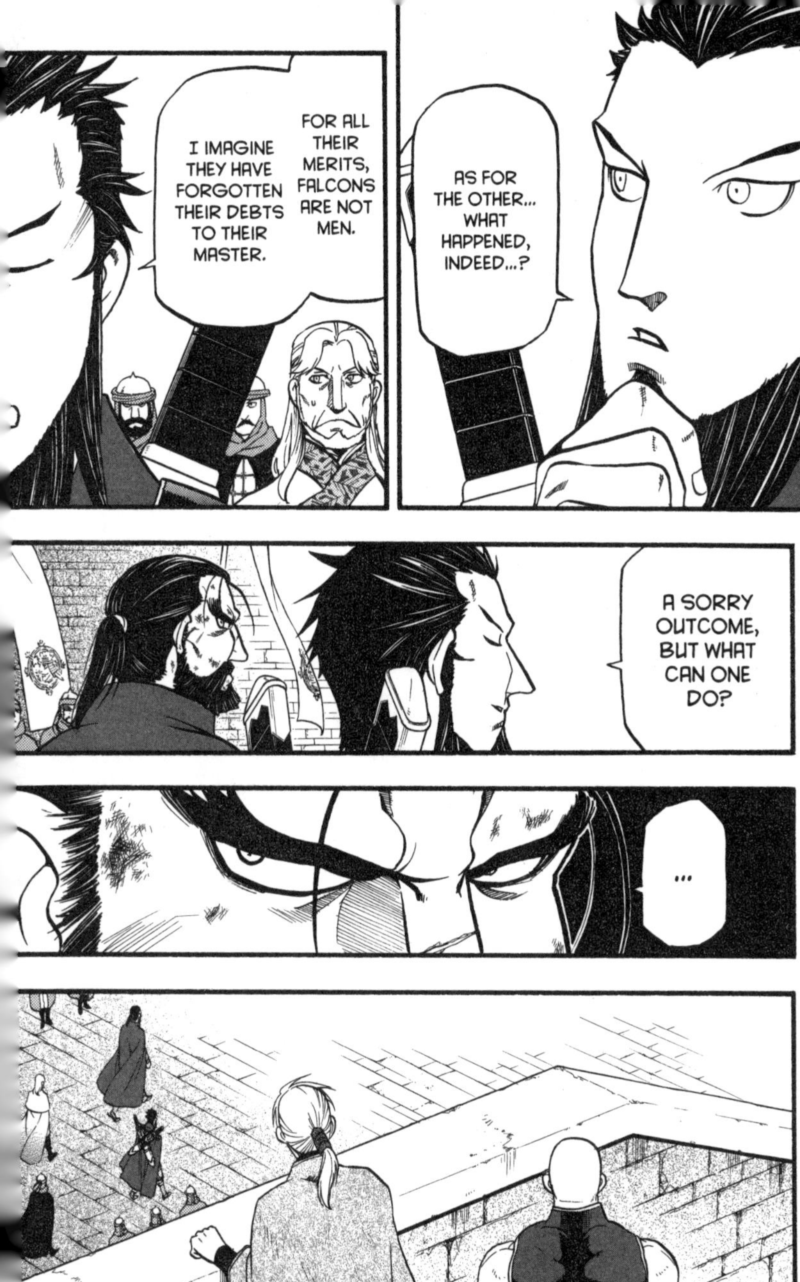
AS FOR THE OTHER... WHAT HAPPENED, INDEED...?
FOR ALL THEIR MERITS, FALCONS ARE NOT MEN.
I IMAGINE THEY HAVE FORGOTTEN THEIR DEBTS TO THEIR MASTER.
A SORRY OUTCOME, BUT WHAT CAN ONE DO?
...

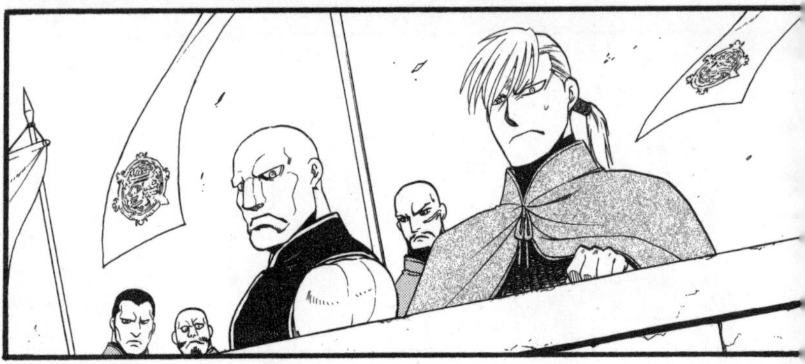

Chapter 92: Night of Solitude

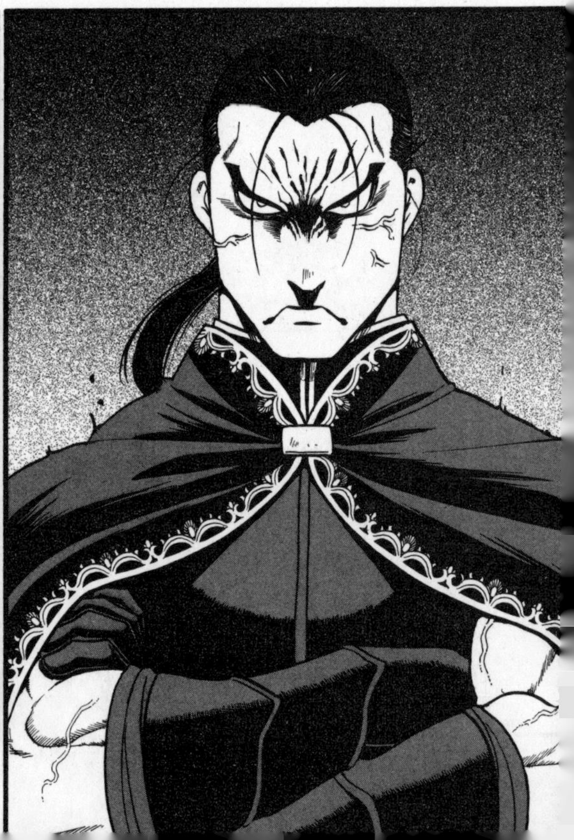

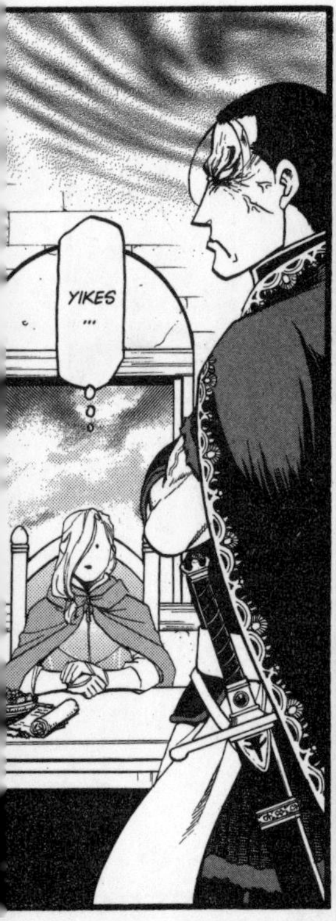
YIKES ...

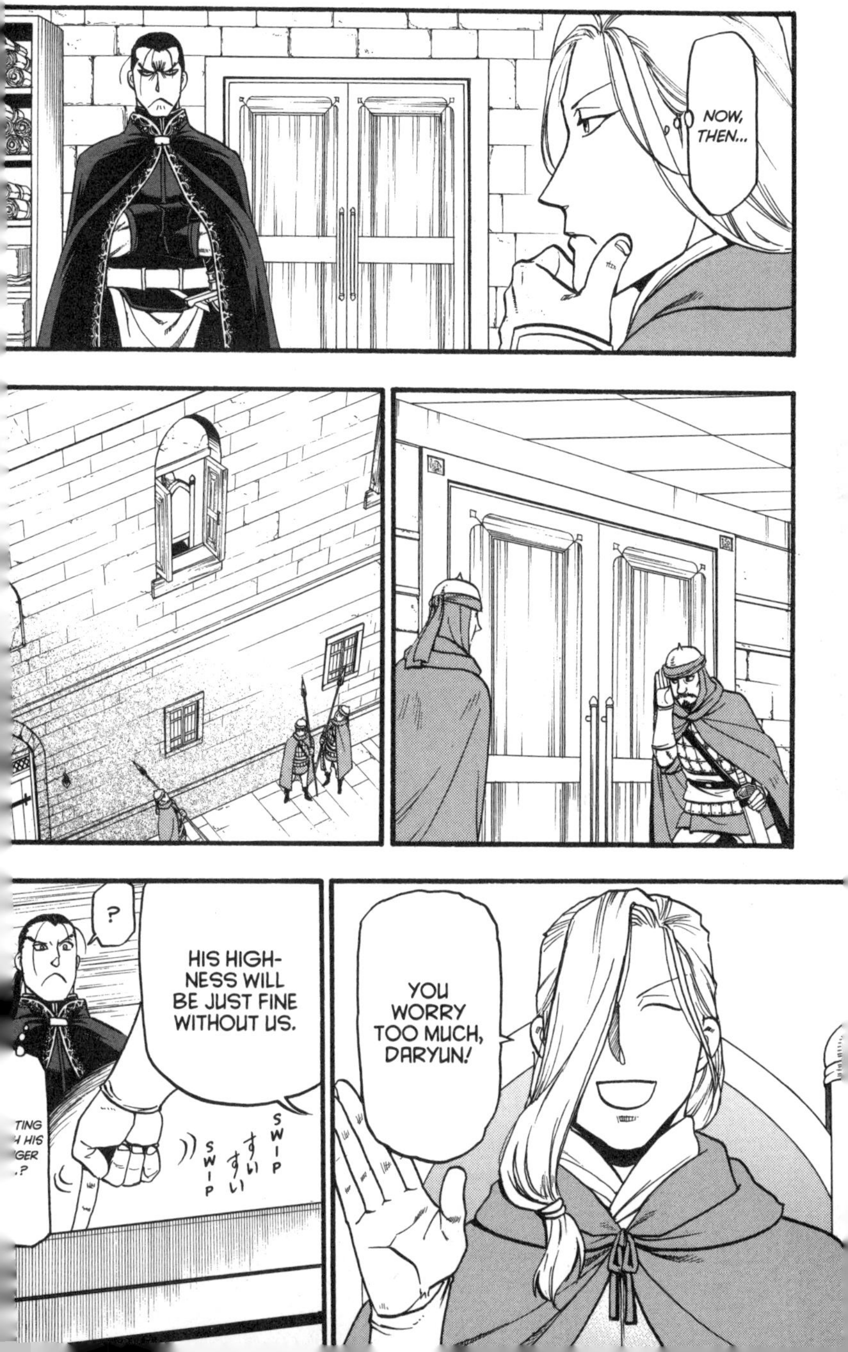
NOW, THEN...
YOU WORRY TOO MUCH, DARYUN!
HIS HIGH-NESS WILL BE JUST FINE WITHOUT US.
?
SWIP SWIP
すい すい

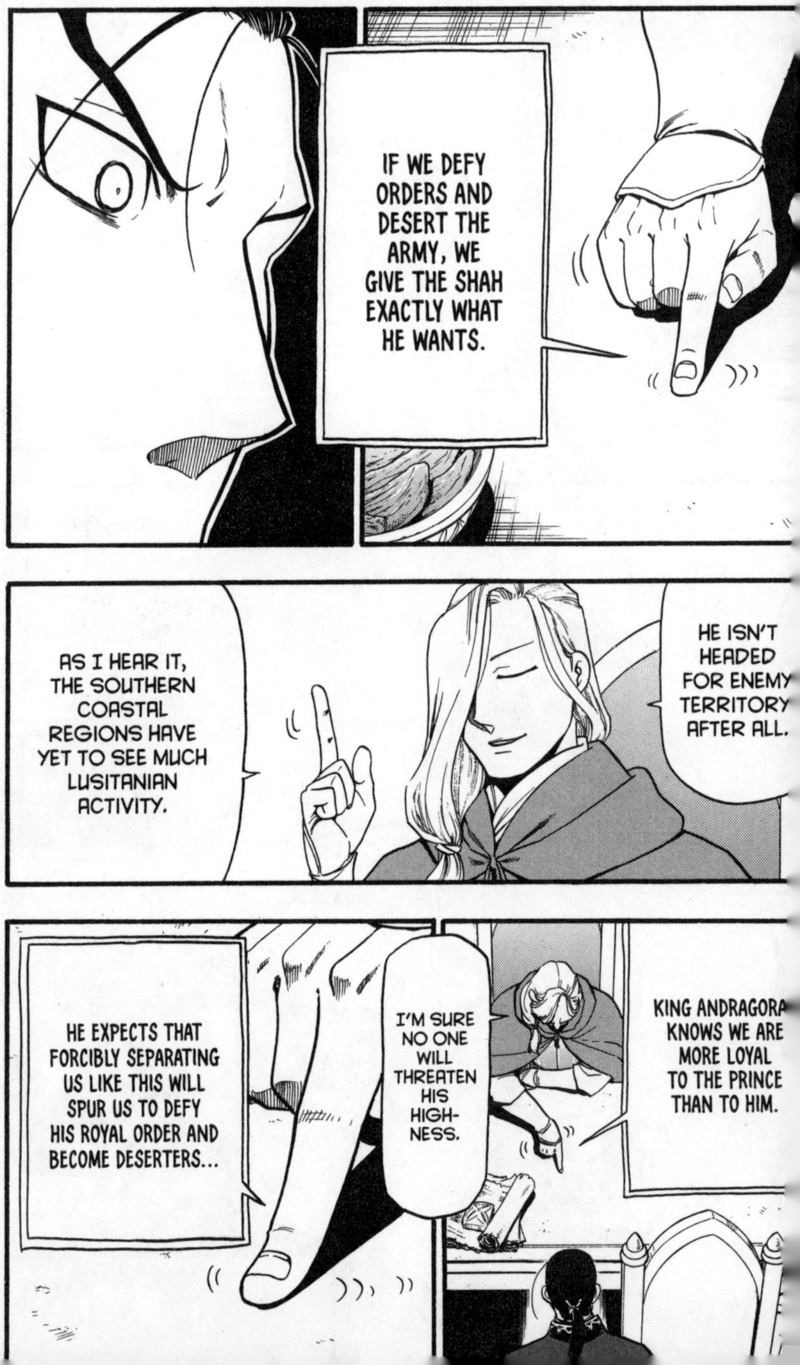
IF WE DEFY ORDERS AND DESERT THE ARMY, WE GIVE THE SHAH EXACTLY WHAT HE WANTS.
HE ISN'T HEADED FOR ENEMY TERRITORY AFTER ALL.
AS I HEAR IT, THE SOUTHERN COASTAL REGIONS HAVE YET TO SEE MUCH LUSITANIAN ACTIVITY.
KING ANDRAGORA KNOWS WE ARE MORE LOYAL TO THE PRINCE THAN TO HIM.
I'M SURE NO ONE WILL THREATEN HIS HIGH-NESS.
HE EXPECTS THAT FORCIBLY SEPARATING US LIKE THIS WILL SPUR US TO DEFY HIS ROYAL ORDER AND BECOME DESERTERS...

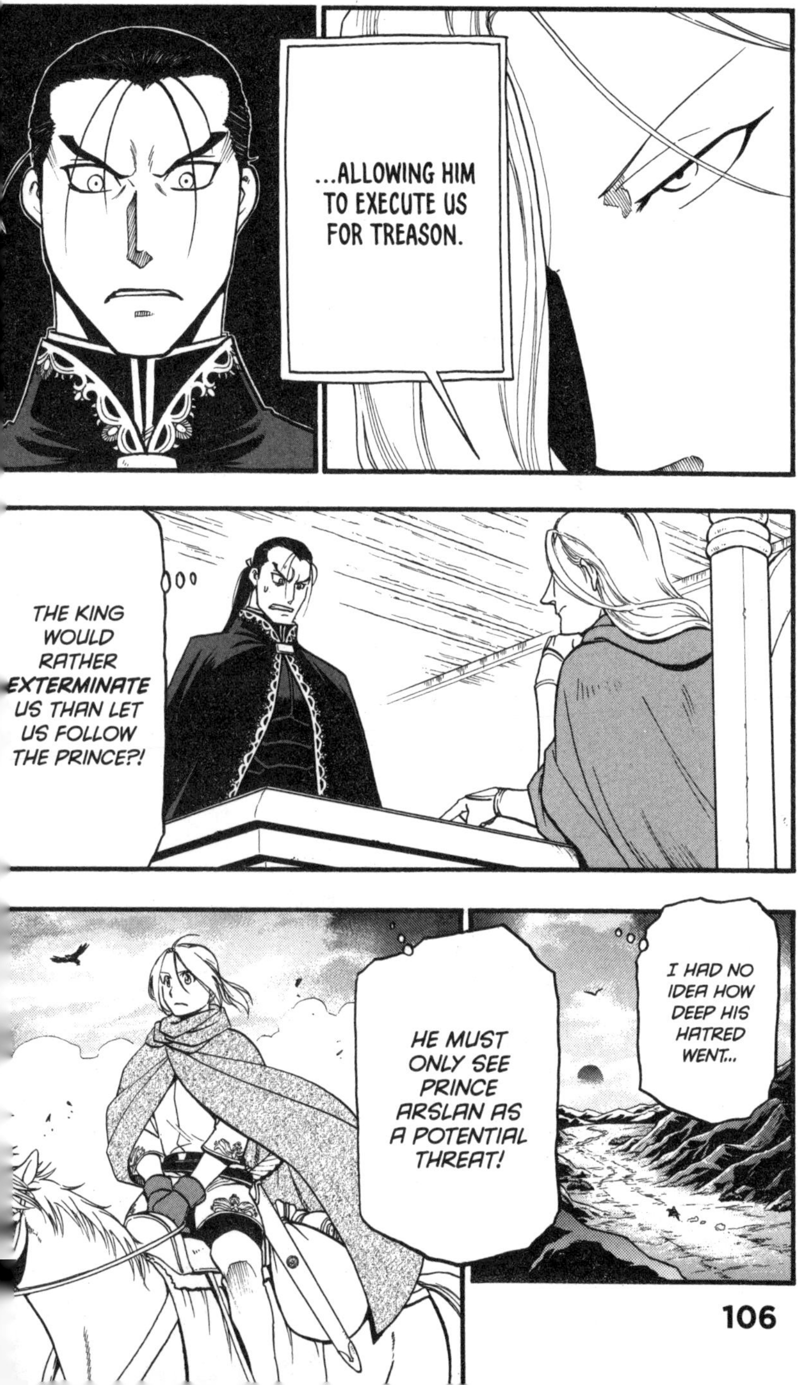
...ALLOWING HIM TO EXECUTE US FOR TREASON.
THE KING WOULD RATHER **EXTERMINATE** US THAN LET US FOLLOW THE PRINCE?!
I HAD NO IDEA HOW DEEP HIS HATRED WENT...
HE MUST ONLY SEE PRINCE ARSLAN AS A POTENTIAL THREAT!

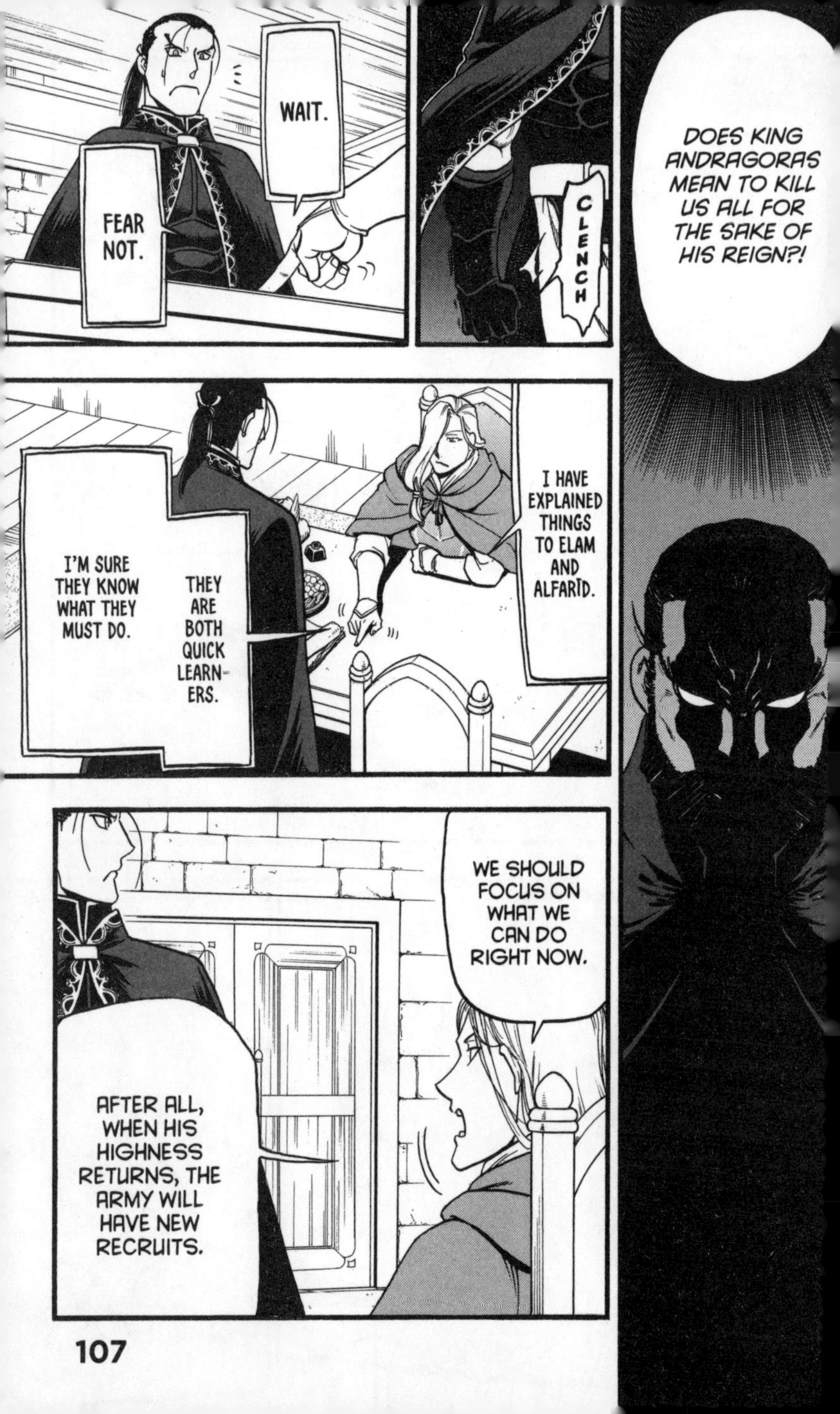
DOES KING ANDRAGORAS MEAN TO KILL US ALL FOR THE SAKE OF HIS REIGN?!
CLENCH
WAIT.
FEAR NOT.
I HAVE EXPLAINED THINGS TO ELAM AND ALFARĪD.
THEY ARE BOTH QUICK LEARNERS.
I'M SURE THEY KNOW WHAT THEY MUST DO.
WE SHOULD FOCUS ON WHAT WE CAN DO RIGHT NOW.
AFTER ALL, WHEN HIS HIGHNESS RETURNS, THE ARMY WILL HAVE NEW RECRUITS.

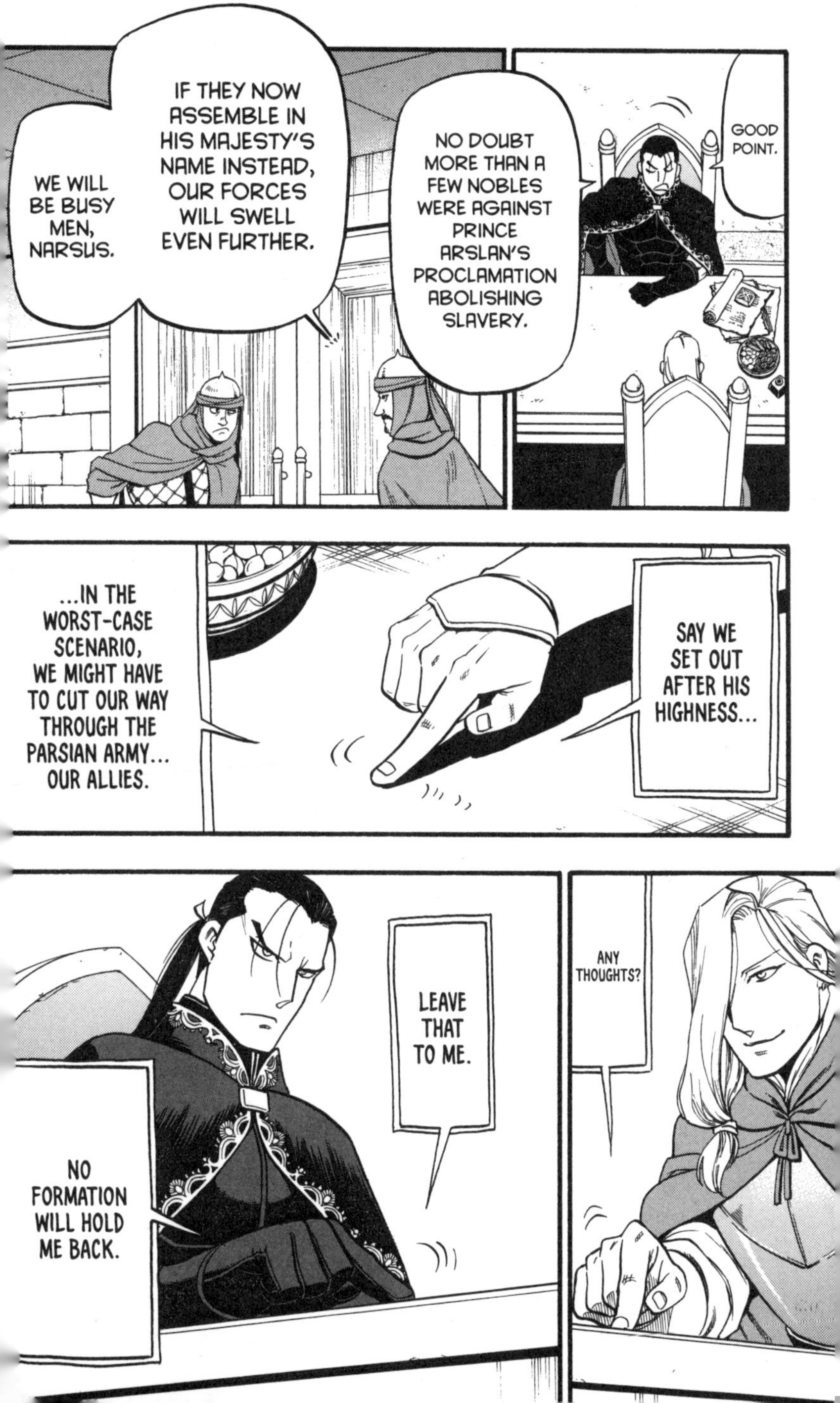
GOOD POINT.
NO DOUBT MORE THAN A FEW NOBLES WERE AGAINST PRINCE ARSLAN'S PROCLAMATION ABOLISHING SLAVERY.
IF THEY NOW ASSEMBLE IN HIS MAJESTY'S NAME INSTEAD, OUR FORCES WILL SWELL EVEN FURTHER.
WE WILL BE BUSY MEN, NARSUS.
SAY WE SET OUT AFTER HIS HIGHNESS...
...IN THE WORST-CASE SCENARIO, WE MIGHT HAVE TO CUT OUR WAY THROUGH THE PARSIAN ARMY... OUR ALLIES.
ANY THOUGHTS?
LEAVE THAT TO ME.
NO FORMATION WILL HOLD ME BACK.

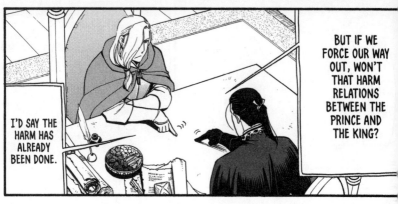

BUT IF WE FORCE OUR WAY OUT, WON'T THAT HARM RELATIONS BETWEEN THE PRINCE AND THE KING?
I'D SAY THE HARM HAS ALREADY BEEN DONE.
A FALLING OUT IS INEVITABL
TO SIT HERE WAITING FOR FATE TO SPRING ITS TRAP WOULD BE IDIOCY.
THESE DATES ARE DELICIOU
TRUE ENOUGH.
YES.
THEY'D GO WELL WITH SOME TEA.
I'LL WAGER LADY FARANGIS WOULD HAVE SOME GOOD TEA.
SPEAKING OF THAT, WHAT ABOUT LADY FARANGIS AND GIEVE? SHOULD WE CONTACT THEM?
YOU MEAN WINE.
NO NEED FOR THAT.

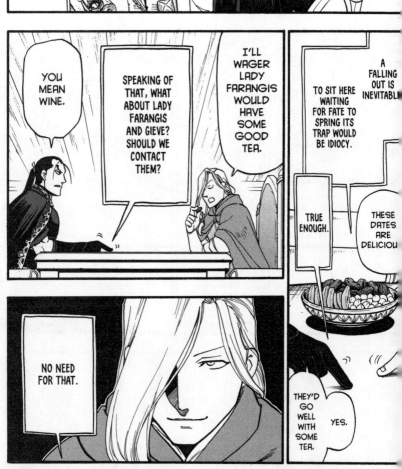

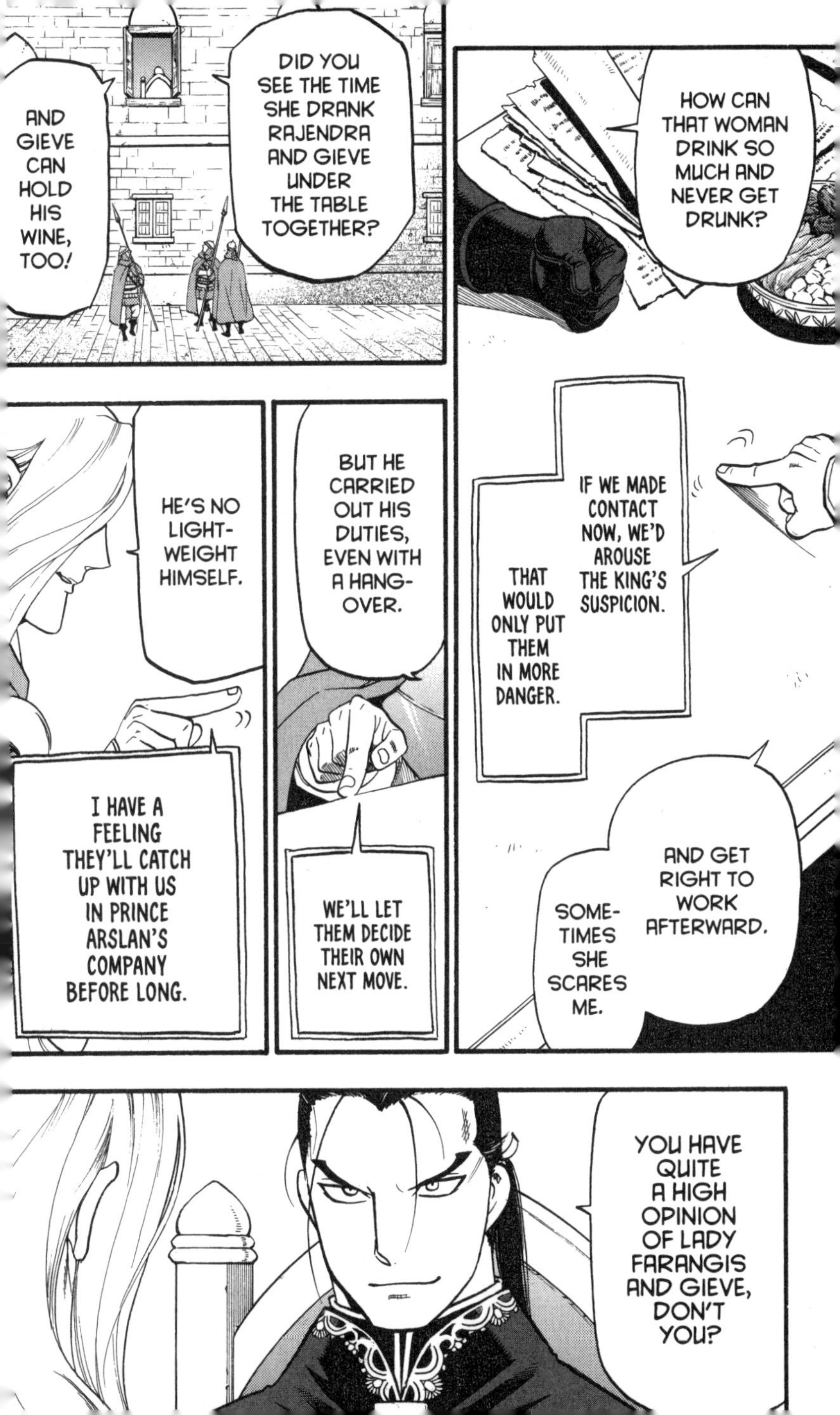
HOW CAN THAT WOMAN DRINK SO MUCH AND NEVER GET DRUNK?
DID YOU SEE THE TIME SHE DRANK RAJENDRA AND GIEVE UNDER THE TABLE TOGETHER?
AND GIEVE CAN HOLD HIS WINE, TOO!
IF WE MADE CONTACT NOW, WE'D AROUSE THE KING'S SUSPICION.
THAT WOULD ONLY PUT THEM IN MORE DANGER.
AND GET RIGHT TO WORK AFTERWARD.
SOMETIMES SHE SCARES ME.
BUT HE CARRIED OUT HIS DUTIES, EVEN WITH A HANGOVER.
WE'LL LET THEM DECIDE THEIR OWN NEXT MOVE.
HE'S NO LIGHTWEIGHT HIMSELF.
I HAVE A FEELING THEY'LL CATCH UP WITH US IN PRINCE ARSLAN'S COMPANY BEFORE LONG.
YOU HAVE QUITE A HIGH OPINION OF LADY FARANGIS AND GIEVE, DON'T YOU?

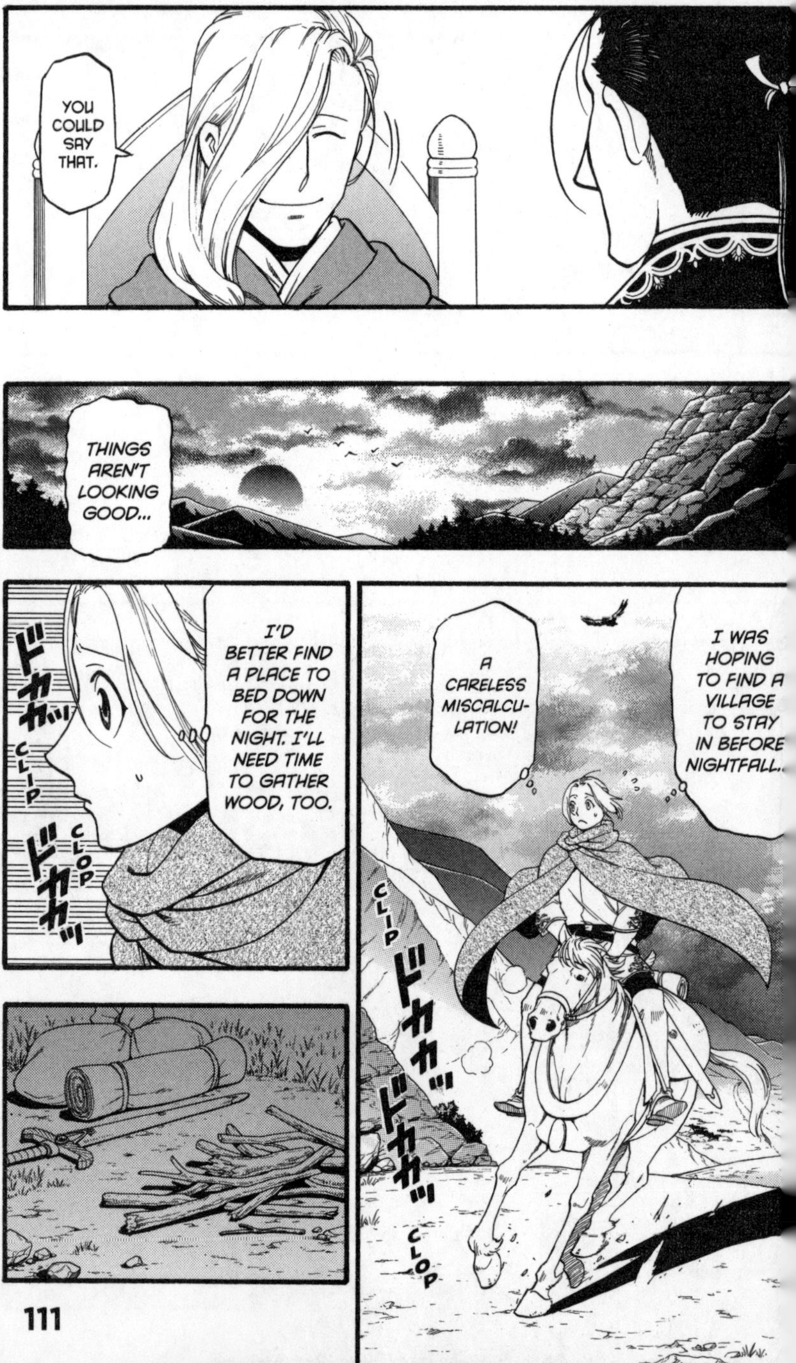
YOU COULD SAY THAT.
THINGS AREN'T LOOKING GOOD...
I WAS HOPING TO FIND A VILLAGE TO STAY IN BEFORE NIGHTFALL...
A CARELESS MISCALCULATION!
CLIP
CLOP
I'D BETTER FIND A PLACE TO BED DOWN FOR THE NIGHT. I'LL NEED TIME TO GATHER WOOD, TOO.
CLIP
CLOP

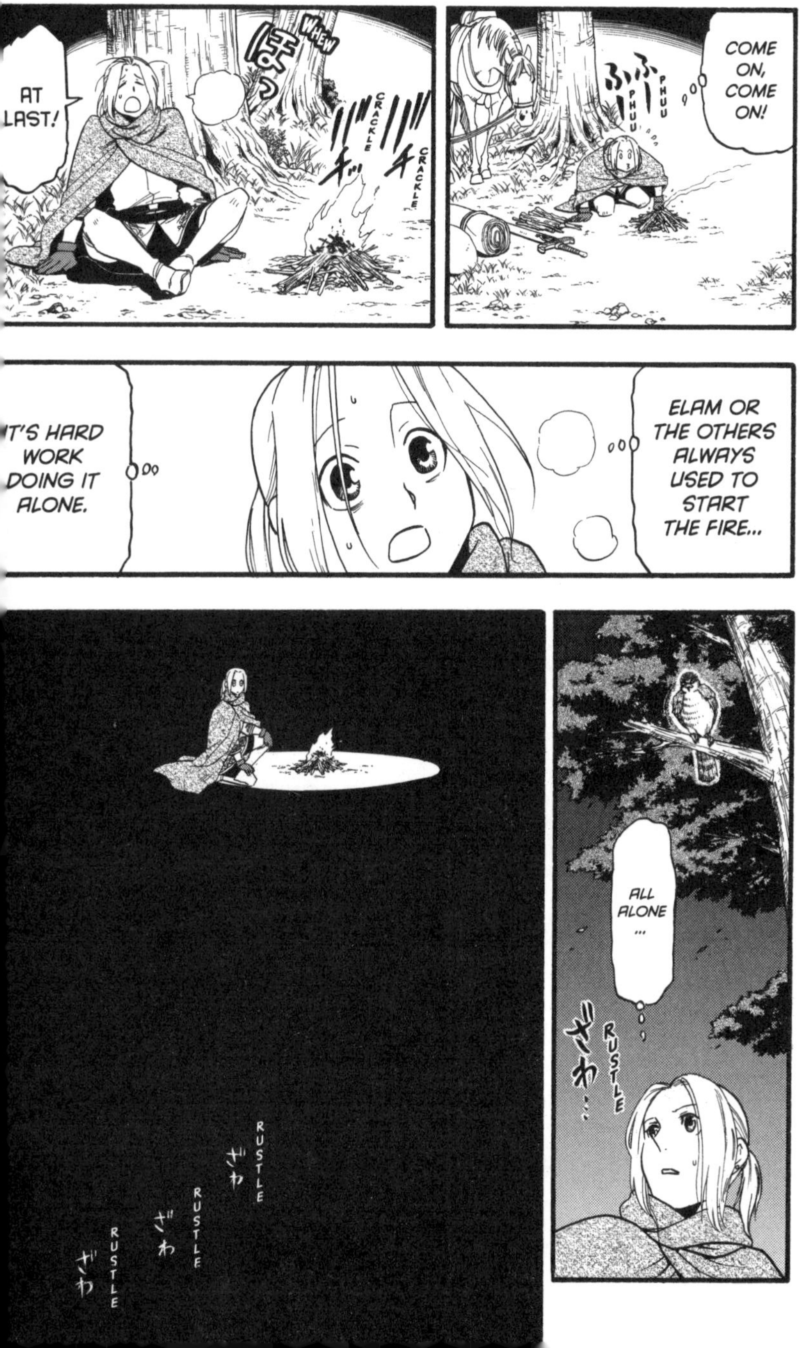
ふーっ
PHUU
PHUU
COME ON, COME ON!
ほっ
WHEW
AT LAST!
チッ
CRACKLE
チ
CRACKLE
ELAM OR THE OTHERS ALWAYS USED TO START THE FIRE...
IT'S HARD WORK DOING IT ALONE.
ALL ALONE ...
ざわ…
RUSTLE
ざわ
RUSTLE
ざわ
RUSTLE
ざわ
RUSTLE

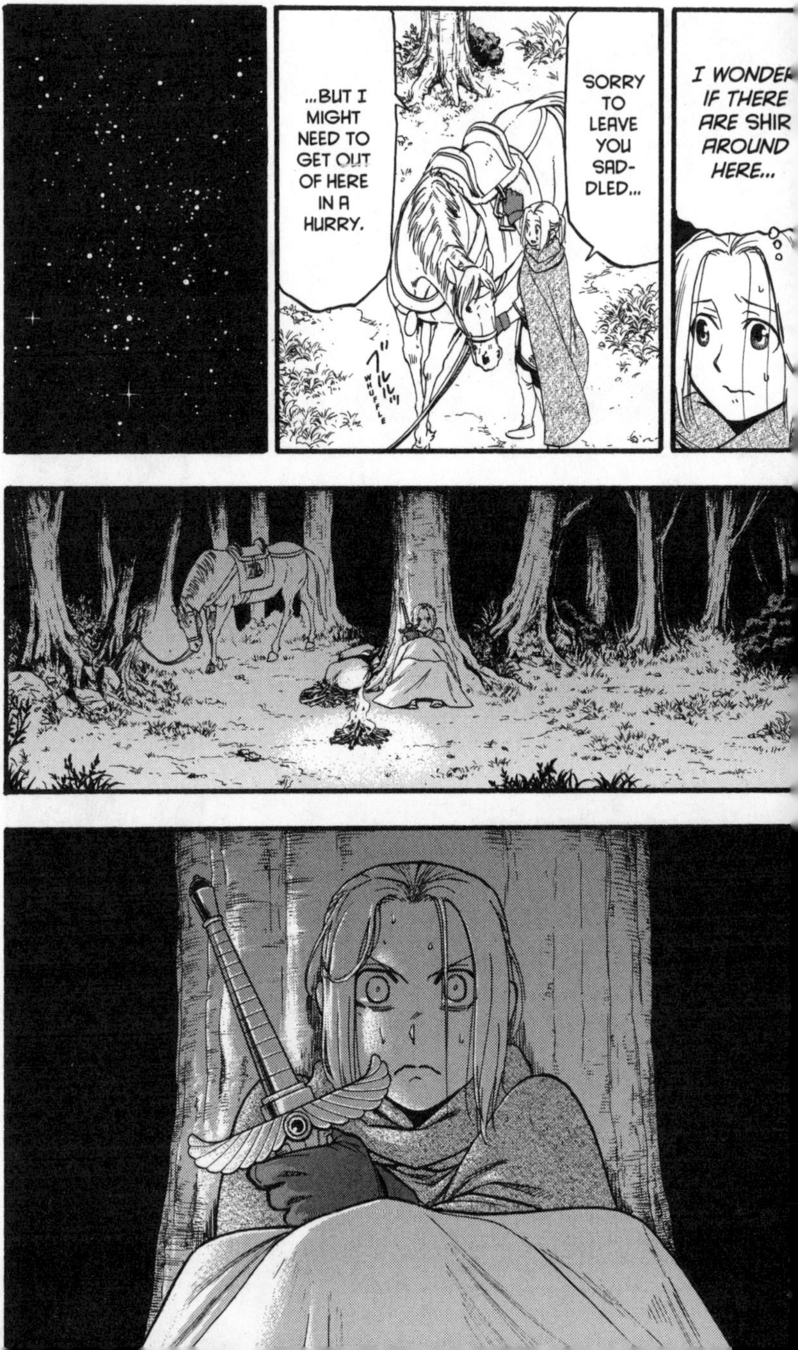
I WONDER IF THERE ARE SHIR AROUND HERE...
SORRY TO LEAVE YOU SADDLED...
...BUT I MIGHT NEED TO GET OUT OF HERE IN A HURRY.
WHUFFLE

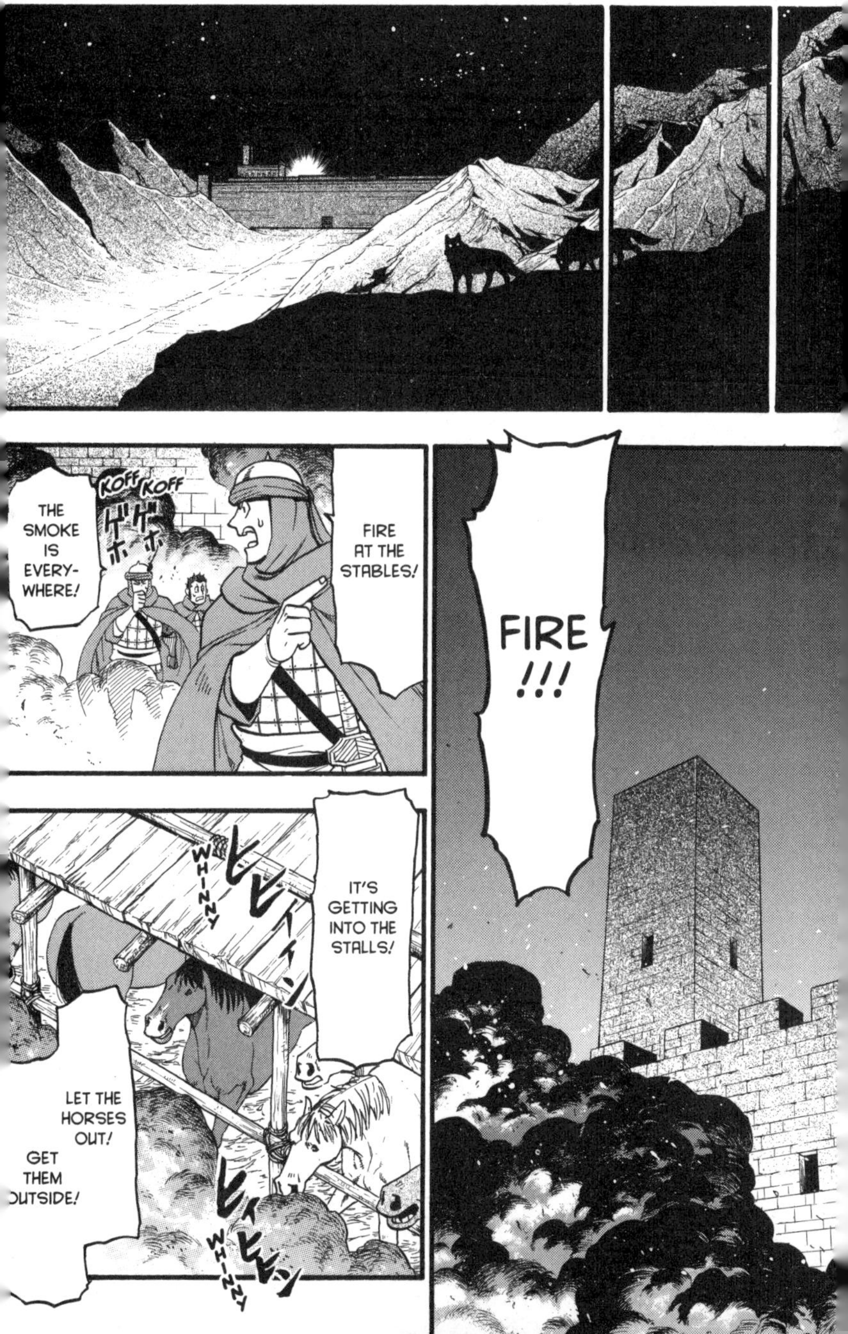
FIRE!!!
FIRE AT THE STABLES!
KOFF KOFF
THE SMOKE IS EVERYWHERE!
IT'S GETTING INTO THE STALLS!
WHINNY
LET THE HORSES OUT!
GET THEM OUTSIDE!
WHINNY

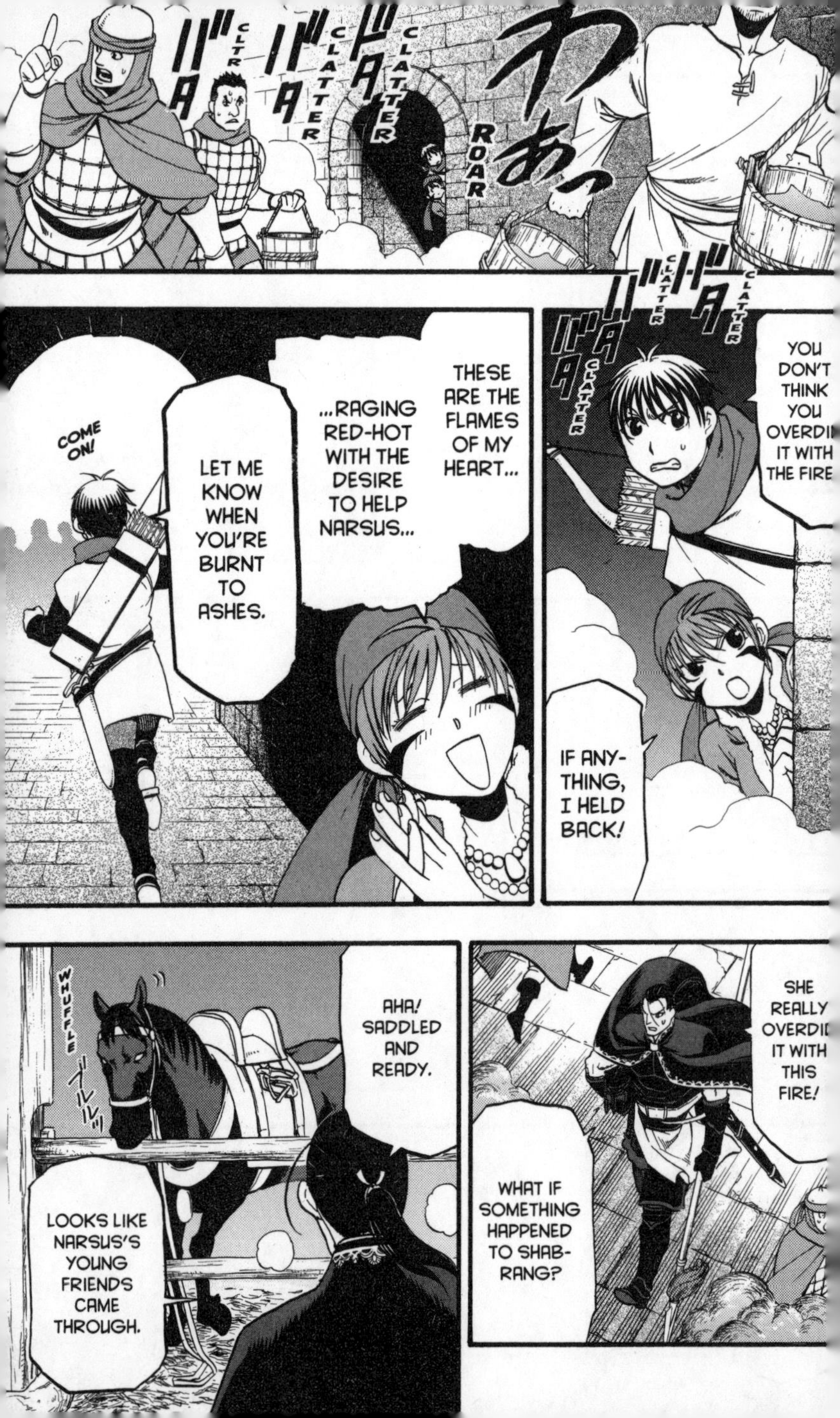
わあっ
ROAR
ドタ
CLATTER
バタ
CLATTER
バタ
CLTR
バタ
CLATTER
バタ
CLATTER
バタ
CLATTER
YOU DON'T THINK YOU OVERDI IT WITH THE FIRE
IF ANY-THING, I HELD BACK!
THESE ARE THE FLAMES OF MY HEART...
...RAGING RED-HOT WITH THE DESIRE TO HELP NARSUS...
LET ME KNOW WHEN YOU'RE BURNT TO ASHES.
COME ON!
SHE REALLY OVERDI IT WITH THIS FIRE!
WHAT IF SOMETHING HAPPENED TO SHAB-RANG?
AHA! SADDLED AND READY.
WHUFFLE
ブルルッ
LOOKS LIKE NARSUS'S YOUNG FRIENDS CAME THROUGH.

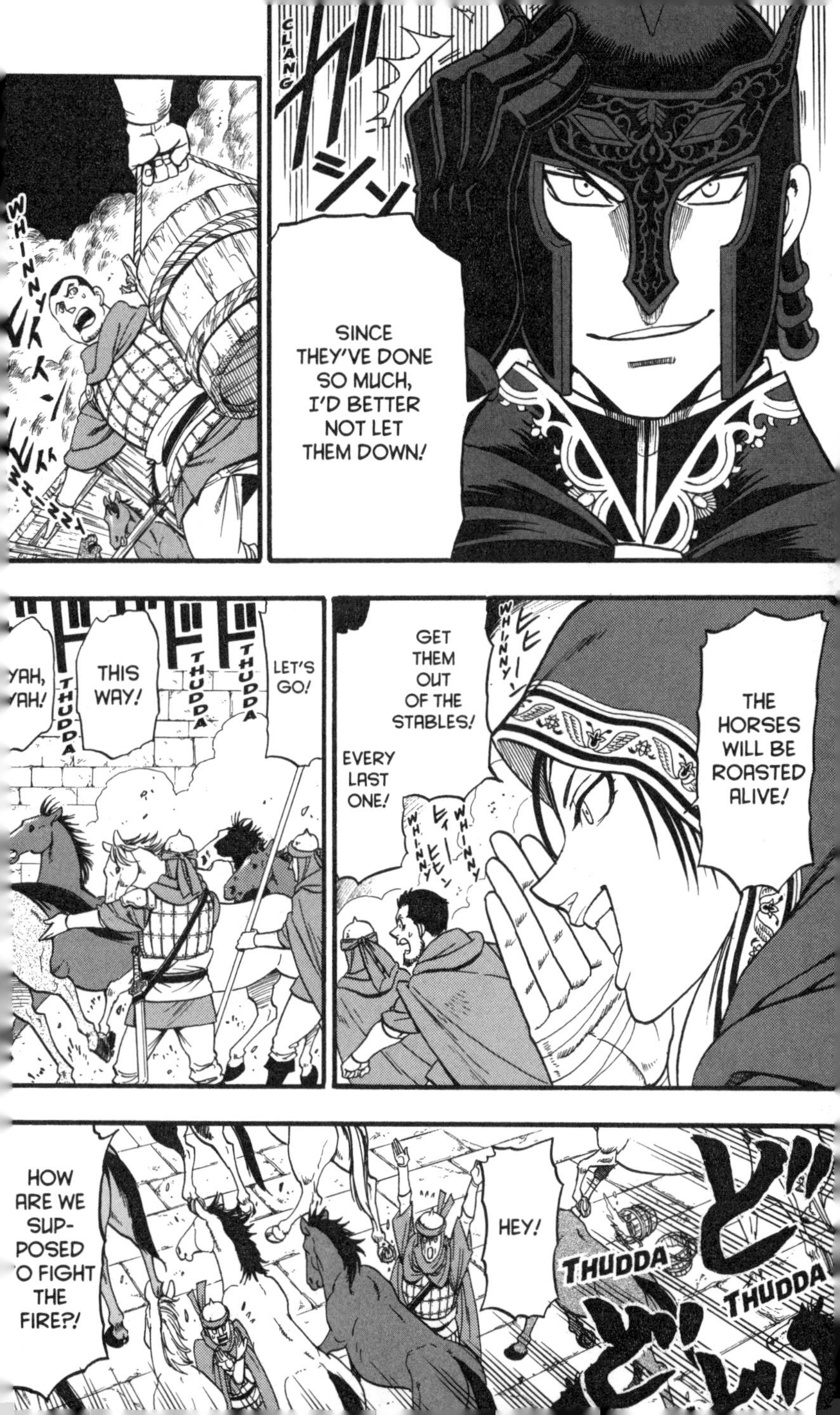
CLANG
SINCE THEY'VE DONE SO MUCH, I'D BETTER NOT LET THEM DOWN!
WHINNY
WHINNY
WHINNY
THE HORSES WILL BE ROASTED ALIVE!
GET THEM OUT OF THE STABLES!
EVERY LAST ONE!
WHINNY
WHINNY
LET'S GO!
THUDDA
THUDDA
THIS WAY!
THUDDA
YAH, YAH!
THUDDA
THUDDA
HEY!
HOW ARE WE SUPPOSED O FIGHT THE FIRE?!

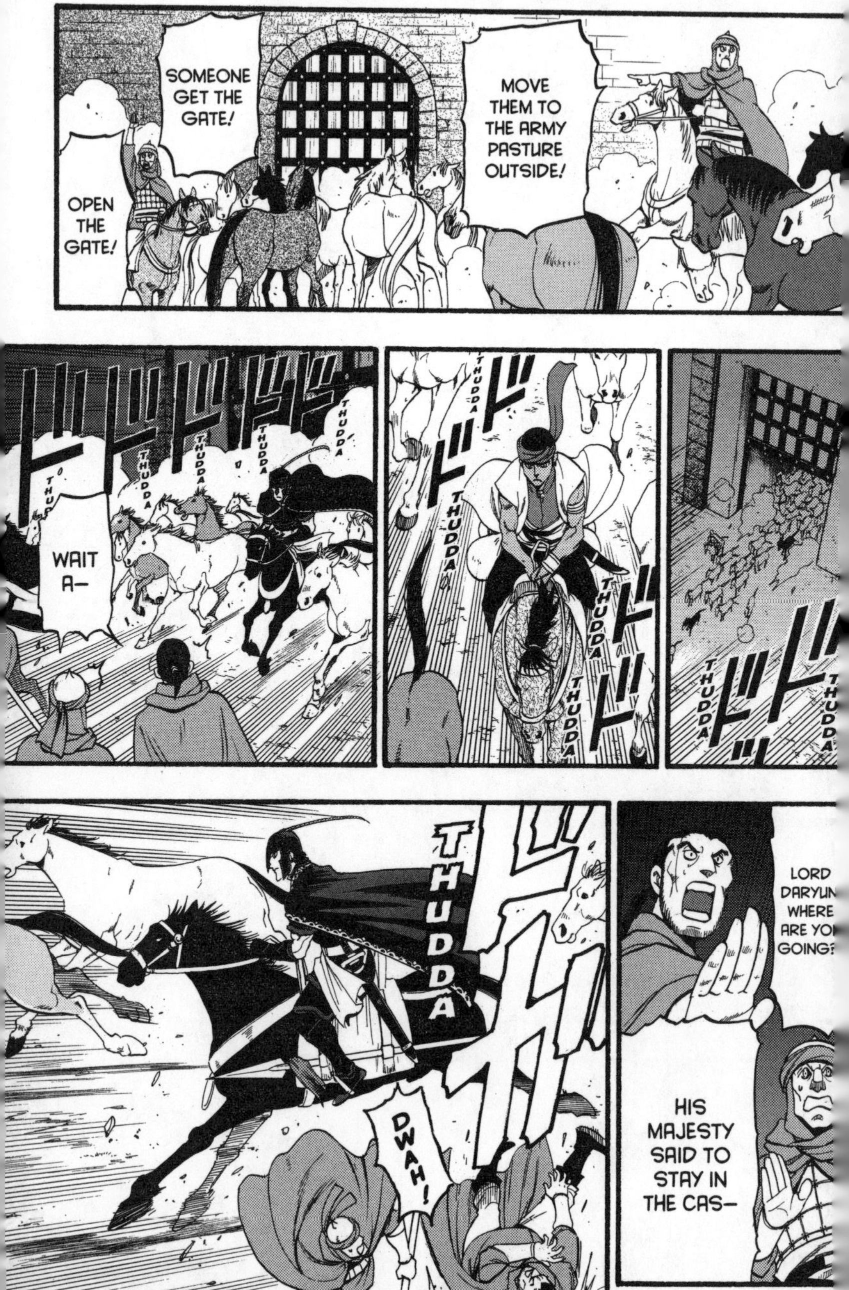
MOVE THEM TO THE ARMY PASTURE OUTSIDE!
SOMEONE GET THE GATE!
OPEN THE GATE!
THUDDA
THUDDA
THUDDA
WAIT A—
LORD DARYUN WHERE ARE YO GOING?
HIS MAJESTY SAID TO STAY IN THE CAS—
THUDDA
DWAH!

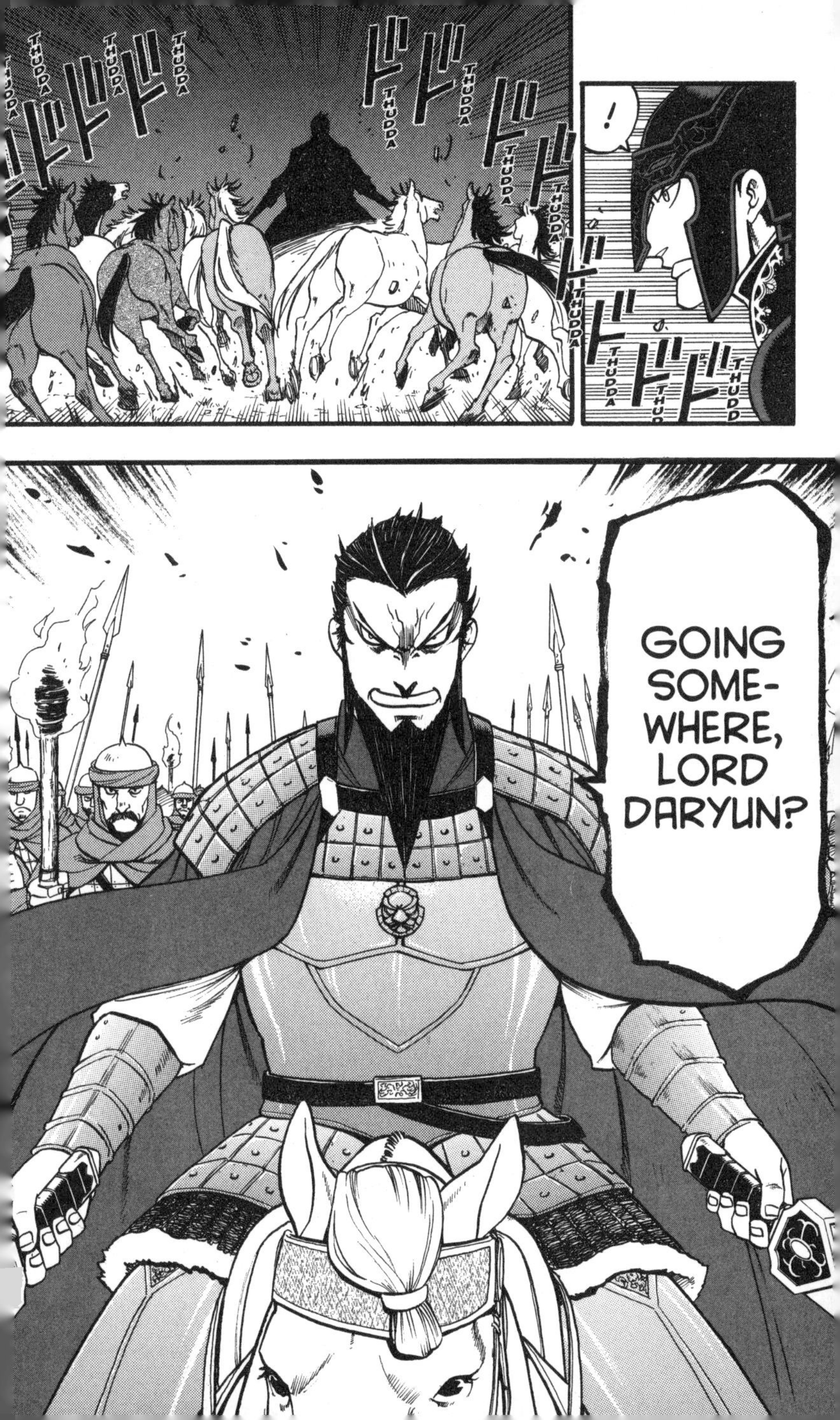
!
ドドド THUDDA THUDDA THUDD
ドドドド THUDDA THUDDA THUDDA THUDDA THUDDA THUDDA THUDDA THUDDA THUDDA
GOING SOME-WHERE, LORD DARYUN?

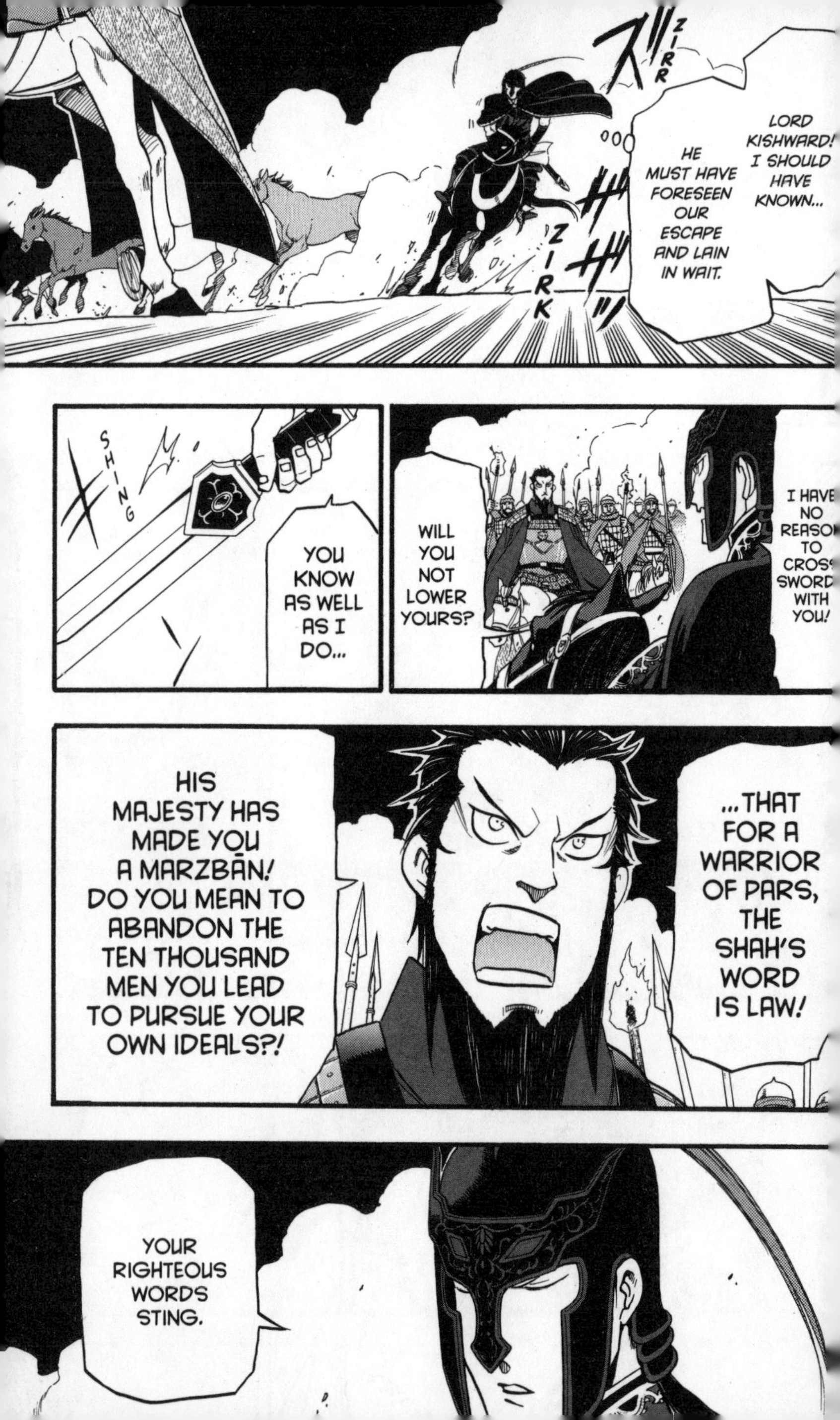
ZIRR
LORD KISHWARD! I SHOULD HAVE KNOWN...
HE MUST HAVE FORESEEN OUR ESCAPE AND LAIN IN WAIT.
ZIRK
I HAVE NO REASON TO CROSS SWORDS WITH YOU!
WILL YOU NOT LOWER YOURS?
SHING
YOU KNOW AS WELL AS I DO...
...THAT FOR A WARRIOR OF PARS, THE SHAH'S WORD IS LAW!
HIS MAJESTY HAS MADE YOU A MARZBĀN! DO YOU MEAN TO ABANDON THE TEN THOUSAND MEN YOU LEAD TO PURSUE YOUR OWN IDEALS?!
YOUR RIGHTEOUS WORDS STING.

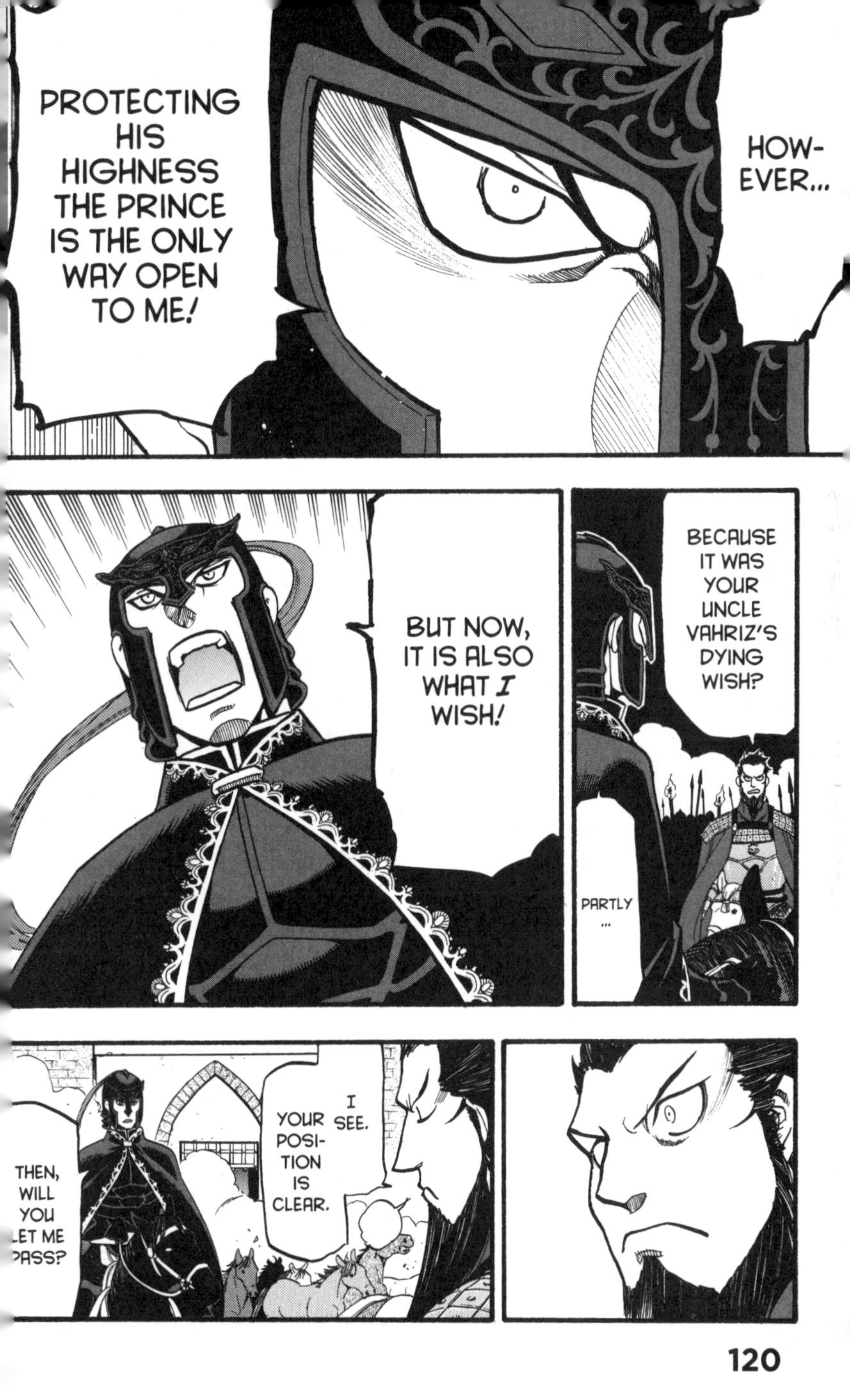
HOW-EVER...
PROTECTING HIS HIGHNESS THE PRINCE IS THE ONLY WAY OPEN TO ME!
BECAUSE IT WAS YOUR UNCLE VAHRIZ'S DYING WISH?
PARTLY ...
BUT NOW, IT IS ALSO WHAT I WISH!
I SEE. YOUR POSITION IS CLEAR.
THEN, WILL YOU ET ME PASS?

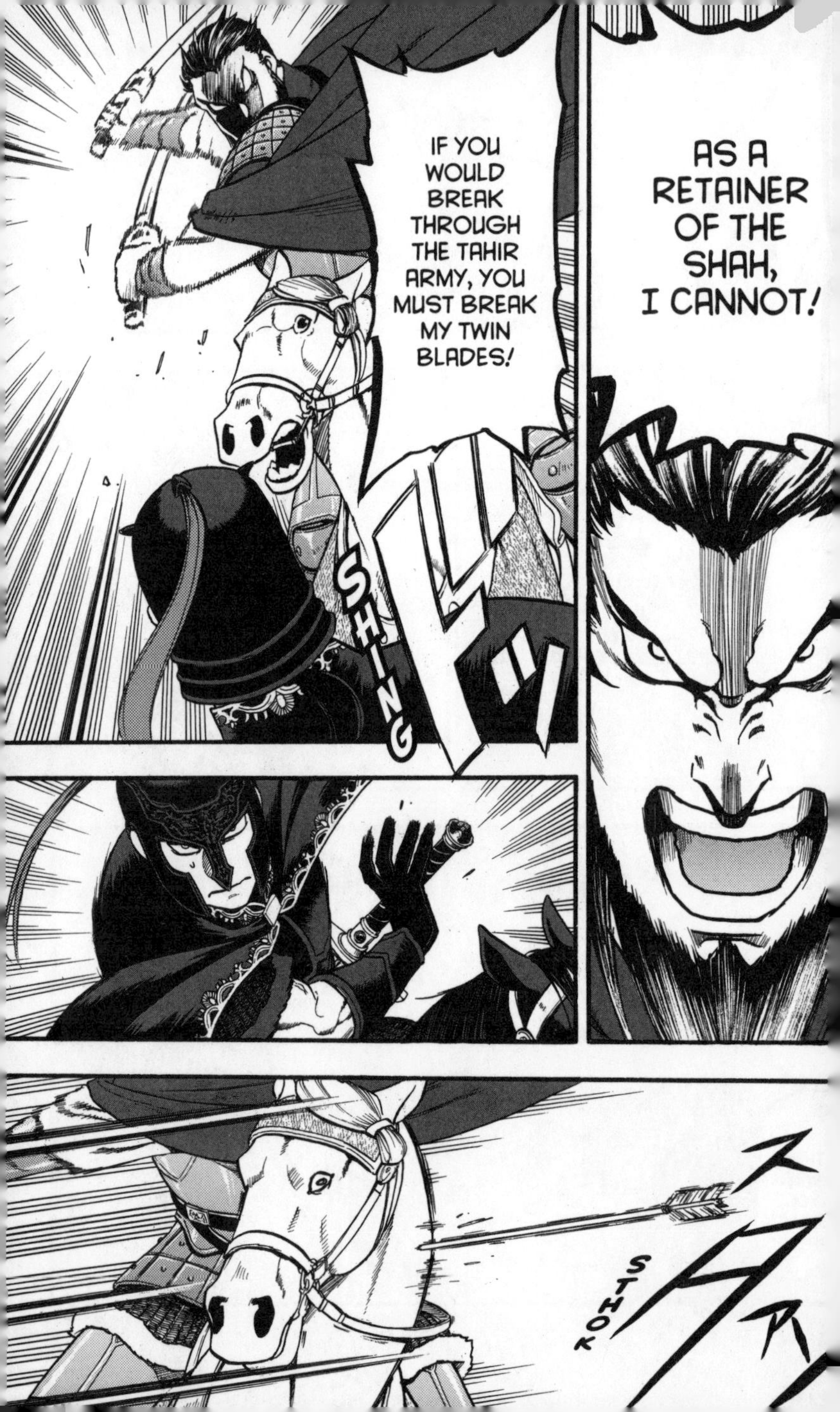
AS A RETAINER OF THE SHAH, I CANNOT!
IF YOU WOULD BREAK THROUGH THE TAHIR ARMY, YOU MUST BREAK MY TWIN BLADES!
SHING
STHOK

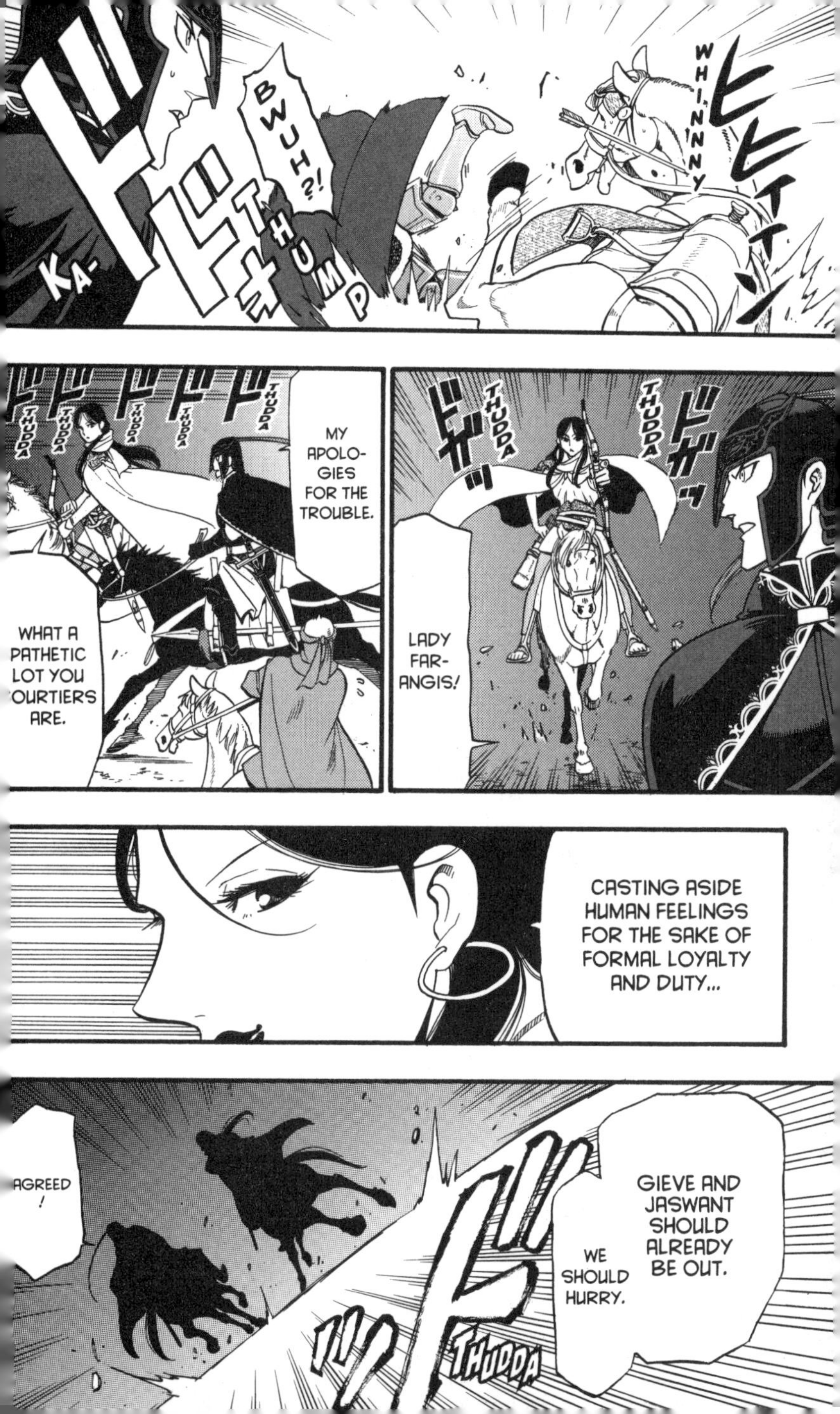
WHINNNY
BWUH?!
THUMP
KA-
THUDDA
THUDDA
LADY FAR-ANGIS!
MY APOLOGIES FOR THE TROUBLE.
THUDDA
THUDDA
THUDDA
THUDDA
THUDDA
WHAT A PATHETIC LOT YOU COURTIERS ARE.
CASTING ASIDE HUMAN FEELINGS FOR THE SAKE OF FORMAL LOYALTY AND DUTY...
GIEVE AND JASWANT SHOULD ALREADY BE OUT.
WE SHOULD HURRY.
AGREED!
THUDDA

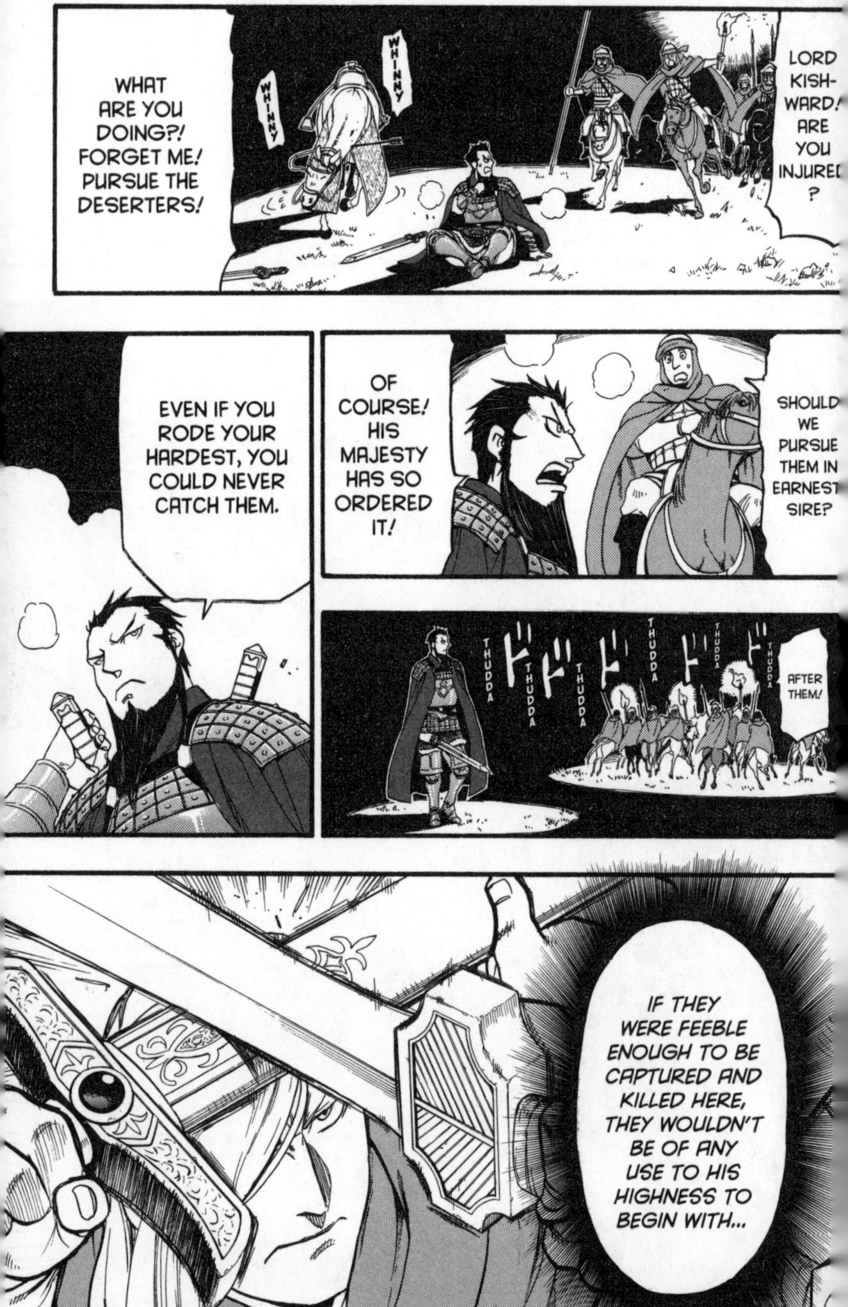
LORD KISHWARD! ARE YOU INJURED?
WHINNY
WHINNY
WHAT ARE YOU DOING?! FORGET ME! PURSUE THE DESERTERS!
SHOULD WE PURSUE THEM IN EARNEST SIRE?
OF COURSE! HIS MAJESTY HAS SO ORDERED IT!
AFTER THEM!
THUDDA ド THUDDA ド THUDDA ド THUDDA ド THUDDA ド THUDDA
EVEN IF YOU RODE YOUR HARDEST, YOU COULD NEVER CATCH THEM.
IF THEY WERE FEEBLE ENOUGH TO BE CAPTURED AND KILLED HERE, THEY WOULDN'T BE OF ANY USE TO HIS HIGHNESS TO BEGIN WITH...

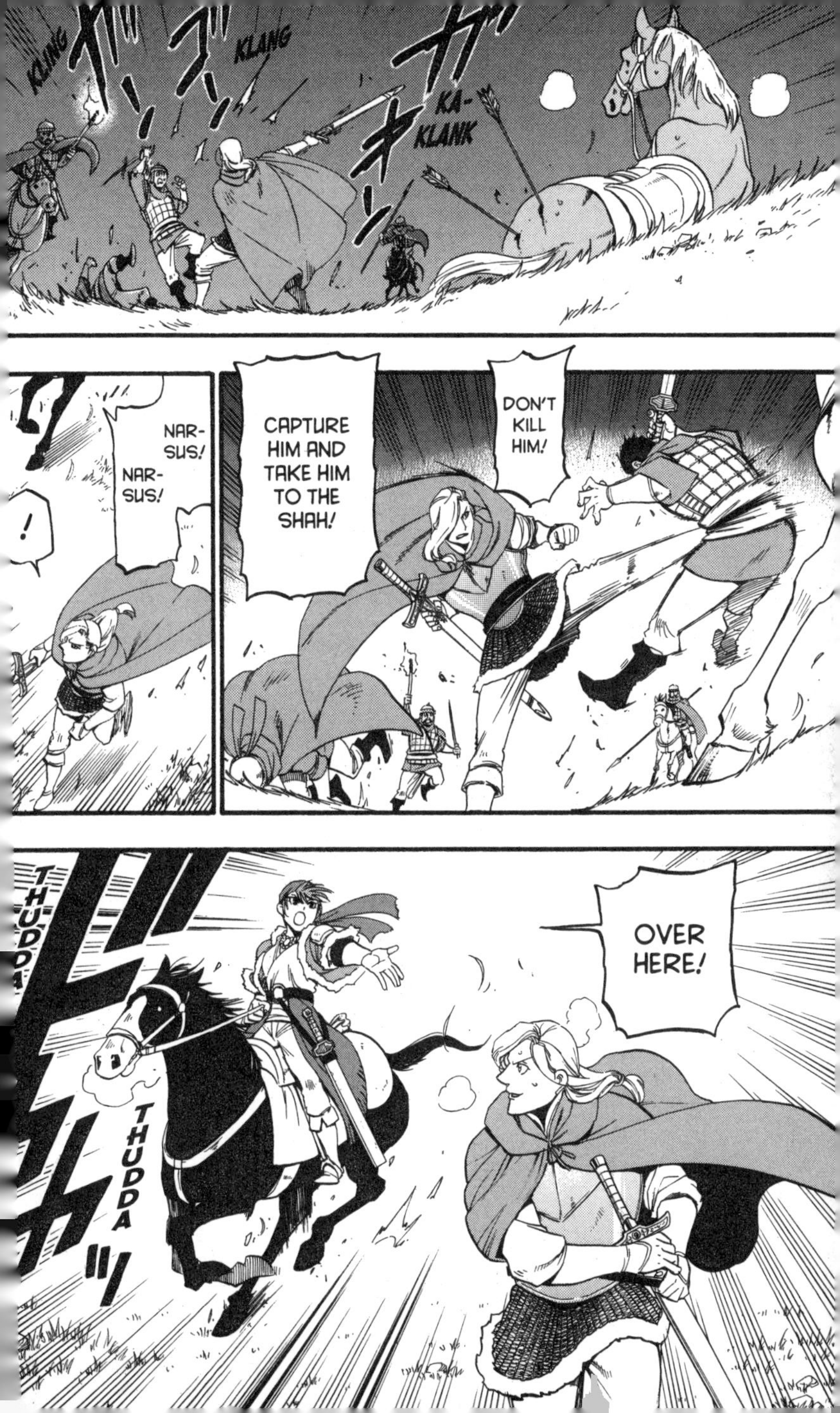

KLING
KLANG
KA-KLANK
DON'T KILL HIM!
CAPTURE HIM AND TAKE HIM TO THE SHAH!
NAR-SUS!
NAR-SUS!
!
OVER HERE!
THUDDA
THUDDA

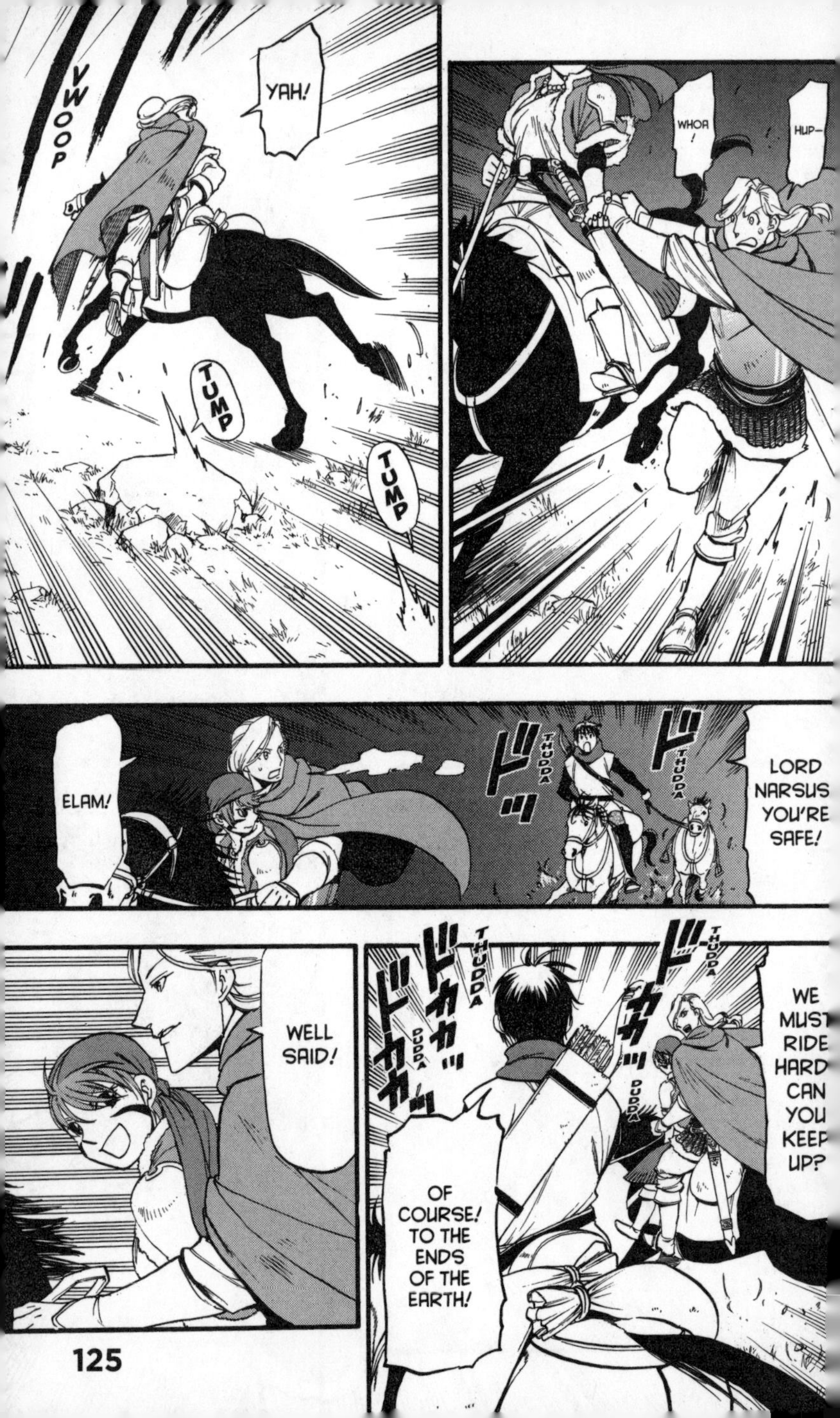
HUP—
WHOA!
YAH!
VWOOP
TUMP
TUMP
LORD NARSUS YOU'RE SAFE!
THUDDA
THUDDA
ELAM!
WE MUST RIDE HARD CAN YOU KEEP UP?
THUDDA
DUDDA
THUDDA
DUDDA
OF COURSE! TO THE ENDS OF THE EARTH!
WELL SAID!

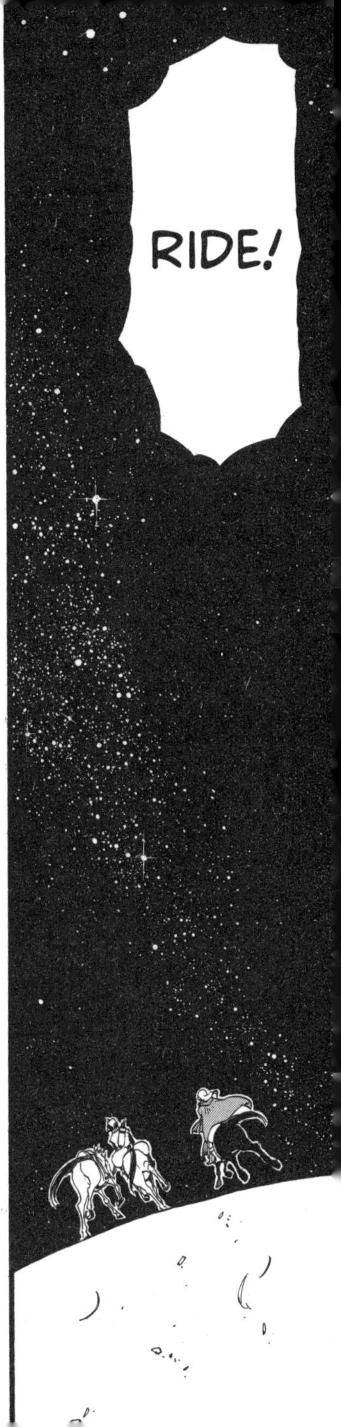
RIDE!

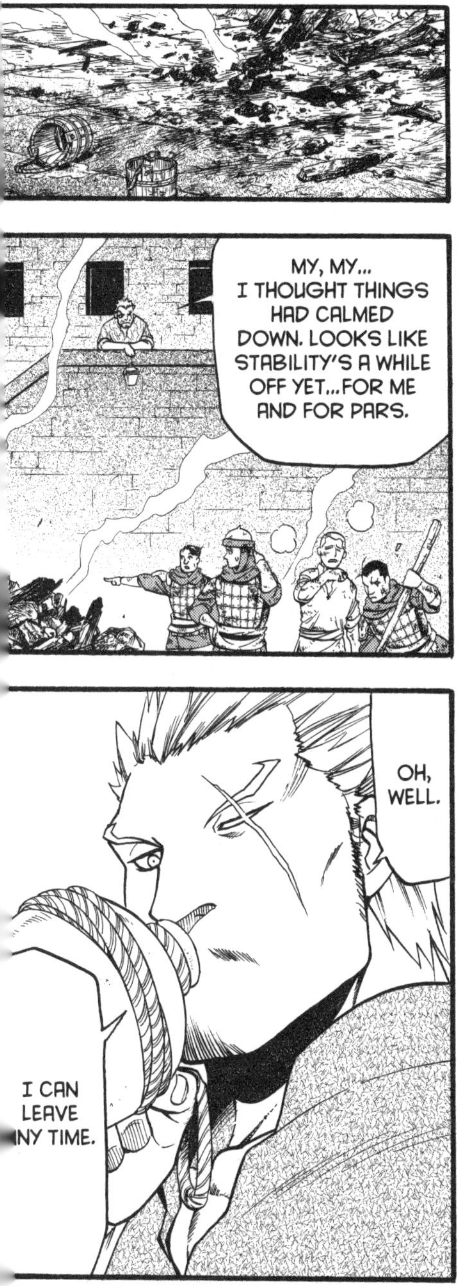
MY, MY... I THOUGHT THINGS HAD CALMED DOWN. LOOKS LIKE STABILITY'S A WHILE OFF YET...FOR ME AND FOR PARS.
OH, WELL.
I CAN LEAVE NY TIME.

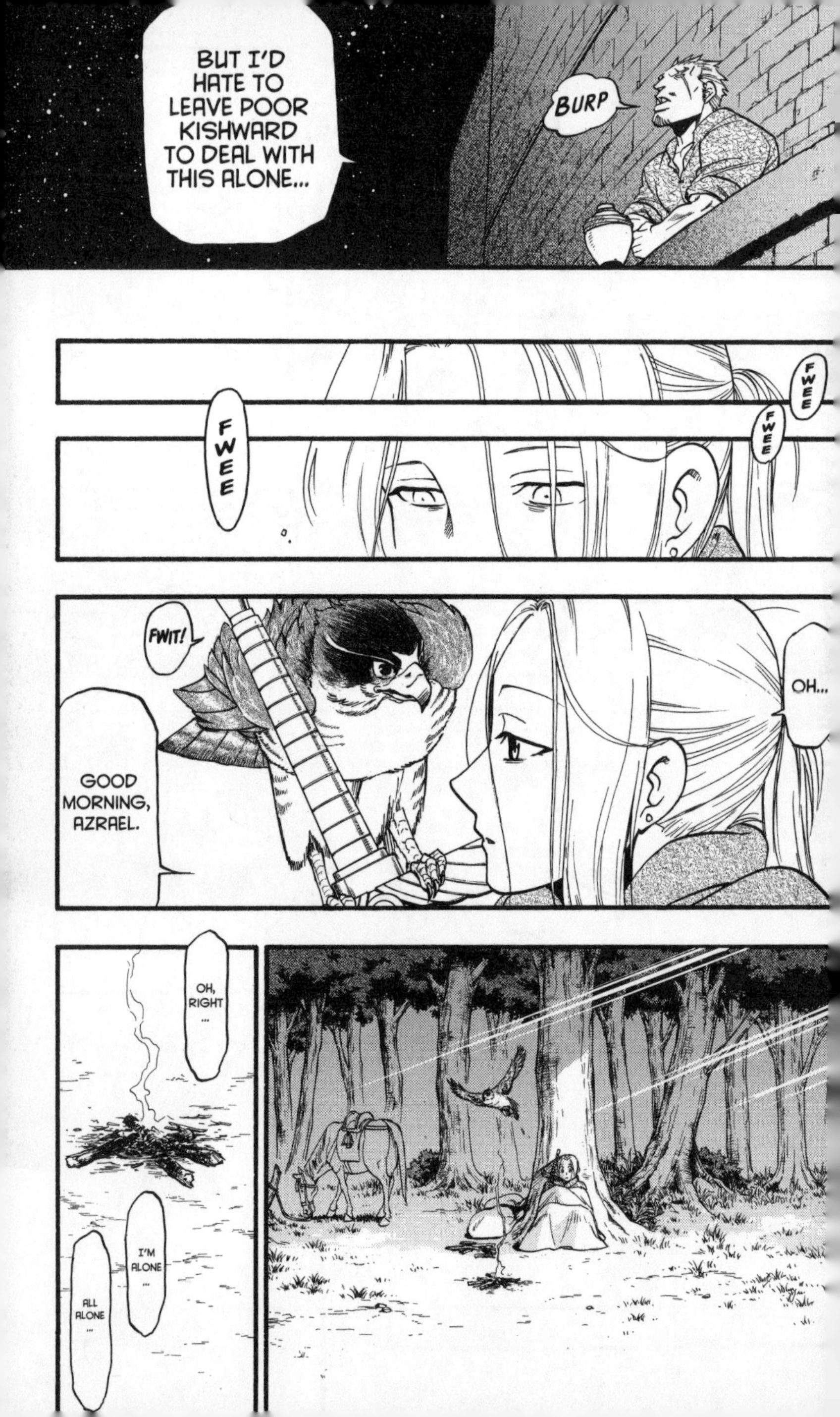
BUT I'D HATE TO LEAVE POOR KISHWARD TO DEAL WITH THIS ALONE...
BURP
FWEE
FWEE
FWEE
OH...
FWIT!
GOOD MORNING, AZRAEL.
OH, RIGHT...
I'M ALONE...
ALL ALONE...

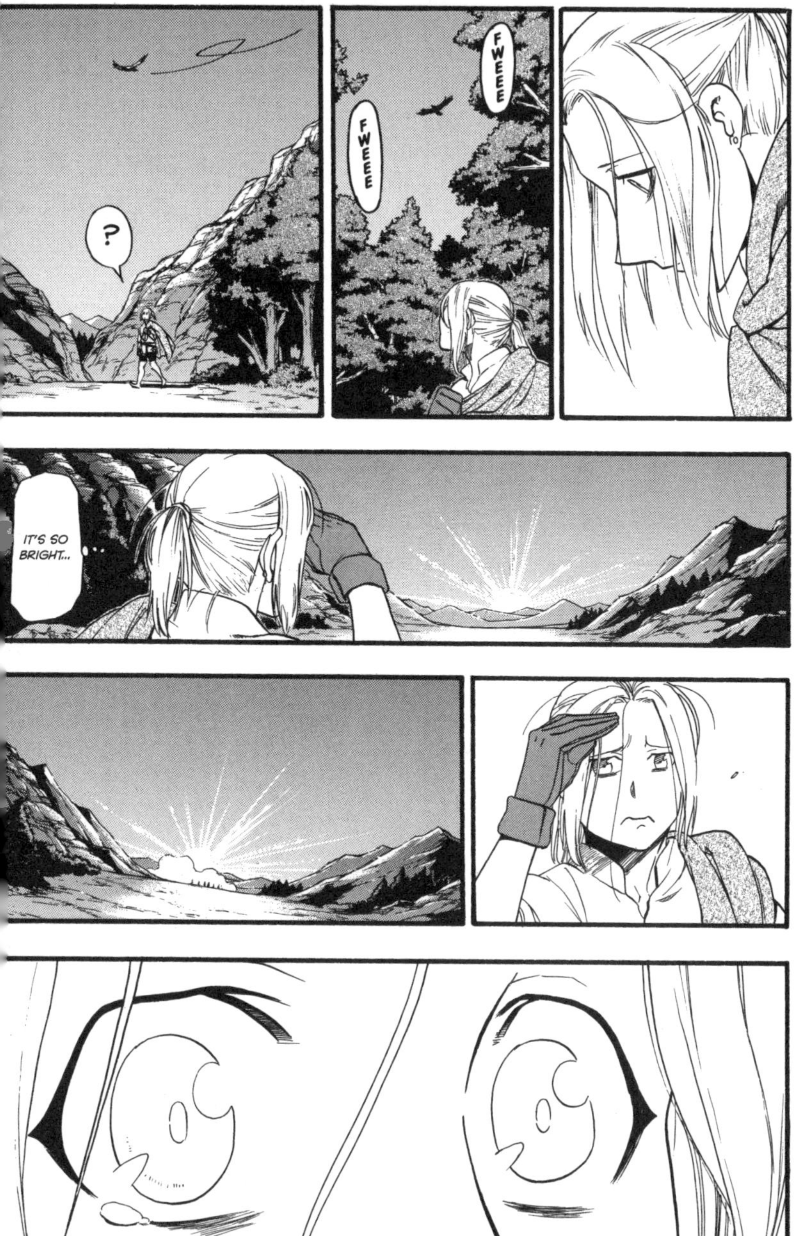
FWEEE
FWEEE
?
IT'S SO BRIGHT...

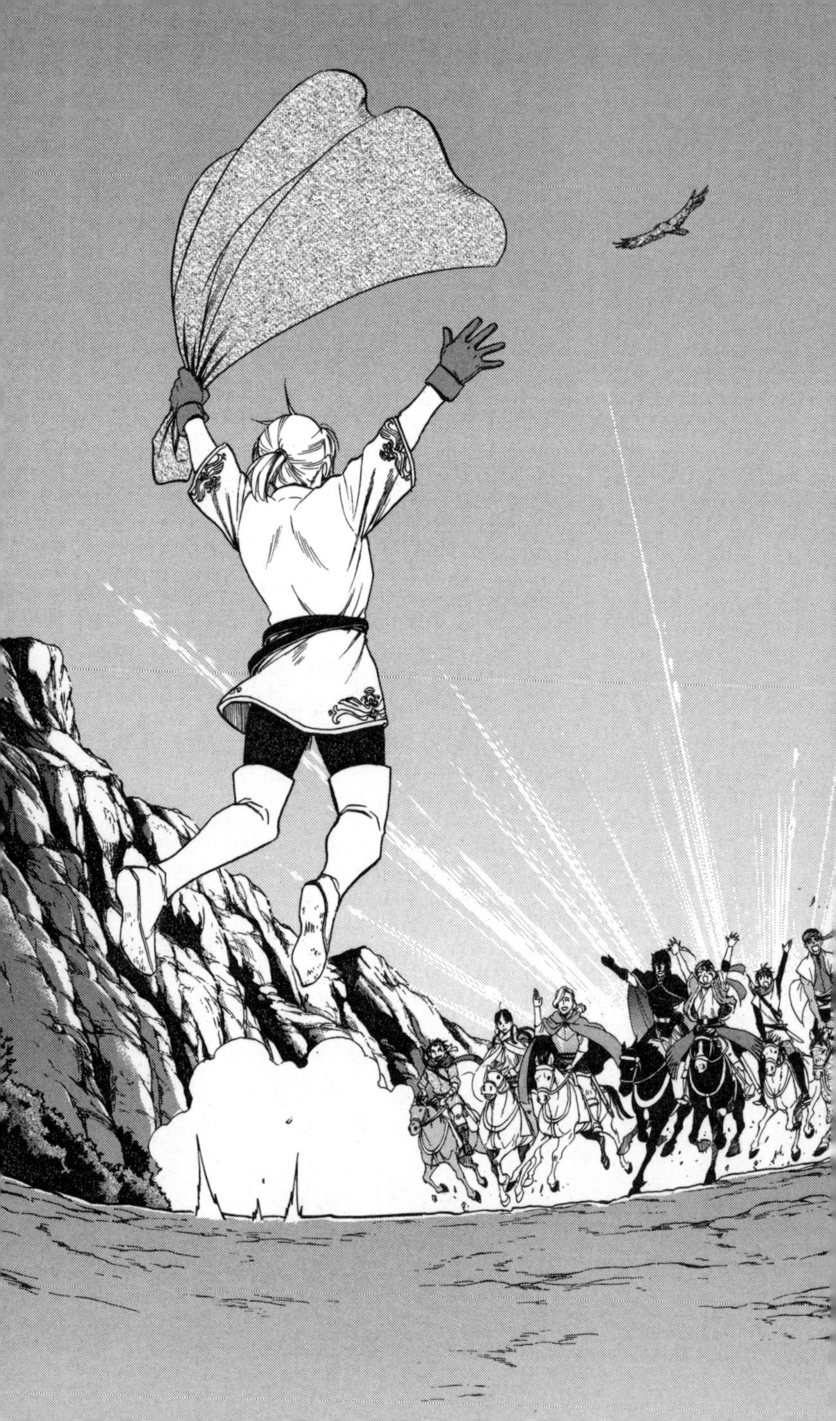

THE HEROIC LEGEND OF
ARSLAN

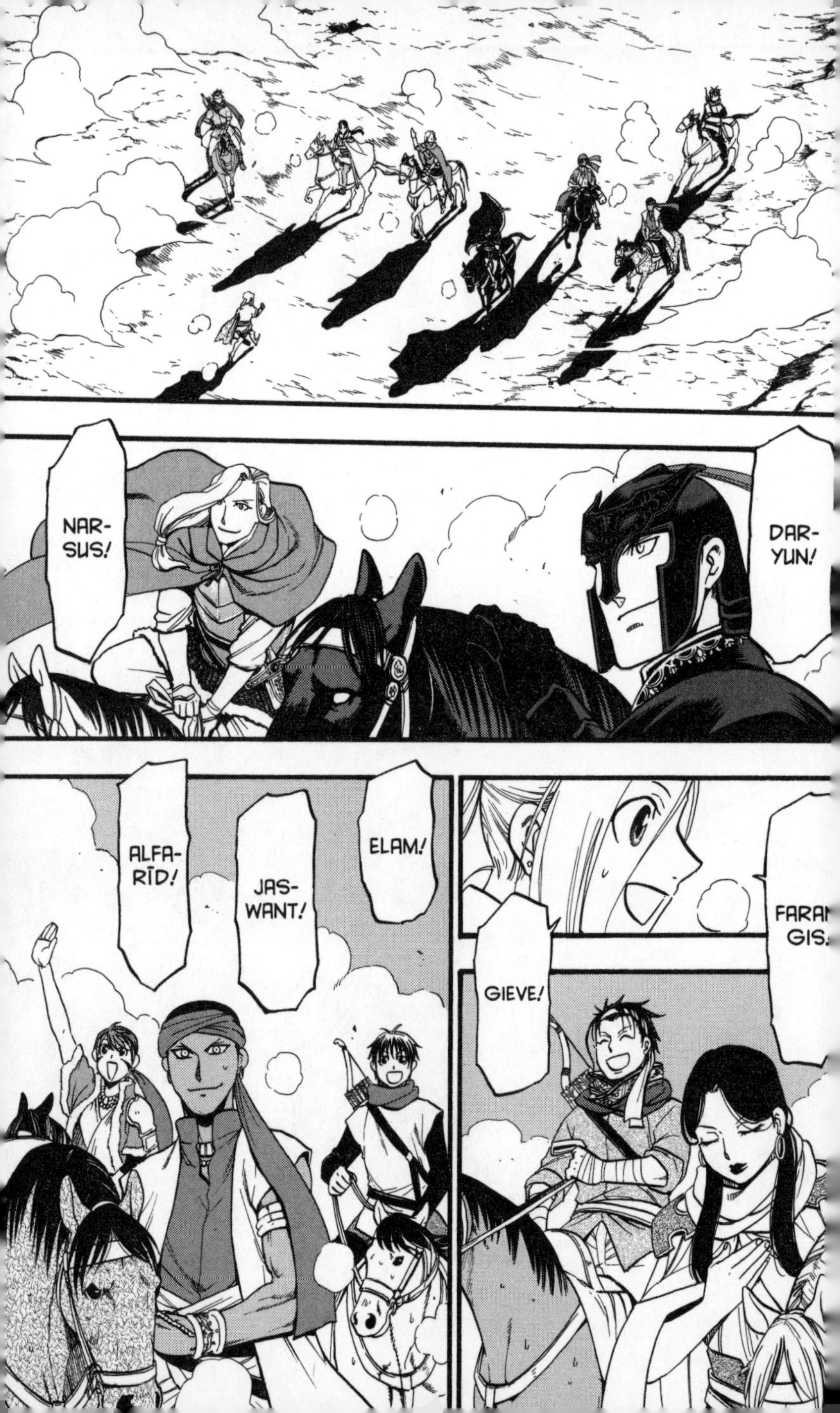
DAR-YUN!
NAR-SUS!
FARAN GIS
GIEVE!
ELAM!
JAS-WANT!
ALFA-RĪD!

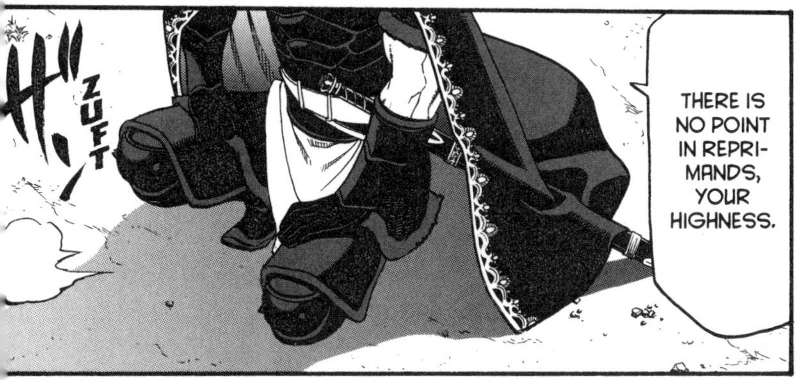
THERE IS NO POINT IN REPRI-MANDS, YOUR HIGHNESS.
ZUFT

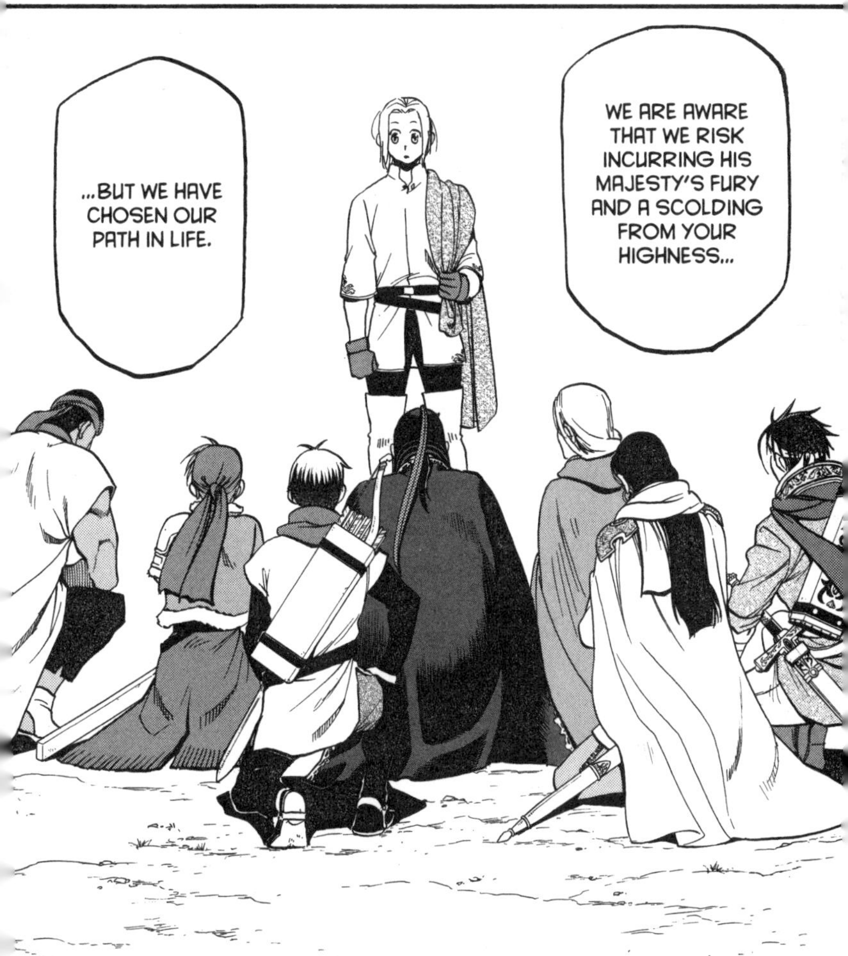
WE ARE AWARE THAT WE RISK INCURRING HIS MAJESTY'S FURY AND A SCOLDING FROM YOUR HIGHNESS...
...BUT WE HAVE CHOSEN OUR PATH IN LIFE.

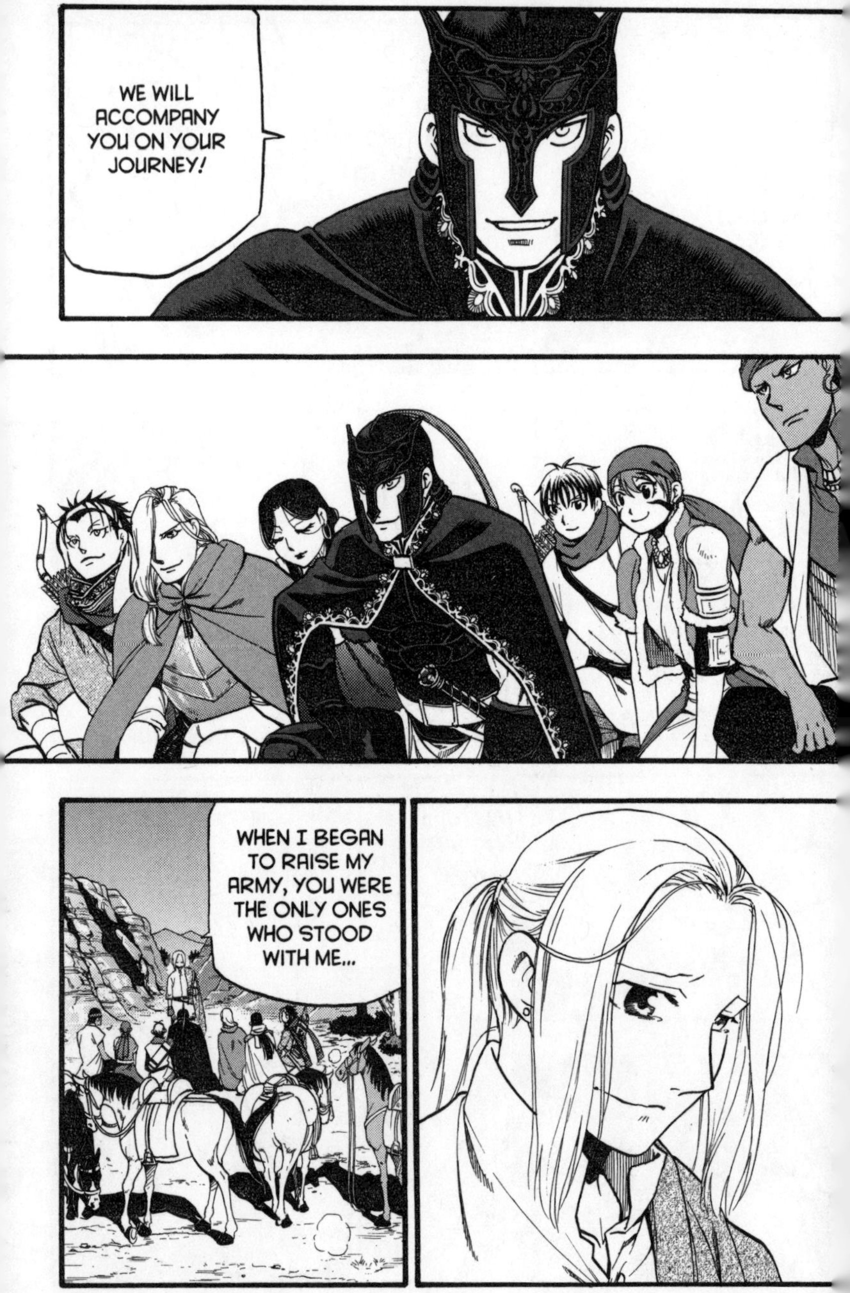
WE WILL ACCOMPANY YOU ON YOUR JOURNEY!
WHEN I BEGAN TO RAISE MY ARMY, YOU WERE THE ONLY ONES WHO STOOD WITH ME...

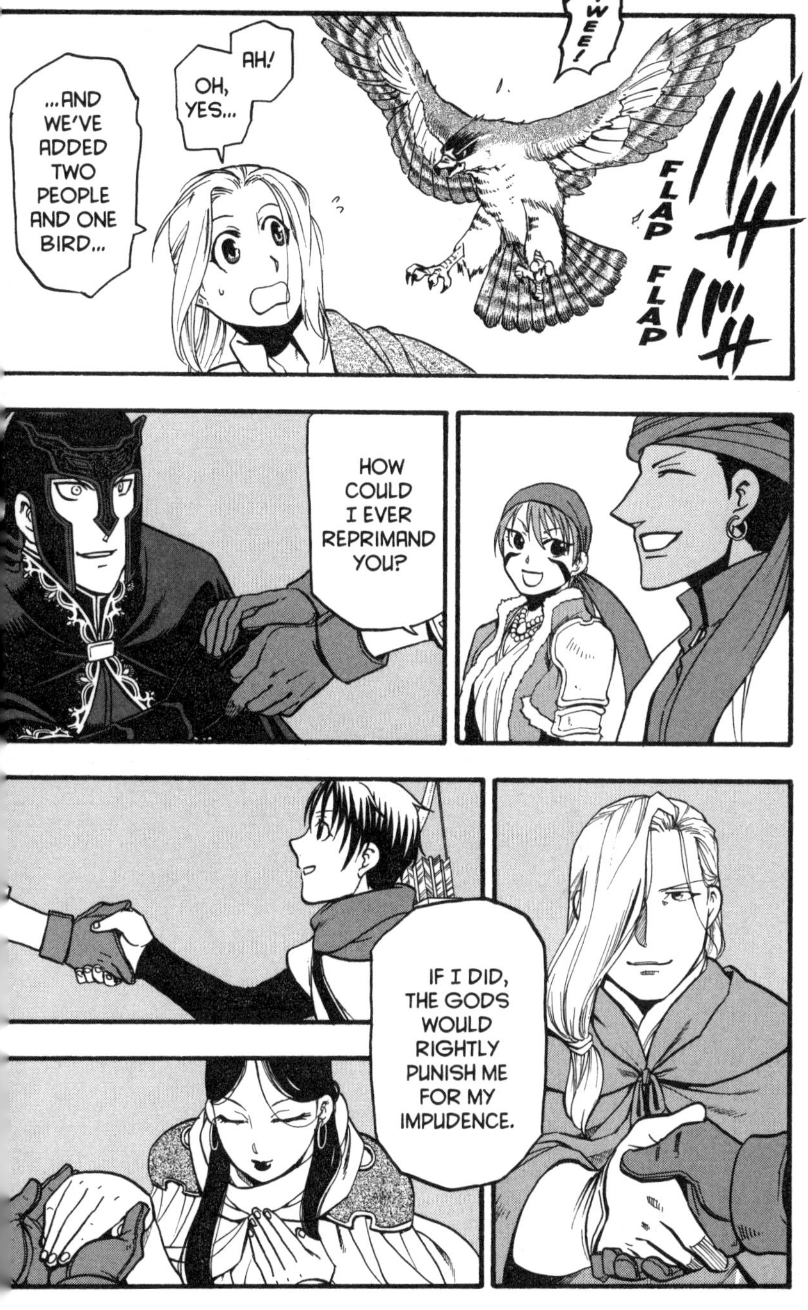
FWEE!
FLAP FLAP
AH!
OH, YES...
...AND WE'VE ADDED TWO PEOPLE AND ONE BIRD...
HOW COULD I EVER REPRIMAND YOU?
IF I DID, THE GODS WOULD RIGHTLY PUNISH ME FOR MY IMPUDENCE.

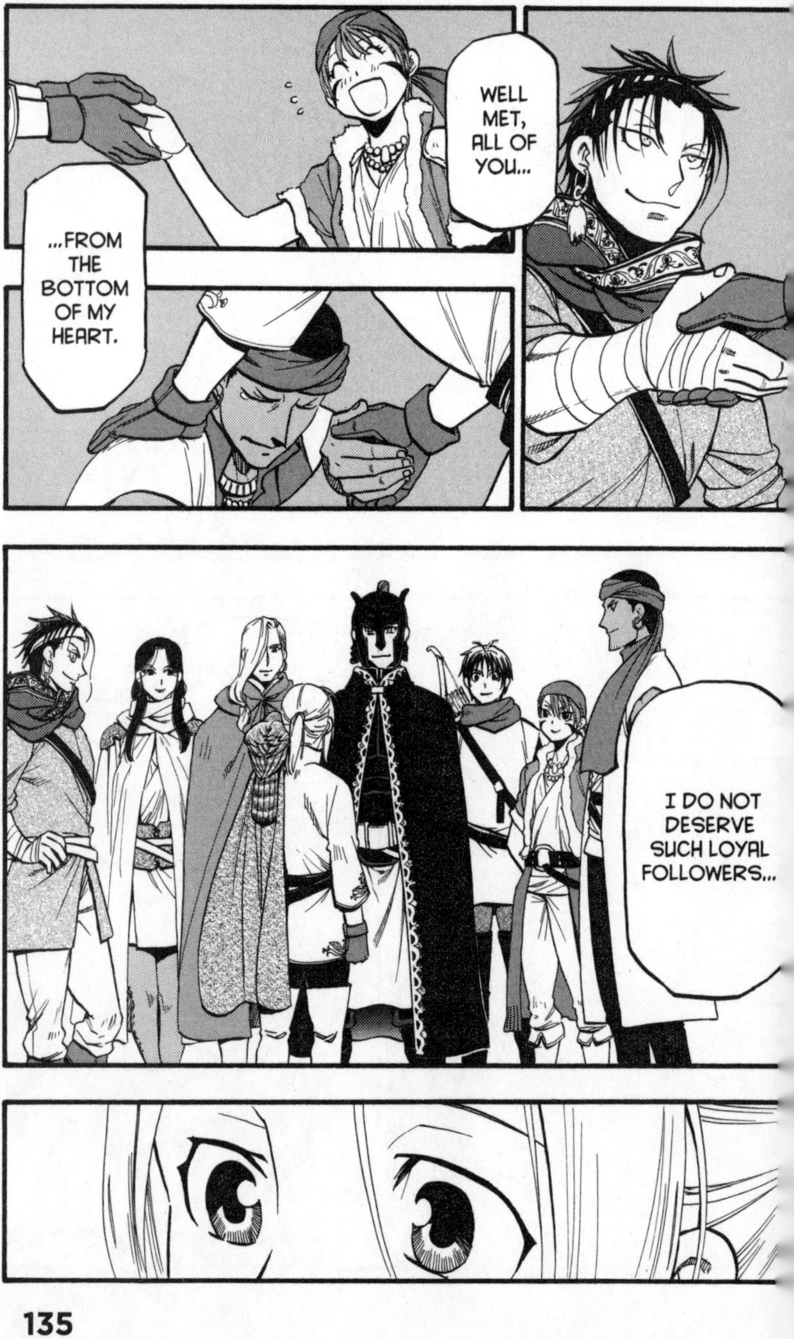
WELL MET, ALL OF YOU...
...FROM THE BOTTOM OF MY HEART.
I DO NOT DESERVE SUCH LOYAL FOLLOWERS...

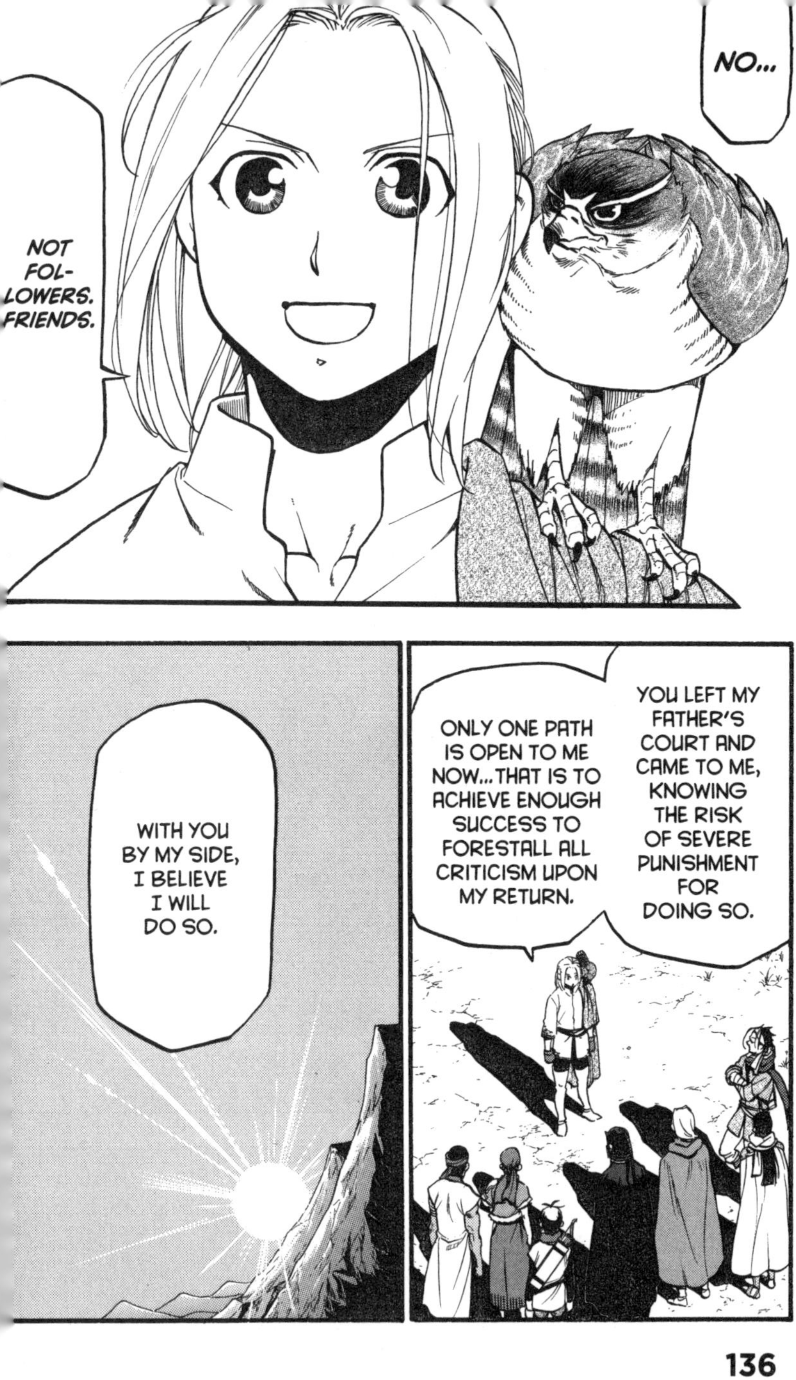
NO...
NOT FOL-LOWERS. FRIENDS.
YOU LEFT MY FATHER'S COURT AND CAME TO ME, KNOWING THE RISK OF SEVERE PUNISHMENT FOR DOING SO.
ONLY ONE PATH IS OPEN TO ME NOW...THAT IS TO ACHIEVE ENOUGH SUCCESS TO FORESTALL ALL CRITICISM UPON MY RETURN.
WITH YOU BY MY SIDE, I BELIEVE I WILL DO SO.

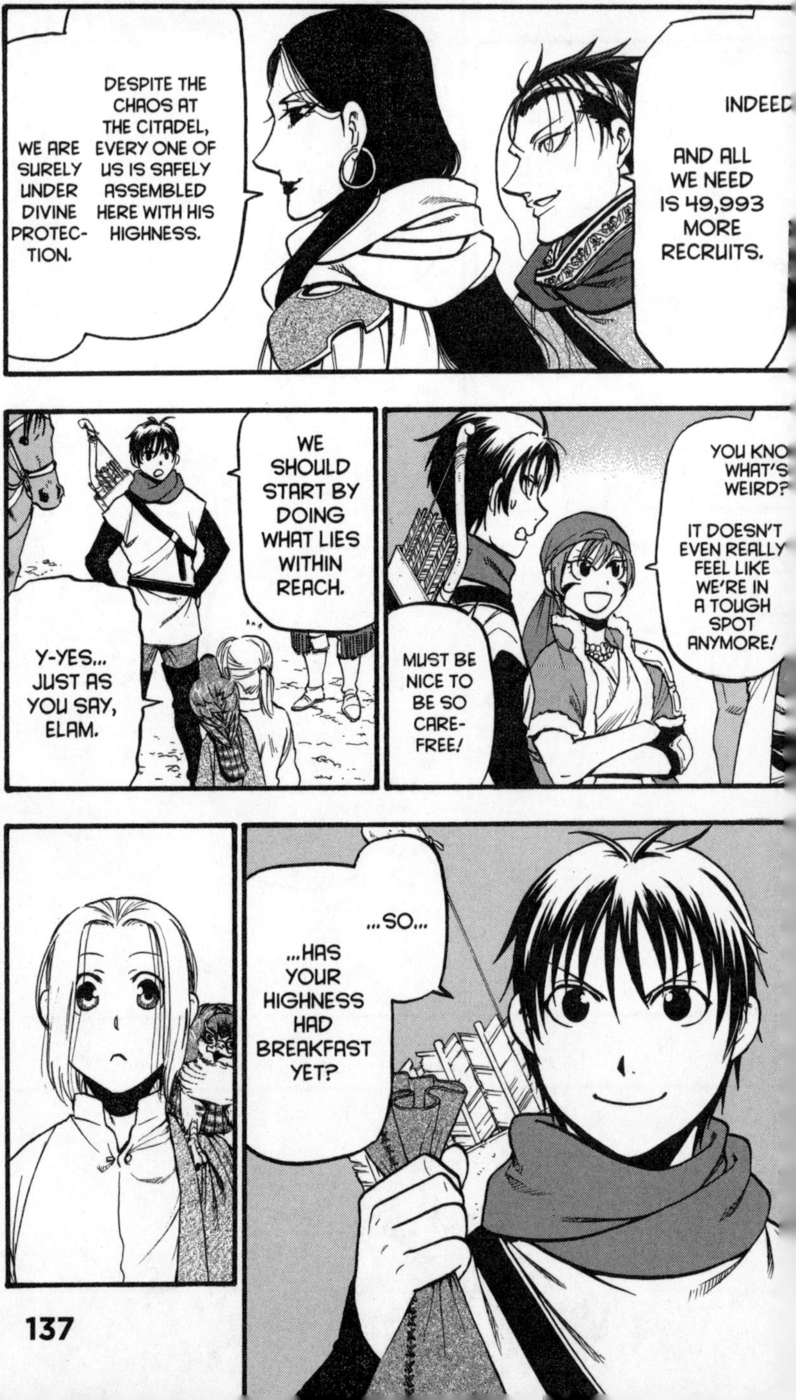
INDEED
AND ALL WE NEED IS 49,993 MORE RECRUITS.
DESPITE THE CHAOS AT THE CITADEL, EVERY ONE OF US IS SAFELY ASSEMBLED HERE WITH HIS HIGHNESS.
WE ARE SURELY UNDER DIVINE PROTECTION.
YOU KNO WHAT'S WEIRD?
IT DOESN'T EVEN REALLY FEEL LIKE WE'RE IN A TOUGH SPOT ANYMORE!
MUST BE NICE TO BE SO CAREFREE!
WE SHOULD START BY DOING WHAT LIES WITHIN REACH.
Y-YES... JUST AS YOU SAY, ELAM.
...SO...
...HAS YOUR HIGHNESS HAD BREAKFAST YET?

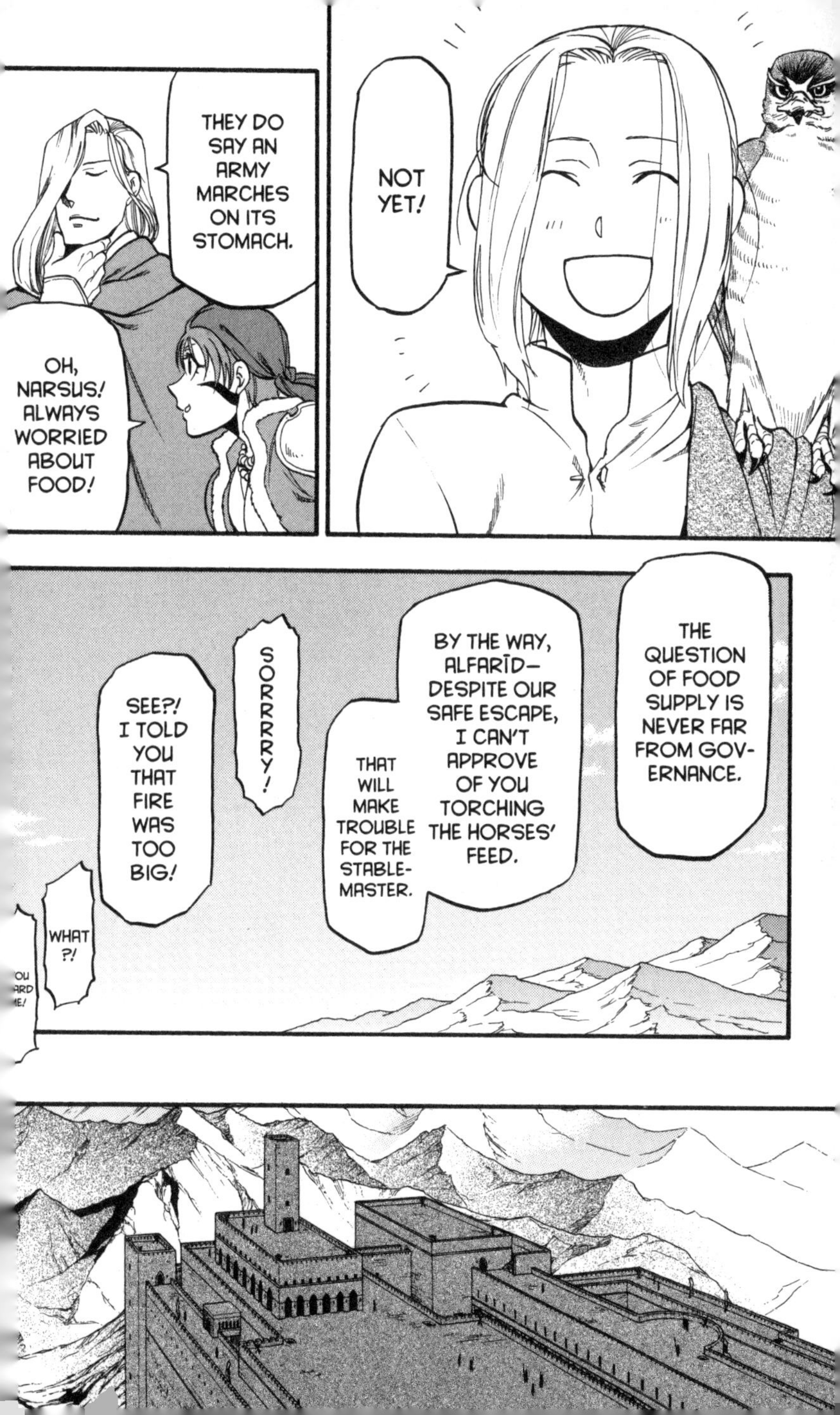
NOT YET!
THEY DO SAY AN ARMY MARCHES ON ITS STOMACH.
OH, NARSUS! ALWAYS WORRIED ABOUT FOOD!
THE QUESTION OF FOOD SUPPLY IS NEVER FAR FROM GOV-ERNANCE.
BY THE WAY, ALFARĪD—DESPITE OUR SAFE ESCAPE, I CAN'T APPROVE OF YOU TORCHING THE HORSES' FEED.
THAT WILL MAKE TROUBLE FOR THE STABLE-MASTER.
SORRRRY!
SEE?! I TOLD YOU THAT FIRE WAS TOO BIG!
WHAT?!

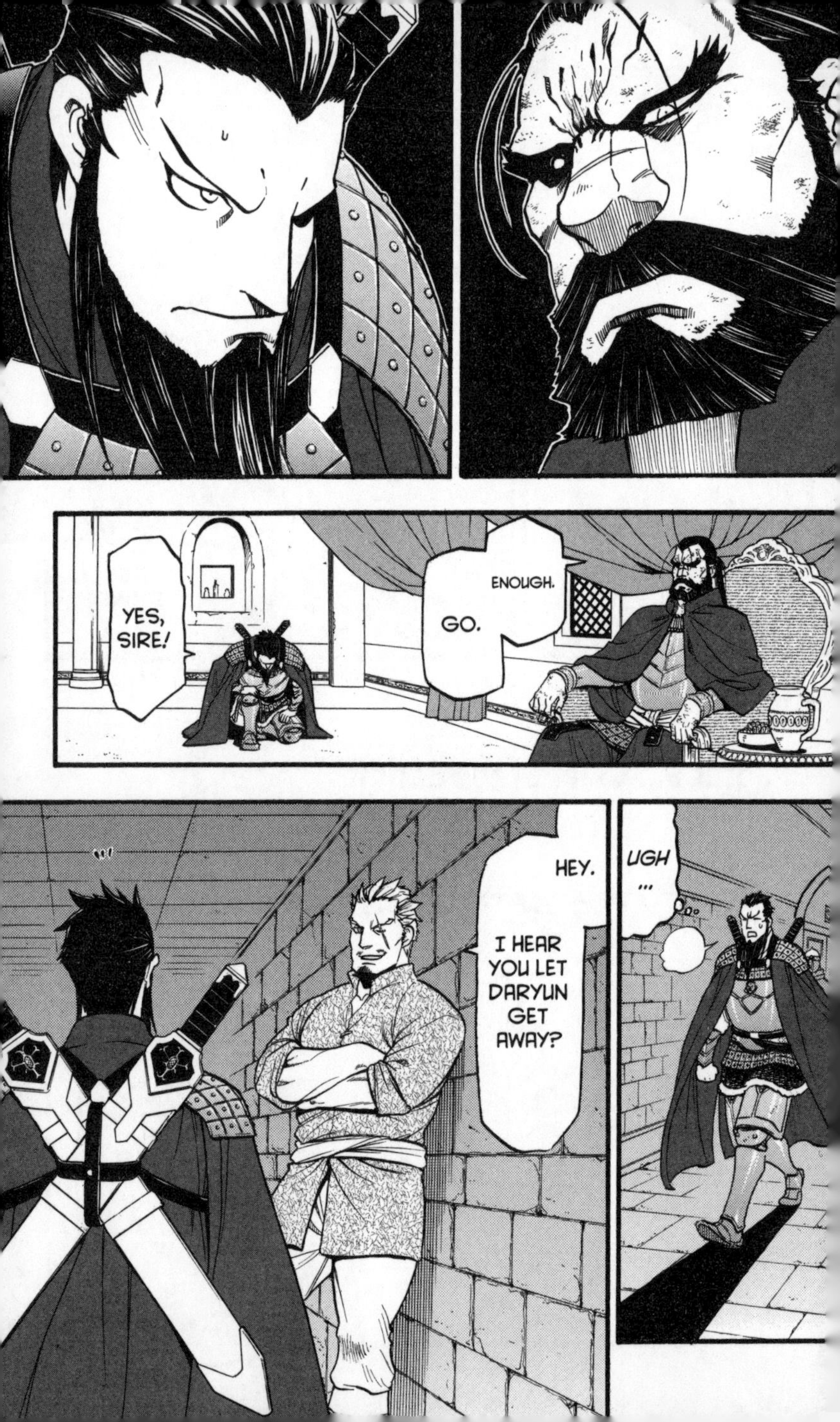
ENOUGH.
GO.
YES, SIRE!
UGH ...
HEY.
I HEAR YOU LET DARYUN GET AWAY?

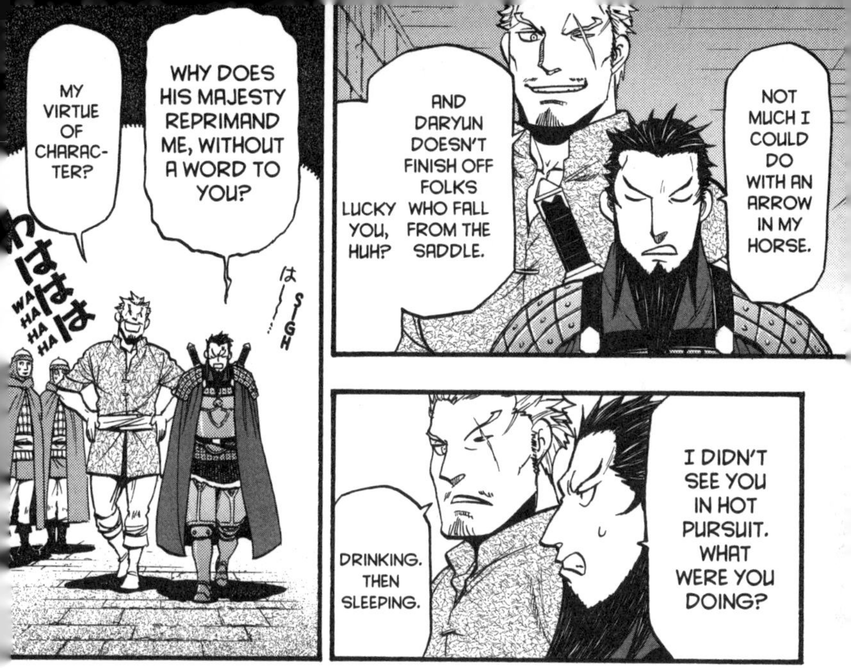
NOT MUCH I COULD DO WITH AN ARROW IN MY HORSE.
AND DARYUN DOESN'T FINISH OFF FOLKS WHO FALL FROM THE SADDLE.
LUCKY YOU, HUH?
I DIDN'T SEE YOU IN HOT PURSUIT. WHAT WERE YOU DOING?
DRINKING. THEN SLEEPING.
WHY DOES HIS MAJESTY REPRIMAND ME, WITHOUT A WORD TO YOU?
MY VIRTUE OF CHARACTER?
わははは
WA HA HA HA
は～…
SIGH

Chapter 93: Chief of the Bandits

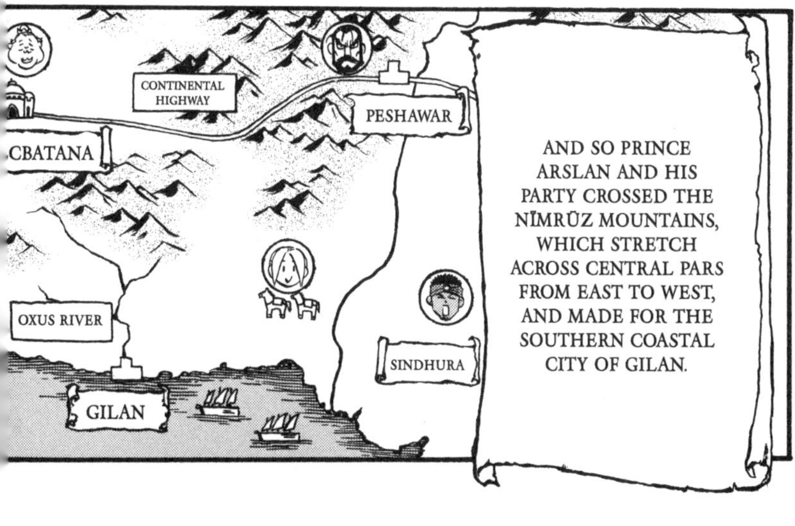
AND SO PRINCE ARSLAN AND HIS PARTY CROSSED THE NĪMRŪZ MOUNTAINS, WHICH STRETCH ACROSS CENTRAL PARS FROM EAST TO WEST, AND MADE FOR THE SOUTHERN COASTAL CITY OF GILAN.
CONTINENTAL HIGHWAY
PESHAWAR
CBATANA
OXUS RIVER
SINDHURA
GILAN

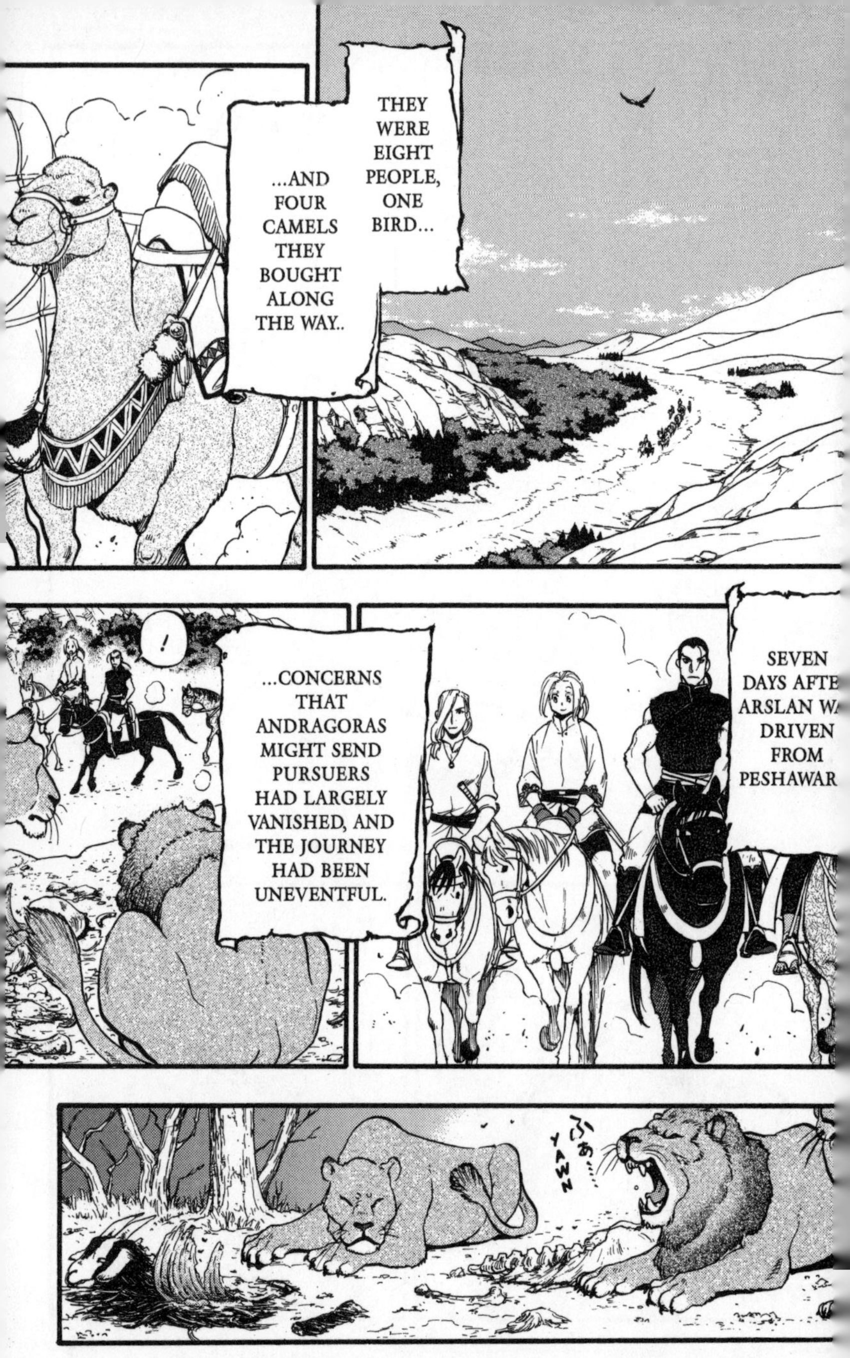

THEY WERE EIGHT PEOPLE, ONE BIRD...
...AND FOUR CAMELS THEY BOUGHT ALONG THE WAY..
SEVEN DAYS AFTE ARSLAN WA DRIVEN FROM PESHAWAR
...CONCERNS THAT ANDRAGORAS MIGHT SEND PURSUERS HAD LARGELY VANISHED, AND THE JOURNEY HAD BEEN UNEVENTFUL.
!
ふあ…… YAWN

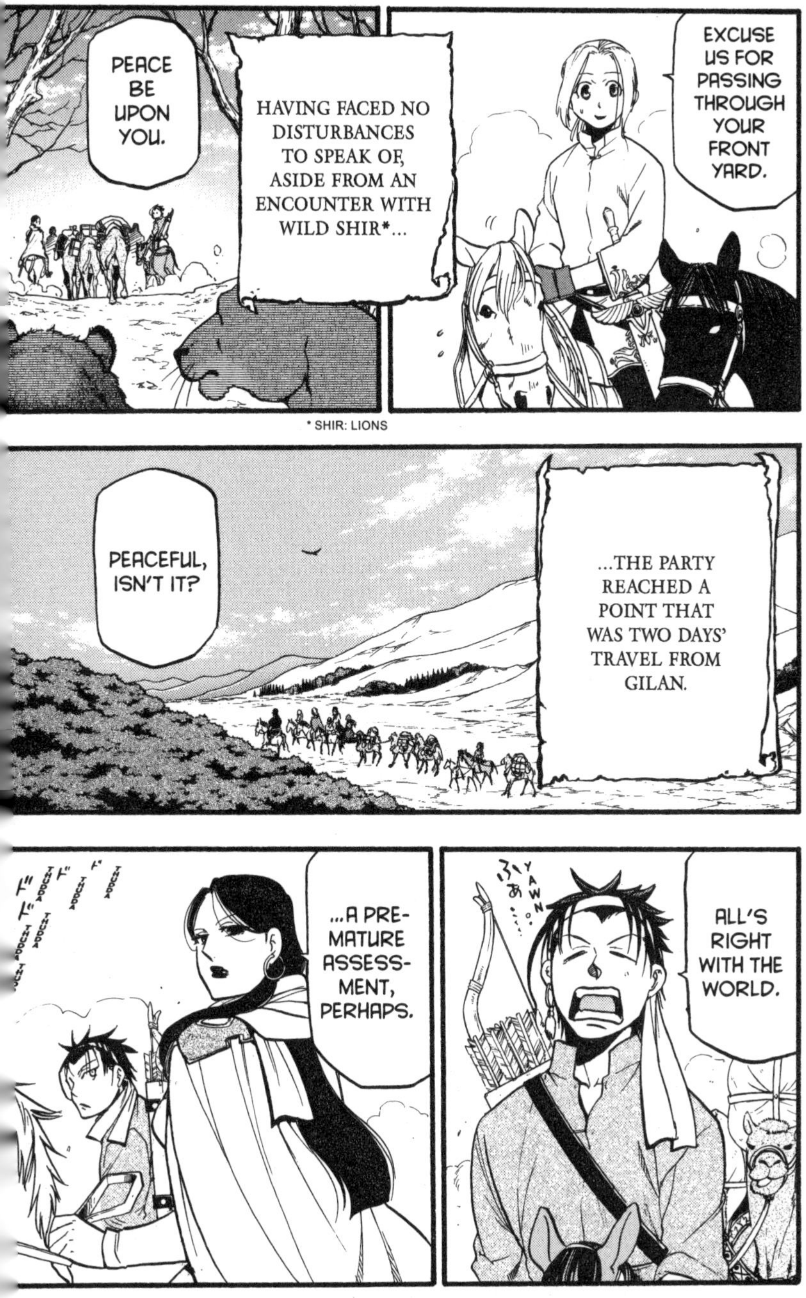
EXCUSE US FOR PASSING THROUGH YOUR FRONT YARD.
HAVING FACED NO DISTURBANCES TO SPEAK OF, ASIDE FROM AN ENCOUNTER WITH WILD SHIR*...
PEACE BE UPON YOU.
* SHIR: LIONS
...THE PARTY REACHED A POINT THAT WAS TWO DAYS' TRAVEL FROM GILAN.
PEACEFUL, ISN'T IT?
ふあ YAWN
ALL'S RIGHT WITH THE WORLD.
ドド THUDDA THUDDA
...A PREMATURE ASSESSMENT, PERHAPS.

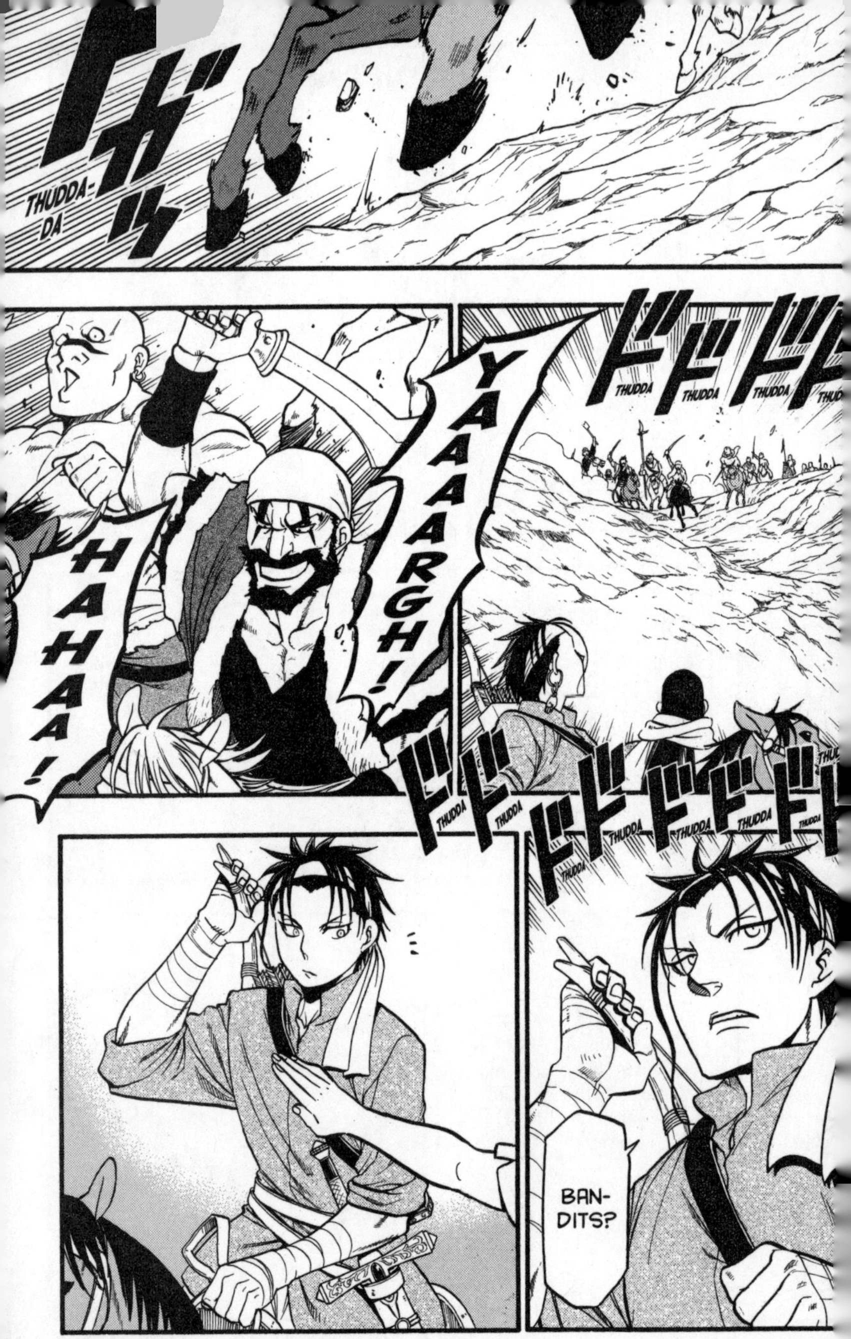

THUDDA-DA
THUDDA THUDDA THUDDA THUDDA
YAAAAARGH!
HAHAHAA!
THUDDA THUDDA THUDDA THUDDA THUDDA THUDDA THUDDA THUDDA
BAN-DITS?

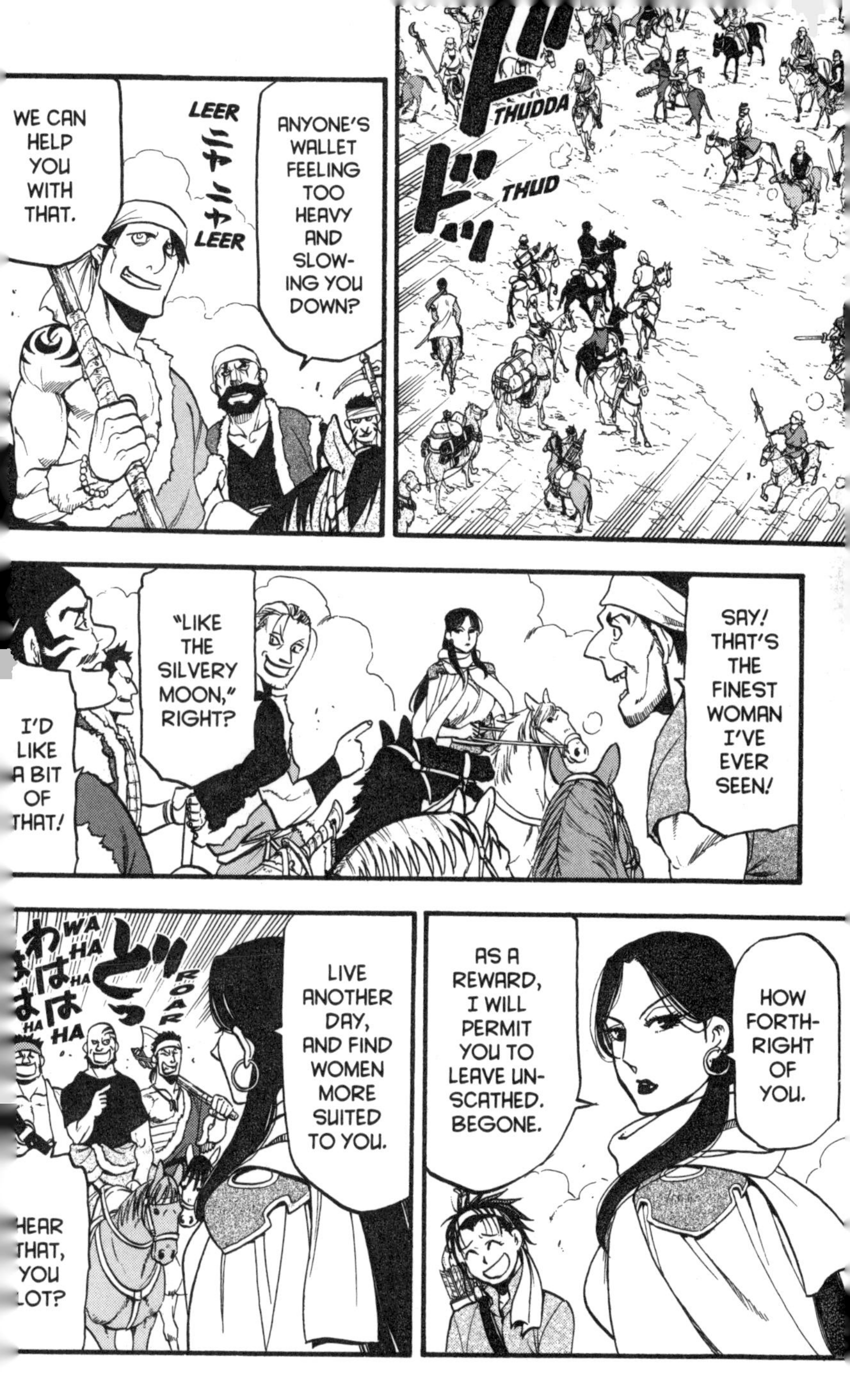

THUDDA
THUD
ANYONE'S WALLET FEELING TOO HEAVY AND SLOWING YOU DOWN?
LEER ニヤニヤ LEER
WE CAN HELP YOU WITH THAT.
SAY! THAT'S THE FINEST WOMAN I'VE EVER SEEN!
"LIKE THE SILVERY MOON," RIGHT?
I'D LIKE A BIT OF THAT!
HOW FORTH-RIGHT OF YOU.
AS A REWARD, I WILL PERMIT YOU TO LEAVE UN-SCATHED. BEGONE.
LIVE ANOTHER DAY, AND FIND WOMEN MORE SUITED TO YOU.
ROAR
WA HA HA HA HA
HEAR THAT, YOU LOT?

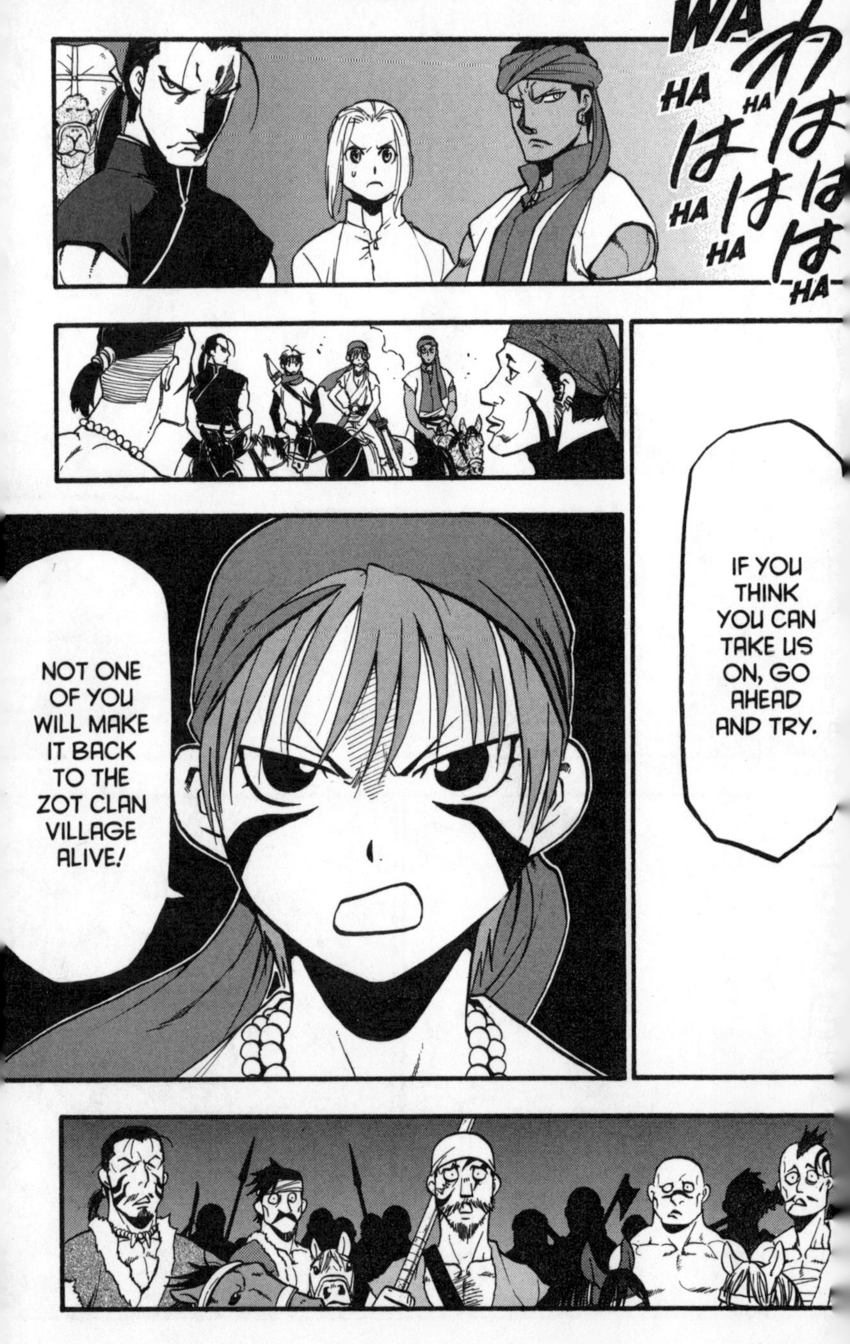

WA HA HA HA HA HA
わははははは
IF YOU THINK YOU CAN TAKE US ON, GO AHEAD AND TRY.
NOT ONE OF YOU WILL MAKE IT BACK TO THE ZOT CLAN VILLAGE ALIVE!

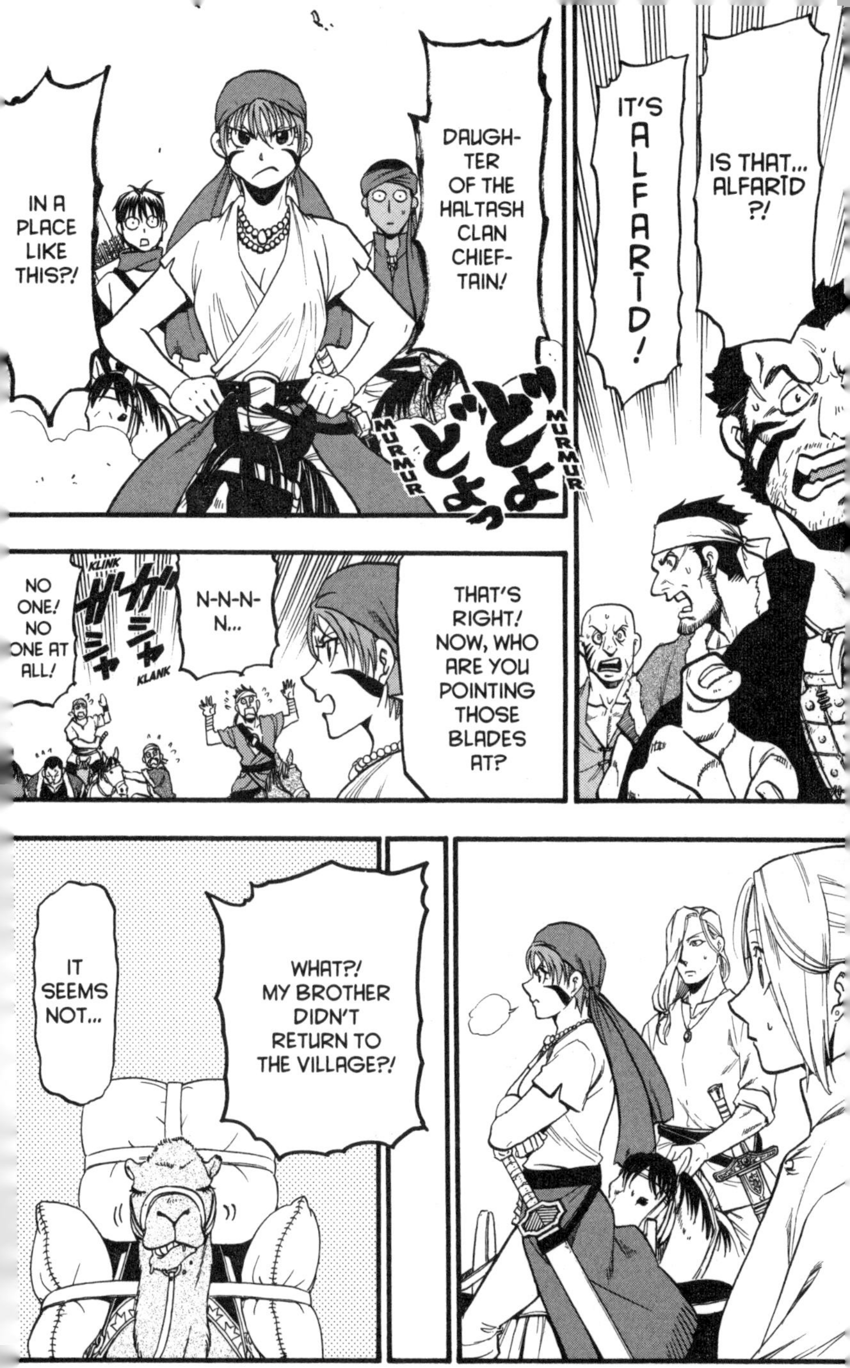
IS THAT... ALFARID ?!
IT'S ALFARID!
DAUGHTER OF THE HALTASH CLAN CHIEFTAIN!
IN A PLACE LIKE THIS?!
MURMUR
どよっ
どよっ
MURMUR
THAT'S RIGHT! NOW, WHO ARE YOU POINTING THOSE BLADES AT?
N-N-N-N...
KLINK
ガシャ
ガシャ
KLANK
NO ONE! NO ONE AT ALL!
WHAT?! MY BROTHER DIDN'T RETURN TO THE VILLAGE?!
IT SEEMS NOT...

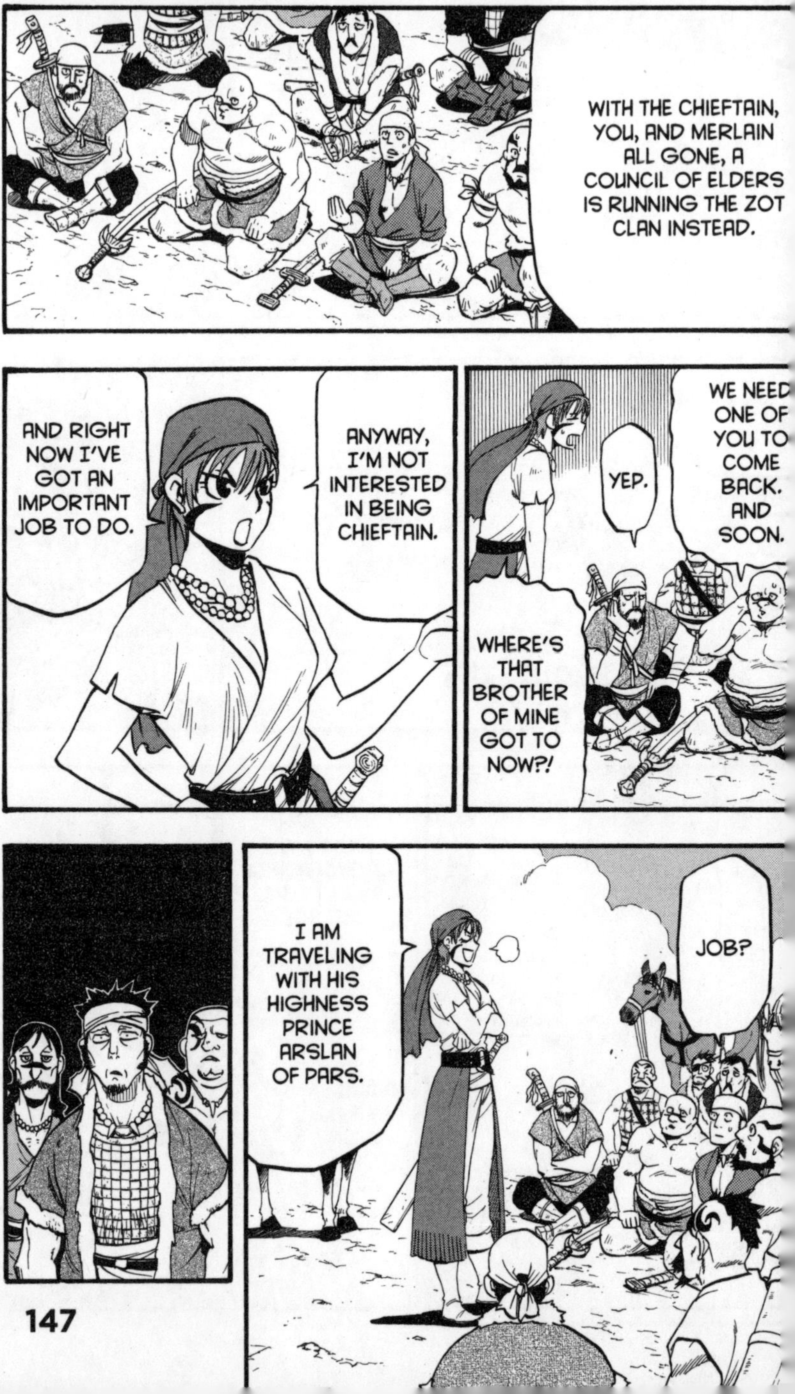
WITH THE CHIEFTAIN, YOU, AND MERLAIN ALL GONE, A COUNCIL OF ELDERS IS RUNNING THE ZOT CLAN INSTEAD.
WE NEED ONE OF YOU TO COME BACK. AND SOON.
YEP.
WHERE'S THAT BROTHER OF MINE GOT TO NOW?!
ANYWAY, I'M NOT INTERESTED IN BEING CHIEFTAIN.
AND RIGHT NOW I'VE GOT AN IMPORTANT JOB TO DO.
JOB?
I AM TRAVELING WITH HIS HIGHNESS PRINCE ARSLAN OF PARS.

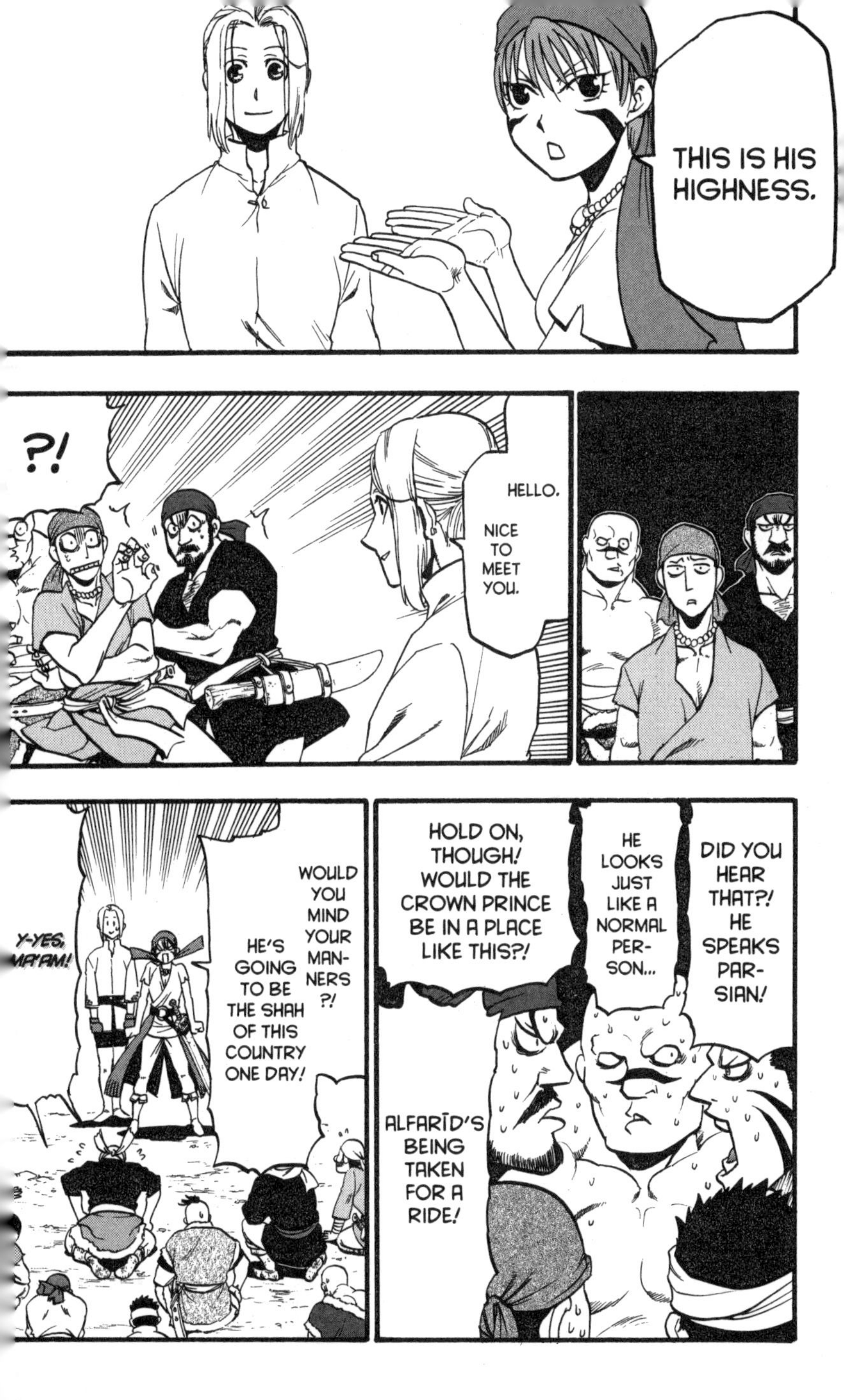
THIS IS HIS HIGHNESS.
HELLO.
NICE TO MEET YOU.
?!
DID YOU HEAR THAT?! HE SPEAKS PAR-SIAN!
HE LOOKS JUST LIKE A NORMAL PER-SON...
HOLD ON, THOUGH! WOULD THE CROWN PRINCE BE IN A PLACE LIKE THIS?!
ALFARĪD'S BEING TAKEN FOR A RIDE!
WOULD YOU MIND YOUR MAN-NERS ?!
HE'S GOING TO BE THE SHAH OF THIS COUNTRY ONE DAY!
Y-YES, MA'AM!

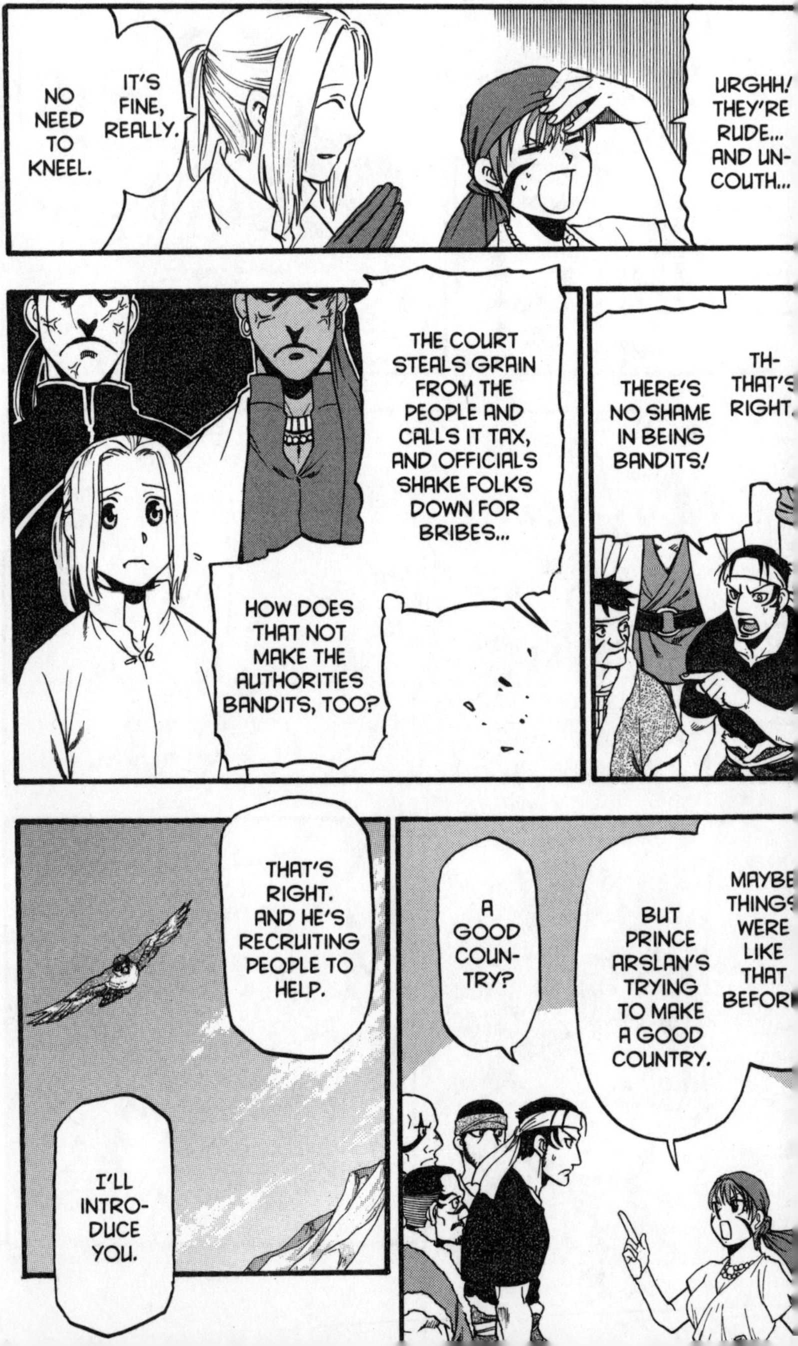
URGHH! THEY'RE RUDE... AND UN-COUTH...
IT'S FINE, REALLY.
NO NEED TO KNEEL.
TH-THAT'S RIGHT.
THERE'S NO SHAME IN BEING BANDITS!
THE COURT STEALS GRAIN FROM THE PEOPLE AND CALLS IT TAX, AND OFFICIALS SHAKE FOLKS DOWN FOR BRIBES...
HOW DOES THAT NOT MAKE THE AUTHORITIES BANDITS, TOO?
MAYBE THINGS WERE LIKE THAT BEFOR
BUT PRINCE ARSLAN'S TRYING TO MAKE A GOOD COUNTRY.
A GOOD COUN-TRY?
THAT'S RIGHT. AND HE'S RECRUITING PEOPLE TO HELP.
I'LL INTRO-DUCE YOU.

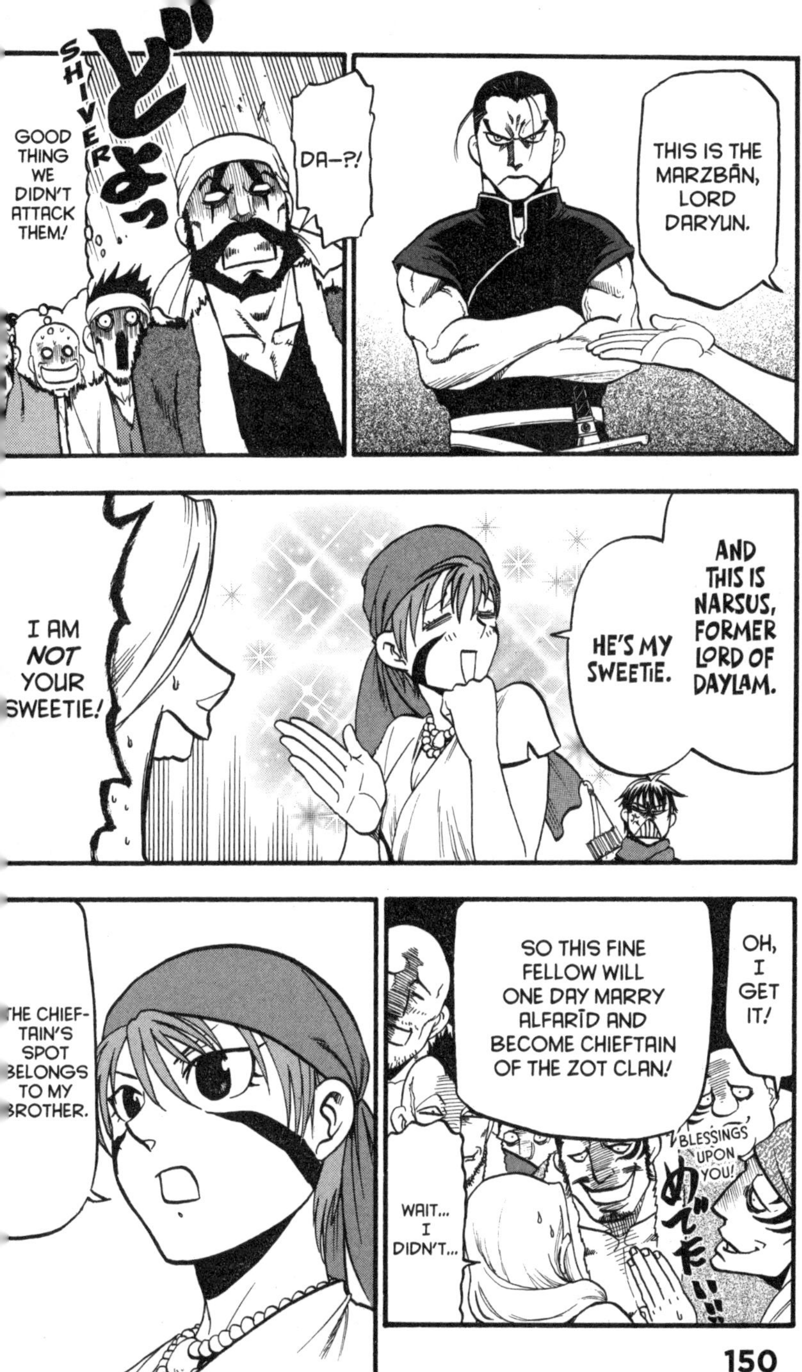
THIS IS THE MARZBĀN, LORD DARYUN.
DA—?!
SHIVER
GOOD THING WE DIDN'T ATTACK THEM!
AND THIS IS NARSUS, FORMER LORD OF DAYLAM.
HE'S MY SWEETIE.
I AM *NOT* YOUR SWEETIE!
OH, I GET IT!
SO THIS FINE FELLOW WILL ONE DAY MARRY ALFARĪD AND BECOME CHIEFTAIN OF THE ZOT CLAN!
BLESSINGS UPON YOU!
WAIT... I DIDN'T...
THE CHIEF-TAIN'S SPOT BELONGS TO MY BROTHER.

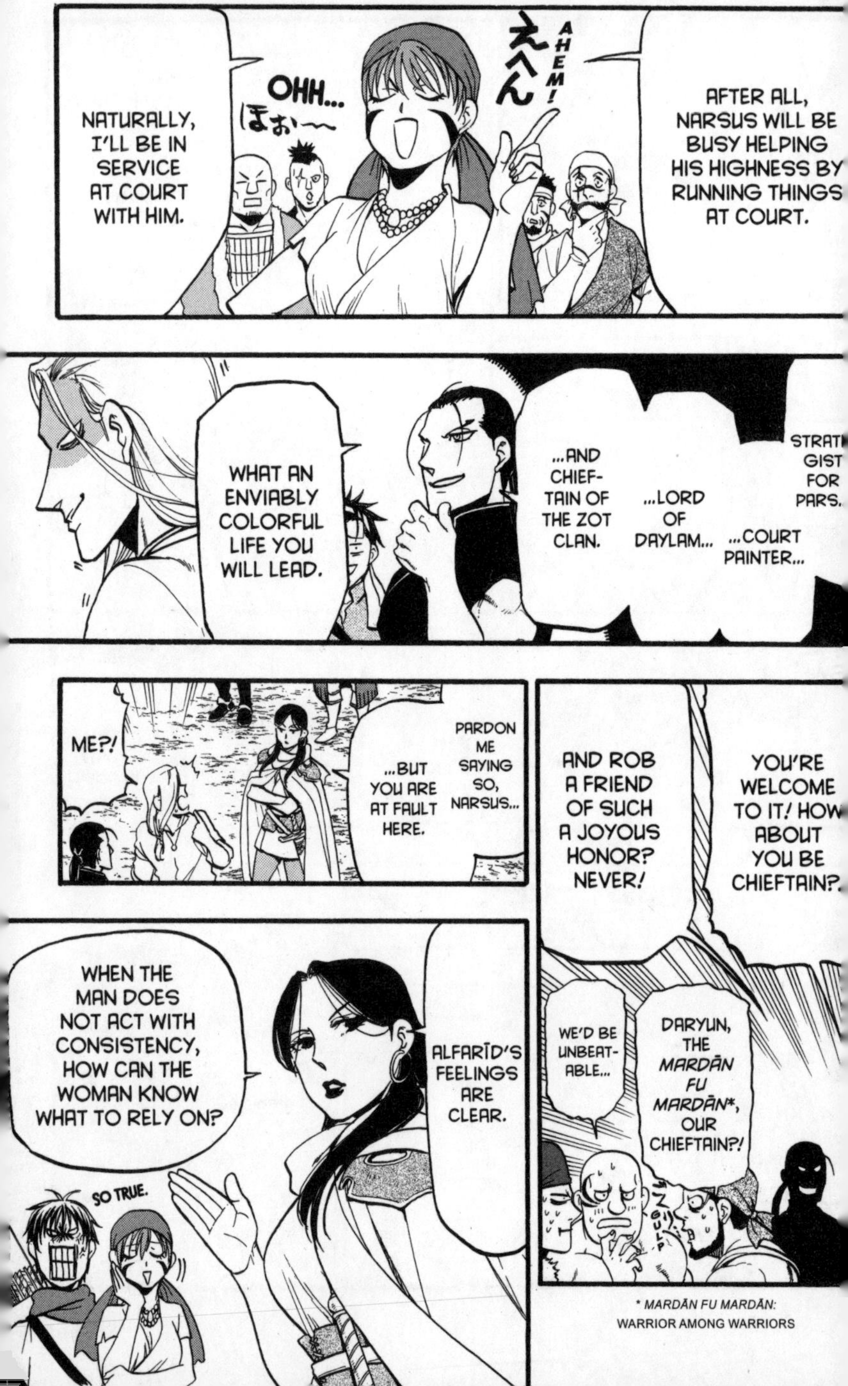
AFTER ALL, NARSUS WILL BE BUSY HELPING HIS HIGHNESS BY RUNNING THINGS AT COURT.
えへん AHEM!
OHH... ほぉ〜〜
NATURALLY, I'LL BE IN SERVICE AT COURT WITH HIM.
STRATEGIST FOR PARS.
...COURT PAINTER...
...LORD OF DAYLAM...
...AND CHIEFTAIN OF THE ZOT CLAN.
WHAT AN ENVIABLY COLORFUL LIFE YOU WILL LEAD.
YOU'RE WELCOME TO IT! HOW ABOUT YOU BE CHIEFTAIN?
AND ROB A FRIEND OF SUCH A JOYOUS HONOR? NEVER!
DARYUN, THE MARDĀN FU MARDĀN*, OUR CHIEFTAIN?!
WE'D BE UNBEATABLE...
GULP
PARDON ME SAYING SO, NARSUS...
...BUT YOU ARE AT FAULT HERE.
ME?!
ALFARĪD'S FEELINGS ARE CLEAR.
WHEN THE MAN DOES NOT ACT WITH CONSISTENCY, HOW CAN THE WOMAN KNOW WHAT TO RELY ON?
SO TRUE.

* *MARDĀN FU MARDĀN:* WARRIOR AMONG WARRIORS

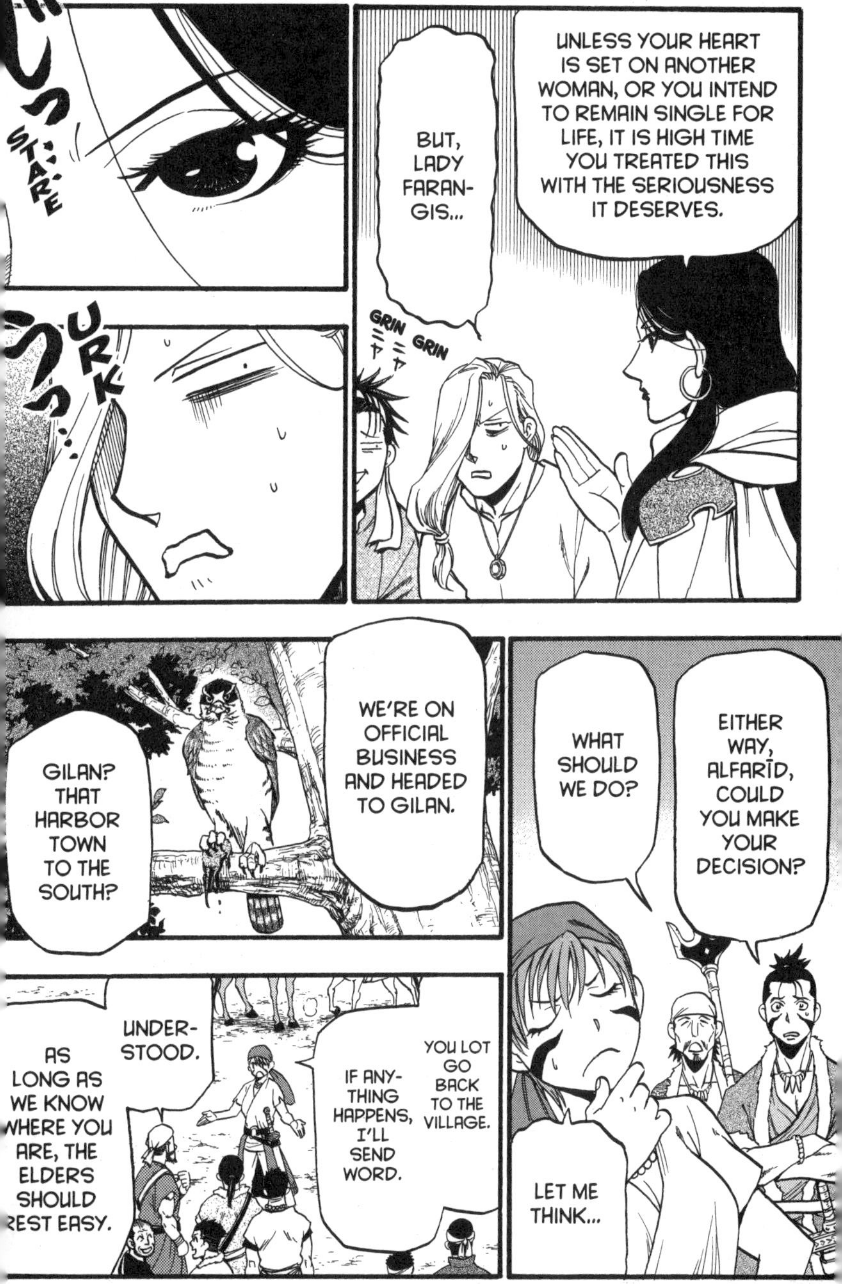
UNLESS YOUR HEART IS SET ON ANOTHER WOMAN, OR YOU INTEND TO REMAIN SINGLE FOR LIFE, IT IS HIGH TIME YOU TREATED THIS WITH THE SERIOUSNESS IT DESERVES.
BUT, LADY FARAN-GIS...
GRIN GRIN
STARE
URK
EITHER WAY, ALFARĪD, COULD YOU MAKE YOUR DECISION?
WHAT SHOULD WE DO?
LET ME THINK...
WE'RE ON OFFICIAL BUSINESS AND HEADED TO GILAN.
GILAN? THAT HARBOR TOWN TO THE SOUTH?
YOU LOT GO BACK TO THE VILLAGE.
IF ANY-THING HAPPENS, I'LL SEND WORD.
UNDER-STOOD.
AS LONG AS WE KNOW WHERE YOU ARE, THE ELDERS SHOULD REST EASY.

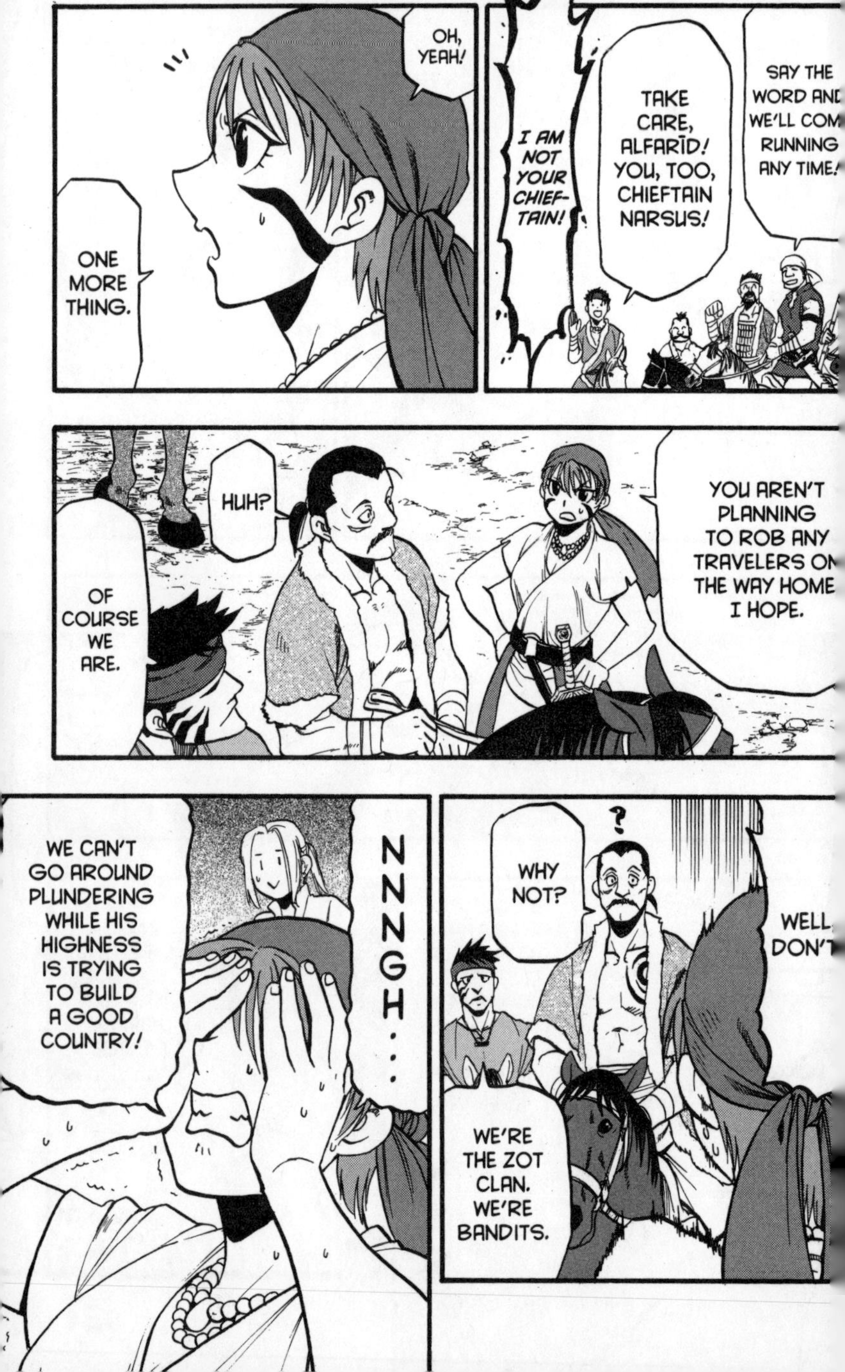
SAY THE WORD AND WE'LL COM RUNNING ANY TIME!
TAKE CARE, ALFARĪD! YOU, TOO, CHIEFTAIN NARSUS!
I AM NOT YOUR CHIEF-TAIN!
OH, YEAH!
ONE MORE THING.
YOU AREN'T PLANNING TO ROB ANY TRAVELERS ON THE WAY HOME I HOPE.
HUH?
OF COURSE WE ARE.
WELL, DON'T
WHY NOT?
WE'RE THE ZOT CLAN. WE'RE BANDITS.
NNNGH...
WE CAN'T GO AROUND PLUNDERING WHILE HIS HIGHNESS IS TRYING TO BUILD A GOOD COUNTRY!

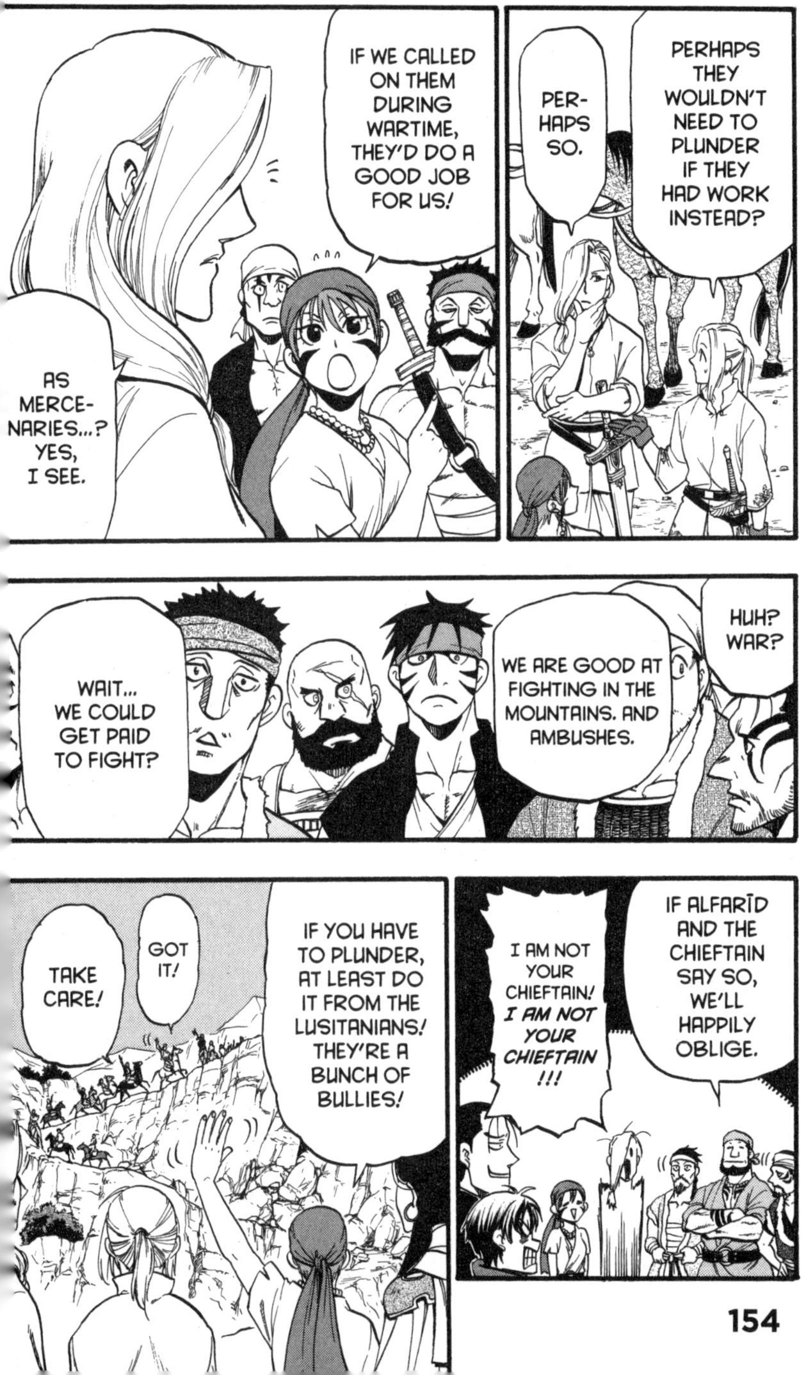

PERHAPS THEY WOULDN'T NEED TO PLUNDER IF THEY HAD WORK INSTEAD?
PER-HAPS SO.
IF WE CALLED ON THEM DURING WARTIME, THEY'D DO A GOOD JOB FOR US!
AS MERCE-NARIES...? YES, I SEE.
HUH? WAR?
WE ARE GOOD AT FIGHTING IN THE MOUNTAINS. AND AMBUSHES.
WAIT... WE COULD GET PAID TO FIGHT?
IF ALFARĪD AND THE CHIEFTAIN SAY SO, WE'LL HAPPILY OBLIGE.
I AM NOT YOUR CHIEFTAIN! *I AM NOT YOUR CHIEFTAIN!!!*
IF YOU HAVE TO PLUNDER, AT LEAST DO IT FROM THE LUSITANIANS! THEY'RE A BUNCH OF BULLIES!
GOT IT!
TAKE CARE!

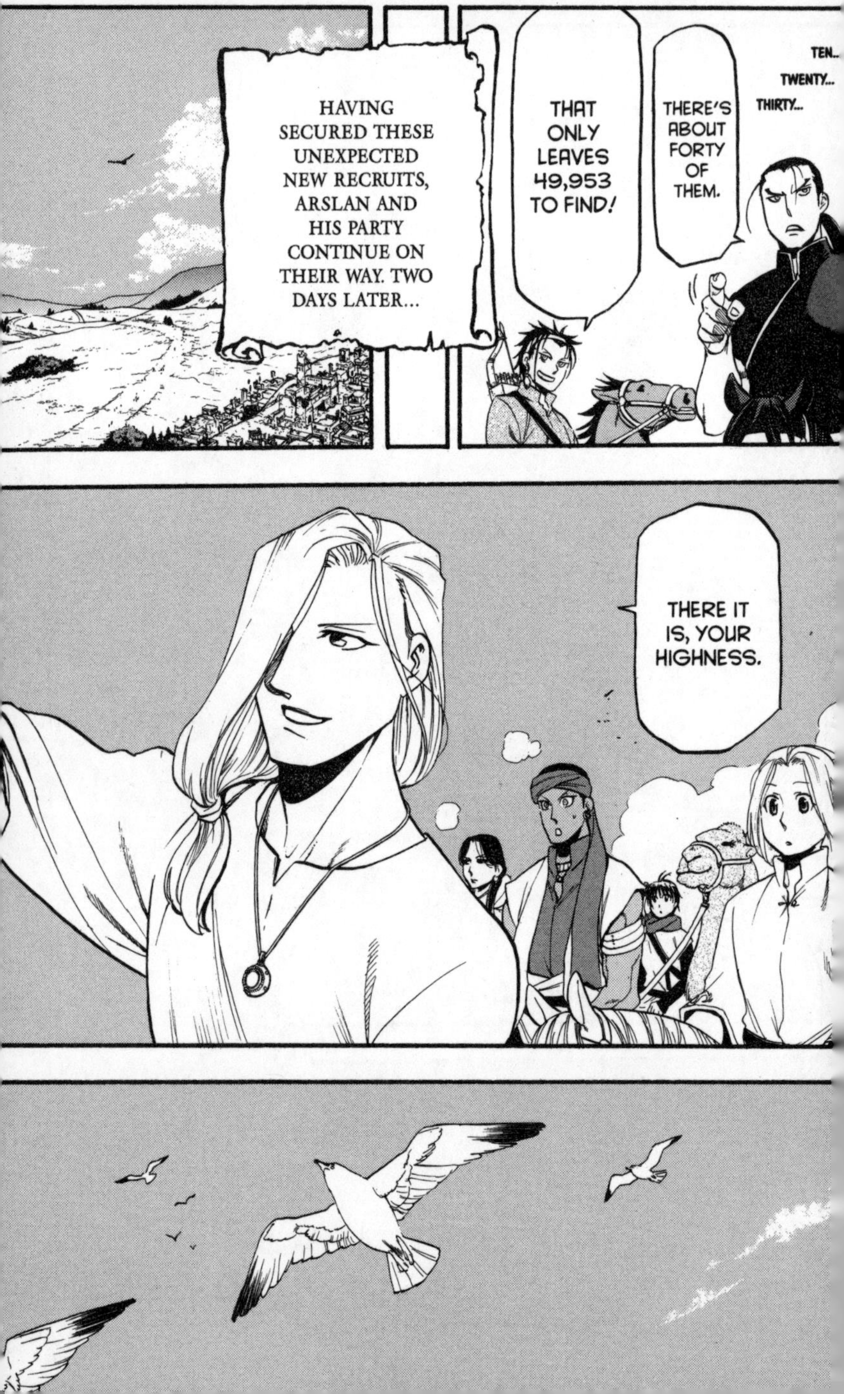
TEN...
TWENTY...
THIRTY...
THERE'S ABOUT FORTY OF THEM.
THAT ONLY LEAVES 49,953 TO FIND!
HAVING SECURED THESE UNEXPECTED NEW RECRUITS, ARSLAN AND HIS PARTY CONTINUE ON THEIR WAY. TWO DAYS LATER...
THERE IT IS, YOUR HIGHNESS.

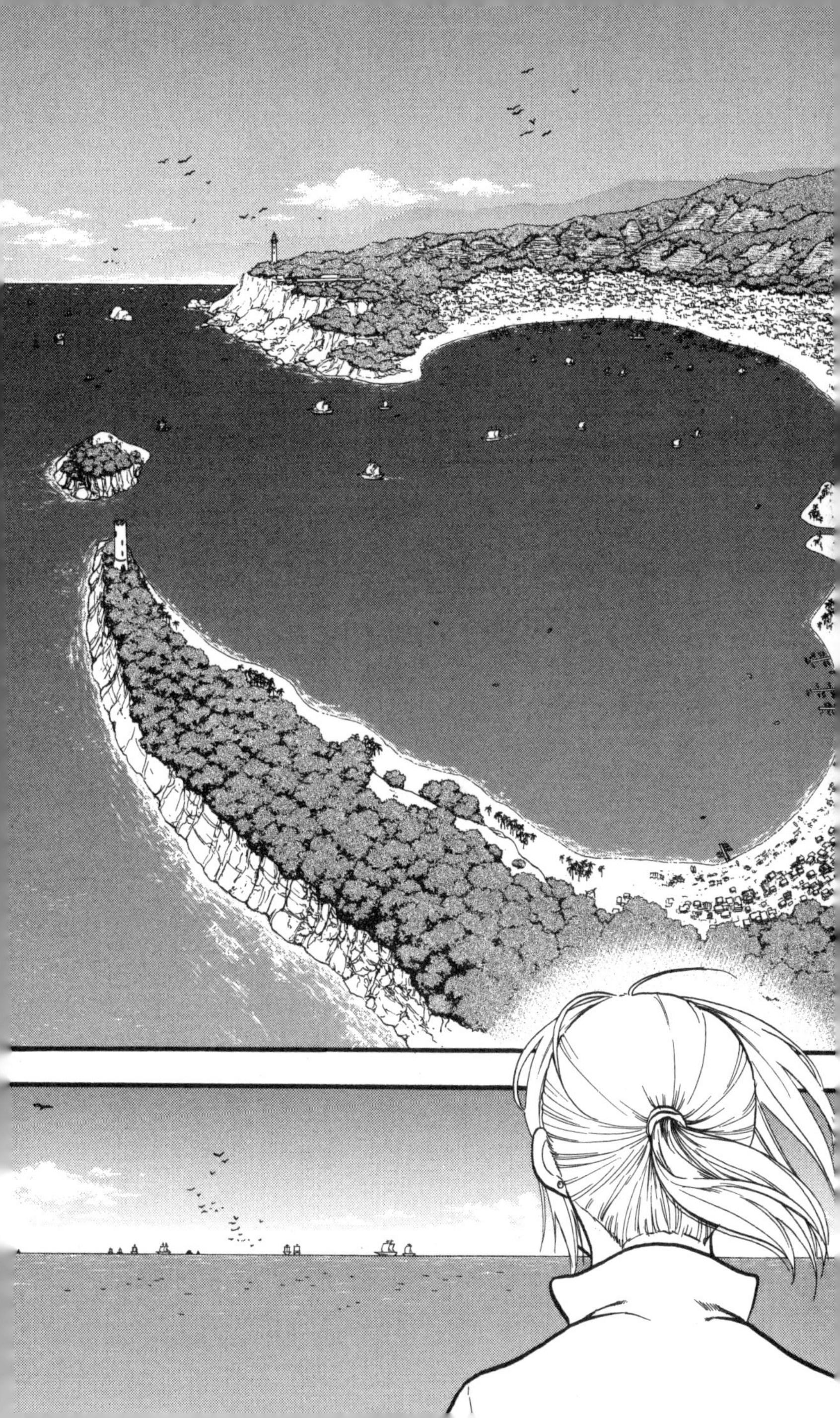

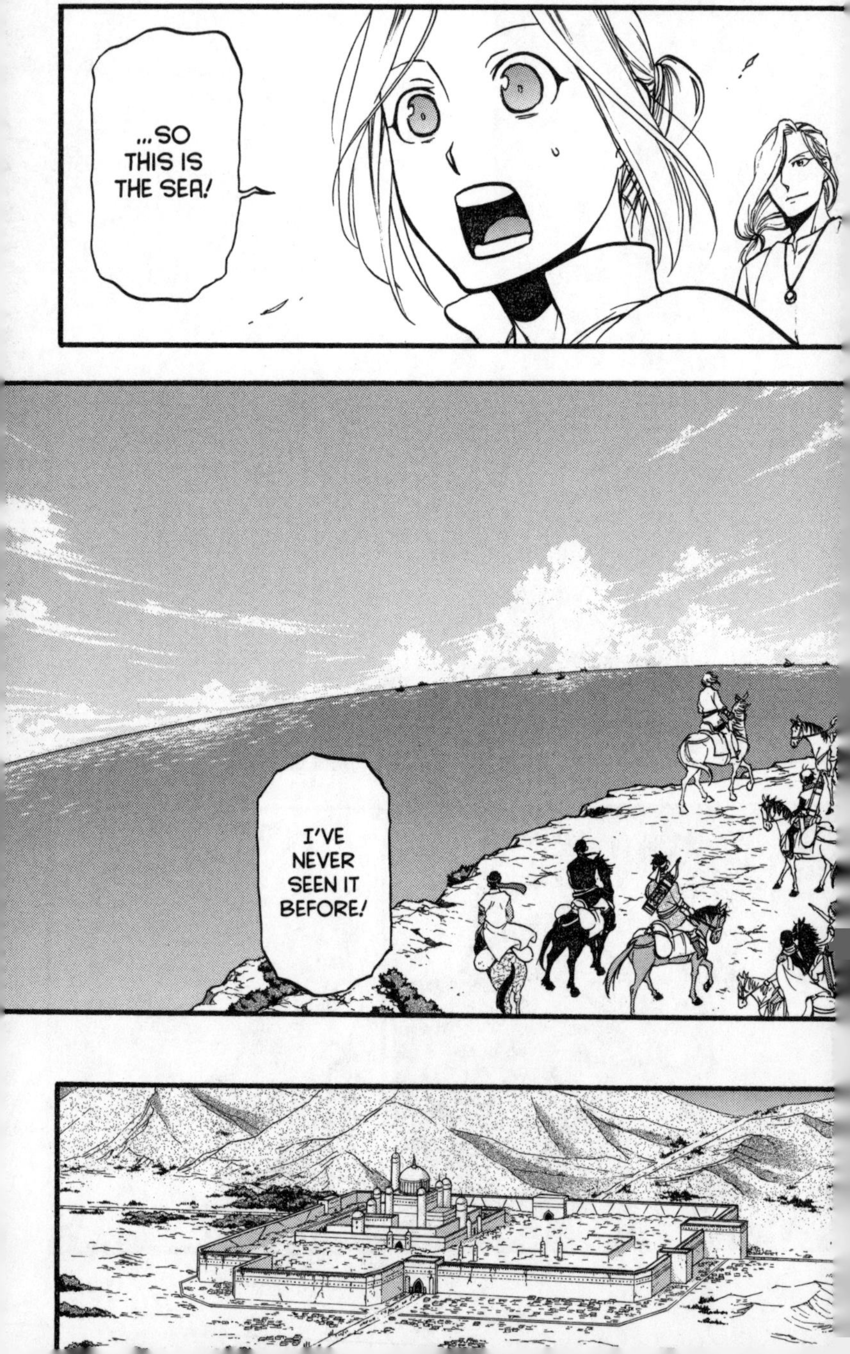
...SO THIS IS THE SEA!
I'VE NEVER SEEN IT BEFORE!

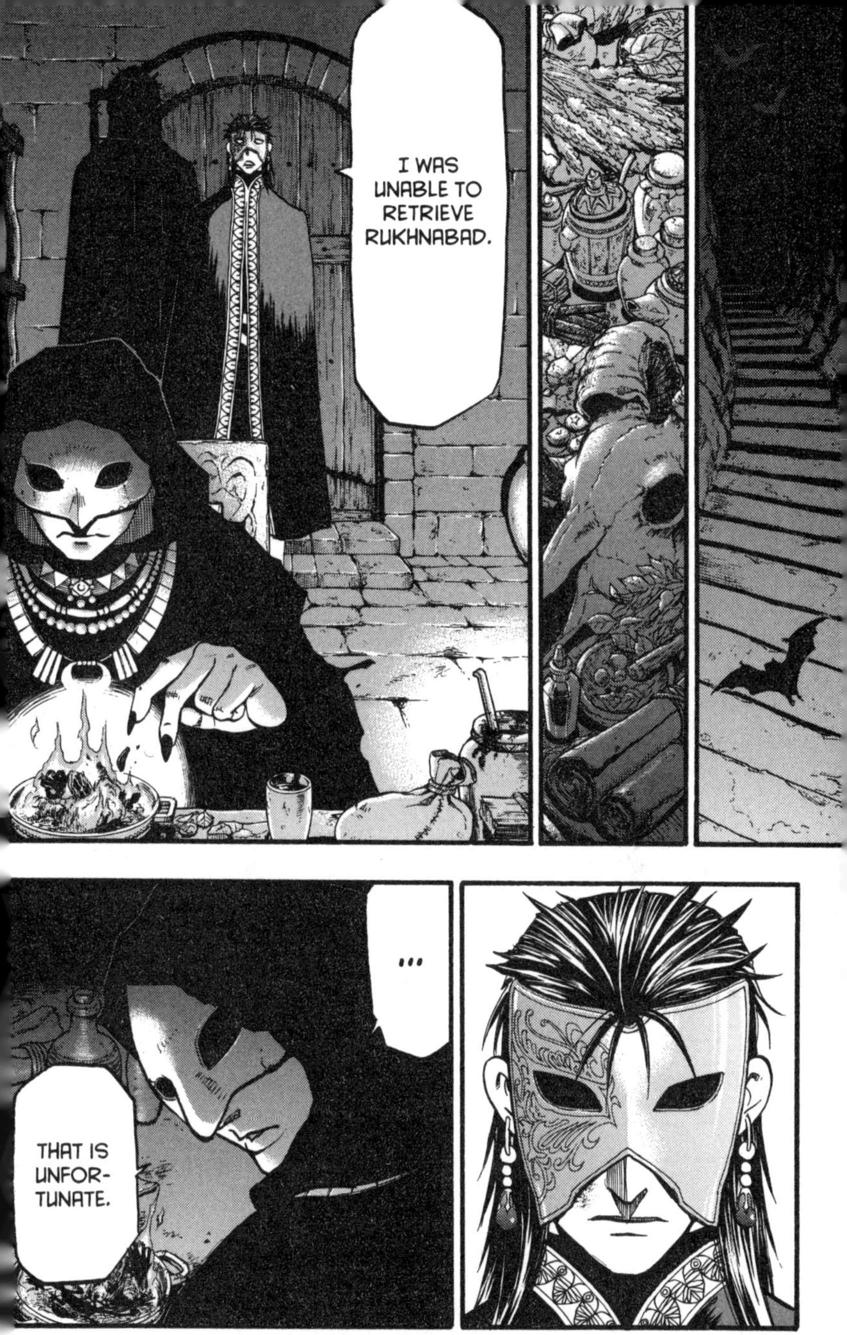
I WAS UNABLE TO RETRIEVE RUKHNABAD.
...
THAT IS UNFOR-TUNATE.

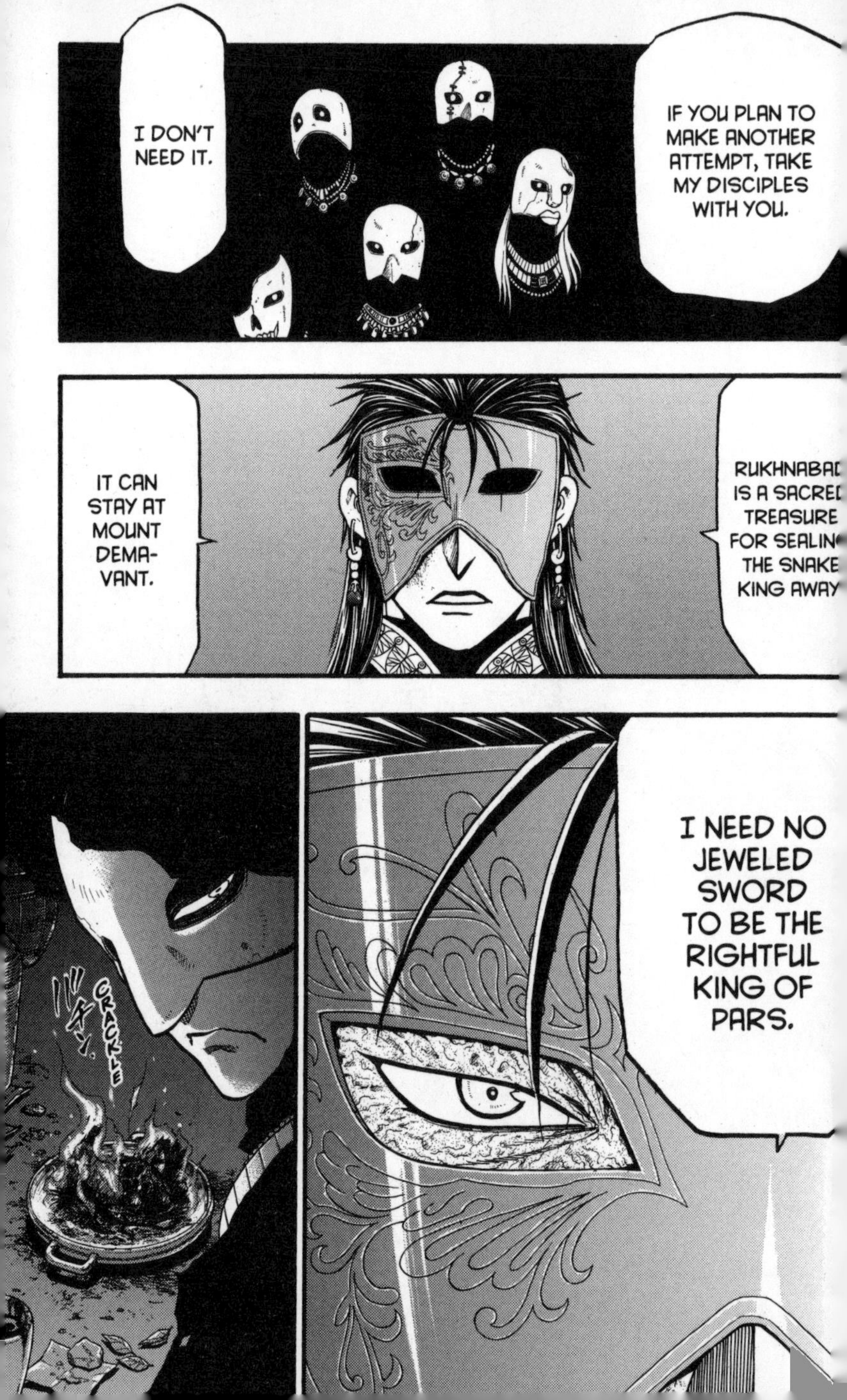
IF YOU PLAN TO MAKE ANOTHER ATTEMPT, TAKE MY DISCIPLES WITH YOU.
I DON'T NEED IT.
RUKHNABAD IS A SACRED TREASURE FOR SEALING THE SNAKE KING AWAY
IT CAN STAY AT MOUNT DEMA-VANT.
I NEED NO JEWELED SWORD TO BE THE RIGHTFUL KING OF PARS.
CRACKLE

THE HEROIC LEGEND OF
ARSLAN

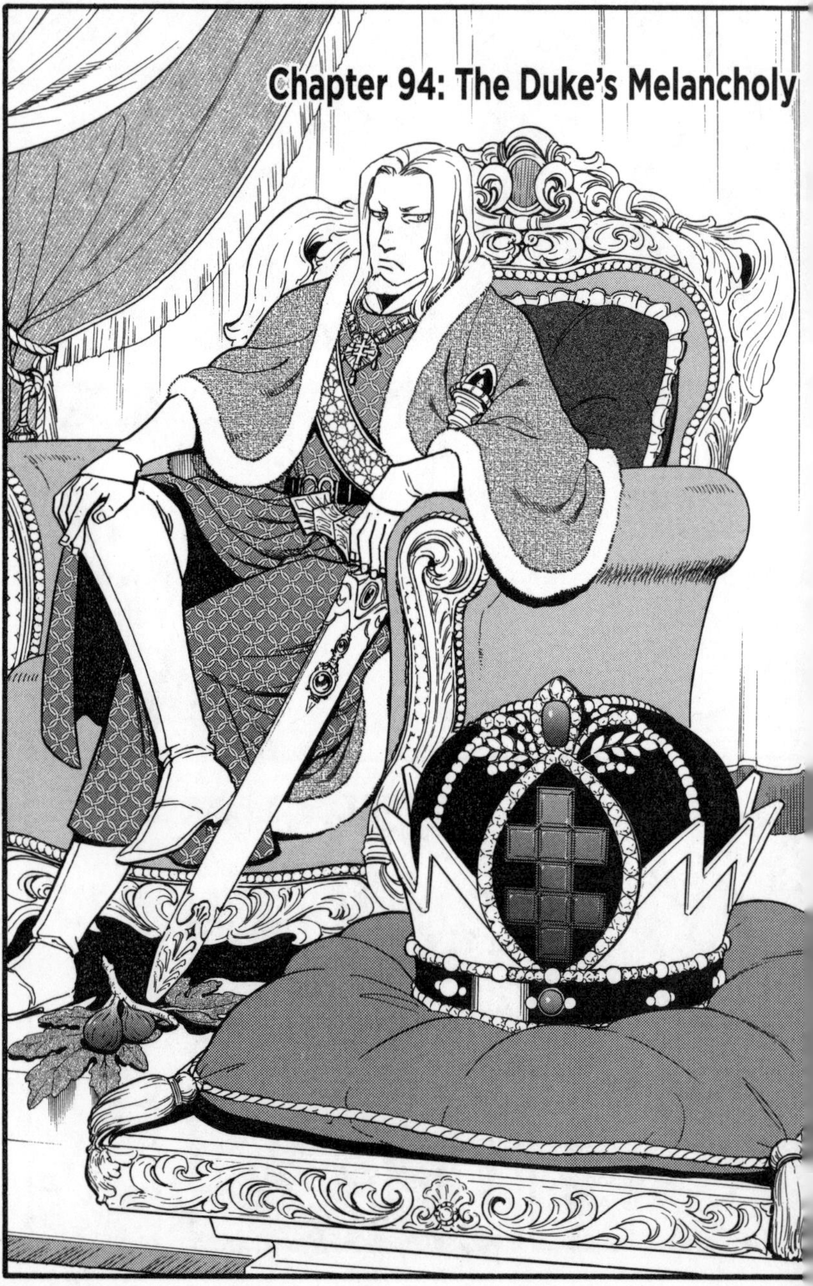
Chapter 94: The Duke's Melancholy

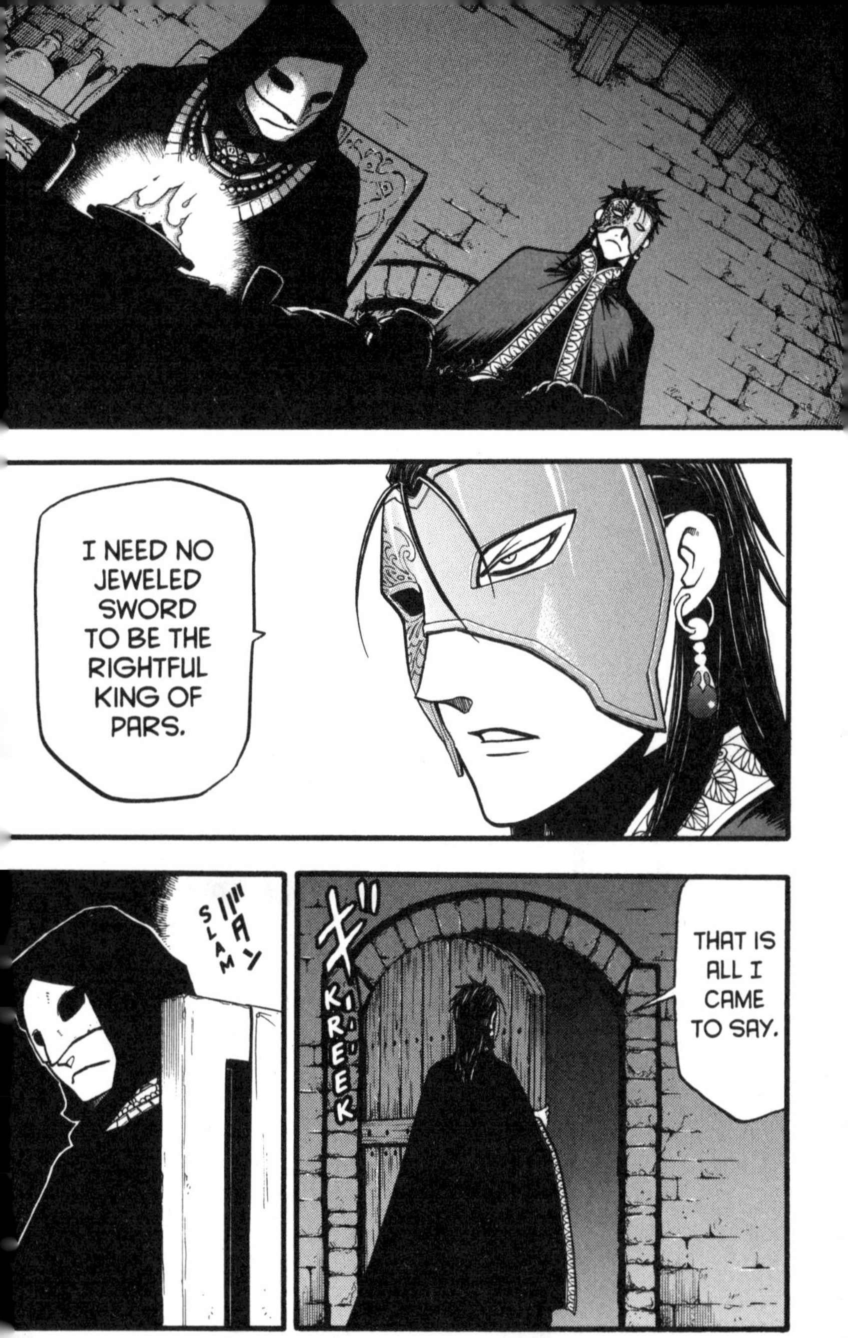
I NEED NO JEWELED SWORD TO BE THE RIGHTFUL KING OF PARS.
THAT IS ALL I CAME TO SAY.
KREEK
SLAM

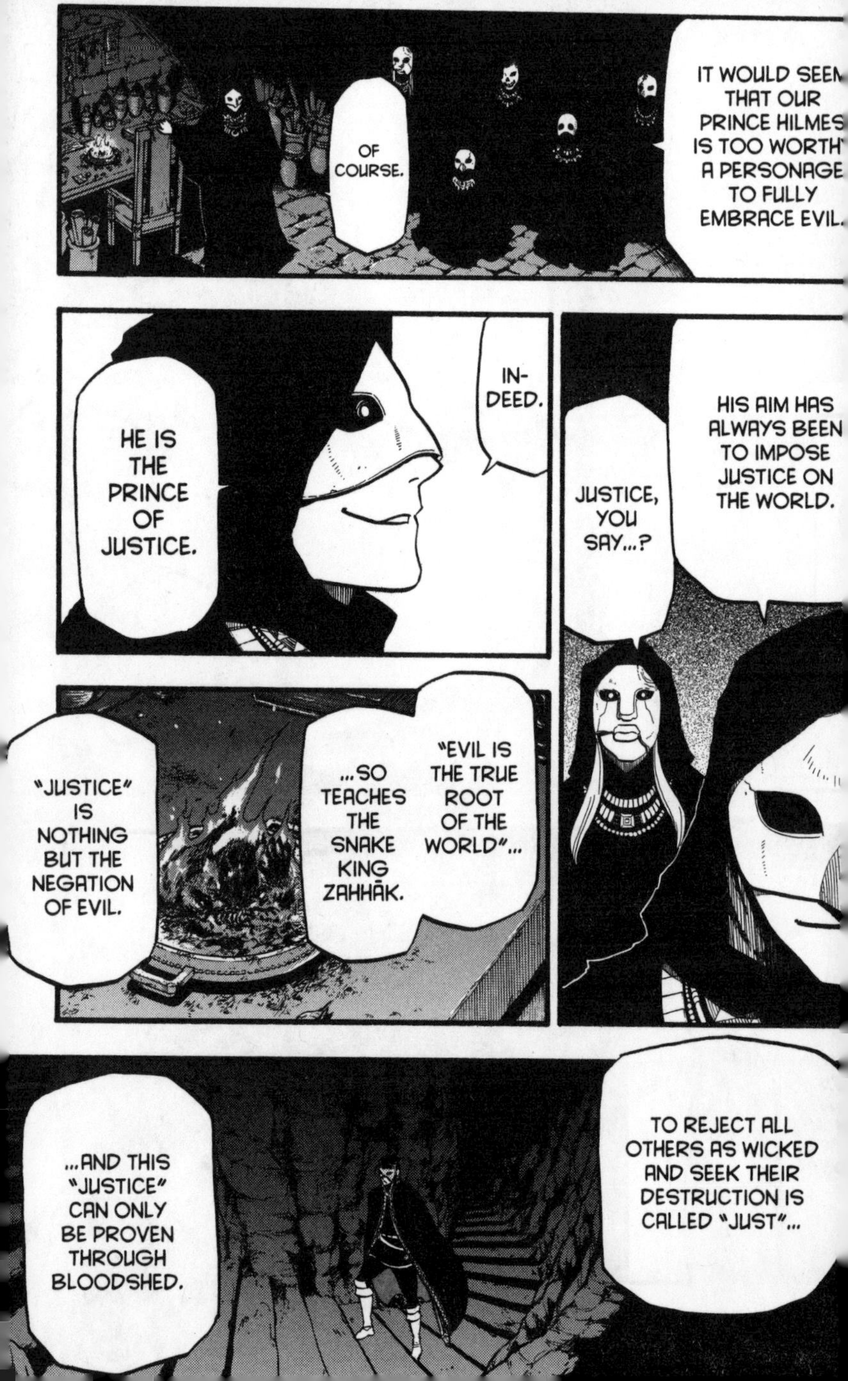
IT WOULD SEEM THAT OUR PRINCE HILMES IS TOO WORTHY A PERSONAGE TO FULLY EMBRACE EVIL.
OF COURSE.
HIS AIM HAS ALWAYS BEEN TO IMPOSE JUSTICE ON THE WORLD.
JUSTICE, YOU SAY...?
IN-DEED.
HE IS THE PRINCE OF JUSTICE.
"EVIL IS THE TRUE ROOT OF THE WORLD"...
...SO TEACHES THE SNAKE KING ZAHHĀK.
"JUSTICE" IS NOTHING BUT THE NEGATION OF EVIL.
TO REJECT ALL OTHERS AS WICKED AND SEEK THEIR DESTRUCTION IS CALLED "JUST"...
...AND THIS "JUSTICE" CAN ONLY BE PROVEN THROUGH BLOODSHED.

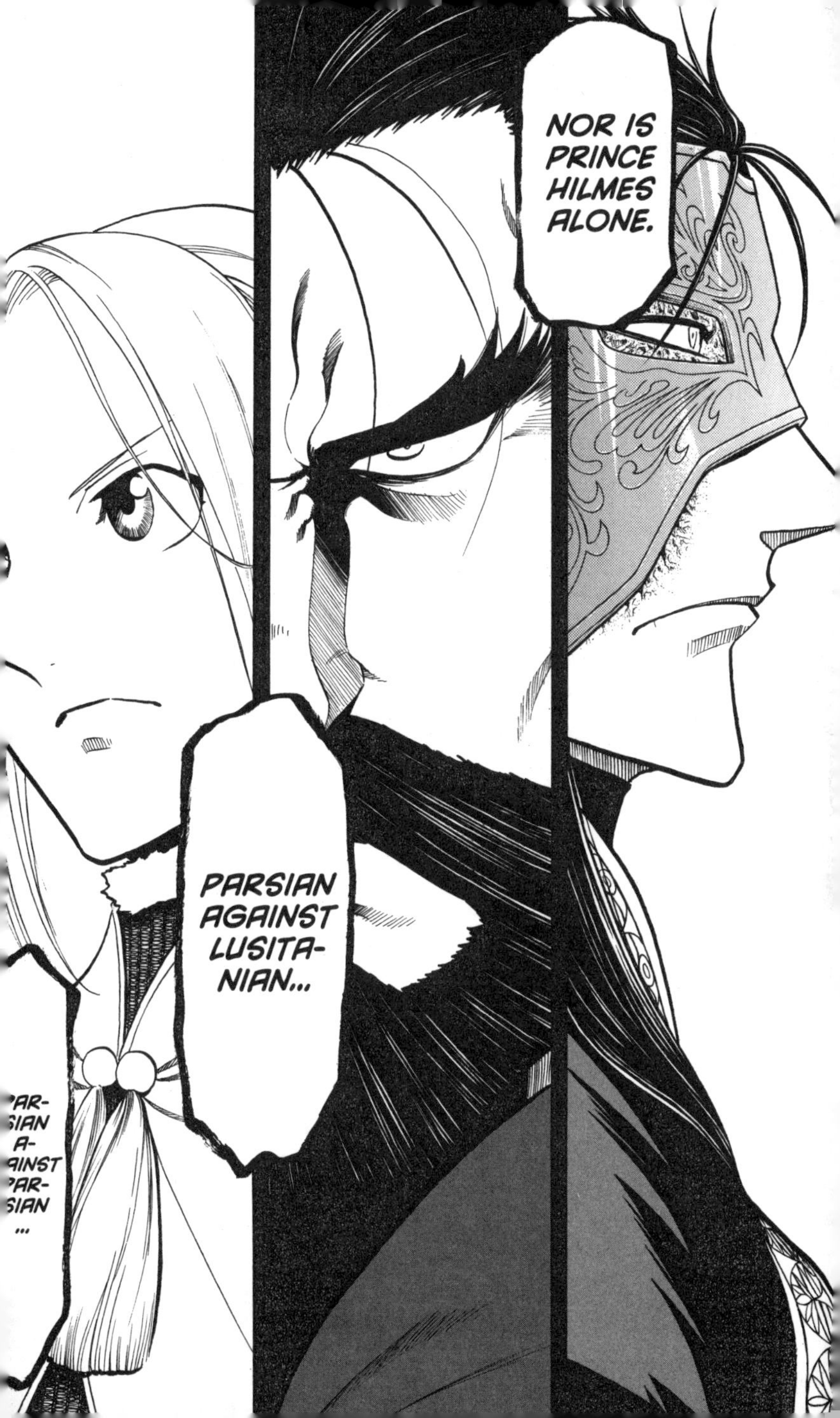
NOR IS PRINCE HILMES ALONE.
PARSIAN AGAINST LUSITA-NIAN...
PAR-SIAN A-AINST PAR-SIAN ...

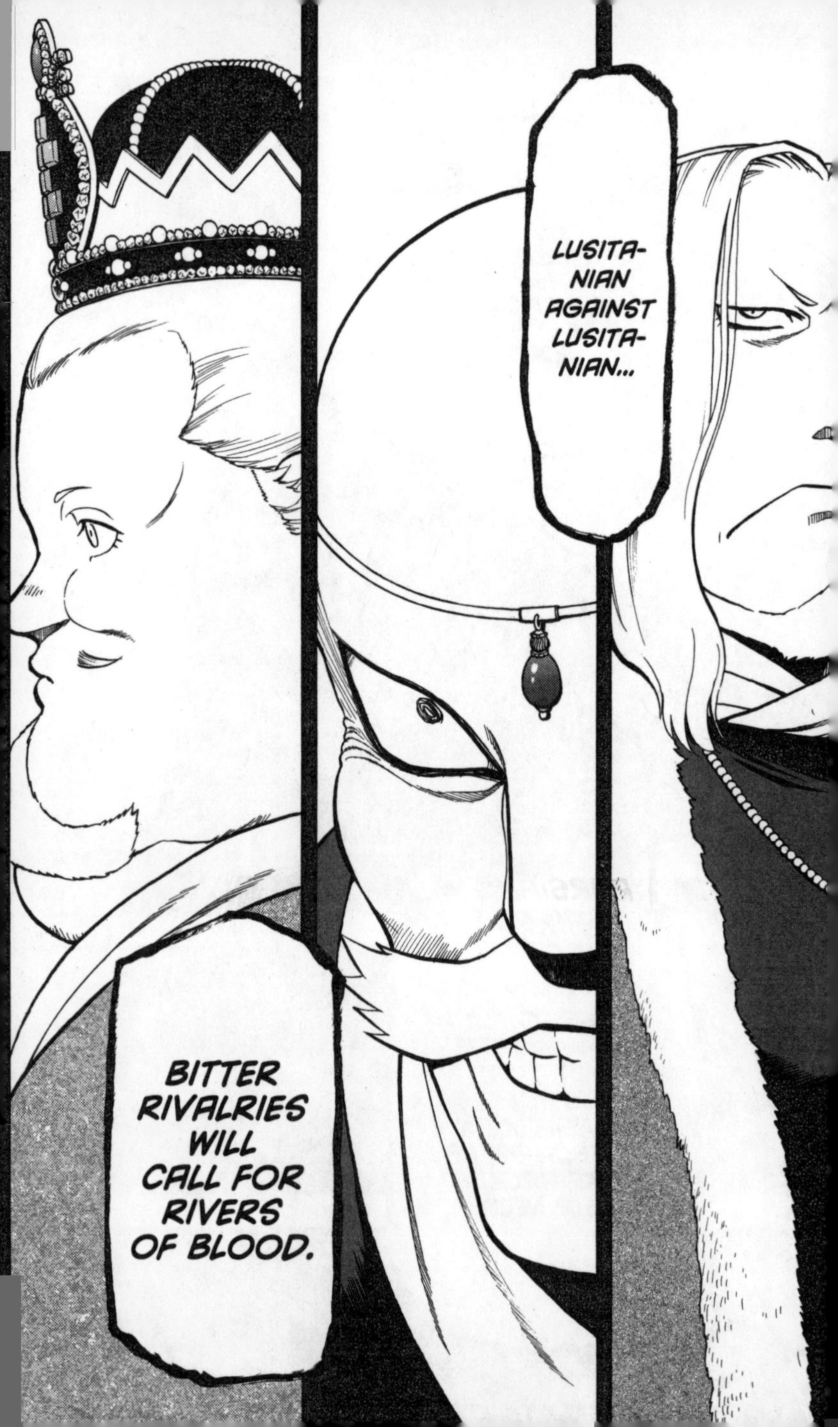
LUSITA-NIAN AGAINST LUSITA-NIAN...
BITTER RIVALRIES WILL CALL FOR RIVERS OF BLOOD.

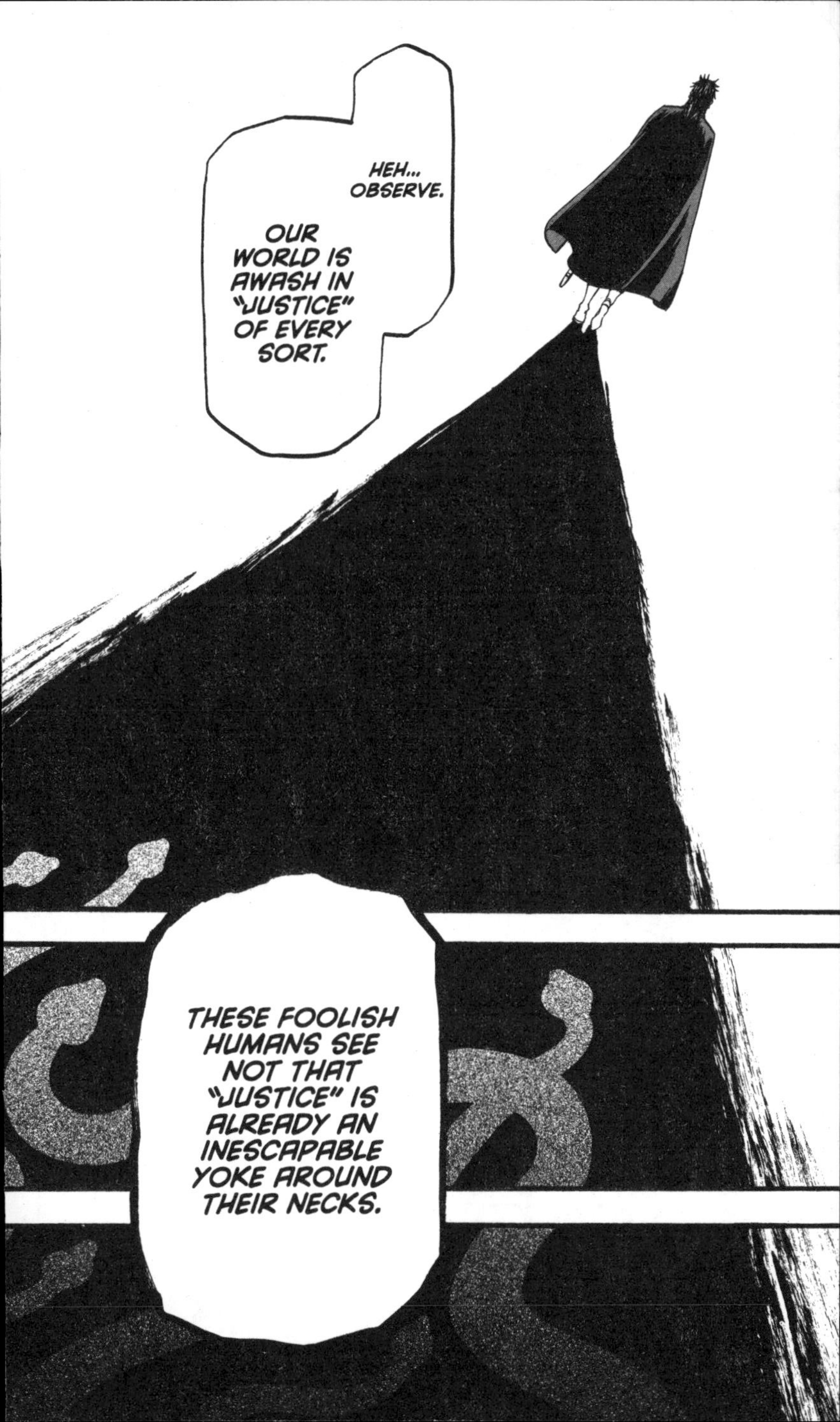
HEH... OBSERVE.
OUR WORLD IS AWASH IN "JUSTICE" OF EVERY SORT.
THESE FOOLISH HUMANS SEE NOT THAT "JUSTICE" IS ALREADY AN INESCAPABLE YOKE AROUND THEIR NECKS.

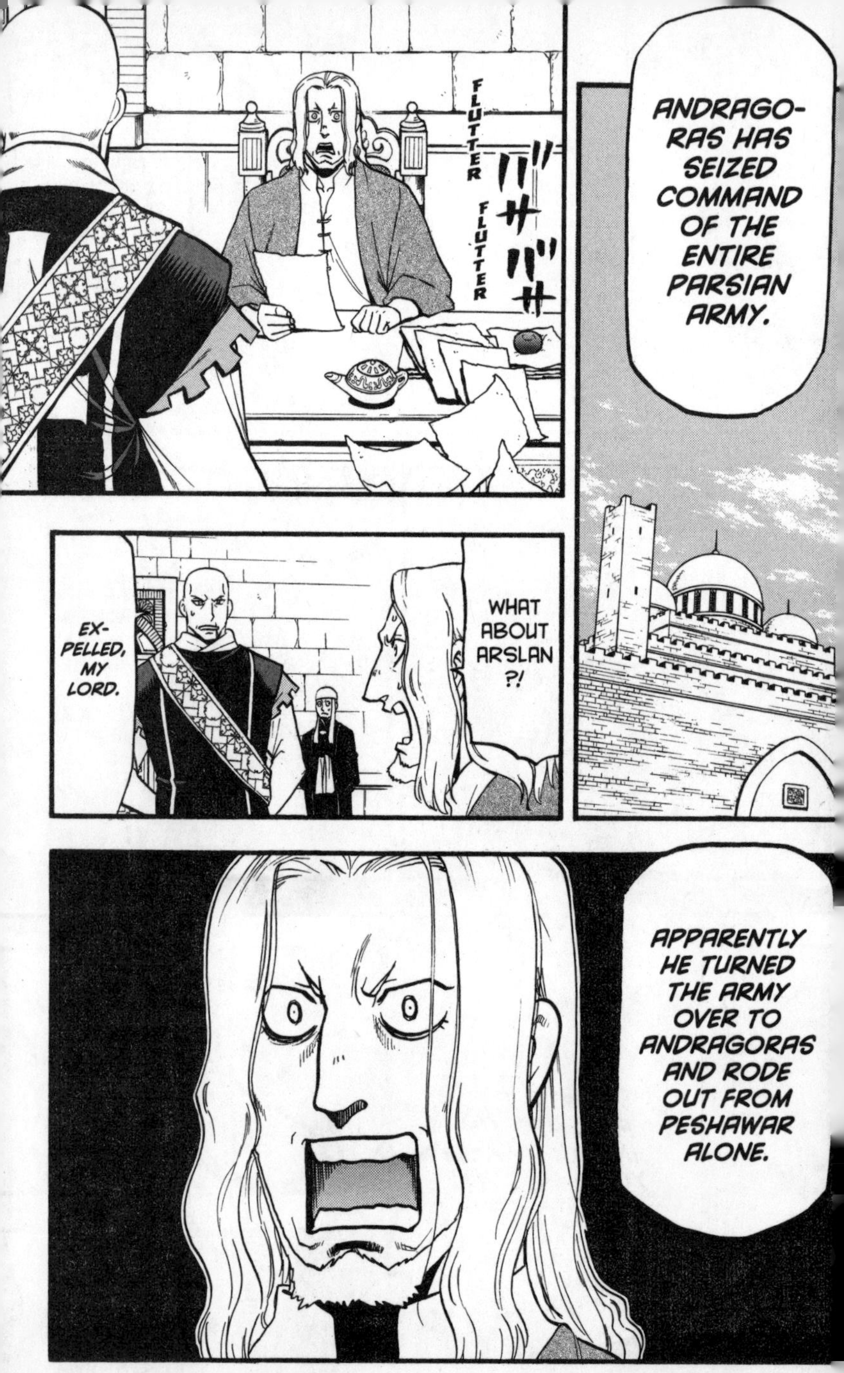
ANDRAGO-RAS HAS SEIZED COMMAND OF THE ENTIRE PARSIAN ARMY.
FLUTTER FLUTTER
WHAT ABOUT ARSLAN?!
EX-PELLED, MY LORD.
APPARENTLY HE TURNED THE ARMY OVER TO ANDRAGORAS AND RODE OUT FROM PESHAWAR ALONE.

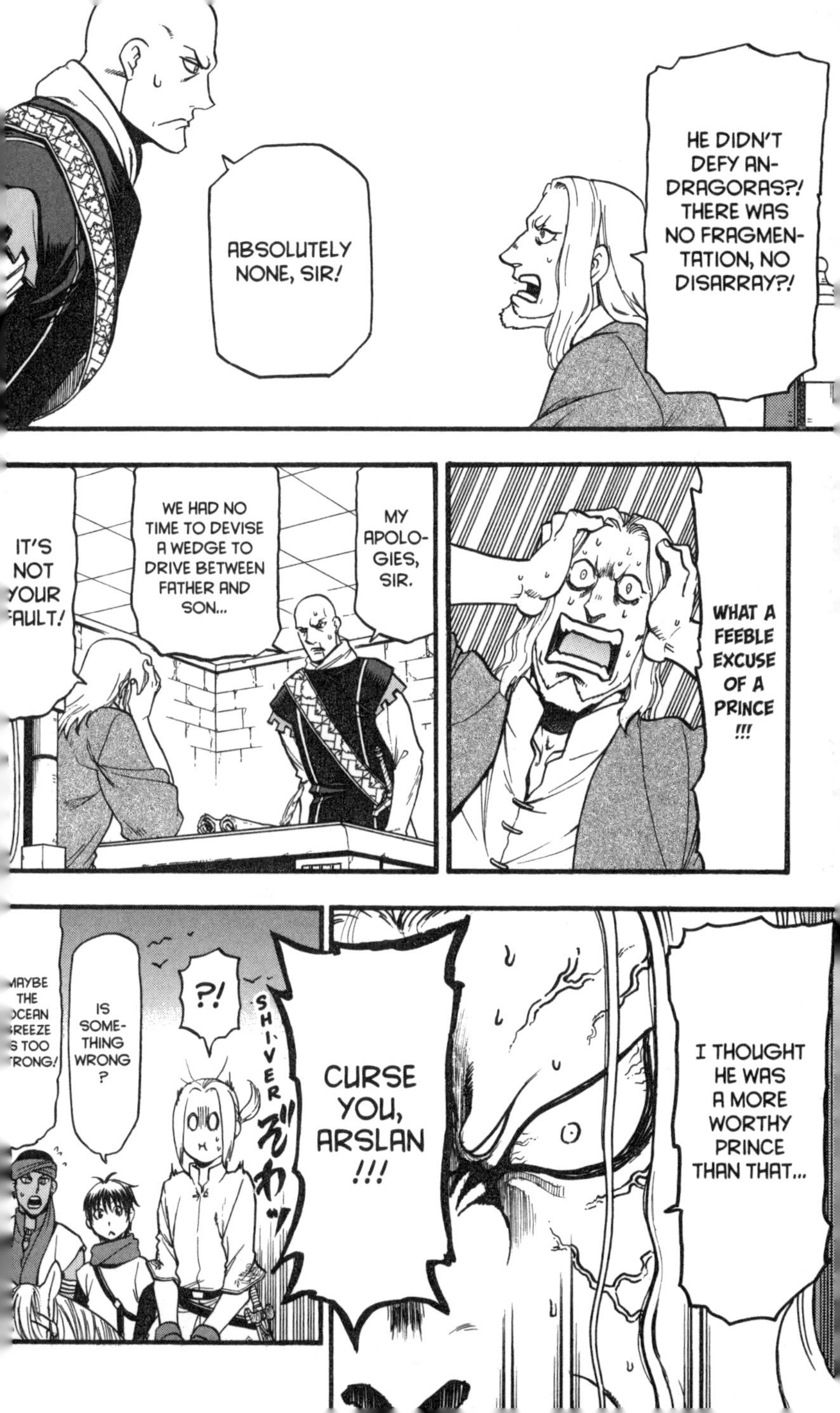

HE DIDN'T DEFY AN-DRAGORAS?! THERE WAS NO FRAGMEN-TATION, NO DISARRAY?!
ABSOLUTELY NONE, SIR!
WHAT A FEEBLE EXCUSE OF A PRINCE !!!
MY APOLOGIES, SIR.
WE HAD NO TIME TO DEVISE A WEDGE TO DRIVE BETWEEN FATHER AND SON...
IT'S NOT YOUR FAULT!
I THOUGHT HE WAS A MORE WORTHY PRINCE THAN THAT...
CURSE YOU, ARSLAN !!!
SHIVER
ぞわッ
?!
IS SOME-THING WRONG ?
MAYBE THE OCEAN REEZE S TOO TRONG!

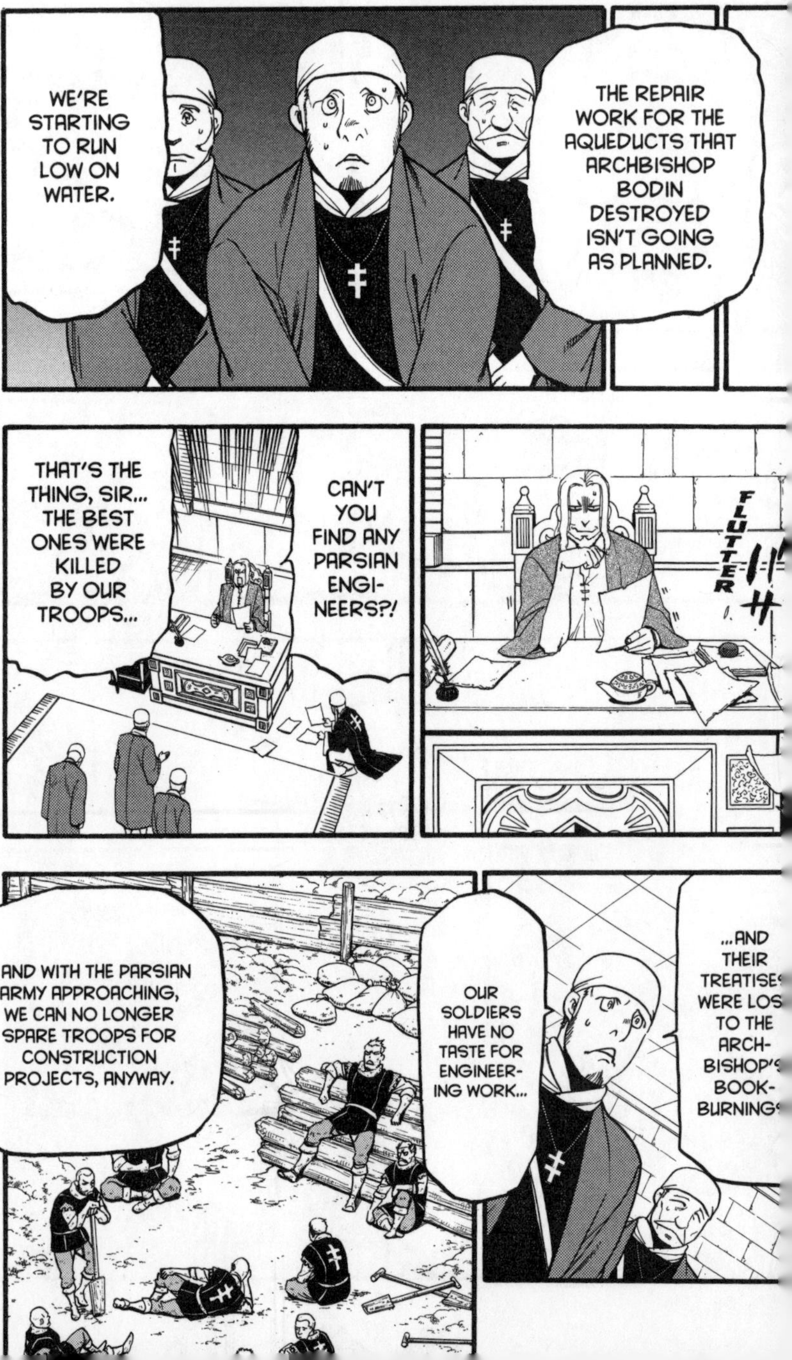
THE REPAIR WORK FOR THE AQUEDUCTS THAT ARCHBISHOP BODIN DESTROYED ISN'T GOING AS PLANNED.
WE'RE STARTING TO RUN LOW ON WATER.
FLUTTER
CAN'T YOU FIND ANY PARSIAN ENGI-NEERS?!
THAT'S THE THING, SIR... THE BEST ONES WERE KILLED BY OUR TROOPS...
...AND THEIR TREATISES WERE LOST TO THE ARCH-BISHOP'S BOOK-BURNINGS
OUR SOLDIERS HAVE NO TASTE FOR ENGINEER-ING WORK...
...AND WITH THE PARSIAN ARMY APPROACHING, WE CAN NO LONGER SPARE TROOPS FOR CONSTRUCTION PROJECTS, ANYWAY.

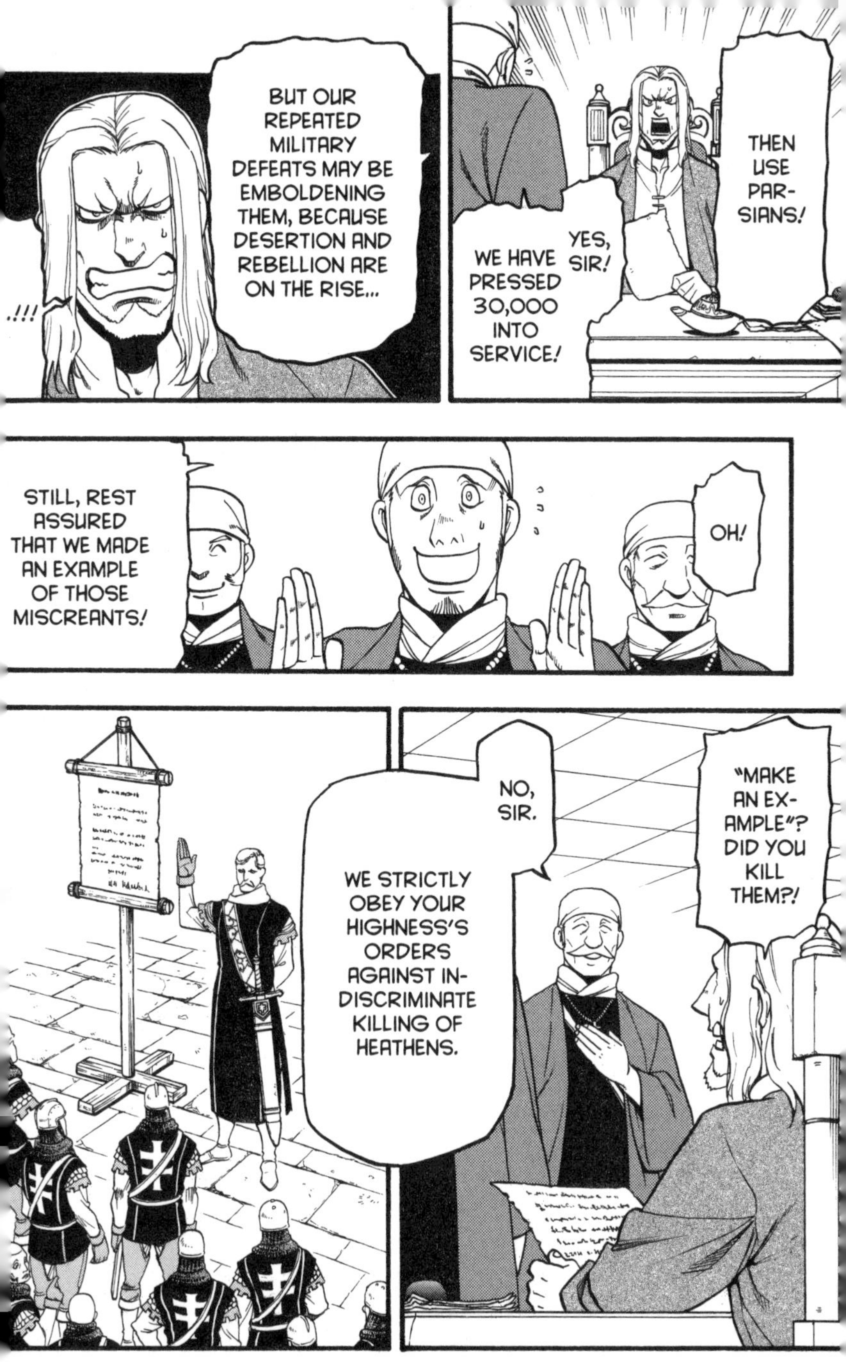
THEN USE PAR-SIANS!
YES, SIR!
WE HAVE PRESSED 30,000 INTO SERVICE!
BUT OUR REPEATED MILITARY DEFEATS MAY BE EMBOLDENING THEM, BECAUSE DESERTION AND REBELLION ARE ON THE RISE...
.!!!
OH!
STILL, REST ASSURED THAT WE MADE AN EXAMPLE OF THOSE MISCREANTS!
"MAKE AN EX-AMPLE"? DID YOU KILL THEM?!
NO, SIR.
WE STRICTLY OBEY YOUR HIGHNESS'S ORDERS AGAINST IN-DISCRIMINATE KILLING OF HEATHENS.

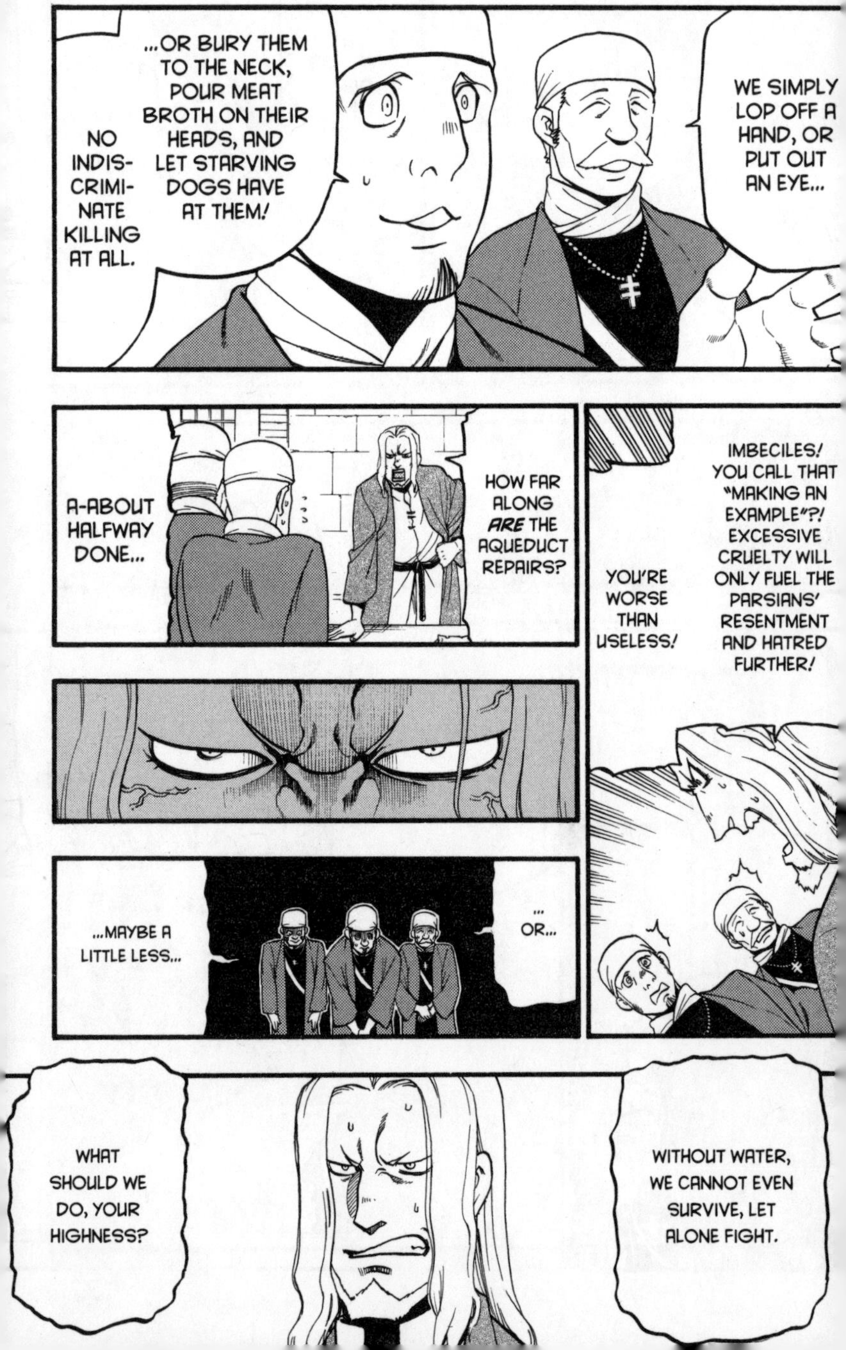
WE SIMPLY LOP OFF A HAND, OR PUT OUT AN EYE...
...OR BURY THEM TO THE NECK, POUR MEAT BROTH ON THEIR HEADS, AND LET STARVING DOGS HAVE AT THEM!
NO INDIS-CRIMI-NATE KILLING AT ALL.
IMBECILES! YOU CALL THAT "MAKING AN EXAMPLE"?! EXCESSIVE CRUELTY WILL ONLY FUEL THE PARSIANS' RESENTMENT AND HATRED FURTHER!
YOU'RE WORSE THAN USELESS!
HOW FAR ALONG *ARE* THE AQUEDUCT REPAIRS?
A-ABOUT HALFWAY DONE...
... OR...
...MAYBE A LITTLE LESS...
WITHOUT WATER, WE CANNOT EVEN SURVIVE, LET ALONE FIGHT.
WHAT SHOULD WE DO, YOUR HIGHNESS?

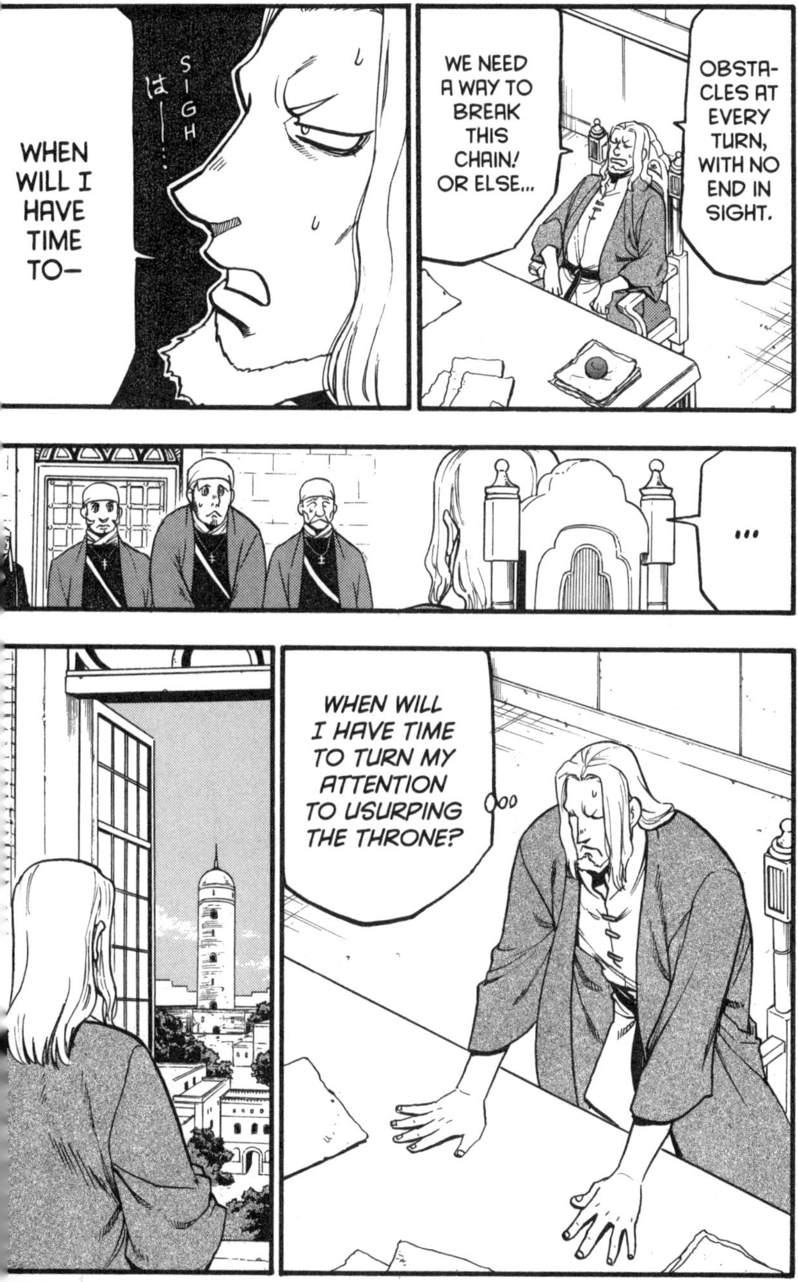
OBSTA-CLES AT EVERY TURN, WITH NO END IN SIGHT.
WE NEED A WAY TO BREAK THIS CHAIN! OR ELSE...
は―…
SIGH
WHEN WILL I HAVE TIME TO—
...
WHEN WILL I HAVE TIME TO TURN MY ATTENTION TO USURPING THE THRONE?

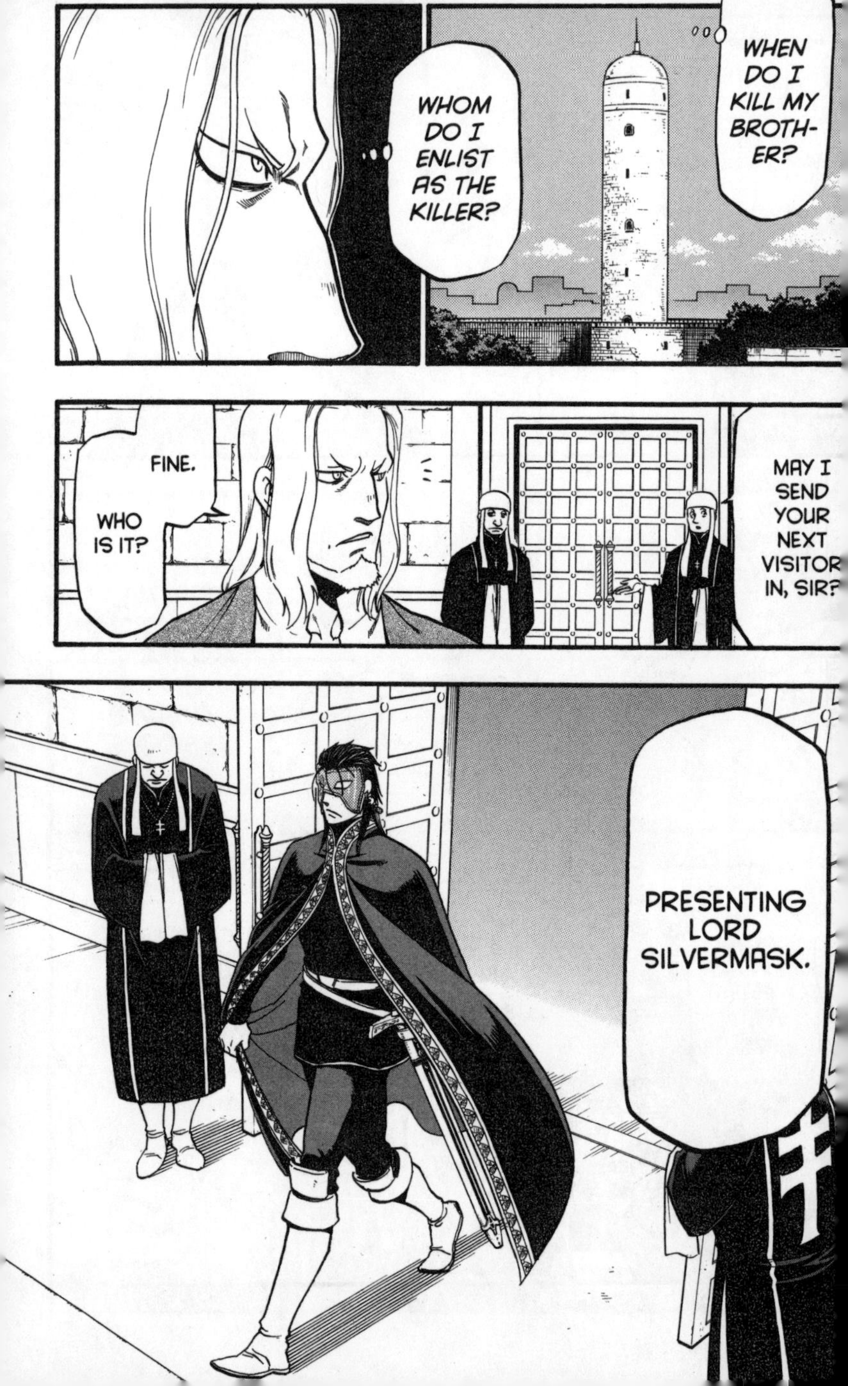
WHEN DO I KILL MY BROTHER?
WHOM DO I ENLIST AS THE KILLER?
MAY I SEND YOUR NEXT VISITOR IN, SIR?
FINE.
WHO IS IT?
PRESENTING LORD SILVERMASK.

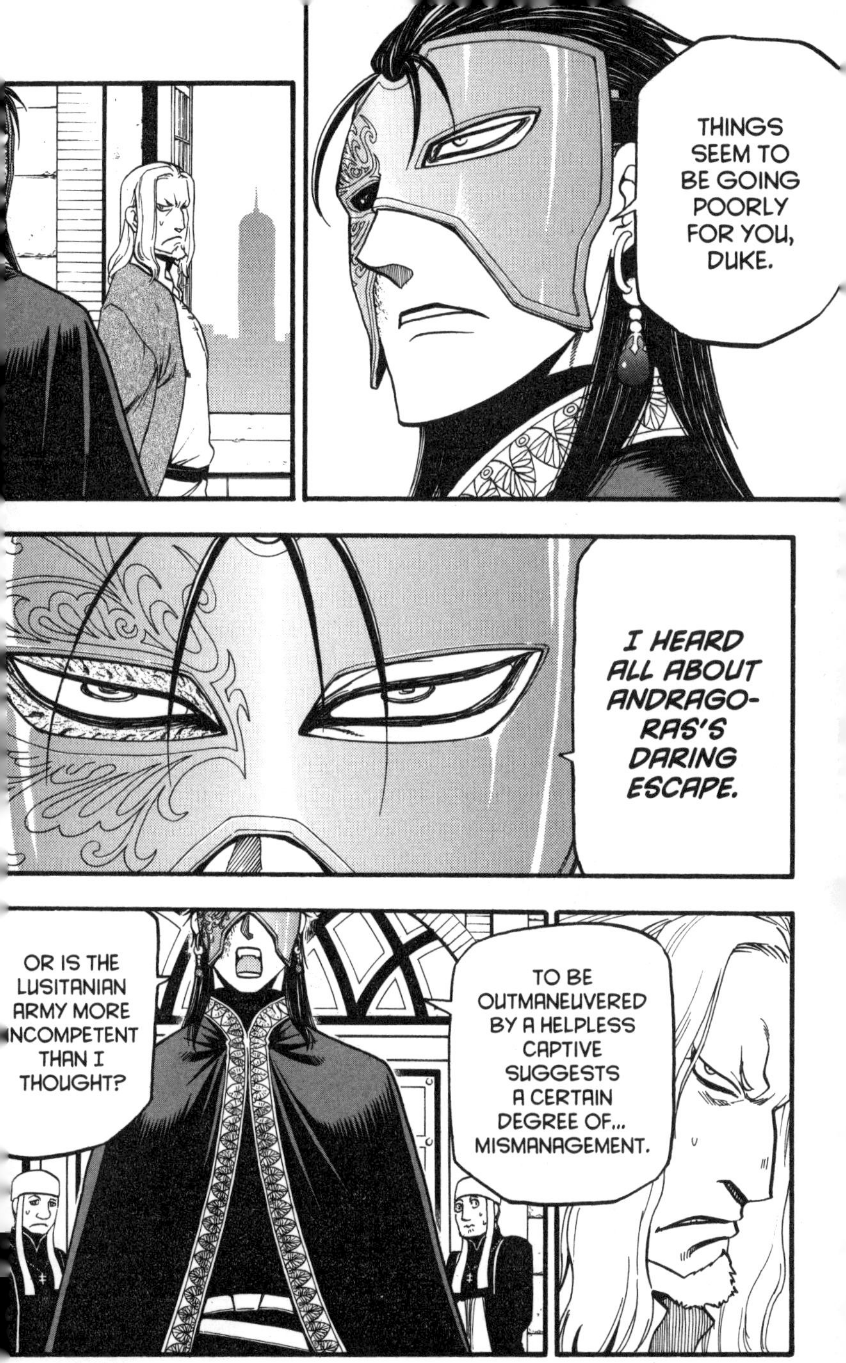
THINGS SEEM TO BE GOING POORLY FOR YOU, DUKE.
I HEARD ALL ABOUT ANDRAGO-RAS'S DARING ESCAPE.
TO BE OUTMANEUVERED BY A HELPLESS CAPTIVE SUGGESTS A CERTAIN DEGREE OF... MISMANAGEMENT.
OR IS THE LUSITANIAN ARMY MORE INCOMPETENT THAN I THOUGHT?

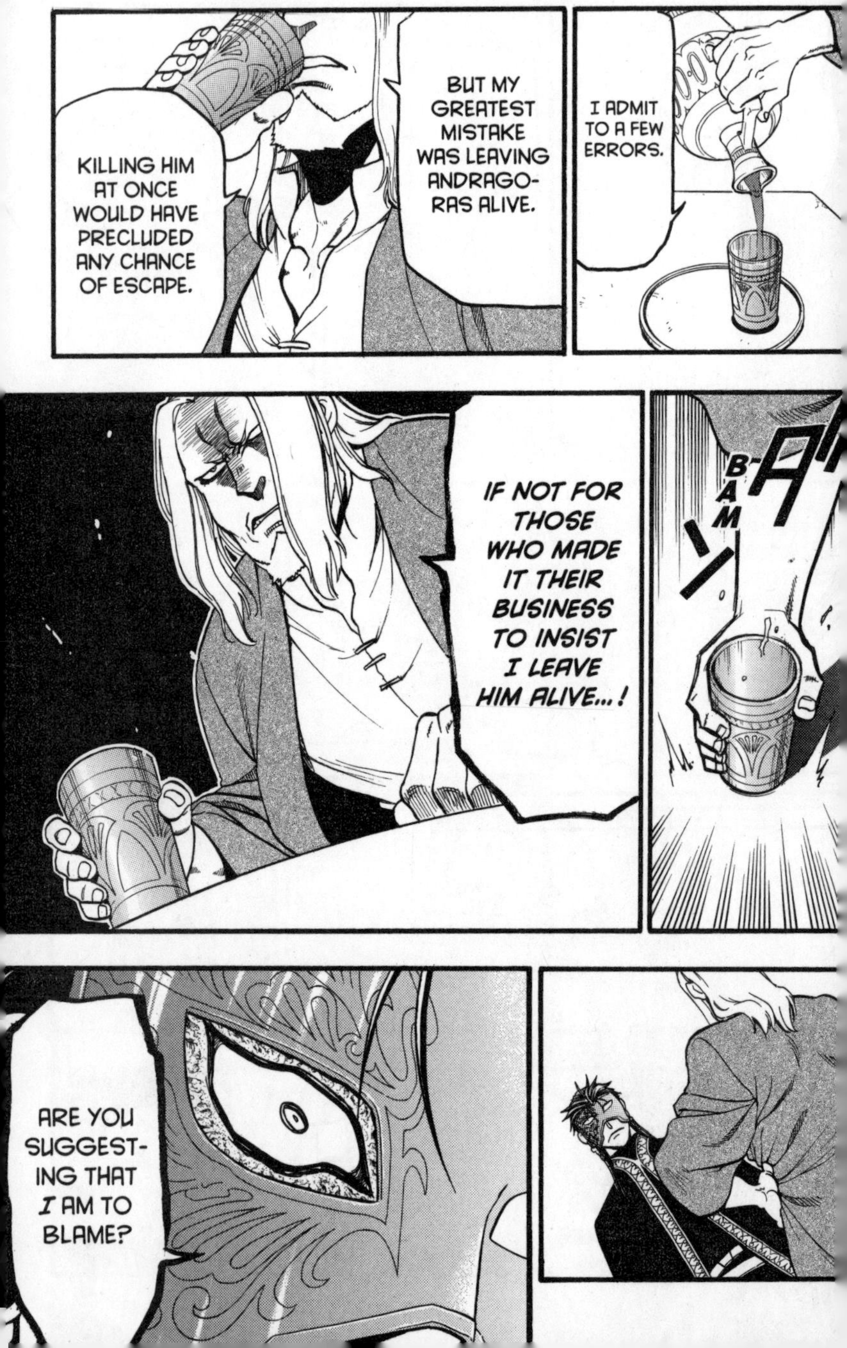
I ADMIT TO A FEW ERRORS.
BUT MY GREATEST MISTAKE WAS LEAVING ANDRAGORAS ALIVE.
KILLING HIM AT ONCE WOULD HAVE PRECLUDED ANY CHANCE OF ESCAPE.
B-BAM
IF NOT FOR THOSE WHO MADE IT THEIR BUSINESS TO INSIST I LEAVE HIM ALIVE...!
ARE YOU SUGGESTING THAT *I* AM TO BLAME?

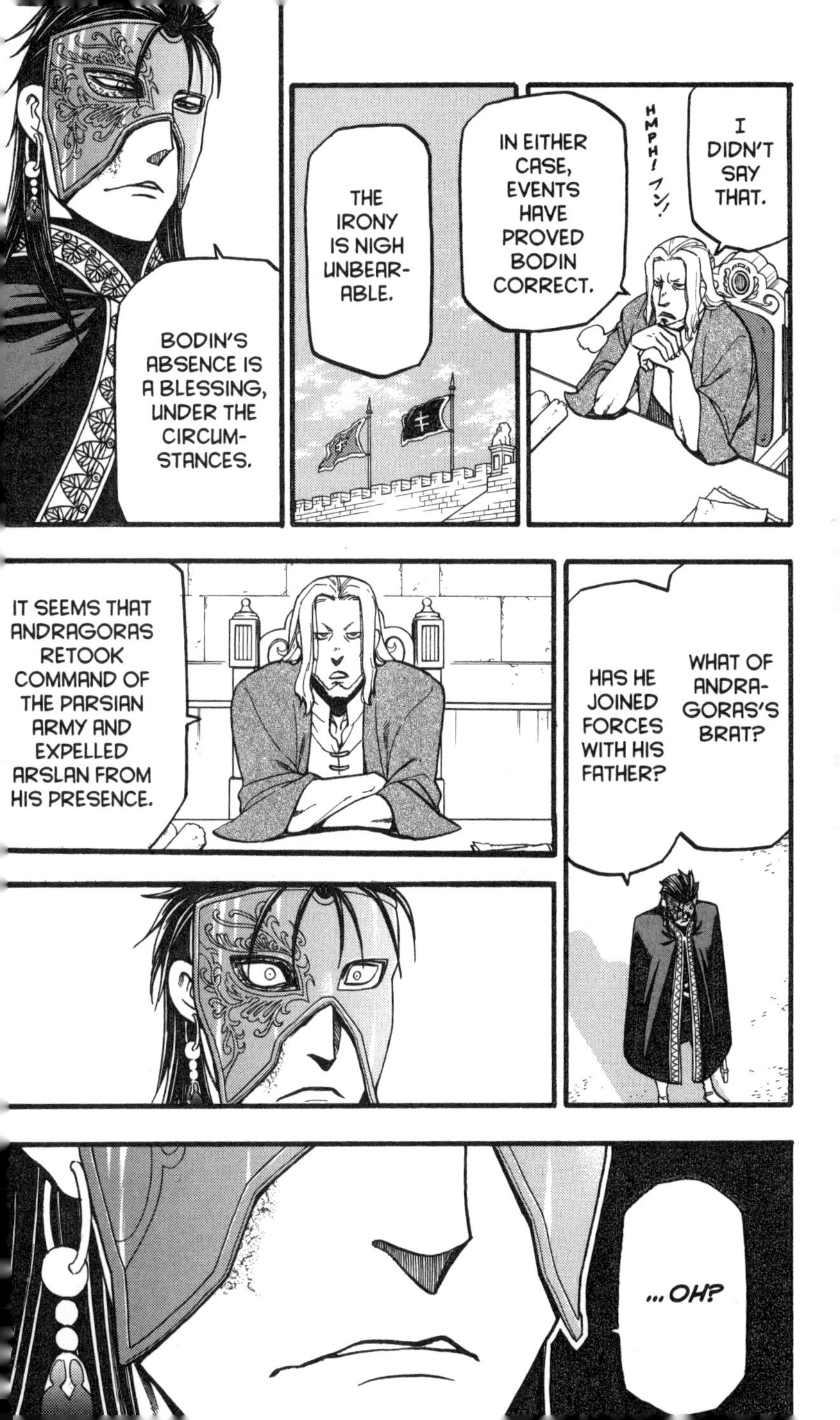
I DIDN'T SAY THAT.
HMPH! フン!
IN EITHER CASE, EVENTS HAVE PROVED BODIN CORRECT.
THE IRONY IS NIGH UNBEAR-ABLE.
BODIN'S ABSENCE IS A BLESSING, UNDER THE CIRCUM-STANCES.
WHAT OF ANDRA-GORAS'S BRAT?
HAS HE JOINED FORCES WITH HIS FATHER?
IT SEEMS THAT ANDRAGORAS RETOOK COMMAND OF THE PARSIAN ARMY AND EXPELLED ARSLAN FROM HIS PRESENCE.
...OH?

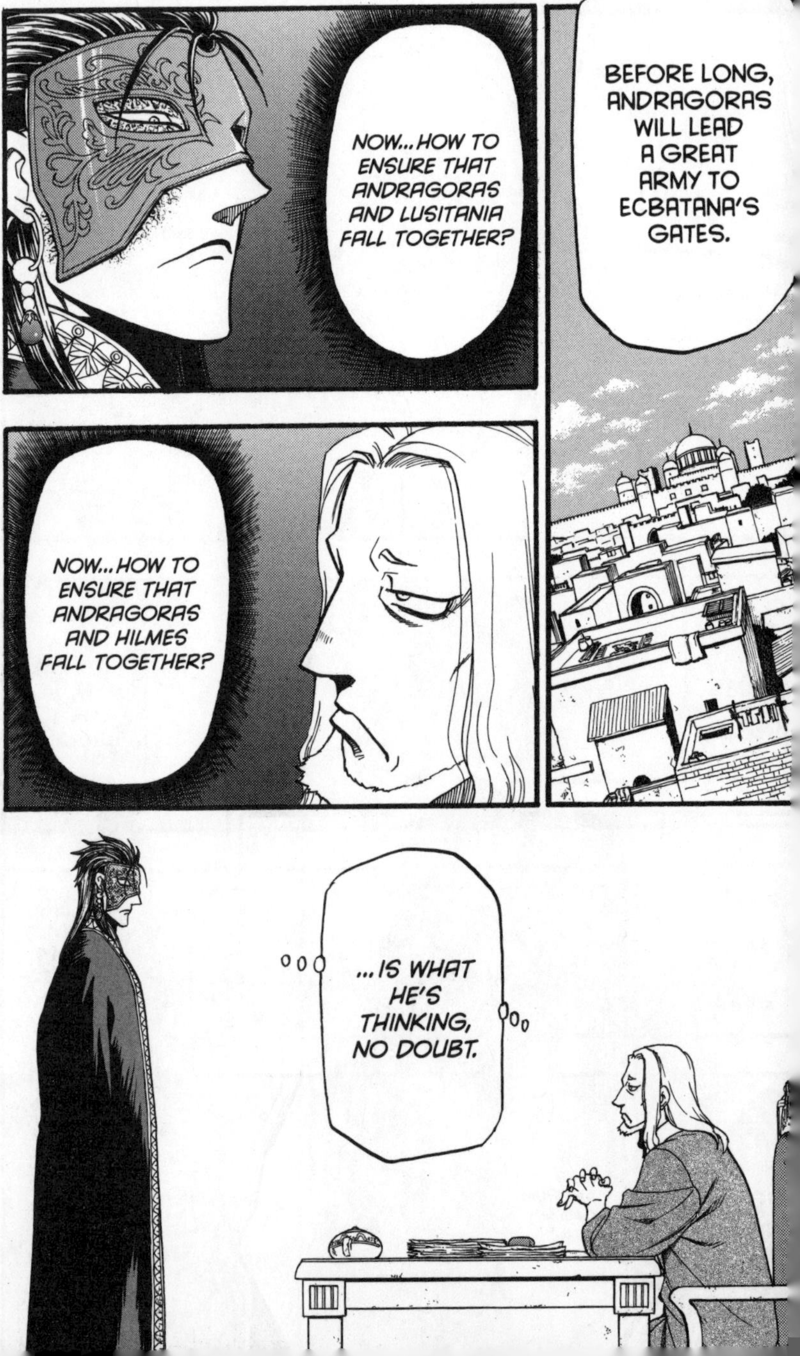
BEFORE LONG, ANDRAGORAS WILL LEAD A GREAT ARMY TO ECBATANA'S GATES.
NOW... HOW TO ENSURE THAT ANDRAGORAS AND LUSITANIA FALL TOGETHER?
NOW... HOW TO ENSURE THAT ANDRAGORAS AND HILMES FALL TOGETHER?
...IS WHAT HE'S THINKING, NO DOUBT.

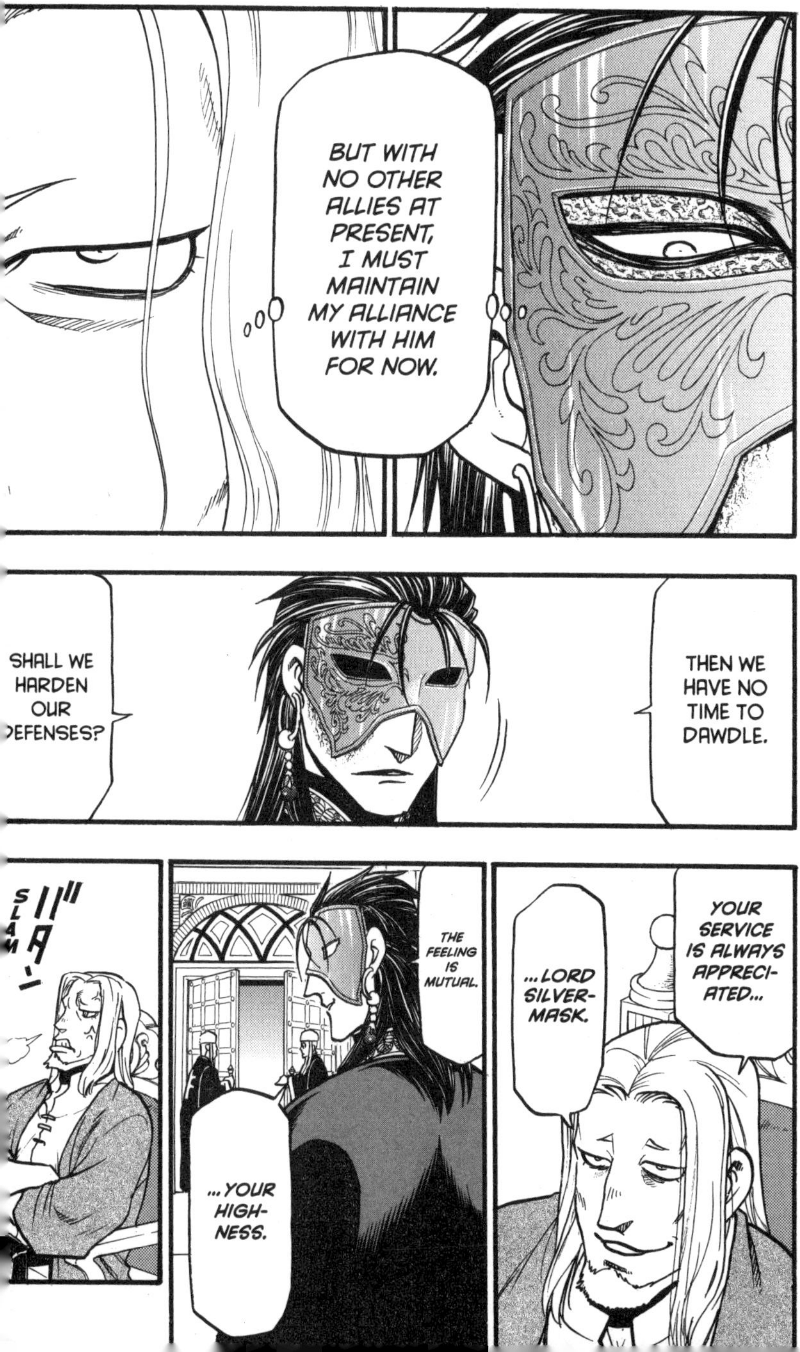
BUT WITH NO OTHER ALLIES AT PRESENT, I MUST MAINTAIN MY ALLIANCE WITH HIM FOR NOW.
THEN WE HAVE NO TIME TO DAWDLE.
SHALL WE HARDEN OUR DEFENSES?
YOUR SERVICE IS ALWAYS APPRECIATED...
...LORD SILVER-MASK.
THE FEELING IS MUTUAL.
...YOUR HIGHNESS.
SLAM

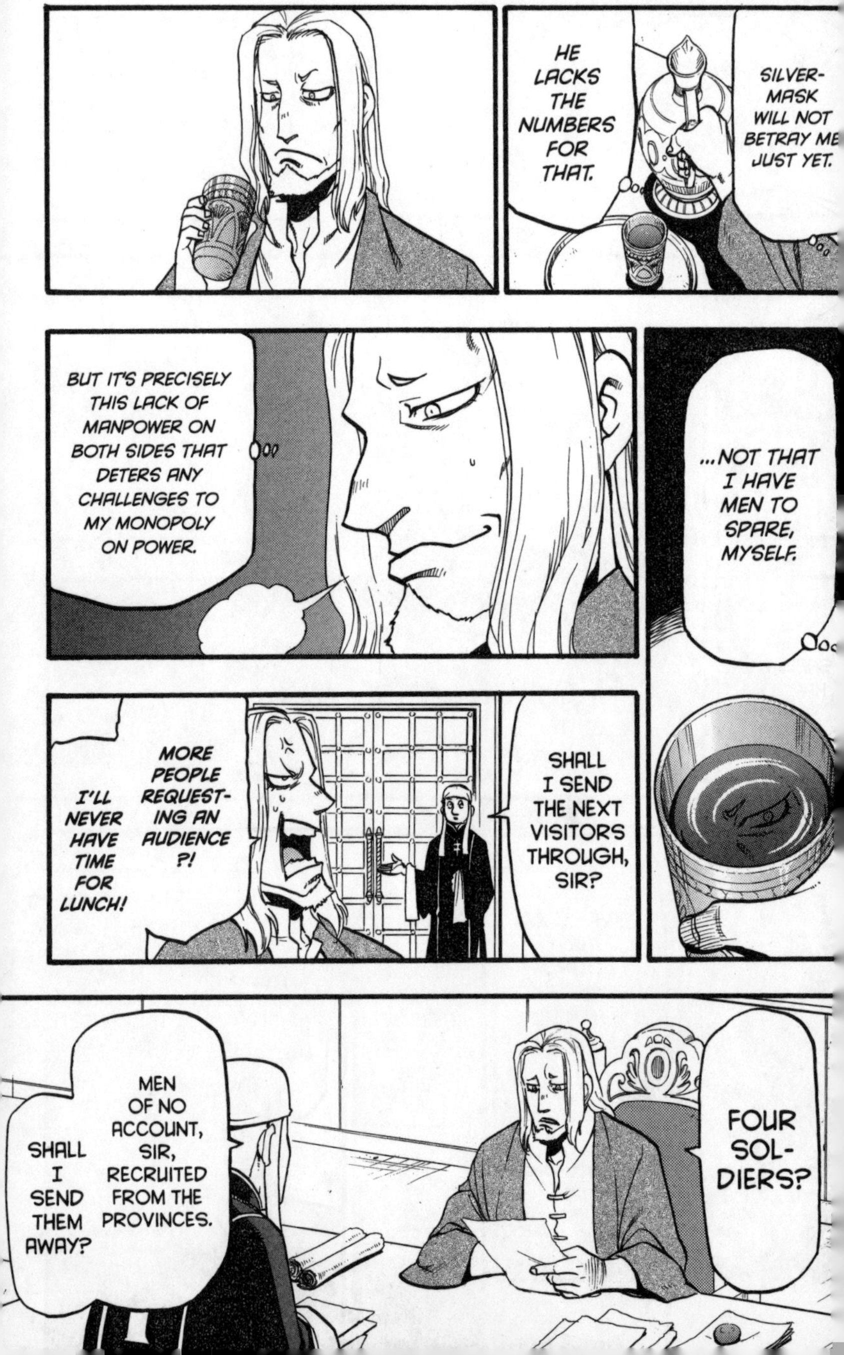
SILVER-MASK WILL NOT BETRAY ME JUST YET.
HE LACKS THE NUMBERS FOR THAT.
...NOT THAT I HAVE MEN TO SPARE, MYSELF.
BUT IT'S PRECISELY THIS LACK OF MANPOWER ON BOTH SIDES THAT DETERS ANY CHALLENGES TO MY MONOPOLY ON POWER.
SHALL I SEND THE NEXT VISITORS THROUGH, SIR?
MORE PEOPLE REQUESTING AN AUDIENCE?!
I'LL NEVER HAVE TIME FOR LUNCH!
FOUR SOLDIERS?
MEN OF NO ACCOUNT, SIR, RECRUITED FROM THE PROVINCES.
SHALL I SEND THEM AWAY?

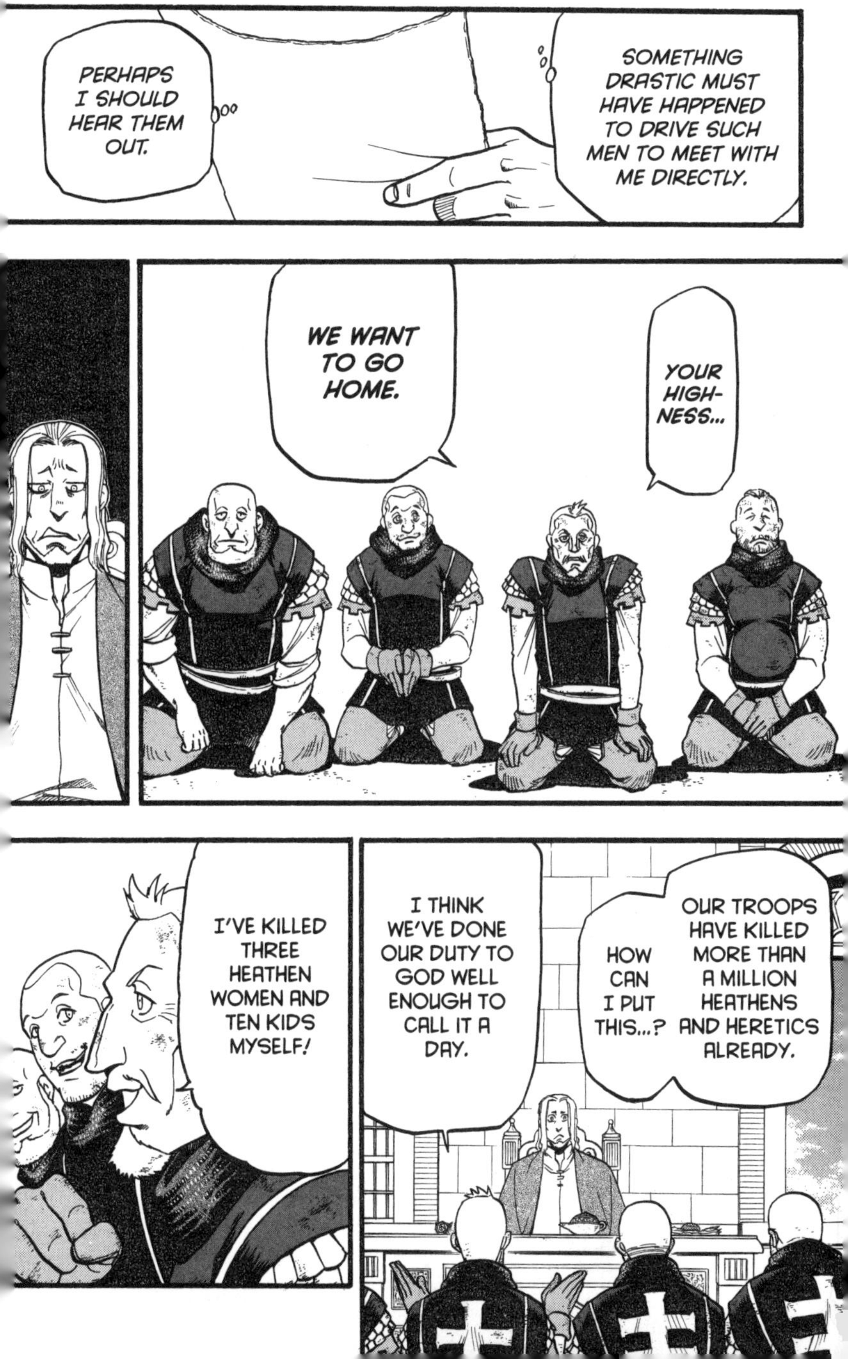
SOMETHING DRASTIC MUST HAVE HAPPENED TO DRIVE SUCH MEN TO MEET WITH ME DIRECTLY.
PERHAPS I SHOULD HEAR THEM OUT.
YOUR HIGH-NESS...
WE WANT TO GO HOME.
OUR TROOPS HAVE KILLED MORE THAN A MILLION HEATHENS AND HERETICS ALREADY.
HOW CAN I PUT THIS...?
I THINK WE'VE DONE OUR DUTY TO GOD WELL ENOUGH TO CALL IT A DAY.
I'VE KILLED THREE HEATHEN WOMEN AND TEN KIDS MYSELF!

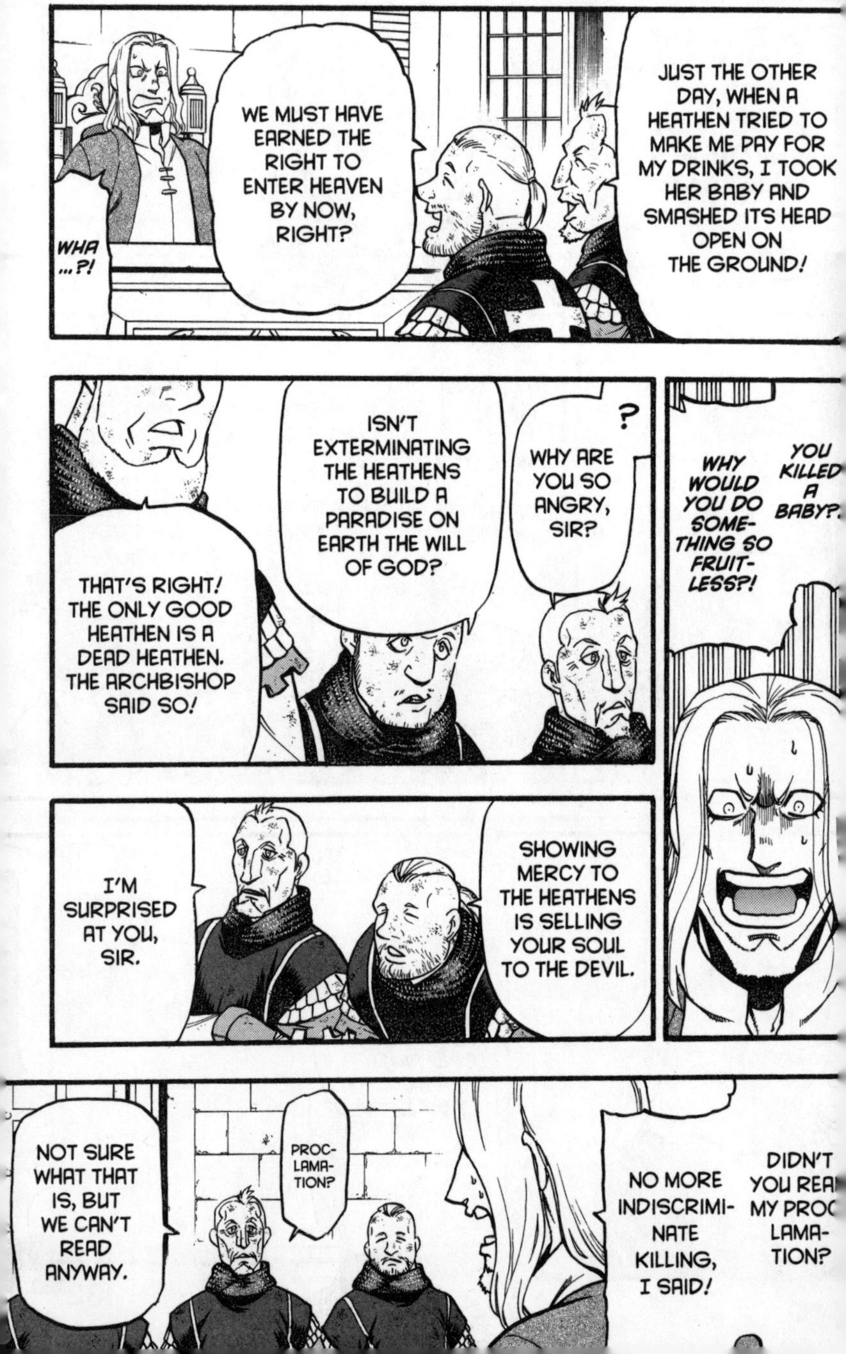
JUST THE OTHER DAY, WHEN A HEATHEN TRIED TO MAKE ME PAY FOR MY DRINKS, I TOOK HER BABY AND SMASHED ITS HEAD OPEN ON THE GROUND!
WE MUST HAVE EARNED THE RIGHT TO ENTER HEAVEN BY NOW, RIGHT?
WHA...?!
YOU KILLED A BABY?!
WHY WOULD YOU DO SOMETHING SO FRUITLESS?!
?
WHY ARE YOU SO ANGRY, SIR?
ISN'T EXTERMINATING THE HEATHENS TO BUILD A PARADISE ON EARTH THE WILL OF GOD?
THAT'S RIGHT! THE ONLY GOOD HEATHEN IS A DEAD HEATHEN. THE ARCHBISHOP SAID SO!
SHOWING MERCY TO THE HEATHENS IS SELLING YOUR SOUL TO THE DEVIL.
I'M SURPRISED AT YOU, SIR.
DIDN'T YOU REA MY PROC LAMATION?
NO MORE INDISCRIMINATE KILLING, I SAID!
PROCLAMATION?
NOT SURE WHAT THAT IS, BUT WE CAN'T READ ANYWAY.

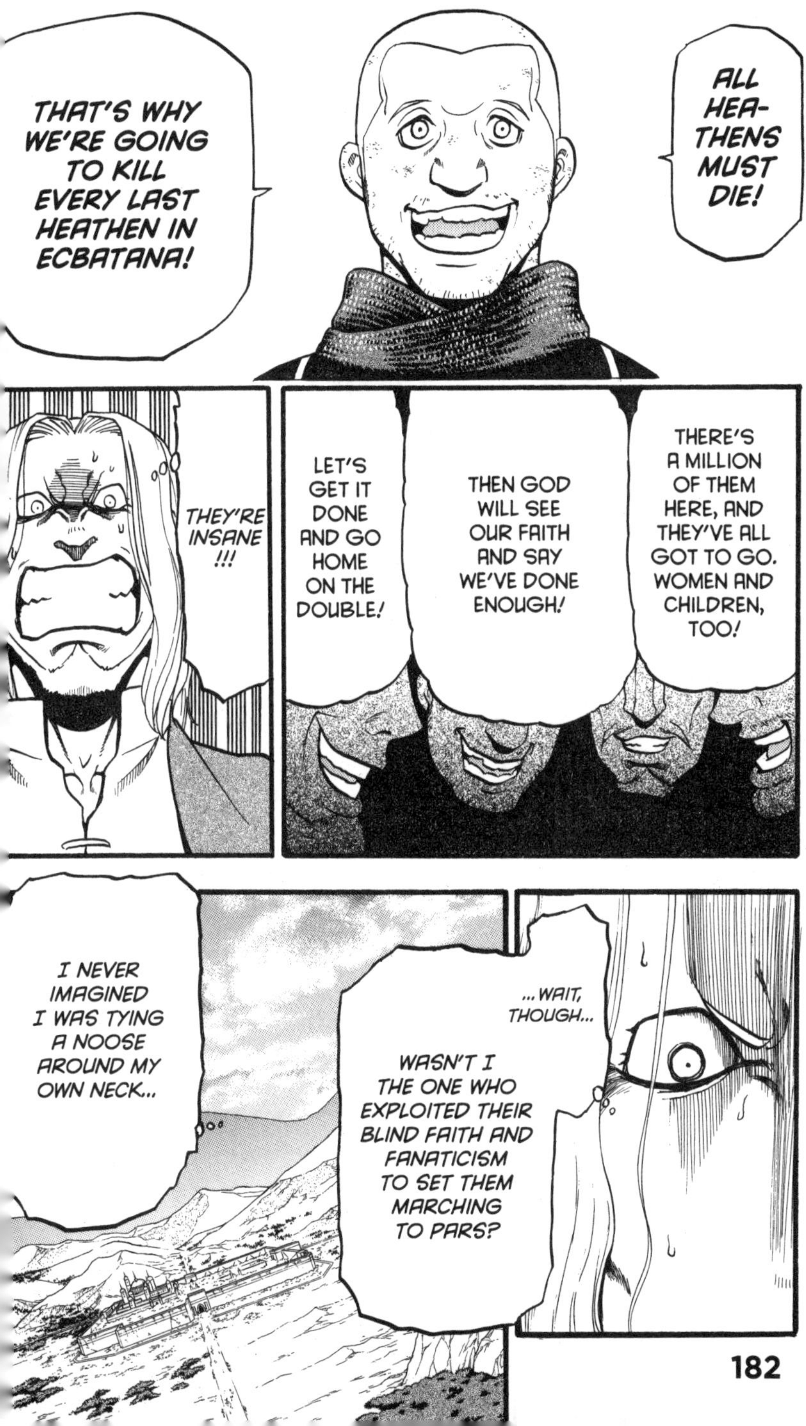
ALL HEATHENS MUST DIE!
THAT'S WHY WE'RE GOING TO KILL EVERY LAST HEATHEN IN ECBATANA!
THERE'S A MILLION OF THEM HERE, AND THEY'VE ALL GOT TO GO. WOMEN AND CHILDREN, TOO!
THEN GOD WILL SEE OUR FAITH AND SAY WE'VE DONE ENOUGH!
LET'S GET IT DONE AND GO HOME ON THE DOUBLE!
THEY'RE INSANE!!!
...WAIT, THOUGH...
WASN'T I THE ONE WHO EXPLOITED THEIR BLIND FAITH AND FANATICISM TO SET THEM MARCHING TO PARS?
I NEVER IMAGINED I WAS TYING A NOOSE AROUND MY OWN NECK...

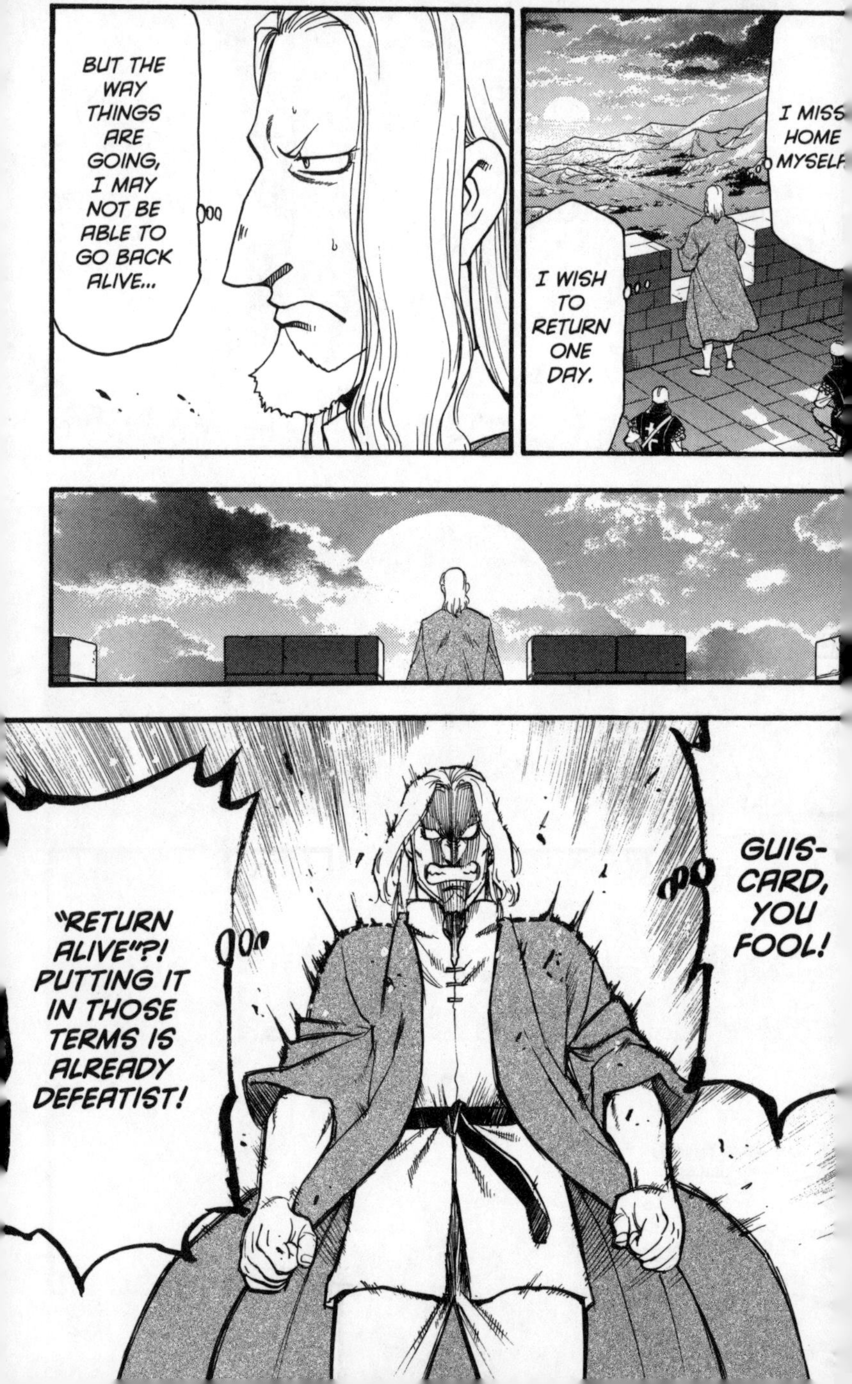
I MISS HOME MYSELF
I WISH TO RETURN ONE DAY.
BUT THE WAY THINGS ARE GOING, I MAY NOT BE ABLE TO GO BACK ALIVE...
GUIS-CARD, YOU FOOL!
"RETURN ALIVE"?! PUTTING IT IN THOSE TERMS IS ALREADY DEFEATIST!

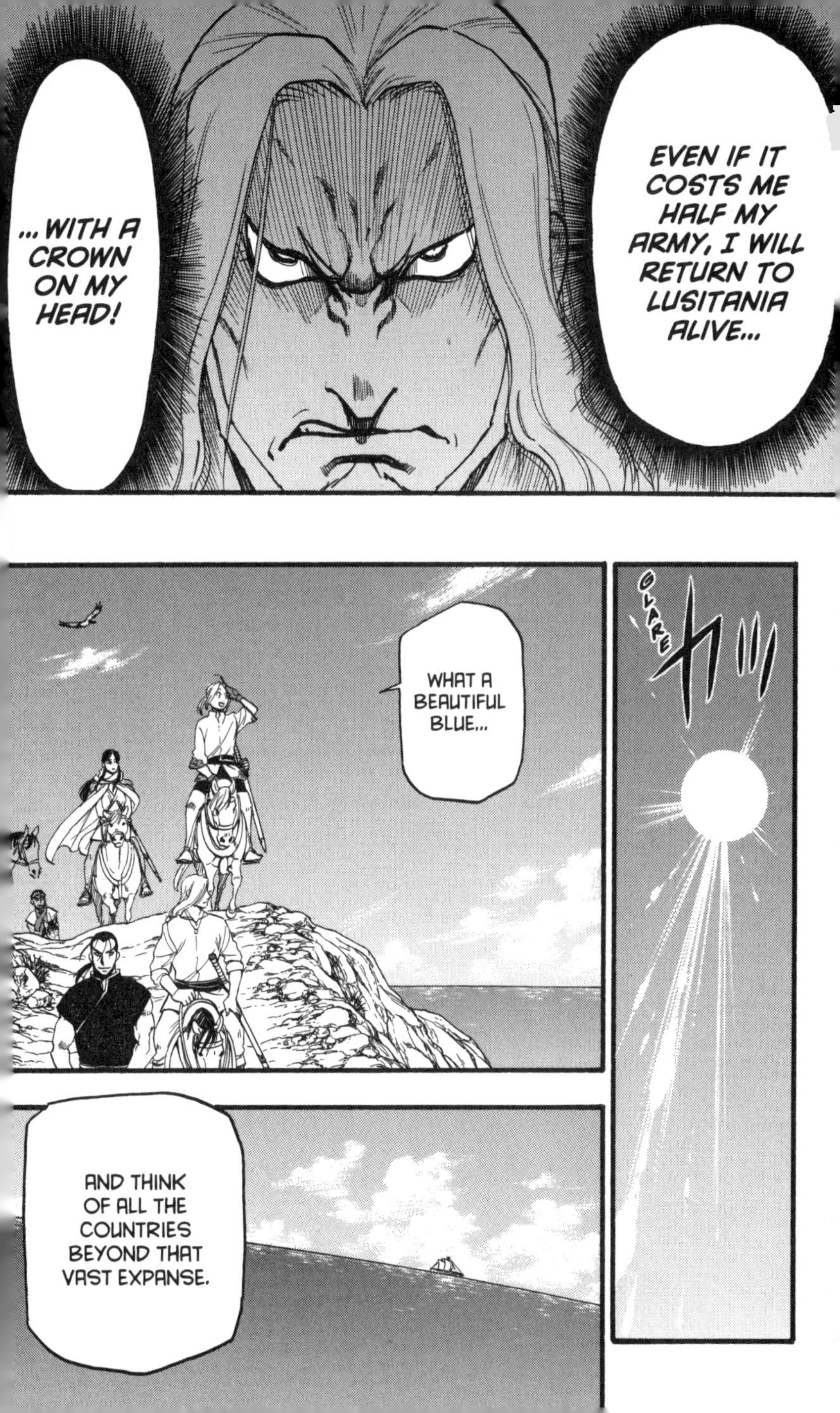
EVEN IF IT COSTS ME HALF MY ARMY, I WILL RETURN TO LUSITANIA ALIVE...
...WITH A CROWN ON MY HEAD!
GLARE
WHAT A BEAUTIFUL BLUE...
AND THINK OF ALL THE COUNTRIES BEYOND THAT VAST EXPANSE.

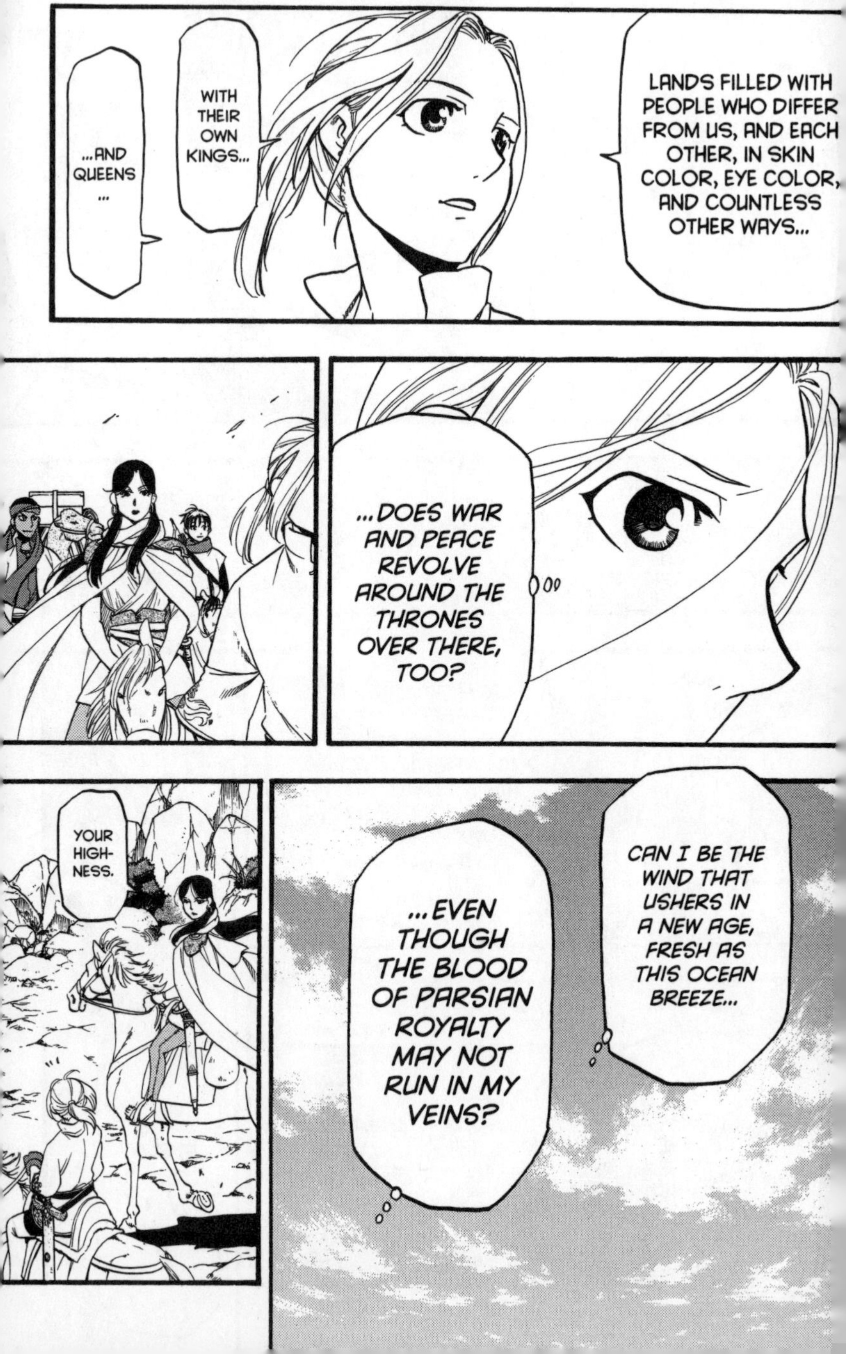
LANDS FILLED WITH PEOPLE WHO DIFFER FROM US, AND EACH OTHER, IN SKIN COLOR, EYE COLOR, AND COUNTLESS OTHER WAYS...
WITH THEIR OWN KINGS...
...AND QUEENS ...
...DOES WAR AND PEACE REVOLVE AROUND THE THRONES OVER THERE, TOO?
CAN I BE THE WIND THAT USHERS IN A NEW AGE, FRESH AS THIS OCEAN BREEZE...
...EVEN THOUGH THE BLOOD OF PARSIAN ROYALTY MAY NOT RUN IN MY VEINS?
YOUR HIGH- NESS.

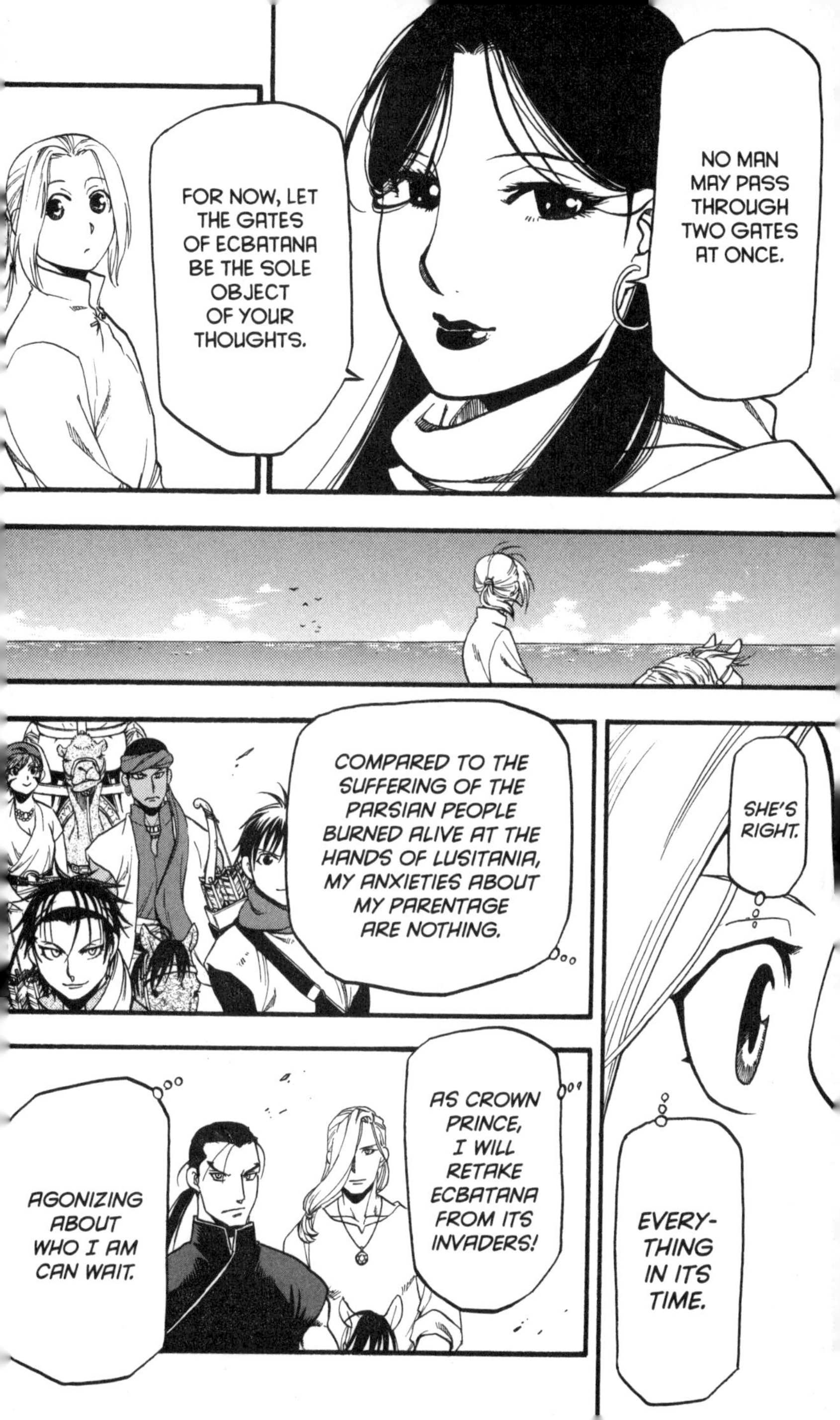
NO MAN MAY PASS THROUGH TWO GATES AT ONCE.
FOR NOW, LET THE GATES OF ECBATANA BE THE SOLE OBJECT OF YOUR THOUGHTS.
SHE'S RIGHT.
EVERY-THING IN ITS TIME.
COMPARED TO THE SUFFERING OF THE PARSIAN PEOPLE BURNED ALIVE AT THE HANDS OF LUSITANIA, MY ANXIETIES ABOUT MY PARENTAGE ARE NOTHING.
AS CROWN PRINCE, I WILL RETAKE ECBATANA FROM ITS INVADERS!
AGONIZING ABOUT WHO I AM CAN WAIT.

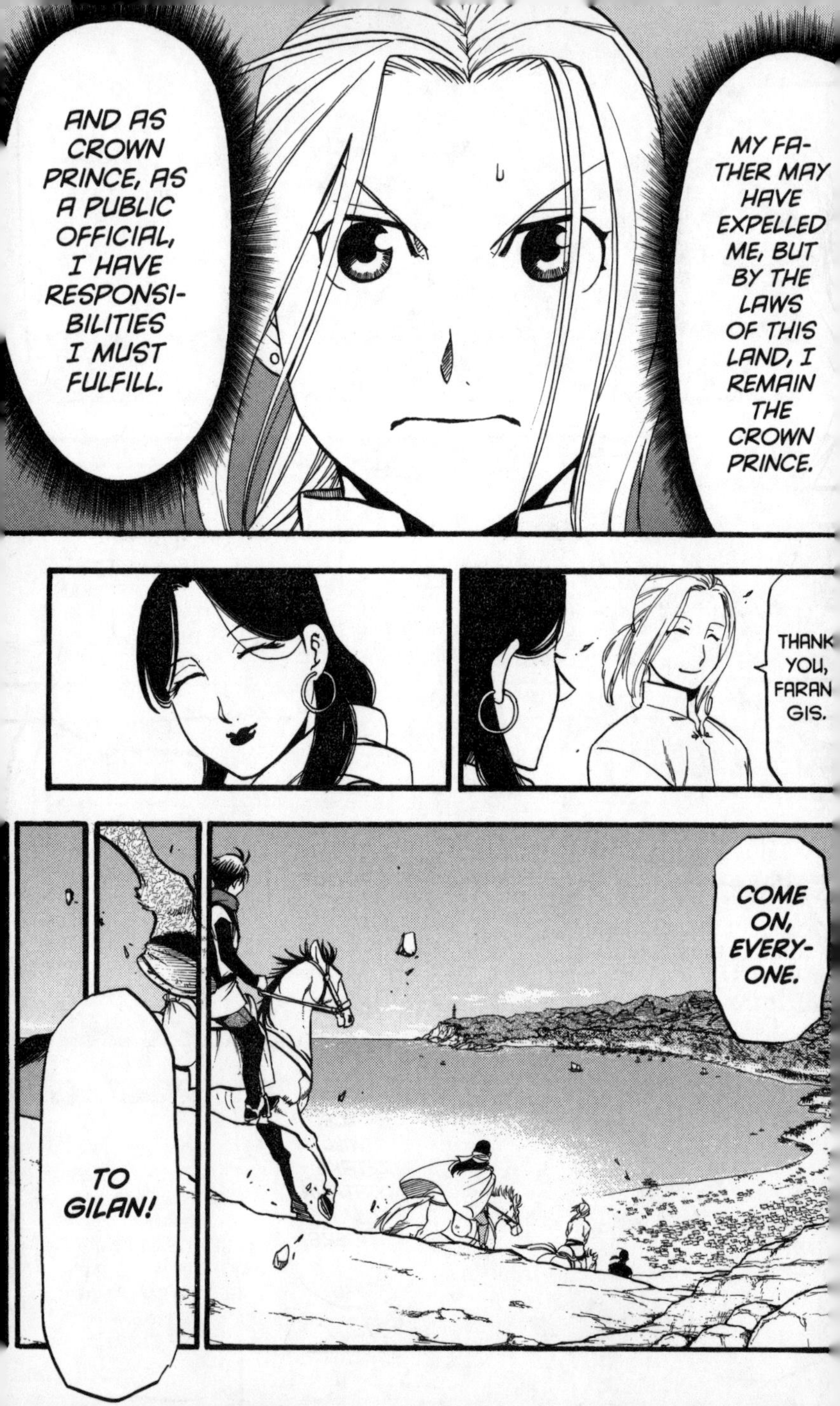
MY FA-THER MAY HAVE EXPELLED ME, BUT BY THE LAWS OF THIS LAND, I REMAIN THE CROWN PRINCE.
AND AS CROWN PRINCE, AS A PUBLIC OFFICIAL, I HAVE RESPONSI-BILITIES I MUST FULFILL.
THANK YOU, FARAN GIS.
COME ON, EVERY-ONE.
TO GILAN!

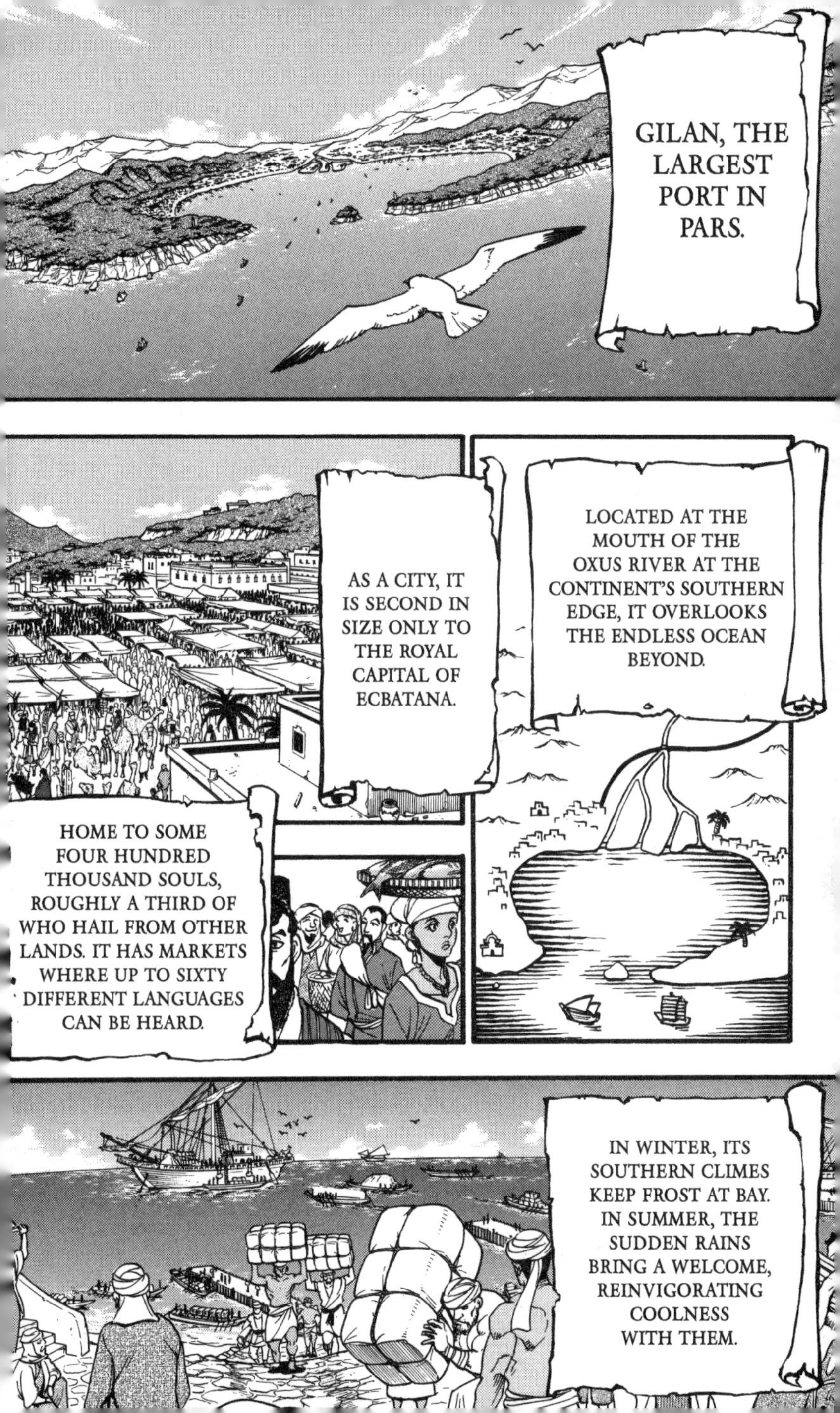
GILAN, THE LARGEST PORT IN PARS.
LOCATED AT THE MOUTH OF THE OXUS RIVER AT THE CONTINENT'S SOUTHERN EDGE, IT OVERLOOKS THE ENDLESS OCEAN BEYOND.
AS A CITY, IT IS SECOND IN SIZE ONLY TO THE ROYAL CAPITAL OF ECBATANA.
HOME TO SOME FOUR HUNDRED THOUSAND SOULS, ROUGHLY A THIRD OF WHO HAIL FROM OTHER LANDS. IT HAS MARKETS WHERE UP TO SIXTY DIFFERENT LANGUAGES CAN BE HEARD.
IN WINTER, ITS SOUTHERN CLIMES KEEP FROST AT BAY. IN SUMMER, THE SUDDEN RAINS BRING A WELCOME, REINVIGORATING COOLNESS WITH THEM.

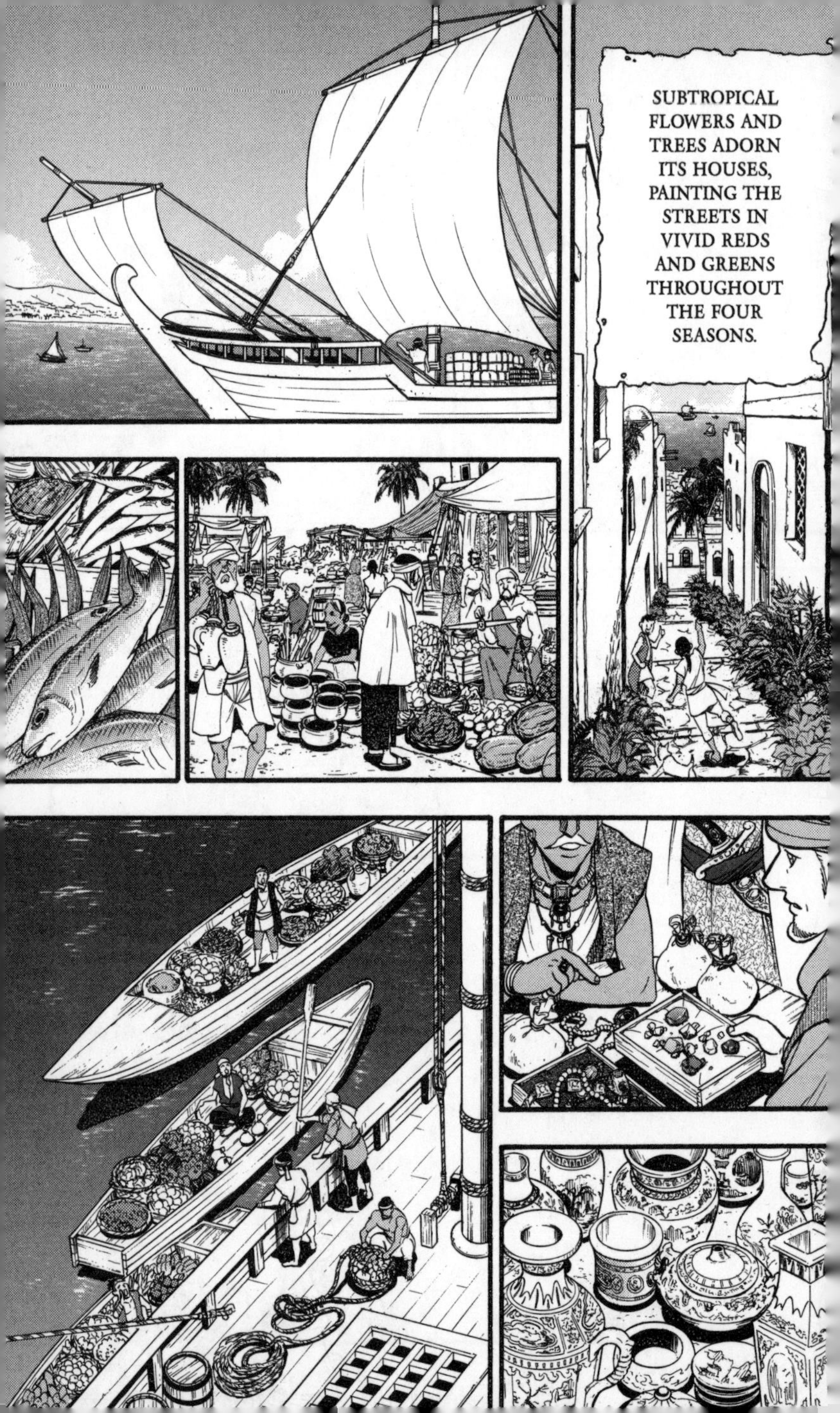
SUBTROPICAL FLOWERS AND TREES ADORN ITS HOUSES, PAINTING THE STREETS IN VIVID REDS AND GREENS THROUGHOUT THE FOUR SEASONS.

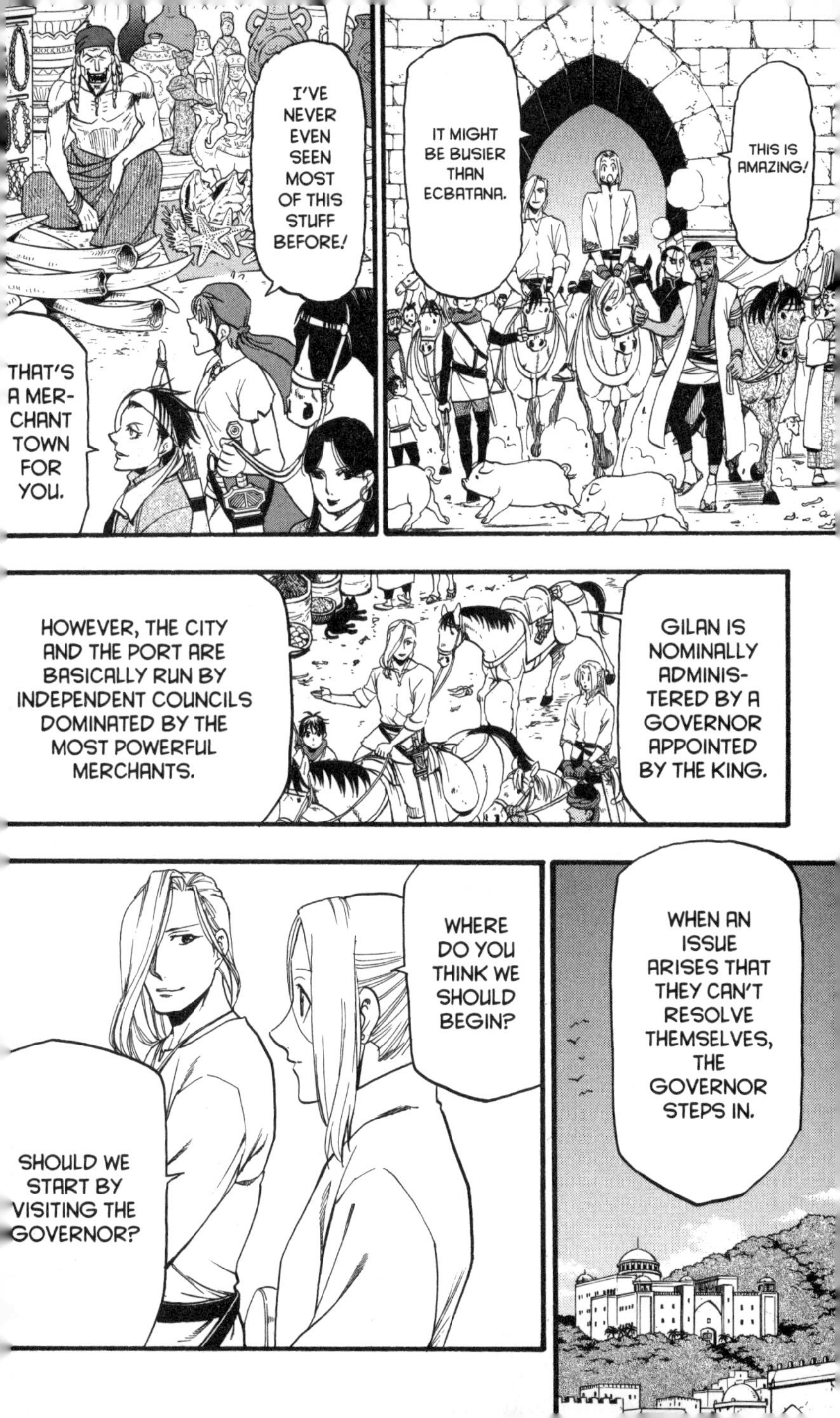
THIS IS AMAZING!
IT MIGHT BE BUSIER THAN ECBATANA.
I'VE NEVER EVEN SEEN MOST OF THIS STUFF BEFORE!
THAT'S A MERCHANT TOWN FOR YOU.
GILAN IS NOMINALLY ADMINISTERED BY A GOVERNOR APPOINTED BY THE KING.
HOWEVER, THE CITY AND THE PORT ARE BASICALLY RUN BY INDEPENDENT COUNCILS DOMINATED BY THE MOST POWERFUL MERCHANTS.
WHEN AN ISSUE ARISES THAT THEY CAN'T RESOLVE THEMSELVES, THE GOVERNOR STEPS IN.
WHERE DO YOU THINK WE SHOULD BEGIN?
SHOULD WE START BY VISITING THE GOVERNOR?

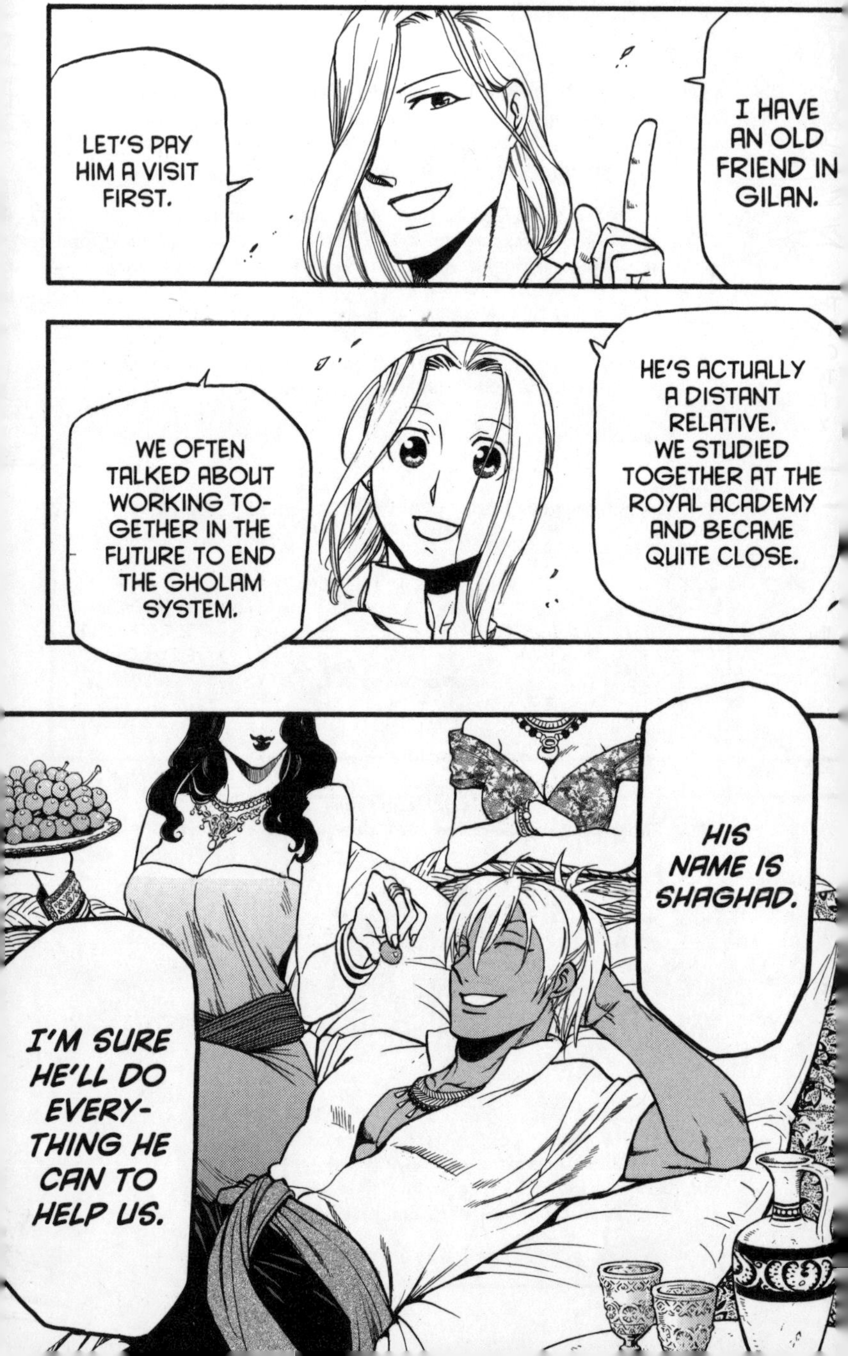
I HAVE AN OLD FRIEND IN GILAN.
LET'S PAY HIM A VISIT FIRST.
HE'S ACTUALLY A DISTANT RELATIVE. WE STUDIED TOGETHER AT THE ROYAL ACADEMY AND BECAME QUITE CLOSE.
WE OFTEN TALKED ABOUT WORKING TO-GETHER IN THE FUTURE TO END THE GHOLAM SYSTEM.
HIS NAME IS SHAGHAD.
I'M SURE HE'LL DO EVERY-THING HE CAN TO HELP US.

A Kodansha Comics Trade Paperback Original
The Heroic Legend of Arslan 15 copyright © 2021 Hiromu Arakawa & Yoshiki Tanaka
English translation copyright © 2021 Hiromu Arakawa & Yoshiki Tanaka

Published in the United States by Kodansha Comics, an imprint of
Kodansha USA Publishing, LLC, New York.

Publication rights for this English edition arranged through
Kodansha Ltd., Tokyo.

First published in Japan in 2021 by Kodansha Ltd., Tokyo
as *Arslan Senki*, volume 15.

ISBN 978-1-64651-295-9

Printed in the United States of America.

www.kodansha.us

1st Printing
Translation: Matt Treyvaud
Lettering: James Dashiell
Editing: Megan Ling
Kodansha Comics edition cover design by Phil Balsman

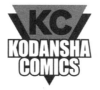

Publisher: Kiichiro Sugawara

Director of publishing services: Ben Applegate
Associate director of operations: Stephen Pakula
Publishing services managing editors: Madison Salters, Alanna Ruse
Production managers: Emi Lotto, Angela Zurlo